Studies in Church History

Subsidia

11

THE MEDIEVAL CHURCH
UNIVERSITIES, HERESY, AND THE RELIGIOUS LIFE

Gordon Leff

THE MEDIEVAL CHURCH: UNIVERSITIES, HERESY, AND THE RELIGIOUS LIFE

Essays in Honour of
Gordon Leff

EDITED BY

PETER BILLER

and

BARRIE DOBSON

PUBLISHED FOR
THE ECCLESIASTICAL HISTORY SOCIETY
BY
THE BOYDELL PRESS
1999

First published 1999

A publication of the Ecclesiastical History Society
in association with The Boydell Press
an imprint of Boydell & Brewer Ltd
PO Box 9, Woodbridge, Suffolk IP12 3DF, UK
and of Boydell & Brewer Inc.
PO Box 41026, Rochester, NY 14604-4126, USA
website: http://www.boydell.co.uk

ISBN 0 9529733 3 2

ISSN 1351-3087

A catalogue record for this book is available
from the British Library

Library of Congress Catalog Card Number: 99-18328

Details of previous volumes are available from Boydell & Brewer Ltd

This book is printed on acid-free paper

Printed in Great Britain by
St Edmundsbury Press Ltd, Bury St Edmunds, Suffolk

CONTENTS

List of Contributors vii
Editors' Preface ix
List of Abbreviations xiii

Gordon Leff: An Appreciation 1
GERALD ALYMER

The Cathars and Christian Perfection 5
BERNARD HAMILTON

Northern Cathars and Higher Learning 25
PETER BILLER

Parisian Theologians and the Jews: Peter Lombard and Peter Cantor 55
JACK WATT

The Instructional Programme of the Mendicant Convents at Paris in the Early Fourteenth Century 77
WILLIAM COURTENAY

William of Ockham and the Michaelists on Robert Grosseteste and Denis the Areopagite 93
DAVID LUSCOMBE

The Medieval Idea of Heresy: What are we to make of it? 111
ARTHUR STEPHEN McGRADE

Fellows and Helpers: The Religious Identity of the Followers of Wyclif 141
JEREMY CATTO

Were the Lollards a Sect? 163
MARGARET ASTON

Cross-Referencing in Wyclif's Latin Works 193
ANNE HUDSON

The 'Mendicant Problem' in the Later Middle Ages 217
ROBERT SWANSON

The Monastic Orders in Late Medieval Cambridge 239
BARRIE DOBSON

The Origins and University Connections of Yorkshire Religious, 1480–1540 271
CLAIRE CROSS

Holy War, Roman Popes, and Christian Soldiers: Some Early Modern Views on Medieval Christendom 293
CHRISTOPHER TYERMAN

Met on the *via moderna* 309
JOHN BOSSY

Bibliography of the Writings of Gordon Leff, 1956–98 325
SIMON DITCHFIELD

Index 343

CONTRIBUTORS

MARGARET ASTON

GERALD AYLMER
Formerly Master of St Peter's College, Oxford

PETER BILLER
Senior Lecturer in History, University of York

JOHN BOSSY
Professor of History, University of York

JEREMY CATTO
Fellow of Oriel College, Oxford

WILLIAM J. COURTENAY
C. H. Haskins Professor of Medieval History, University of Wisconsin

CLAIRE CROSS
Professor of History, University of York

SIMON DITCHFIELD
Lecturer in History, University of York

BARRIE DOBSON
Professor of Medieval History, University of Cambridge

BERNARD HAMILTON
Formerly Professor of Medieval History, University of Nottingham

ANNE HUDSON
Professor of Medieval English, University of Oxford

DAVID LUSCOMBE
Leverhulme Personal Research Professor of Medieval History, University of Sheffield

ARTHUR STEPHEN McGRADE
Professor Emeritus, Department of Philosophy, University of Connecticut

ROBERT SWANSON
Reader in Medieval Church History, University of Birmingham

CHRISTOPHER TYERMAN
Lecturer, Hertford College, Oxford, and Head of History, Harrow School

JOHN A. WATT
Formerly Professor of Medieval History, University of Newcastle

EDITORS' PREFACE

This volume is presented to Professor Gordon Leff by several of his many admirers in recognition of his exceptional contributions to the history of medieval thought and religion during a scholarly career of more than forty years. Gordon Leff, almost invariably known as Bunny to his closest friends and colleagues since his undergraduate years at Cambridge in the early 1950s, would think it in the worst possible taste to publicize his own remarkable achievements. But remarkable they have certainly been. With the appearance of his celebrated article on 'The fourteenth century and the decline of Scholasticism' (*Past and Present*, 1956) and of his Penguin survey of *Medieval Thought: St Augustine to Ockham* two years later, the name of Gordon Leff immediately became familiar among medievalists on both sides of the Atlantic. At the same time his engagement with the deepest issues in the philosophy of history, as well as the publication in 1961 of his *The Tyranny of Concepts*, put him in the forefront of fundamental debates outside the confines of medieval thought and on both sides of the iron curtain. During the following decades his awe-inspiring talents for the elucidation of theological, philosophical, and political thought were applied in rapid succession to the work of many of the most important figures in the history of medieval intellectual endeavour, and in 1969 he turned again to another probing analysis of history's epistemological problems in his *History and Social Theory*. The ten substantial books and many articles written by Bunny Leff between his first monograph, *Bradwardine and the Pelagians*, and his *William of Ockham: the Metamorphosis of Scholastic Discourse* eighteen years later will be a permanent memorial not only to his unique contribution to scholarship and intellectual debate but also to a creative energy not easily rivalled among English historians of his own or indeed any other generation.

The two editors of this volume first came to know Bunny Leff only after he had left the History Department of the University of Manchester for the Department of History at the then new University of York in 1965. One of us was a working colleague from his first meeting with Bunny, and the other was the latter's research student who later became his colleague too. We are therefore all the more grateful to Gerald Aylmer, our own first Head of Department at York, for the reminiscences of Bunny's eventful nine years at Manchester between 1956 and 1965 which he has included in his tribute to his long-time friend. During the early, often exciting but sometimes volatile, years of the University of York, the respect in which Bunny himself held Gerald Aylmer as well as his other colleagues was to make a much greater contribution to the exhilarating self-confidence of his new department than he probably ever realized. Too dedicated a scholar to be always immediately accessible, for many of his students he became – as Gerald Aylmer points out – the near-legendary 'sage of Strensall', once unforgettably parodied by another colleague, the late Gwyn Williams, as 'St Gordon, the hermit of Strensall'. Strensall, it should be explained, is the village six miles north of York where Bunny has lived for more than thirty years. It is therefore hardly surprising that his ability to compose the lecture he was about to give during his long early morning walk from home to the University, and then to deliver it without notes at 9.00 am, was a never failing source of envy among his colleagues until his retirement in 1988. However, as a Professor Emeritus for the last decade (he had been promoted to a Chair of History in 1969), Bunny continues to maintain almost as benevolently watchful an eye on the affairs of his University as on his garden and – of course – the history of medieval thought.

As many friends and colleagues of Bunny Leff will vividly recall, most conversations with him about historical matters tend to conclude with a wry smile and a denial on his part that he is a 'real' historian at all. Such a remark, in the case of a scholar who approaches nearly all issues historically and has consistently argued that 'the criteria of intellectual change can in the end only be contextual', should hardly be taken too seriously. We are therefore not too apprehensive that Bunny himself will raise serious objections to the fact that almost every contributor to this book is or has been a member of a history department. But then any *Festschrift* which tried to reflect this particular honorand's intellectual interests in full would have had to double the scope and size of this volume. Many scholars, especially Bunny's past and present colleagues at York, would have wished to participate in this collection of papers. However, we decided at an early stage to prepare a collection of articles which would represent only the medieval scholar. Contributors were accordingly asked to write on subjects relating to the medieval themes upon which Bunny has written, namely either speculative thought, the universities, the religious orders, or heresy. We hope that our deliberate emphasis on these themes sufficiently explains not only the contents but also the title of this volume. To all the contributors themselves we are extremely grateful, not only for the pleasure they immediately expressed to us in accepting our original invitation to participate in this volume but also for the care they have taken to submit such immaculate texts of their papers.

We are also most grateful to Professor John Bossy, Professor Claire Cross, Mr John Fuggles and Professor Jack Watt for their advice at the early stages of preparing this volume. Our thanks are also due to Dr Simon Ditchfield for his labours in compiling the Bibliography, labours all the more out of the ordinary in the case of as exceptionally a productive writer and reviewer as Bunny Leff. Dr Allen Warren has given invaluable support towards this book; and to Dr Robert Swanson, the Publications Editor of the Ecclesiastical History Society, we owe more than we can adequately say. Our final thanks must be to the Committee of that Society itself for its enthusiasm in supporting us in this work of celebration.

Peter Biller
Barrie Dobson

ABBREVIATIONS

Abbreviated titles are adopted within each paper after the first full citation. In addition, the following abbreviations are used throughout the volume.

ABMA	*Auctores Britannici Medii Aevi* (London, 1969–)
AFP	*Archivum Fratrum Praedicatorum* (Rome, 1931–)
AHDLMA	*Archives d'histoire doctrinale et littéraire du moyen âge* (Paris, 1926–)
AHR	*American Historical Review* (New York, 1895–)
AL	*Aristoteles Latinus*, Corpus Philosophorum Medii Aevi (Rome, Cambridge, etc., 1939–)
Anselm, *Tractatus*	Anselm of Alessandria, *Tractatus de hereticis*, ed. A. Dondaine, 'La hiérarchie cathare en Italie, II', *AFP*, 20 (1950), pp. 308–24
ASI	*Archivio storico italiano* (Florence, 1842–)
BL	London, British Library
Borst, *Katharer*	A. Borst, *Die Katharer, MGH Schriften*, 12 (Stuttgart, 1953)
BRUC	A. B. Emden, *A Biographical Register of the University of Cambridge to 1500* (Cambridge, 1963)
BRUO	A. B. Emden, *A Biographical Register of the University of Oxford to A. D. 1500*, 3 vols (Oxford, 1957–9)
BRUO 1501–1540	A. B. Emden, *A Biographical Register of the University of Oxford A. D. 1501–1540* (Oxford, 1974)
CaF	*Cahiers de Fanjeaux* (Toulouse, 1966–)
Canterbury College	*Canterbury College: Documents and History*, ed. W. A. Pantin, 4 vols (Oxford Historical Society, new ser, 6–8 [1947–50]; 30, ed. W. T. Mitchell, [1985])
CAS	Cambridge Antiquarian Society
Catto, 'Wyclif'	J. I. Catto, 'Wyclif and Wycliffism at Oxford 1356–1430', *Late Med. Oxford*, pp. 175–261
CclR	*Calendar of the Close Rolls preserved in the Public Record Office 1272–1509*, 61 vols (London, 1900–63)
CChr.SL	*Corpus Christianorum, series Latina* (Turnhout, 1953–)
Cooper, *Annals*	C. H. Cooper, *Annals of Cambridge*, 5 vols (Cambridge, 1842–1908)
CPL	*Calendar of Entries in the Papal Registers relating to Great Britain and Ireland: Papal Letters, 1198–1492*, ed. W. H.

	Bliss *et al.*, 15 vols in 16 (London, 1893–1960, Dublin, 1978)
CSEL	*Corpus scriptorum ecclesiasticorum latinorum* (Vienna, 1866–)
CUP	*Chartularium Universitatis Parisiensis*, ed. H. Denifle, A. Chatelain, 4 vols (Paris, 1889–97)
CYS	*Canterbury and York Society* (London, 1907–)
DDC	*Dictionnaire de droit canonique*, ed. R. Naz, 7 vols (Paris, 1935–65)
Dobson, 'Religious (Oxford)'	R. B. Dobson, 'The Religious Orders 1370–1540', *Late Med. Oxford* (Oxford)', pp. 539–79
DSP	*Dictionnaire de Spiritualité*, ed. M. Villier, 16 vols (Paris, 1937–94)
DTC	*Dictionnaire de théologie canonique*, ed. E. Vacant *et al.*, 15 vols (Paris, 1903–50)
Duvernoy, *Histoire*	J. Duvernoy, *Le Catharisme: l'histoire des Cathares* (Toulouse, 1979)
Duvernoy, *Religion*	J. Duvernoy, *Le Catharisme: la religion des Cathares* (Toulouse, 1976)
EETS	*Early English Text Society* (London, 1864–)
EHR	*English Historical Review* (London, 1886–)
EWS	*English Wycliffite Sermons*, ed. A. Hudson and P. Gradon, 5 vols (Oxford, 1979–96)
Friedberg	*Corpus iuris canonici*, ed. E. Friedberg, 2 vols (Leipzig, 1879)
FS	*Franciscan Studies* (New York, 1924–)
Grace Book A	*Grace Book A, containing the proctors' accounts and other records of the University of Cambridge, 1454–1488*, ed. S. M. Leathes, CAS, Luard Memorial Series, I (Cambridge, 1897)
Grace Book B	*Grace Book B, Part 1, containing the proctors' accounts and other records of the University of Cambridge, 1488–1511*, ed. M. Bateson, CAS, Luard Memorial Series, II (Cambridge, 1903)
Gray, *St Radegund*	A. Gray, *The Priory of St Radegund, Cambridge*, CAS, XXXI (Cambridge, 1898)
Greatrex	J. Greatrex, *Biographical Register of the English Cathedral Priories of the Province of Canterbury* (Oxford, 1997)
Hudson, *Books*	A. Hudson, *Lollards and their Books* (London, 1985)
Hudson, *PR*	A. Hudson, *The Premature Reformation. Wycliffite Texts and Lollard History* (Oxford, 1988)
JEH	*Journal of Ecclesiastical History* (Cambridge, 1950–)
JThS	*Journal of Theological Studies* (London, 1899–)

Knighton	*Knighton's Chronicle* 1337–1396, ed. and transl. G. H. Martin (Oxford, 1995)
Knowles, *Rel. Orders*	M. D. Knowles, *The Religious Orders in England*, 3 vols (Cambridge, 1948–59)
Lambert, *Heresy*	M. D. Lambert, *Medieval Heresy. Popular Movements from the Gregorian Reform to the Reformation*, 2nd edn (Oxford, 1992)
Late Med. Oxford	*Late Medieval Oxford* (vol. 2 of *The History of the University of Oxford*), ed. J. I. Catto and R. Evans (Oxford, 1992)
Leader	D. R. Leader, *The University to 1546* (vol. 1 of *A History of the University of Cambridge*, Cambridge, 1988)
Leff, 'Apostolic ideal'	G. Leff, 'The Apostolic ideal in later medieval ecclesiology', *JThS*, ns, 18 (1967), pp. 58–82
Left, *Bradwardine*	G. Leff, *Bradwardine and the Pelagians* (Cambridge, 1957)
Leff, 'Decline'	G. Leff, 'Heresy and the decline of the medieval Church', *P&P*, 20 (1961), pp. 36–51
Leff, *Dissoluiton*	G. Leff, *The Dissolution of the Medieval Outlook* (New York, 1976)
Leff, *Gregory*	G. Leff, *Gregory of Rimini* (Manchester, 1961)
Leff, *Heresy*	G. Leff, *Heresy in the Later Middle Ages. the Relation of Heterodoxy to Dissent c. 1250–c. 1450*, 2 vols (Manchester, 1967)
Leff, *Medieval Thought*	G. Leff, *Medieval Thought: St Augustine to Ockham* (Harmondsworth, 1958)
Leff, *Ockham*	G. Leff, *William of Ockham: the Metamorphosis of Scholastic Discourse* (Manchester, 1975)
Leff, *Paris and Oxford*	G. Leff, *Paris and Oxford Universities in the Thirteenth and Fourteenth Centuries* (New York, 1968)
Leff, *Tyranny*	G. Leff, *The Tyranny of Concepts* (London, 1961)
Letters and Papers	*Letters and Papers, Foreign and Domestic illustrative of the reign of Henry VIII, 1509–47*, ed. J. S. Brewer and J. Gairdner, 21 vols (HMSO, 1862–1910)
Lollardy and Gentry	M. Aston and C. Richmond, eds, *Lollardy and the Gentry in the Later Middle Ages* (Stroud, 1997)
Magdalene College	P. Cunich, D. Hoyle, E. Duffy and R. Hyam, *A History of Magdalene College Cambridge, 1428–1988* (Cambridge, 1994)
Mansi	J. D. Mansi, *Sacrorum conciliorum nova et amplissima collectio*, 31 vols (Florence, 1759–98)
Matthew Paris, *CM*	Matthew Paris, *Chronica majora*, ed. H. R. Luard, 7 vols, *RS*, 57 (1872–83)

MGH	*Monumenta Germaniae historica inde ab a. 500 usque ad a. 1500*, ed. G. H. Pertz *et al.* (Hannover, Berlin, etc., 1826–)
Schriften	*Schriften der MGH* (Stuttgart, 1938–)
SS	*Scriptores* (in folio), 30 vols (Hannover, 1824–1924)
Moore, *Dissent* (1977) or (1985)	R. I. Moore, *The Origins of European Dissent*, 1st edn (London, 1977) or 2nd edn (Oxford, 1985)
Moorman, *Grey Friars*	J. R. H. Moorman, *The Grey Friars in Cambridge, 1225–1538* (Cambridge, 1952)
MS	*Medieval Studies* (Toronto, 1939–)
Moneta	Moneta of Cremona, *Adversus Catharos et Valdenses Libri Quinque*, ed. T. Ricchini (Rome, 1743)
Mullinger	J. B. Mullinger, *The University of Cambridge from the earliest times to the royal injunctions of 1535* (Cambridge, 1873)
ns	new series
Pantin, *Chapters*	*Documents illustrating the activities of the General and Provincial Chapters of the English Black Monks, 1215–1540*, ed. W. A. Pantin, Camden Third Series, 45, 47, 54 (1931–7)
P&P	*Past and Present: A Journal of Scientific History* (London, 1952–)
PBA	*Proceedings of the British Academy* (London, 1904–)
PL	*Patrologia Latina*, ed. J. P. Migne, 217 + 4 index vols (Paris, 1841–61)
Rashdall, *Universities*	H. Rashdall, *The Universities of Europe in the Middle Ages*, new edn by F. M. Powicke and A. B. Emden, 3 vols (Oxford, 1936)
RBPH	*Revue Belge de Philologie et d'Histoire* (Brussels, 1922–)
R.C.H.M.	Royal Commission on Historical Monuments
Reg. Repingdon	*The Register of Bishop Philip Repingdon*, 1405–1419, ed. M. Archer, 3 vols, Lincoln Record Society 57–8, 74 (1963–82)
Reg. Trefnant	*Registrum Johannis Trefnant*, ed. W. W. Capes, *CYS*, 20 (1916)
RH	*Revue historique* (Paris, 1876–)
Roth	F. Roth, *The English Austin Friars*, 1249–1538 (New York, 1966)
RS	*Rerum Brittanicarum medii aevi scriptores*, 99 vols (London, 1858–1911) = *Rolls Series*
Sacconi	Rainier Sacconi, *Summa de Catharis et Pauperibus de Lugduno*, ed. F. Sanjek, *AFP*, 44 (1974), pp. 50–7
SC	Sources chrétiennes (Paris, 1940–)

SCH	*Studies in Church History* (London/Oxford, 1964–)
SCH.S	*Studies in Church History: Subsidia* (Oxford, 1978–)
SOPMA	T. Kaeppeli and E. Panella, *Scriptores Ordinis Praedicatorum medii aevi*, 4 vols (Rome, 1970–93)
ST	Thomas Aquinas, *Summa theologiae*, Blackfriars edn, 61 vols (London, New York, 1964–81)
Szittya, *Antifraternal*	P. R. Szittya, *The Antifraternal Tradition in Medieval Literature* (Princeton, NJ, 1986)
Tanner, *Decrees*	N. P. Tanner, ed., *Decrees of the Ecumenical Councils* (London, Washington, 1990)
Thomson, *Lollards*	J. A. F. Thomson, *The Later Lollards 1414–1520* (Oxford, 1965)
TRHS	*Transactions of the Royal Historical Society* (London, 1871–)
VCH	*Victoria History of the Counties of England*
Wilkins, *Concilia*	D. Wilkins, *Concilia magnae Britanniae et Hiberniae*, 4 vols (London, 1737)
Willis and Clark	R. Willis and J. W. Clark, *The Architectural History of the University of Cambridge and the Colleges of Cambridge and Eton*, 4 vols (Cambridge, 1886)
WS	Wyclif Society, 35 vols (London, 1883–1922)

GORDON LEFF: AN APPRECIATION

by GERALD AYLMER

GORDON LEFF and I first met in 1955 or 1956. I was already at the University of Manchester as an Assistant Lecturer in Modern History when he arrived from Cambridge to take up an Assistant Lectureship in Medieval History. He explained to me that he had already crossed swords with the University Registrar about continuing to hold a Prize Fellowship at King's College. Gordon had taken a firm line, saying that he was only receiving (as I recollect) £50 a year from King's; and, if he was not allowed to go on holding the fellowship, he would have to withdraw his acceptance of the post at Manchester. This was a bold thing to do in the mid-1950s when academic jobs were scarce, not least in that he had already been asked by the new Professor of Medieval History there about his membership of the Communist Party. He also told me that, in conversation with one of his Cambridge mentors, he had said that, if he were unable to pursue an academic career, he would apply to become the college gardener. A sad loss to horticulture at King's!

In retrospect it is a comment on the ideological climate of the mid-twentieth century that a scholar like Gordon Leff should ever have been a Marxist, let alone a member of the Communist Party. Having discarded political communism sharply and decisively by the time that he reached Manchester, his evolution away from Marxist thought and historiography was a more gradual and complex process. My understanding has always been that his original commitment to Marxism had been largely due to the impact, emotional as well as intellectual, of military service in India at the end of the Second World War, rather than to the influence of anyone in Cambridge. Whether the largely self-educative school system which he had experienced at A. S. Neill's Summerhill made him readier to embrace a comprehensive set of doctrines which offered answers to all the world's problems, I do not know. At Cambridge his undergraduate contemporaries were clearly in awe of him. His admirers were much relieved that a promising career was saved from being cut short when an amplifier, with which he was supposed to be disrupting some solemn occasion as a political gesture, providentially failed to work and his technical skills were unequal to putting it right. A useful reminder of the role of contingency in biography as in history. By the time that he was doing research on medieval philosophy under the supervision of Professor David Knowles, some sense of contradiction, or at least of paradox, in his attitude to Marxism was clearly perceived. So far as I can remember, his political evolution was confirmed but by no means precipitated with the Hungarian uprising of 1956 and its subsequent repression by Soviet forces.

Our friendship ripened through a common concern with ideas, although his range of interests was always much wider than mine, extending to cricket and to music. At a more practical level, it was the Campaign for Nuclear Disarmament in Manchester during the years 1958–62 which brought us together. Whether due to his training in the Army debating societies of 1945–6 or to his phase as a political activist, he has a marvellous gift for public oratory: he spoke consistently and coherently without notes (as has almost invariably also been true of his academic lecturing). At street corners and factory gates it was normally my role to distribute leaflets while Gordon orated. During these years CND was emphatically 'a house of many mansions', a broad church; he and I always belonged to the non-pacifist and non-fellow-travelling section of the movement, and continued to support the then Labour Party in ordinary domestic politics. Outside our normal academic duties we tried to entertain students at home. Such was the pay of university staff in those years that we calculated how to share the cost by the use of a measuring-rod, to see how much cider was left in the barrel when the party was over.

It must have been around this time that he was working on *The Tyranny of Concepts*, which he had wanted – following an aphorism in Hobbes – to call 'The Money of Fools'; this was first published in 1961. It constituted an explicit and systematic rejection of Marxism, in which he was none the less still distancing himself from the liberalism of both Karl Popper and Isaiah Berlin. The book is a polemic, concluding with a stirring re-affirmation of socialist humanism as the alternative to Marxism. The sequel to this work, *History and Social Theory* (published simultaneously with a second, revised edition of *Tyranny* in 1969), was relatively long in coming, but is surely among the most underrated works of our time. It offers a positive alternative, within an empirical framework, to the great system-builders of modern thought, whether Christian, Marxist, or liberal. As the title suggests, it attempts a synthesis of historical (*not* historicist) thinking with a concern for the pressing problems of modern society. Perhaps the most positive line of argument is the insistence on meaningful periodization as the strongest single element in successful historical understanding. Compared with the earlier book, it could be called more academic, certainly more directly related to the author's own teaching and to his practice as a historian; it is written with less urgency but with at least equal cogency of reasoning. Since it has become fashionable in some circles to sneer at the culture and the universities of the 1960s, it is well to note that a historian in the North of England produced these two books over and above his output of works on medieval thought and scholastic philosophy, a reminder that commitment and hard work are characteristics of the individual, not of the decade or of the supposedly prevailing climate of opinion.

It is difficult for a non-medievalist to relate this polymathic range of interests to Gordon Leff's specific studies, on medieval philosophers, heresy, the rise of universities, and so on. It may indeed be an impertinence to try to do so; but a possible approach lies in relation to his professional career. His move from a lectureship at Manchester to a Readership at the then three-year old University of York in 1965 might have been thought foolhardy by some at the time; certainly it was a calculated risk. His arrival coincided with the launching of a new second-year undergraduate course a little grandiosely entitled (though not so named by him) 'The Discipline of History'. I believe it was the first of its kind to be offered in a British university. Not only did he teach one of the options within this course every year from 1966 to his final retirement in the 1990s, but his seminars were less concerned with historiography, and closer indeed to something more like 'History and Social Theory'. This course remains one of his most enduring memorials because of its impact on successive generations of students who chose to take it. The nearest to a kindred spirit among the York historians of the early days was W. E. S. Thomas, until his return to Oxford in 1967. Later, in the 1970s, Gordon Leff and I taught a joint first-year introductory course on 'The Origins of the Western Political Tradition', which ran from Plato to Locke, relating each thinker in turn to the historical background of their times. Whether or not predictably, it was Augustine and Hobbes who emerged as the 'men for all seasons', holding the grimmest mirror up to humanity, while yet offering an ultimate message of Hope. Although superficiality and over-simplification are scarcely to be avoided in a course such as this, Gordon was superb on the Greeks as well – naturally – on Augustine and Aquinas. At the same time we were both engaged on research and writing of what might be considered a fairly technical nature, although in very different fields of history. Likewise these were the years marked by some of the bizarre and extravagant features of 'student power' – another lost world only a generation later. Meanwhile Gordon Leff developed a remarkable rapport with York's first Vice-Chancellor, Eric James (Lord James of Rusholme), from whose periodic strictures on over-narrow, even trivial, research in the humanities he was always somehow excepted.

It seems a fair question to ask whether he should have been – or indeed is – a philosopher and not a historian. His occasional impatience with the minutiae of scholarly references, together with the fact that (thanks to Summerhill) his Latin was wholly self-taught, occasionally led some reviewers to pounce on technical errors. No doubt he might have received even more formal recognition if it had always been fully appreciated that his mind is indeed more that of a theorist than of an empirical investigator. But then this is his strength as a lecturer: the capacity to grasp a subject as a whole and to keep control of it in his own mind for the purposes of clear, rounded exposition. The so far unpublished Carlyle Lectures, delivered in Oxford, exemplified the effectiveness of this technique. The more human touch has certainly not been lacking. One ex-student remembers Gordon's son (now a highly successful schoolteacher) sitting at the back of a lecture, swinging his legs and reading boys' comics. Since some of my colleagues at York sometimes remonstrated with me that Gordon did not always do his share of one-to-one or one-to-two tutorial teaching, I may venture to quote another ex-pupil (*in vino veritas*): 'but an hour with Dr Leff is worth three or four with most of the others'. Nor is it usual to find a scholar with such an extraordinary variety and breadth of interests, and depth of reading, so ready to listen sympathetically to other people and to offer wisely considered advice when it is sought. As he has been well-named, veritably 'the sage of Strensall'.

THE CATHARS AND CHRISTIAN PERFECTION

by BERNARD HAMILTON

THE Church's Founder enjoined the life of perfection on all his followers, but the Cathars were unique in describing themselves as perfect or as 'good men'.[1] In all other forms of Christianity it is an observable fact that the more devout church members are, the more they are conscious of their imperfections and lack of goodness. This suggests that Cathar spirituality was very different from that of the mainline Christian churches, and it is this which I want to investigate here.

Although a great deal has been written about Cathars, there is still no very satisfactory account of their spirituality. An earlier generation of scholars have given detailed analyses of the beliefs and religious practices of the Cathars, based of necessity almost entirely on Catholic sources which are not concerned to give a rounded picture of the Cathar faith.[2] More recently historians, using the Cathars' own writings as well as those of their opponents, have examined Catharism in its social context[3] and have traced in detail the roots of the Cathar faith,[4] but they have not tried to explain why many people found it compelling as a religion. Even Jean Duvernoy, whose magisterial *Le Catharisme: la religion des Cathares* deals with every aspect of Cathar life, nevertheless devotes only two pages to spirituality, and his assessment is very negative:

> Ce qui frappe le plus, au contact de cette littérature comme en présence des documents judiciaires, c'est l'aspect purement

[1] Matt. 5. 48; in the Cathar rite of initiation the celebrant speaks of 'Aquest Sanh babtisme . . . a tengut la gleisa de Deu desl Apostols en sa, et es vengutz de bos homes en bos homes entro aici . . .'; in the same *Ritual* the opening words of St John's Gospel contain this revealing scribal error at John 1 9: 'Erat lux vera que illuminat bonem [*sic*] hominem venientem in hunc mundum'; L. Clédat, *Le Nouveau Testament traduit au XIIIe siècle en langue provençale suivi d'un Rituel cathare* (Photolithographie. Bibliothèque de la Faculté des Lettres de Lyon, IV, Paris, 1887) (reprinted Geneva, 1968), pp. xvii, 470.

[2] E.g. J. Guiraud, *Cartulaire de Notre Dame de Prouille, précédé d'une étude sur l'Albigéisme languedocien au xiie et xiiie siècles*, 2 vols (Paris, 1907); E. Broeckx, *Le Catharisme* (Universitas catholica Lovaniensis. Dissertationes, Series 11, vol. 10, Hoogstraten, 1916).

[3] E.g. R. Nelli, *La vie quotidienne des Cathares du Languedoc au xiiie siècle* (Paris, 1969).

[4] H. Söderberg, *La Religion des Cathares. Étude sur le Gnosticisme de la basse antiquité et du moyen âge* (Uppsala, 1949).

> logique, voire ratiocinateur, de la théologie, qui apparait beaucoup plus comme une conviction que comme une foi. Rien de ce qui nous est parvenu ne permet de supposer quail y ait eu une mystique cathare.[5]

Anne Brenon has presented Catharism as a living faith set in a geographical and historical context, emphasising what is known about the individuals who made up the Cathar Church.[6] This is a fruitful approach, but I want to examine here the spiritual dynamic of the faith which those men and women held and to try to answer the question: why did almost all the Cathar perfect consider that their own distinctive religious insights were so important and unique that they were worth dying very painfully to affirm?

An understanding of Cathar spirituality can only be gained through a study of the Cathars' own writings. The Catholic sources remain, of course, of great importance. The works of polemicists, while needing cautious handling, contain much valuable factual information, while the Inquisition records are the most important single source of evidence. The inquisitors had no wish to misrepresent their opponents' teaching and practice: on the contrary, they were concerned to identify it as precisely as possible in order to refute the errors it contained. But the Inquisition records, like the Catholic sources in general, are principally concerned with establishing in what ways Cathar beliefs differed from those of orthodox Christianity, and they therefore pay little attention to Cathar religious experience.

But it is now possible to know something about this because a quite substantial number of Cathar texts are available. These are the Occitan translation of the New Testament and the *Ritual* written in the fly-leaves of the same work; *The Book of the Two Principles*, to which a Latin text of the Cathar *Ritual* is annexed; two Cathar works, a *Gloss on the Lord's Prayer*, and an *Apologia for the Church of God*, found in Trinity College Dublin by Th. Venckeleer among the Ussher manuscripts; the sections of a Cathar treatise embedded in a polemical work of Durand of Huesca; the passages from the lost work of the Cathar Tetricus (perhaps Thierry) quoted by Moneta de Cremona; and the parts of the lost Cathar treatise called *Stella* which are used by Salvo Burci in his polemical work called *Suprastella*.[7] It is not possible to exclude Catholic

[5] Duvernoy, *Religion*, p. 269.

[6] Anne Brenon, *Le vrai visage du Catharisme* (Toulouse, 1988).

[7] Occitan New Testament and Ritual: Clédat, *Nouveau Testament*; *Book of the Two*

sources completely from this discussion, because the Cathar evidence is still not comprehensive enough to answer all the questions which need to be addressed. What I intend to do is to use the Cathar sources as a focus, in order to determine what the Cathars themselves thought was of central importance in their faith, and to use Catholic sources only where there are gaps in the Cathar evidence.

As readers will be aware, the Cathars were divided over questions of doctrine. Although they were all Christian dualists, some were absolute dualists and some were moderate dualists. The latter believed that there was one God, but that this world had been fashioned from the four elements which God had made by the devil, who was an evil demiurge but was also himself a creature of the Good God. Absolute dualists believed that there were two co-eternal creative principles, one Good and one Evil, and that the evil God had made the phenomenal universe. I shall be dealing with the absolute dualists, because the sources written by the Cathars which I have listed above derive from them.[8]

The Cathars of Languedoc were absolute dualists, and so were one group of Italian Cathars, the Albanenses, also known as the Church of Desenzano.[9] They based their teaching entirely on the Bible, accepting the whole of the New Testament, with the addition of the Epistle to the Laodiceans, an apocryphal work attributed to St Paul. This was not heretical, merely uncanonical, consisting of a catena of passages from Paul's other letters.[10] Absolute dualists also accepted part of the Old Testament. They rejected the Pentateuch and the historical books as

Principles: C. Thouzellier, ed., *Livre des deux principes*, SC, 198 (Paris, 1973) [henceforth *Liber*]; Latin *Ritual*: C. Thouzellier, ed., *Rituel Cathare*, SC 236 (Paris, 1977); the *Gloss* and the *Apologia*: ed. Th. Venckeleer, 'Un Recueil cathare, le manuscrit A.6.10 de la "collection vaudoise" de Dublin: 1. "Une Apologie"', *RBPH*, 38 (1960), pp. 815–34; 'Une Glose sur le Pater', 39 (1961), pp. 759–93; Cathar Treatise: C. Thouzellier, ed., *Un Traité cathare inédit du début du XIIIe siècle, d'après le "Liber contra Manicheos" de Durand de Huesca*, Bibliothèque de la *RHE*, 37 (Louvain and Paris, 1961) [henceforth *Traité*]; Tetricus: in Moneta de Cremona, *Adversus Catharos et Valdenses Libri Quinque*, ed. T. Ricchini (Rome, 1743); *Stella* in Salvo Burci, *Liber supra Stella*, ed. Ilarino da Milano, *Aevum*, 19 (1945), pp. 307–41. I have not included in this list *The Secret Book of St John* translated by the Cathars from Old Slavonic, because it was only read by one group of Italian Cathars and was considered heretical even by some of them.

8 R. Nelli, *La Philosophie du Catharisme: le dualisme radical au xiiie siècle* (Paris, 1975).

9 Rainier Sacconi, *Summa de Catharis et de Pauperibus de Lugduno*, ed. F. Sanjek, *AFP*, 44 (1974), pp. 50–7, 59.

10 M. R. Harris, 'The Occitan Epistle to the Laodiceans: towards an edition of PA 36', in A. Cornagliotti *et al.*, eds, *Miscellanea di Studi Romanzi offertà a Giuliano Gasca Queirazza*, 2 vols (Alessandria, 1988), 1, pp. 428–46.

the work of the evil God, but accepted the Wisdom Books and the Prophets as divinely inspired.[11] Among the Albanenses, John of Lugio and his followers accepted the whole of the Old Testament canon: in this they were unique among the Cathars, but they seem to have read the historical books in the same sense as other Cathars did, as an account of the work of the evil creator God, albeit an account inspired by the Good God.[12] No copy of the Cathar Old Testament has ever been identified, and only one text of the New Testament, an Occitan translation, is known, and this has never yet been edited.[13]

While sharing with their Catholic opponents a common belief that that the Bible was divinely inspired, the Cathars interpreted it in a way which was consonant with their belief that the creation was the work of an evil God who was co-eternal with the Good God. The key text to the understanding of scripture in their view was: 'All things are double, one against another.'[14] As there were two gods so there were two creations. The Good God had indeed created the heaven and the earth, but these were not the heaven and the earth which we can see, but the new heaven and the new earth described by St John in the Book of Revelation.[15] The prophets had referred to that 'new earth' when they spoke of 'the land of the living'.[16] The Good God had created men to live in that world, and they were not simply spiritual beings, but had bodies which were part of the good creation.[17] But the visible heavens and earth were, according to the Cathars, the creation of the evil God. So in their cosmogony there existed two universes, mirror-images of each other.

Originally the two creations had been distinct, but the forces of evil had invaded the Land of the Living. The Cathars taught that it was this event which is described in the Revelation of St John: 'And there was war in heaven: Michael and his angels fought against the dragon; and

[11] Sacconi, pp. 51–2.

[12] 'Item iste Ioannes [de Lugio] recipit totam Bibliam, sed putat eam fuisse scriptam in alio mundo et ibidem fuisse formatos Adam et Euam', Sacconi, p. 56; *Liber, Contra Garatenses, De omni creatione, De manifestatione fidelium*, pp. 376–8.

[13] Clédat published only a lithographic edition of the manuscript. M. R. Harris has been working for many years on this text, see n. 10 above.

[14] Ecclus. 42. 25. For the Cathar understanding of it, *Traité*, ch. xii, p. 209.

[15] Rev. 21. 1; *Traité*, ch. vi, pp. 147–8.

[16] Ps. 116. 9 (Vulgate, 114. 9); *Traité*, ch. xvi, pp. 244–5.

[17] Absolute dualists 'credunt quod iste Deus sanctus et verus suum populum habuerit caelestem constantem ex tribus scilicet corpore et anima et spiritu': Moneta de Cremona, 1, I, p. 3.

the dragon fought and his angels, and prevailed not: neither was their place found any more in heaven.'[18] Yet before this defeat occurred, St John relates that the dragon's 'tail drew the third part of the stars of heaven and did cast them to the earth'. The Cathars understood this to refer to the angelic men who had lived in the realm of the Good God and who were drawn down to the universe of his evil adversary.[19]

In the Cathar view it was not force alone which caused these beings to fall. They cited the words of Jeremiah: 'As you have forsaken me and served a strange god in your own land, so shall you serve strange gods in a land which is not your own.'[20] This was the Cathars' understanding of original sin. They held that the creatures of the Good God were composed of body, soul, and spirit, and that it was only their souls which fell: their lifeless bodies and their dissociated spirits remained in the Land of the Living,[21] while their captive souls were imprisoned by the evil God in the material bodies of men and women, birds, and warm-blooded animals.[22] In the Cathar view not all life-forms in this creation possessed angelic souls. Vegetables had no spiritual content, and neither did fishes. The Cathars accepted the teaching of classical Greek scientists that fish grow in the water just as vegetables grow in the soil.[23] They also believed that there were some creatures with souls which were the creation of the evil God: reptiles, toads, and rats were in that category, while some Cathars supposed that there might also be some men who had evil souls.[24] An angelic soul was immortal, and when its body died it sought refuge in some other warm-blooded

[18] Rev. 12. 7–8. Sacconi lists among the beliefs of the Albanenses: 'Item quod dyabolus cum suis angelis ascendit in celum et, facto ibi prelio cum Michaele archangelo et angelis boni dei, extraxit inde tertiam partem creaturarum dei, et infundit eas cotidie in humanis corporibus et in brutis et etiam de uno corpore eas transmittit in aliud, donec omnes reducentur in celum', *Summa*, p. 51.

[19] Rev. 12. 4; cf. *Liber, Compendium, Quod deus non sit potens in malis*, pp. 310–12.

[20] Jer. 5. 19; *Traité*, ch. xvi, p. 255; *Liber, Compendium, De deo alieno*, p. 322 (where the prophecy is wrongly attributed to Isaiah).

[21] The very complex theology of the Cathars about the relationship between the heavenly and earthly bodies, souls, and spirits of the fallen angels is most clearly described by J. Duvernoy, 'La Religion cathare en Occitanie', in R. Lafont and R. Pech, eds, *Les Cathares en Occitanie* (Paris, 1982), pp. 211–24.

[22] Cf. Sacconi, n. 18 above.

[23] The evidence about Cathars eating fish is summarized by Borst, *Katharer*, p. 184 and n. 16.

[24] 'Quidam homo est [qui] nunquam habuit scientiam discernendi bonum a malo, verum a falso, ut valeat salvari, nec habet nec habebit unquam, *et sine dubio multi inveniuntur in hoc mundo. . . .* ergo non fuit in eo potentia salvandi . . .' (italics mine), *Liber, De arbitrio, De ignorantia multorum*, p. 394. For evil animals see n. 25 below.

creature which was about to be born, which might be a man or a beast or a bird.[25] The Cathars, in other words, believed that the angelic souls were trapped in the evil world by a perpetual round of reincarnation.

The spiritual condition of man and of many other living creatures in the Cathar view was therefore a very depressing one. They had been created to live in the Land of the Living, but they found themselves imprisoned in alien, material bodies in a hostile universe made by the evil God. They identified their condition with the Babylonian Captivity of the Jews described by the Old Testament prophets.[26] Death was no solution to their problems, nor did they seek Nirvana, like the Buddhists, but a restoration to their former state. So they prayed in the words of the *Miserere*: 'Restore unto me the joy of thy salvation.'[27]

In their prayers the Cathars regularly used Trinitarian forms, like 'Let us adore the Father, the Son, and the Holy Spirit.'[28] Nevertheless, the inquisitors doubted whether they believed in the Holy Trinity in an orthodox way, and their doubts seem to have been well founded. For the Cathars did make a distinction between God the Father who was uncreated, and the Son and the Spirit who were subordinate to Him and were either created beings or emanations of the Father.[29] But it seems clear that however unorthodox their explanations of the doctrine of the Trinity were, their experience of the Good God in their lives took a Trinitarian form as Creator, Redeemer, and Comforter.[30]

For Cathars, as for all Christians, salvation had come through Jesus Christ, but many modern scholars have misunderstood Cathar teach-

[25] 'Credunt etiam quod quando anima egreditur de corpore humano, transit ad aliud sive humanum sive bestiale . . .', *Manifestatio haeresis Albigensium et Lugduniensium*, perhaps written by Ermengaud of Béziers, ed. A. Dondaine, 'Durand de Huesca et la polémique anti-cathare', *AFP*, 24 (1959), p. 270. But an angelic soul could not be reborn in a rat, a toad, or a reptile, which were considered creatures of the evil god. Duvernoy, *Religion*, pp. 93–7.

[26] The Cathars applied to themselves the laments of the Jews captive in Babylon: Ps. 137. 4 (Vulgate, 136. 4); *Traité*, ch. xv, pp. 244–5.

[27] Ps. 51. 12 (Vulgate, 50. 14); *Traité*, ch. xix, p. 298.

[28] Clédat, *Nouveau Testament*, pp. vi, 470.

[29] E.g. '. . . ipse deus et filius eius Ihesus Christus qui unum et idem sunt secundum illos [Catholicos]', *Liber, De Libero Arbitrio, Reprobatio sententie*, p. 190. The Cathar teaching about the Holy Spirit was very complex: Moneta de Cremona describes it and explains that the Spirit whom they invoked in Trinitarian formulae was the *Spiritus principalis*. Cf. 'spiritu principali confirma me', Ps. 50. 14 (Vulgate). But they held: 'Filium majorem Spiritu Sancto, et ab ipso substantialiter diversum', Moneta, I, 1, pp. 4–5.

[30] This is shown most clearly by the discourses of the celebrant at the *consolamentum*: Clédat, *Nouveau Testament*, pp. xi–xxii, 473–9; *Rituel Cathare*, pp. 194–261.

ing about the Incarnation. Because Cathars wrote that Christ came into this world only in a spiritual form and did not take human flesh, their view of him has been described as Gnostic. If he did not have flesh, then he could not truly have suffered, died, and risen from the dead, and he was therefore a Teacher rather than a Saviour.[31] Now the Cathars undoubtedly did say those things about Christ's presence in this world, but they also said that the events described in the Gospels really took place in the Land of the Living. Catholic writers in the Middle Ages admitted this:

> [The Cathars] believe that Christ was born of Joseph and Mary, whom they call Adam and Eve, in the Land of the Living, and he suffered and rose again [there] and thence ascended to the Father; and did and said those things which have been written about him in the New Testament; and with the same Testament and with the disciples and his father and mother, he passed through seven worlds and then freed his people.[32]

The Cathars did not doubt that the Incarnation and the sacrifice of Calvary had really taken place: they speak of Christ redeeming the Kingdom with his blood.[33] We do not know precisely how they understood the doctrine of the atonement, but in that regard it is worth remembering that no mainstream church has ever ratified one particular theory of the atonement as authoritative, and the Cathars may have been like most other Christians and considered Christ's sacrifice a *magnum mysterium*, inexpressible in human language.[34]

The confusion of modern scholars about the Cathar doctrine of the Incarnation is a consequence, I think, of their unwillingness to accept the Cathar belief that because this world was the creation of the evil God it was, in Christian terms, Hell. Christ's descent through the seven heavens of the phenomenal world to free his people thus corresponds to orthodox Christian belief in the Harrowing of Hell.[35] His work in

[31] E.g. Duvernoy, *Religion*, pp. 82–9.

[32] *Manifestatio haeresis*, p. 270.

[33] '. . . lo nostre Segnor Yesu Christ . . . aisicom es scrit al vangeli, he reymu lo regne sobre dit al sio sanc . . .', 'Une Glose', p. 783.

[34] '. . . there has never been any official formulation in orthodox Christianity of the mystery of the Lord's redemptive work and . . . there is every likelihood that a variety of emphases and interpretations will continue': 'Atonement', F. L. Cross and E. A. Livingstone, eds, *The Oxford Dictionary of the Christian Church*, 3rd edn (Oxford, 1997), p. 123.

[35] Salvo Burci asserts of the Albanenses: 'Item dicunt in hoc mundo infernum esse, idest

this world was indeed exemplary: he could not take a human body created by the evil God, and he could only represent his Incarnation for the edification of men, but the spiritual validity of that representation derived from the fact that the Incarnation had really happened, though in another world.

Having manifested his life to men, Christ returned to the Land of the Living. In this world he left his Church, the Cathar Church, to continue his work.[36] He gave its members his teaching, a spiritual understanding of the Cathar version of the Bible, which in their view had been written in the Land of the Living and brought into this world by Christ.[37] He also gave his Church the power to forgive sins and to reconcile men to God through the one sacrament of salvation, the *consolamentum*. This could be conferred at need by any Cathar, although the normal minister was a Cathar bishop or one of his coadjutors. The Cathars believed that this was the true baptism of Christ, 'with the Holy Spirit and with fire', spoken of in St Luke's Gospel.[38]

Membership of the Cathar Church was confined to adults[39] and involved a long period of training in the belief and practice of the Christian faith. The candidates were received in the course of a public liturgy, the *consolamentum*, at the climax of which the officiant held a Gospel book over each candidate's head and said: 'Pater sancte susciper [sic] servum tuum in tua justicia et mite [sic] gratiam tuam et Espiritum Santum tuum super eum. [Holy Father receive thy servant in thy righteousness and send thy grace and thy Holy Spirit upon him.]' These words were always said in Latin.[40] The candidates then became consoled Cathars, and were known as the perfect. It was believed that through this sacrament they had received once more the spirits which they had left in the Land of the Living and that they were able, through the work of the Holy Spirit, to communicate once more with

hic esse ignem et frigus et omne malum et non alius infernus nec fuit nec erit', *Aevum*, 19, p. 313.

36 'Apologie', ch. 1, *RHPB*, 38, pp. 820–2.

37 This view seems to have been quite widely held: 'Credunt ... [Christum] cum eodem [novo] testamento . . . per septem terras transisse et inde populum suum liberasse', *Manifestatio haeresis*, *AFP*, 24, p. 270; John of Lugio: 'recipit totam Bibliam, sed putat eam fuisse scriptam in alio mundo . . .', Sacconi, p. 56.

38 Luke 3. 16; Occitan *Ritual*, ed. Clédat, *Nouveau Testament*, pp. xvi, 476.

39 There was no infant baptism, but children as young as ten or twelve were sometimes consoled; examples in Guiraud, *Cartulaire*, 1, pp. cclxxvi–cclxxix.

40 Occitan *Ritual*, ed. Clédat, *Nouveau Testament*, pp. xx, 479.

the Good God, even though they still lived in an evil cosmos. At death they would be freed from the round of reincarnation: their souls and spirits would return to the Land of the Living and there be reunited with their bodies which the Good God had made. It was in this sense that they understood St Paul's teaching about the resurrection of the body: 'It is sown a natural body, it is raised a spiritual body.'[41]

The consoled Cathar was called to a life of perfection. In a way there is nothing unusual about that, for Christ enjoined on all his followers the counsel: 'Be ye perfect even as your Father which is in Heaven is perfect.'[42] Nevertheless, the way in which the Cathars sought to obey the Lord's commandment was an unusually harsh one, for it involved a total change of life. Once they were consoled they had to renounce all family and social ties, give away all their property, observe a lifelong rule of celibacy, and place themselves entirely under the orders of the Cathar bishop. They were bound to say set prayers at regular hours of the day and night and to observe strict dietary laws, with long periods of fasting each year. They were forbidden to take the life of men or of warm-blooded creatures, even in self-defence; and they undertook never to tell a lie or take an oath even though their lives might depend on doing so.[43] Now there were in the Catholic Church religious orders like the Carthusians and the Grandmontines whose members followed rules of almost equal austerity, but in the Catholic tradition such mortification was perceived as a special vocation for some Christians.[44] In Catharism there was no option: the rule of life was designed to enable the Cathar to wage war on his body, because that body was the creation of an evil God. The sexual and aggressive instincts, the appetite for food and the need for sleep were all, in the Cathar view, functions of an evil body over which the redeemed soul had to gain the mastery.

There were many people who, while admiring the dedicated lives of the Cathars and believing their teaching, were not willing or able to undertake the total commitment which membership of the Cathar

[41] I Cor. 15. 44; Moneta de Cremona discusses the Cathar understanding of this text, IV, VIII, iv, p. 360.

[42] Matt. 5. 48.

[43] The principles underlying these obligations are set out in detail in the Latin *Ritual* for receiving the *consolamentum*, *Rituel Cathare*, pp. 246–60.

[44] Carole A. Hutchinson, *The Hermit Monks of Grandmont* (Kalamazoo, MI, 1989); Un Certosino and J. Dubois, 'Certosini', *Dizionario degli Istituti di Perfezione* (Rome, 1975), 2, cols 782–821.

Church demanded. Such people were known as believers: they were not bound by any of the rules of the Cathar Church because they did not belong to it, but they could, when dying, summon the Cathar perfect and be consoled by them. In the thirteenth century in Languedoc the practice developed of believers entering into a contract with the Cathar Church, the *convenanza*, stating their wish to be received before they died.[45] Deathbed converts experienced no difficulty about keeping the rules of the Church.

It seems relevant to ask why, since they did not believe that their bodies were the creation of the Good God, the Cathar perfect who were received into the Church when they were in good health did not commit suicide, thus releasing their souls from temptation. Some nineteenth-century scholars, notably Douais, did accuse them of encouraging their followers to commit suicide through the use of the *endura*, but such criticism was ill-founded.[46] The *endura*, by which a Cathar consoled during a terminal illness entered upon a fast to death, arose only during the time of persecution in the thirteenth century as a way by which those who had been consoled when extremely ill might avoid post-baptismal sin, since it was difficult to find a perfect who could administer the sacrament a second time. There is no evidence that the *endura* formed a normal part of Cathar practice, and, indeed, healthy Cathars never discussed the possibility of suicide. The vocation of the perfect was to remain in this world and carry on the redeeming work of Christ by ministering to their fellow men, for as the *Gloss on the Lord's Prayer* explains when commenting on 'forgive us our trespasses': 'And it should be known that from the beginning [this people] was in debt, that is to say [the debt] of loving one another.'[47] Moreover, it would be wrong to imply that Cathar spirituality was simply a matter of stoical endurance. In the discourse addressed to the candidates at their consoling the officiant reminds them: 'Wherefore you must understand that you should love God in truth, in kindliness, in humility, in mercy, in chastity and in other virtuous ways.'[48] This love of God lay at the centre of the Cathar life of perfection.

[45] Duvernoy, *Religion*, pp. 159–60.

[46] C. Douais, *Les Albigeois. Leur Origine. Action de l'Église aux XIIIe siècle* (Paris, 1879), p. 253; for a refutation, Borst, *Katharer*, p. 197.

[47] 'E deven saber que els eran debitor de lo comencament . . . co es a saber l'un l'aotre que se amesan entre lor . . .', 'Une Glose', *RBPH*, 39, p. 777.

[48] *Rituel Cathare*, p. 248.

The Cathars recognized that some element of compromise with the physical world was essential if they were to carry out their ministry. Thus although individual perfect might own no property, the Cathar Church corporately owned the houses in which they lived and administered their means of livelihood.[49] The perfect might eat very sparingly, but they had to eat something; they might sleep very little, but they could not dispense with sleep entirely.

Nevertheless, no Cathar could be complacent. At his initiation he was told: 'And if you shall have done well to the end [of your life], we hope that your soul will have everlasting life.'[50] Perseverance was by no means certain, for the Cathar's redeemed soul inhabited a body which remained under the dominion of the evil God who had created it, and it continued to fight against the soul, seeking to entrap it once more. Moreover the Cathar perfect were very conscious of the importance of integrity of life and cited St James: 'Whosoever shall keep the whole law but offend in one point is become guilty of all.'[51]

So far as I am aware, the Cathars were unique among western Christians in not producing any literature which aimed to give training in the cultivation of the spiritual life. Catholic monastic clergy, whom in many ways the Cathar perfect closely resembled, produced a huge literature about how to live the virtuous life: the theology of the seven contrary virtues as antidotes to the seven deadly sins may serve as an example of this. But there is not the slightest indication either in their own surviving works, or in those of their opponents, or in the voluminous depositions made to the Inquisition by their supporters, that the Cathars had any writings of this kind. It is dangerous to argue from silence, but I would tentatively suggest that this gap was a direct consequence of the Cathar view of the nature of the soul. Whereas Catholics assumed that each human soul was a new creation which needed to grow in the knowledge and love of God, Cathars believed that their souls were very ancient[52] and that knowledge of God and of

[49] This element of compromise about possessions is very evident in the opening rubrics of the form for consoling a dying believer, where the conferring of the sacrament is made dependent on his payment of outstanding monetary debts to the Cathar Church: 'E si deu lunha re e o pod pagar far o deu. E si far no o vol, no deu esser receubutz.' Clédat, *Nouveau Testament*, pp. xxii, 480.

[50] 'E si be o faitz entro a la fi, avem esperansa que la vostra arma aia vida durable', ibid. pp. xix, 478.

[51] Jas. 2. 10; 'Apologie', ch. 9, *RBPH*, 38, p. 827.

[52] Moneta de Cremona cites the Albanensian Cathar Tetricus, commenting on 1 Pet. 3.

the virtuous life formed part of their natural properties. Once the link between the Good God and the soul had been re-established, the soul could discern clearly what was virtuous, and needed no further training.

But as their awareness of the possibility of committing grave sins shows, the Cathars were very conscious of the need of God's grace to protect their human frailty. One very important way in which they experienced the presence of God was in His Church.[53] The Cathar Church was perceived as being the centre of the Good God's activity in a universe made by and subject to the God of Evil. Perhaps for that reason an initiated Cathar was never left on his own except in a case of grave emergency. At his consoling he became a member of a single-sex community, a house of the perfect, and if it was necessary for him to travel as part of his ministry, then a companion was normally assigned to him. It was not, of course, always possible to observe this practice in time of persecution, but it remained the ideal.[54] This rule was designed not merely to afford the perfect human companionship and moral support, it also had a sacramental value. For Christ had said: 'For where two or three are gathered together in my name, there am I in the midst of them.'[55] Thus Christ was sacramentally present in the lives of the Cathar communities, or companions, who constituted a permanent church.

There has been much debate about whether the Cathars celebrated the Eucharist.[56] At the beginning of every meal the presiding Cathar took bread, wrapped it in a napkin, recited the Lord's Prayer over it, and distributed it to the company, whether they were initiates or not. But although their lay adherents attached a sacramental significance to this ceremony, the perfect did not.[57] They regarded bread as part of the

18–19: 'Ex qua etiam auctoritate voluit esse miser haereticus Tetricus nomine quod populus Dei antiquus sit, non novus, id est de novo creatus', I, IV, v, p. 61.

53 'Apologie', ch. 1, *RBPH*, 38, 820–2.

54 Before the time of persecution the perfect went to considerable lengths to seek the companionship of other Cathars when they left their communities. E.g. the evidence of an Inquisition witness cited by Duvernoy: 'As this heretic did not wish to eat without a companion . . . I went and fetched another heretic who kept him company during the meal', 'La religion', in Lafont and Pech, eds, *Les Cathares en Occitanie*, p. 239.

55 Matt. 18. 20; cf. Clédat, *Nouveau Testament*, pp. xviii, 477.

56 A. V. Solovjev, 'La Messe cathare', *Cahiers d'études cathares*, 12 (1951–2), pp. 199–206.

57 'Albanenses dicunt quod panis ille non benedicitur corporalis nec potest accipere aliquam benedictionem, cum ipse panis sit creatura dyaboli . . .', Sacconi, p. 44. Examples of believers' devotion to the blessed bread of the Cathars, Duvernoy, *Religion*, p. 216.

evil creation, and one can only infer that they performed this ceremony because they had derived it from some more orthodox tradition of worship and believed it to be of apostolic origin. The Latin *Ritual* explains at some length how the Cathars understood the eucharistic texts in the New Testament:

> 'Verily, verily, I say unto you, except ye eat the flesh of the Son of man', that is unless you keep the commandments of the Son of God, 'and drink his blood', that is unless you receive the spiritual sense of the New Testament, 'ye have no life in you.'

They glossed the narrative of the Last Supper in the same way.[58] The sacramental presence of Christ in the life of the perfect was therefore experienced through devout meditation on holy scripture in the light of the revelation which he had given to his Church.

The Cathars had access to God the Father through the Lord's Prayer around which their liturgy was built. They recited this with the doxology, and in the fourth petition used the form 'give us this day our supersubstantial bread'.[59] There was nothing heretical about this: St Jerome had been in some doubt about how to render *epiousios* in the Vulgate texts of the Lord's Prayer, and has used *supersubstantialem* in St Matthew's Gospel and *cotidianum* in that of St Luke.[60] The Cathars preserved both forms in their translation of the New Testament, but used the Matthew version liturgically. Obviously 'supersubstantial bread' accorded better with their beliefs than 'daily bread', for ordinary bread was under the dominion of evil and not within the power of the Good God to give. It should be noted, however, that the nuns at the Paraclete under the direction of Heloise, the wife of Peter Abelard, also used the form 'panem nostrum supersubstantialem' in the Lord's Prayer.[61]

[58] '"Amen, amen dico vobis, nisi manducaveritis carnem filii hominis", id est nisi observaveritis precepta filii Dei, "et eius sanguinem biberitis", id est nisi spiritualem intentionem novi testamenti receperitis, "non habetis vitam in vobis"' (commenting on John 6. 53). *Rituel Cathare*, p. 206.

[59] All known Cathar versions use this form, e.g. Clédat, *Nouveau Testament*, p. 470.

[60] 'Panem nostrum supersubstantialem da nobis hodie', Matt. 6. 11; 'Panem nostrum cotidianum da nobis hodie', Luke 11. 3.

[61] For the use of 'supersubstantialem' in the Pater Noster by the nuns of the Paraclete, see Peter Abelard, *Epistola*, X, *PL* 178, cols 335–40; C. Waddell, 'Peter Abelard's Letter 10', *Cistercian Medieval History*, 2, Cistercian Studies, 24 (Kalamazoo, MI, 1976), pp. 75–86. I should like to thank Dr J. M. B. Porter for drawing my attention to this source.

By supersubstantial bread the Cathars understood divine love, which is the nature of God Himself: 'Therefore this people prays that this supersubstantial bread, which is God's love, may be given them by the Father, in order that after they have received it they may be found perfect in the sight of their God . . .'.[62]

Love is not a quality associated with the Cathars by Catholic writers, who never mention it when discussing them, possibly because the importance of God's love in the Christian life was not a point at issue between them. Divine Love was central to the Cathar religion: the *consolamentum* was intended to restore the believer to God's love,[63] and the fullest exposition of the Cathar understanding of the way in which God's love operated is found in the *Gloss on the Lord's Prayer*. The author, meditating on Holy Scripture, has discerned there a hierarchy of spiritual powers who draw the individual soul to God with cords of love. His conception is not dissimilar from that set out in orthodox terms by the pseudo-Dionysius in his *Celestial Hierarchy* except that, because the writer is a Cathar, he has also discerned a parallel diabolical hierarchy who stretch cords to hinder the soul in its ascent. The author concludes: 'Thus the God of all grace commanded His beloved Son [to bring] the gift of His Love to . . . the people, to perfect and strengthen and confirm them.'[64]

But bodily mortifications did not enable the Cathars to overcome all temptations. The Cathar Church claimed the power to forgive sins committed after consoling and in effect made the same distinction as the Catholic Church did between mortal and venial sins, while not using that terminology. Trivial sins were absolved at monthly meetings at which all the Cathars of a district made a general confession in a set form to a deacon, representing the bishop. Most of the sins they confessed were those common to all Christians: distraction at prayer, worldly conversation, making uncharitable remarks about each other. But one venial sin was peculiar to Cathars: 'With our tongue we fall

[62] 'Per co aquest poble prega aquest pan sobresostancial, co es la carita, esser dona a si del Paire per co que, cant ille la haoran recebua, ille sian troba perfeit en l'esgardement del lor Dio . . .', 'Une Glose', ch. vi, *RBPH*, 39, p. 777.

[63] At the administration of the *consolamentum* in the Latin rite the minister made this comment on I Cor. 13. 3: '"Et si distribuero in cibos pauperum omnes facultates meas, et si tradidero corpus meum ita ut ardeam, caritatem autem non habuero, nichil mihi prodest', id est sine hoc baptismate spiritus caritatis.' *Rituel Cathare*, p. 246.

[64] 'Enaisi lo Dio de tota gracia ordene lo sio Fill ama e lo don de la carita a . . . lo poble perfar, consodar e confermar', 'Une Glose', ch. v, *RBPH*, 39, p. 775.

into idle words, into frivolous talk, into laughter.'[65] Laughter is inappropriate in Hell, and that is where the Cathars believed that they were living. They received formal penances for trivial sins, usually consisting of a few additional days of fasting.[66]

Grave sins arose from a wilful failure to keep the Cathar Church's laws, and consisted of offences like theft, taking life, fornication, lying, swearing an oath, or eating meat. Such sins broke the communion between the perfect and the Good God, and only a bishop could absolve them, for they necessitated re-consoling and the imposition of a heavy penance. The offender was deprived of office in the Church for life, and, like an unfrocked Catholic priest, was only allowed to exercise his ministry *in extremis*. It is not known whether such absolution could be received more than once. It should also be noted that if a Cathar felt a vehement and persistent desire to break the Church's law and consented to it in will, though not in deed, he was required to do severe penance and was stripped of office.[67]

The inquisitor Rainier Sacconi criticizes the Cathar penitential system and his strictures deserve attention because he had been a Cathar minister for seventeen years before being converted to Catholicism and joining the Dominican Order. He comments that during all his years as a Cathar:

> I have not seen any of them pray privately apart from the others, or look sad because of his sins, or burst into tears, or beat his breast and say 'Be merciful, O Lord, to me a sinner', or anything else of this kind which might be a sign of contrition.[68]

There is no reason to disbelieve Rainier's evidence, and it suggests that Cathars understood penance in a different way from other Christians. Penance in the medieval Catholic Church was seen as an act of satisfaction offered by the sinner to the justice of God; other Christians have regarded it as an expression of sorrow offered by the sinner to

[65] 'De las nostras lengas cazem em par ulas ossiossas, en vas parlementz, en ris . . .', Clédat, *Nouveau Testament*, pp. x, 470.

[66] Sacconi, 'De confessione venalium', p. 46.

[67] Anselm of Alessandria, *Tractatus de hereticis*, ch. 6, ed. A. Dondaine, 'La Hiérarchie cathare en Italie, II', *AFP*, 20 (1950), p. 315.

[68] '. . . non vidi aliquem ex eis orare secreto seorsum ab aliis, aut ostendere se tristem de peccatis suis, siue lacrimari vel percutere pectus et dicere: "Propitius esto, Domine, [michi] peccatori", sive aliquid aliud huiusmodi, quod sit signum contritionis.' Sacconi, *Summa*, *AFP*, 44, p. 45.

God's Love. But the Cathars seem to have viewed it as remedial: a means of restraining their evil bodies from increasing their hold over their redeemed souls. No doubt, as they believed that this world was Hell, they considered that during the millennia spent here they had already performed all necessary penance for the true sin which they had committed once when they had rebelled against the Good God in the Land of the Living.[69]

The Cathar perfect had a vocation to minister to the other imprisoned spirits and this ministry took various forms determined by their bishop. The opinion sometimes expressed by modern writers that the Cathars spent all their time preaching is quite unfounded.[70] Some Cathars, almost exclusively men, were seconded to that work by their bishop,[71] to bring news of salvation to those who were ignorant of it; others ran small communities which provided instruction to postulants; some women brought up orphaned children in an understanding of the Cathar faith; some Cathars seem to have led contemplative lives;[72] but all of them had a ministry to pray for others. This was particularly important in the Cathar Church since it was believed that only the initiated had access to God. Other people might pray, but their prayers could not be heard and they only profaned God's name by making them.[73] Cathar believers, when they met Cathar perfect of either sex, knelt before them and said:

[69] This appears to be the opinion of the absolute dualists: 'Item nota quod quidem doctor Albanensium, scilicet Lanfrancinus de Vaure, dicit, et est opinio Albanensium, quod non omnes oves sive anime que descenderunt vel ceciderunt de celo incorporantur, sed aliqui purgantur in aere isto caliginoso sine corpore aliquo, et maiorem penam sustinent quam ille que sunt in corporibus, sed cicius salvantur; et ille sunt de quibus dicitur in evangelio: "Alias oves habeo que non sunt ex etc."' (John 10. 16), Anselm of Alessandria, *Tractatus de hereticis*, *AFP*, 20, p. 312.

[70] E.g. 'The "perfect" were the ministers of the Cathar Church; usually they wandered in pairs through the country . . . and so were able to keep in close touch with their followers.' J. R. Strayer, *The Albigensian Crusades* (Ann Arbor, MI, 1971), p. 32.

[71] This appears from the very detailed analysis of Inquisition records by R. Abels and E. Harrison, 'The participation of women in Languedocian Catharism', *MS*, 41 (1979), pp. 215–51; Anne Brenon rightly emphasises that there was no theoretical distinction made between the sexes in regard to the preaching ministry: *Les Femmes Cathares* (Paris, 1992), pp. 210–15.

[72] Berbeigueira, the wife of Lobenx of Puylaurens, told the inquisitors that she had seen a Cathar perfect who 'For a very long time remained seated on a chair, unmoving, like the trunk of a tree, unaware of what was going on around him', cited by Guiraud, *Cartulaire*, I, p. lxiv.

[73] When the angelic souls fell from grace they lost the right to pray: 'Aquest poble ofrent aquesta oracion al Segnor laide lo nom del sio Dio entre las genz a las cals el intre, aisicom lo Segnor dis per Ezechiel profeta: "Non per vos yo faray maison de Israel, mas per lo mio saint

'Bless us, Good Christians, grant us God's blessing and yours. Pray God for this sinner that he may be delivered from an evil death and be brought to a good end.' The Cathar replied: 'God grant your prayer. May he make you a good Christian and bring you to a good end.'[74]

This intercessory prayer for those who could not pray themselves formed an important part of the Cathars' ministry. Even more important, of course, was the administration of the *consolamentum* to dying believers. This could be undertaken by any perfected Cathar of either sex, and was a particularly dangerous ministry during the time of persecution, and one which led to the arrest and death of many perfect. But in this the Cathars were following the precepts of their Lord: 'Greater love hath no man than this than that he lay down his life for his friends. Ye are my friends . . .'[75]

Nevertheless, there were severe limits to the power of the Cathar perfect as intercessors. All that they could do was to pray for God's grace that the believer might die consoled and achieve liberation. The Good God could not be asked for any kind of material aid – protection from pain, or illness, or even persecution – because he had no authority over the physical world, which was entirely subject to the God of Evil. This was a very significant difference between the religious practice of the Cathars and that of their Catholic contemporaries.[76]

Not all the fallen souls from the Land of the Living could be reached by Cathar ministers, for some were in the bodies of birds and animals. Although the Cathars could do nothing to help such souls, they could refrain from harming them: hence their absolute prohibition on taking the life of a bird or a warm-blooded beast. The Cathars took that injunction very seriously. Catholic authorities occasionally asked those whom they suspected of being Cathars to wring the neck of a chicken and took it as evidence of guilt if they refused to do so. This was a perfectly reasonable assumption in an agrarian society, but

nom lo cal vos laides entre las genz a-las cals vos intre"' (Ezek. 36. 22). 'Une Glose', ch. ii, *RBPH*, 39, p. 765. This right was restored to the Cathar at his consoling.

[74] This form is reported in Inquisition records, Duvernoy, *Religion*, pp. 209–10.

[75] John 15. 13–14.

[76] Salvo Burci, possibly on the authority of the *Stella*, attributes to the Albanenses the beliefs that: '. . . bonus Deus non sanaret opera diaboli' (and therefore Christ cannot have performed miracles of corporal healing); and 'Mundus iste et corpora ista sunt a Deo non bono, et bonus Deus non habet aliquid ad faciendum in istis in aliquo casu . . .', *Aevum*, 19, pp. 310, 339.

there were Cathars who died rather than kill a chicken.[77] I think that the Cathar prohibition about eating animal produce, including eggs and milk, may have been similarly motivated. Catholic writers supposed that these food taboos were connected with the Cathars' horror of coition,[78] but I suspect that the Cathars were more deterred from milking a cow by the knowledge that it had a soul of equal value to their own, and that it too was in exile from the heavenly kingdom.[79] Cathar respect for the animal creation also took more positive forms. A rubric in the Occitan *Ritual* enacts that if Cathars are travelling and find an animal in a trap they should disregard it, but this implies that their normal reaction would be to release and care for it.[80]

One way in which Catharism differed a great deal from medieval Catholicism and, indeed, from most other traditional kinds of Christianity, was in its attitude towards death. Catholics viewed death with apprehension: it would be followed by judgement and therefore by the possibility of damnation or the near certainty of Purgatory. The Cathar had no such fears, for the day of judgement had already happened.[81] He was already living in Hell, and the worst that could happen when he died was that he would remain there. Cathars did not believe in Purgatory: there was no need of further purgation for souls which had already endured millennia of torments. The Cathar Church did not pray for the dead.[82] There was no point in

[77] The Cathar Church's understanding of the prohibition of killing is explained in 'Apologie', ch. iii, *RBPH*, 38, p. 823. Examples from the Inquisition records of how Cathars refused to kill animals even when in danger of death, in Duvernoy, *Religion*, pp. 191–2.

[78] 'Item credunt quod comedere carnes et oua vel caseum, etiam in urgenti necessitate sit mortale peccatum, et hoc ideo quia nascuntur ex coito.' This opinion of Sacconi must be given weight because he had been a professed Cathar, though a moderate dualist: Sacconi, p. 43.

[79] Moneta de Cremona accuses the Albanensian theologian Tetricus of making no distinction between men and beasts: '. . . Tetricus Haereticus in quadam parte cujusdam Libri sui cap. II . . . [asserit] quod omnis creatura Deum laudat, volens hoc habere ex eo quod legitur Apoc. 5, vv.13–14 . . . Ignoravit autem . . . quod creatura rationalis laudet, et etiam aliae creaturae; sed differenter, quia creatura rationalis, id est Homo, vel Angelus, effective, aliae autem creaturae materialiter . . .', I, VII, ii, p. 79.

[80] M. R. Harris has made a conjectural restoration of this rubric, which he believes has been wrongly copied, to suggest that the animal should only be left in the trap if the Cathars are unable to follow their normal practice of leaving monetary compensation for the huntsman when they release it: 'Le problème des bonshommes devant l'animal piégé dans le Rituel cathare occitan', *Heresis*, 2 (1984), pp. 15–19.

[81] 'Et dicunt quod sententia iudicii iam data est, pro eo quod dicitur: "Princeps mundi huius iam iudicatus est"' (John 16. 11), *De Heresi Catharorum in Lombardia*, ed. A. Dondaine, 'La hiérarchie cathare d'Italie, I', *AFP*, 19 (1949), p. 309.

[82] 'O miseri tapini, vos multum nugamini de corporibus humanis, cum mortua sint, et

doing so, because either they had achieved salvation and did not need prayers, or they had been reincarnated and were no longer dead.

The Cathars did not fear death, they feared life. Given their premisses they had reason to do so. The Good God was all-loving, but he was not almighty and he had no jurisdiction over the kingdom of darkness in which they lived. The odds were heavily weighted against their salvation: the whole universe, the vastness of the heavens as well as the earth, was the creation of the evil God, and the Cathars' souls were imprisoned in bodies made by and subject to that God. It was this fear which, I would argue, explains the Cathars' readiness to face execution by burning alive with calm indifference. Cathars condemned to the stake were always offered a reprieve if they would recant, but only a handful availed themselves of that clemency. I do not wish to deny that it took great physical courage voluntarily to accept death by burning, but I would suggest that the Cathars had a spiritual motivation in doing so. To die for one's faith is good evidence of final perseverance, and death, for the Cathar, marked the end of bodily imprisonment. The spirit was already perfect: if it resisted temptation to the end it was assured of restoration to a place in the Land of the Living, there to be reunited with its spiritual body. A Cathar facing death at the stake could therefore apply to himself St Paul's words to Timothy:

> I have fought the good fight, I have finished my course, I have kept the faith. Henceforth there is laid up for me a crown of life, which the Lord, the righteous judge, will give back to me [*reddet mihi*, Vulgate] at that day; and not to me only, but unto all them also that love his appearing.[83]

University of Nottingham

ponitis ea in foveas huc et illuc privatim . . .', wrote Salvo Burci, addressing all the main schools of Cathars, *Aevum*, 19, p. 337; but it would seem that in times of peace the families of believers consoled on their deathbeds often insisted on more conventional funerals: W. L. Wakefield, 'Burial of heretics in the Middle Ages', *Heresis*, 5 (1985), pp. 29–32.

[83] 2 Tim. 4. 7–8; *Traité*, ch. xix, p. 298; Moneta de Cremona also reports the Cathar use of this text: I, IV, i, p. 50.

NORTHERN CATHARS AND HIGHER LEARNING[1]

by PETER BILLER

THE confluence between speculative thought and universities on the one hand and broad-based heretical movements on the other hand was a predominant theme in Bunny Leff's great and monumental *Heresy in the Later Middle Ages*, notably in the case of Wyclif, Hus, and the popular propagation of their ideas. The first arm of this theme, university learning, seems to have no place in the history of Catharism. Where are there equivalent Cathar masters? In a university setting we do have *Catholic* theologians' discussion of *dualism*, but is this more than a footnote in the history of Catharism? Take for example the University of Paris, its theology faculty, and the bachelor's exercise of lecturing on the *Sentences* of Peter Lombard, where the question of there being one or several principles of things arose in the first distinction of the second book, and take three 1250s commentators. Tackling this question during his bachelor years (1252–6), St Thomas states five arguments in favour of plurality of principles, citing one logical and three natural works of Aristotle. He postpones naming the proponents of plurality until his response. Here he combines Aristotle's survey of them in the first book of the *Metaphysics* and the Church's experience of dualist heresy in a list:[2] early natural philosophers, Empedocles and Pythagoras, and the heresy of the Manichees. Such a sentence commentary, showing us a formal proposition, one among several philosophical dualisms which were being ventilated in the theological schools of Paris, seems remote from the inquisitor's register through which we see Cathar perfects and their followers living out theological dualism in fortified villages down south in Languedoc.

In such scholastic discussion, where heretical dualism is at issue, the erroneous 'opinion' is likely to be identified as Manichean and its description may entirely derive from patristic refutations of the

[1] I am extremely grateful to John Baldwin, Barrie Dobson, and Mark Smith for their close and constructive comments, and I am especially indebted to Bernard Hamilton for the quite remarkable generosity of time and attention he devoted to this paper.

[2] St Thomas Aquinas, *Scriptum super libros sententiarum*, II, i, 1, 1, *Opera omnia*, 25 vols (Parma, 1852–73), 6, pp. 384–86.

Manichees, in particular St Augustine's. Since the discussion is general and timeless, an author, who may know of the doctrines of the Cathars, may still feel no need to refer to such contemporary dualists; even if he *does* refer to them, he may call them 'Manichees', as churchmen had been doing since the mid-twelfth century, possibly as far back as Guibert de Nogent in the early years of the century;[3] and if he wished to import material from contemporary dualism, there would be no obvious reason to distinguish it from early Church dualism. A second commentator, St Bonaventure, differed from St Thomas in identifying the proponents of a plurality of principles, beginning with Manichees. 'The Manichees say' several propositions, grounded partly on Holy Scripture and partly on *rationes*.[4] A third commentator, Peter of Tarentaise,[5] broadly followed St Thomas, both in not identifying the proponents of plurality and in some of the propositions which he ascribed to them. However, he also inserted into his list two *rationes*, which are not from St Thomas. They are similar in content, but not in precise wording, to those which St Bonaventure attributed to the Manichees. Now, we can look forward from these 1250s commentaries, whose influence and large numbers of copies established commonplaces for many decades to come. These commentaries provide some of the raw material for 'the later history of scholastic discussion of dualism', which is likely to be the history of a confined and 'intertextual' world, remote from the contemporary dualists, who survived in Languedoc until the 1320s.

From the 1250s we can also look back to an *earlier* period, when we can argue that the opposite of 'remoteness' prevailed. Some of the 1250s statements, those of Peter of Tarentaise, are rooted in statements which were attributed to 'Manichees' by Guillaume d'Auxerre (died *c.*1231) in his *Summa aurea*, which was written around 1220.[6] Several points indicate that these 'Manichees' were contemporary Cathars. These are Guillaume's knowledge of Cathars; the attribution to them of one quotation which does not, in its Latin form, predate the twelfth

[3] B. Hamilton, 'Wisdom from the East: the reception by the Cathars of Eastern dualist texts', P. Biller and A. Hudson, eds, *Heresy and Literacy in the Middle Ages, 1000–1530* (Cambridge, 1994, reprinted with corrections, 1996), p. 45.

[4] St Bonaventure, *Commentaria in quatuor libros sententiarum*, II, i, 1, 1, *Opera omnia*, 11 vols (Quaracchi, 1882–1902), 2, pp. 25–7.

[5] Peter of Tarentaise, *In quattuor libros sententiarum commentaria*, II, i, 2, 1, 4 vols (Toulouse, 1649–52), 2, pp. 8–9.

[6] See nn. 14 and 20 below.

century; and the extensive similarity of their propositions to those which were described as Cathar around 1241 in a treatise written by the Italian Dominican polemicist Moneta of Cremona (died *c.*1250). The following section contains further details of these men and their writings. What emerges from a closer look at the Guillaume/Moneta parallels should be added to some observations which Arno Borst made about higher theology and the Cathars. Together they point to connections with the schools of Paris. While previous work on Catharism has concentrated heavily on its southern branches, in Languedoc and Lombardy, this underlines the importance of northern Catharism within the Catharism of Latin Christendom, a point to which I return at the end of this paper.

GUILLAUME D'AUXERRE, MONETA OF CREMONA, AND 'MAXIMS'

I begin with the treatment of Cathars by one northern theologian, Guillaume d'Auxerre, in his *Summa aurea.*[7] In his preface Guillaume gives 'defense of the faith against heretics' as one of the three grounds for using human reasoning to prove faith,[8] and the overall role of heresy in the *Summa aurea* warrants independent study.[9] Here we can only conjecture the broader context such a study would supply, while turning to Guillaume's main formal statements of dualist opinions, which occur at two points, one on resurrection and the other on the principle of the first created things. At issue in the one was denial of the resurrection of bodies, and in the other belief in two principles of created things rather than one. In both cases Guillaume presents heretics using 'argument' (*ratio*) as well as scriptural 'authority' (*auctoritas*). These heretics' 'arguments' are presented by Guillaume, one on the question of resurrection and three on the theme of two principles. There is striking similarity between Guillaume's restatement of these heretics' 'arguments' and the presentation of some of

[7] The *Summa aurea* was edited by J. Ribailler in the series *Spicilegium Bonaventurianum* (Paris and Grottaferrata, 1980–7), with the *Summa*'s book numbers and the series numbers co-ordinating thus: Lib. 1 = 16; Lib. 2 parts 1–2 = 17 (in two parts not differentiated by number); Lib. 3 part 1 = 18a; Lib.3 part 2 = 18b; Lib. 4 = 19; *Introduction* = 20.

[8] *Summa aurea*, I, Prologue, *Spicilegium Bonaventurianum*, 16, p. 16: defensio fidei contra haereticos.

[9] F. Droes, 'Guillaume d'Auxerre et les cathares?', *Annuaire-Bulletin de l'École Pratique des Hautes Études VIe Section*, 84 (1979–80), pp. 427–8, reports research on the possibility of Guillaume of Auxerre being the *Magister G* referred to in the Italian Cathar *Liber de duobus principiis*.

them by two other Catholic writers who described and refuted Cathar doctrines, Alain de Lille and Moneta of Cremona. Two treatises by Alain are in question here, *Quoniam homines*, which he wrote between 1155 and 1165, and probably around 1160,[10] and *De fide*,[11] which he wrote between 1185 and 1200, and for convenience these will be referred to as Alain I and Alain II. Here are the parallels in my translation – these and other parallels are given in Latin in the appendix at the end of this paper.

Guillaume's restatement of the heretics' 'argument' denying resurrection runs thus. 'The soul uses a body like an instrument. But nothing is owed to an instrument – for it merits nothing of itself, only the one using the instrument [merits anything]. Therefore since the body merits nothing, nothing is owed it; therefore resurrection is not owed it.'[12] Moneta's restatement of Cathar belief goes like this. 'They believe that these bodies are only organs, that is to say, instruments of souls, for good or evil things are done, so they say, through bodies as instruments. Therefore just as only the artisan is rewarded, not the instrument which he uses, so only the soul will be rewarded, not the body.'[13]

In a chapter on the theme of 'created things and their principles', Guillaume's treatise attributes to 'Manicheus' or 'the Manichees' three propositions and deductions from them. The first is parallelled by descriptions of Cathar doctrine in both Alain II and Moneta, and the third by Moneta alone. Here are the parallels.

Guillaume's treatise introduces the propositions and deductions, and states the first thus. 'They want to prove their opinion by certain maxims. The first [maxim] is "What has an invariable cause is itself invariable". Since therefore the benign God is an invariable cause, He is not the cause of variable things.'[14] In Alain II the argument runs thus. '"If the cause [is] immutable the effect [is] immutable"; but it is clear that these corporeal things are mutable, therefore their cause is

[10] Ed. in P. Glorieux, 'La somme "Quoniam homines" d'Alain de Lille', *AHDLMA*, 20 (1954), pp. 111–364 (119–364); for discussion of date, see p. 116.

[11] M.-T. d'Alverny, *Alain de Lille. Textes inédits, avec une introduction sur sa vie et ses oeuvres* (Paris, 1965), p. 156.

[12] *Summa aurea*, IV, xviii, 1, 1, *Spicilegium Bonaventurianum*, 19, p. 460.

[13] Moneta, *Adversus Catharos*, IV, viii, 1, p. 346b.

[14] *Summa aurea*, II, viii, 1, *Spicilegium Bonaventurianum*, 17, part 1, p. 168. I am confining my discussion of arguments about two principles to the three restated by Guillaume here, and excluding those which are given later, pp. 170–1, whose contemporary or patristic origin is not clear.

mutable.'[15] In Moneta: 'They introduce a certain proposition: "If the cause [is] invariable, so also [are] its effects". Since therefore these visible things are variable, it cannot be that their cause is the holy and true God, who is invariable.'[16]

In Guillaume's treatise the third goes like this. 'The third [maxim is]: "The principles of contraries are contraries." Since therefore good and evil are contraries, they have contrary principles. Since therefore the highest good is the cause of good, the highest evil is the cause of evil.'[17] In Moneta: 'They want [this, that is to say, two principles] to be held on the basis of this dictum of Aristotle: "The principles of contraries are contraries." Since therefore good and evil are contraries, they have contrary principles. Since therefore the highest good is the cause of good, the principle of evil will be the highest evil.'[18]

So far, passages have been presented in which the parallels are very close. We have only been looking at Alain II (between 1185 and 1200). If we extend the survey to include the earlier Alain I (probably *c.*1160), we find a general theological treatise which at one point turns to the 'opinion of [the] Manichee' [Manichei [. . .] opinionem]'. We will discuss later the issue of the mixture of old and contemporaneous in Alain I, and note here only the further parallels which it provides. Alain I's version of an invariable or immutable cause and its effects should be compared to those quoted above. It runs like this. 'Item, that which has an invariable cause and is also itself invariable. But God is an invariable and immutable cause; however visible things are variable and mutable. Therefore [God] is not the cause of visible things.' In addition Alain I provides a parallel – as Alain II and Moneta do not – to the second argument concerning the principles of created things which Guillaume described, which has not yet been quoted. Alain I runs thus. 'Item, God is a constructive cause and not a destructive cause. But wickedness pertains more to destruction than construction. Therefore

[15] Alain de Lille, *De fide catholica contra haereticos*, I, iii, *PL* 210, col. 309.

[16] Moneta, *Adversus Catharos*, I, viii, 1, p. 83a. In Peter of Tarentaise, cited in n. 5 above: 'Cuius causa est inuariabilis, ipsum est inuariabile; quia idem similiter se habens natum est omnino facere idem, ut dicitur in lib. de gen. & corrup. Ergo, cum Deus sit causa inuariabilis, ab ipso non sunt variabilia.'

[17] *Summa aurea*, II, viii, 1, *Spicilegium Bonaventurianum*, 17, part 1, p. 168.

[18] Moneta, *Adversus Catharos*, I, I, 3, p. 23b. Compare also Guillaume d'Auvergne's presentation of 'Manichean' argument against one principle, in his *De universo*, VIII, *Opera omnia*, 2 vols (Paris, 1674), 1, p. 601: 'Horum [= reasons] igitur primum est quia ex altero contrariorum non potest esse alterum: malum igitur ex bono esse non potest: erit igitur ex malo.'

evil things are not from God; but they are from something; therefore from another.'[19] Guillaume's words are these. 'The second thing [or 'ground' which they advance] is this. "What is constructive and destructive of something is not the same." Since therefore God is the destructive cause of evil men, He is not the constructive cause of the same men.'[20] In my translation 'destructive', translating both *destructiva* and *peremptoria*, is exaggerating similarity. While the first set of parallels we have noted, those between Alain II, Guillaume, and Moneta are extremely close, those we are noting here between Alain I and the later texts (including Alain II) are perceptibly more distant.[21]

Problematic are both of Alain's treatises – Alain I because of the use of patristic material and Alain II because of uncertainty about the source of Alain's knowledge of Cathars (southern or northern?) – and also the dicta other than *contrariorum contraria*, because their origin is unknown. In order to control the enquiry into the parallels, then, I am going to confine its first part to the two less problematic authors, Guillaume and Moneta, and the least problematic dictum, *contrariorum contraria sunt principia*.

In his chapter 'On created things and their principles' Guillaume does not produce a contemporary name for the proponents of the arguments he describes, and refers to them as *Manichei*, but he does include in the chapter a Paris chancellor's reminiscence of experience 'among them' ('inter eos'). 'They' are clearly Cathars (the passage is discussed later), and the combination of this and the parallels with Moneta's Cathars show that the arguers in Guillaume's chapter were Cathars. However, there is more than just common identity at stake: what precisely explains the closeness of Guillaume and Moneta? One possibility is that Moneta is copying Guillaume. The other possibility is that Guillaume and Moneta are independently acquiring information about Cathar doctrines, one in northern France and the other in Lombardy. A third possibility is that Moneta was turning his attention both to the Cathars of Lombardy and to the *Summa aurea* (or another source which was based on the *Summa aurea*).

Let us begin with the possibility of copying by Moneta. It is not difficult to show the circumstances which could have made it easy for

19 Glorieux, 'Quoniam homines', p. 130.

20 In Peter of Tarentaise, cited in n. 5 above: 'Nihil est causa constructiua, & destructiua: ergo oportet ponere duo prima principia, vnum constructionis, alterum destructionis.'

21 D'Alverny, *Alain de Lille*, p. 158, observed an overlap.

him to be aware of and use the *Summa aurea*. The *Summa aurea* was written substantially earlier than the 1241 date which is given for Moneta's treatise. Although 1215 and 1229 are the firmest extreme termini for Guillaume's work, its use in book 4 of Gui de Orchelles' *Tractatus de sacramentis* pushes the earlier terminus to 1216–17, and it is usually and plausibly assumed that the later terminus should be pushed back, to 1222.[22] The *Summa aurea* circulated quickly, diffused in several early abbreviations as well as numerous unabridged full or part copies, of which 125 still survive.[23] Although many of these manuscripts bear earlier marks of ownership from Paris and northern European cathedral chapters and monasteries, the work also spread quickly both among Dominicans and in the south. Thus one copy was given to Dominicans in Magdeburg some time after 1235; other copies made in the thirteenth century bear marks of ownership (themselves not necessarily, of course, indicating *earliest* ownership) by Dominican convents in Cambridge, Frankfurt, Pettau, Kassa (present-day Kosice), and Dubrovnik.[24] Among Italian manuscripts three are currently in Bologna, and one of these, a thirteenth-century copy, was once owned by Moneta's own convent in Bologna.[25] Further, one of the earliest treatises to grapple with the *Summa aurea* was written in Paris by Moneta's fellow Dominican, Roland of Cremona. Before this, in 1228, Roland had been in Moneta's company in the foundation of a convent at Cremona,[26] and Roland was back in Italy between 1233 and 1244 to deal with heresy, based in Bologna;[27] Moneta's treatise implies

[22] On the date of the *Summa aurea*, see J. Ribailler's *Introduction Générale* to his edition, *Spicilegium Bonaventurianum*, 20, p. 16; A. M. Landgraf, *Introduction á l'histoire de la littérature théologique naissante* (Montréal and Paris, 1973), pp. 173–4. See the editors' comments in Gui de Orchelles, *Tractatus de sacramentis*, D. and O. Van den Eynde, eds (New York, Louvain, and Paderborn, 1953), p. xli: the ignoring of important canon-legal material on marriage of 1216–17 suggests a date for Gui's *Tractatus* hardly after 1216–17 – and thus not after 1220 – and Guillaume's use of Gui's work in the fourth book of the *Summa aurea* (but not in earlier books) suggests a date for the *Summa aurea*'s completion a little after 1220, that is to say, between 1222 and 1225. There seems no clear ground for the double chronological slide. On the reasoning of the Van den Eyndes, the fourth book of the *Summa aurea*, in this picture, could have been undergoing influence from a Gui work composed in 1216–17. Why could it not be as early as 1218?

[23] They are described by Ribailler, *Introduction*, pp. 42–184.

[24] Ibid., pp. 42, 47, 80–1, 139, 157; see also p. 93, for a Naples copy which was once in Dominican hands.

[25] Ibid., pp. 50–2.

[26] *SOPMA*, 3, p. 137.

[27] Ibid., p. 330.

engagement with Cathars in the 1230s, and he also was in Bologna. There could be no more obvious channel for the mediation to Moneta of the ideas of the *Summa aurea* than Roland.

However, this only shows that it is highly plausible that Moneta had access to the *Summa aurea* and *could* have used it: not that he *did*. Although Moneta was a very sober writer, there seems considerable force, even passion, in the plea to his readers which he advances in the preface to his work. 'One thing however I beg of the readers of this work [unum autem peto a lectoribus istius operis].' His readers must not attack him for the frailty of his arguments against heretics. And,

> where they will have seen me positing certain arguments against the Church or replies on behalf of heretics, they [the readers] should not tear into me, saying that these [propositions and replies] did not originate with the heretics, [and alleging] that out of my own *ingenium* I have thought up the sort of things which could give comfort and succour to heretical wickedness. For [in fact] I have got these [propositions and replies] from their [the heretics'] mouths and writings [ubi etiam viderint me ponere argumenta aliqua contra ecclesam, aut responsiones pro haereticis, non me lacerent dicentes ea non ab haereticis duxisse originem, sed me proprio ingenio adinvenisse hujusmodi, quae possent nutrire, et augere haereticam pravitatem, quia vel ex ore eorum, vel ex scripturis suis illa habui].[28]

Providing the form and some of the substance of Moneta's statements are the topos of the author's modesty about his knowledge,[29] and an anxiety about the dissemination of heresies, through the restatement of heresies which such refutation requires, which recalls the topos of confessors' manuals – the danger of teaching how to sin when asking a penitent about sin. There may well be echoes of the words and thoughts of a tradition about the rhetoric used by historians, which goes back to Cicero's *De oratore* and beyond, in Moneta's contrasting of thinking up something out of one's own *ingenium* (perhaps best translated as 'inventive talent') and the implied authenticity of the *ipsissima verba* of the heretics and their own writings. That is to say, Moneta may be writing in the form and language of this historio-

[28] Moneta, *Praefatio*, p. 2.

[29] E. R. Curtius, *European Literature and the Latin Middle Ages*, trans. W. R. Trask (London, Henley, 1953), pp. 83–5. Moneta is being modest about the strength of his counter-arguments, not about his knowledge of heretics' arguments.

graphical rhetoric, while adapting 'the historian representing the past' to 'the polemicist representing his opponents'. Perhaps: but while his words may be anchored in such rhetorical traditions, Moneta is *at the same time* making a simple claim about his sources and the truthfulness of his representation of Cathar arguments.

When we turn to read the enormous treatise which follows this preface, what do we see? First, we need to stand back and set Moneta's treatise alongside other mid-thirteenth-century Italian Catholic authors, especially Dominicans, who were arguing with the Cathars, in a world which has recently been illuminated in Lorenzo Paolini's account of the culture of Italian Cathars.[30] Paolini shows a world of communication across polemical battle-grounds, in which Catholic theologians were engaging directly and knowledgeably with the extensive high and written theology of the Italian Cathars. It is not a closed 'intertextual' world of Catholic writers aridly dependent on each other. Secondly, Moneta himself was one of the least dependent of authors. The lack of a modern edition of his work and its great size (560 folio-size pages in the eighteenth-century edition) imposes caution. Only an impression can be given – but this impression is strong and points in one direction. We see an immense array of propositions ascribed to heretics' statements and writings. Some of the latter are very specific, with two Cathar authors cited by name (Tetricus and Desiderius), and specific reference: 'as the heretic Tetricus [claims] in a certain part of a certain book of his, chapter 2 of that part [sicut Thetricus haereticus in quadam parte cujusdam Libri sui cap.ii illius partis]'.[31] The copying of other Catholic authors on heretics is not only not obvious in Moneta's treatise, it is entirely out of character. Moneta seems to have been quoting the words or writings of Cathars from his Italian milieu, and such direct reliance is precisely what he claimed in his preface.

Turning now to Guillaume, we move to a figure associated with the city of Auxerre, its diocese, and the schools of Paris.[32] Seventeen years after Guillaume's death, his house in Auxerre was still identified as Guillaume's to Salimbene, when he visited Auxerre in 1248. The *Summa aurea* bears many marks of Guillaume's participation in

30 L. Paolini, 'Italian Catharism and written culture', Biller and Hudson, eds, *Heresy and Literacy*, pp. 61–82.

31 Moneta, I, vii, 2, p. 79b; see further Paolini, 'Italian Catharism', p. 101.

32 On his life, see Ribailler, *Introduction*, pp. 1–5.

intellectual life in Paris, and it is precisely this which Salimbene recalled from his conversation with 'the priests of the diocese of Auxerre', who preserved the memory of Guillaume and told Salimbene this: 'when he disputed in Paris, no-one disputed better than him'.[33]

Behind Guillaume and the *Summa aurea* stand the Cathars, their presence in the diocese of Auxerre, and concern about them both in this diocese and the university of Paris. Attentive to the Cathars and efforts to repress them was a chronicle written by Robert (*d.* 1212), a member of the Premonstratensian house of St Marien in Auxerre.[34] Several bishops of Auxerre had to pay attention to the Cathars of the diocese, in particular the obstinately persisting Cathars of La Charité,[35] although only one of them immediately stands out as zealous in their repression: Hugh of Noyers (1183–1206). Writing Hugh's biography in the *Gesta* of the bishops of Auxerre some time between 1207 and 1220, Eustache, a canon of the cathedral of Auxerre, presented Hugh as a *hereticorum malleus*, a 'hammer of the heretics' of the diocese of Auxerre, in particular the Cathars at La Charité.[36] During Hugh's episcopate the episode which made the headlines came in 1201. The man accused of Cathar heresy, Évrard of Chateauneuf, was a knight, 'great and powerful [*magnus et potens*]' and 'a man experienced in things of the world [*vir in rebus seculi versutus*]', in the descriptions of the *Gesta* and Robert of Auxerre:[37] after serving a cousin of the king of France, Pierre de Courtenay, the count of Auxerre, he had managed the lands of Hervé, count of Nevers. The papal legate Cardinal Octavian convoked a council at Paris to hear Évrard's case. There Évrard appeared before the legate, the archbishops and bishops of the French realm, and the 'theology' masters of Paris. The case was pressed

[33] Quoted by Ribailler, *Introduction*, p. 4: 'ut referebantur mihi sacerdotes de episcopatu Altissiodorensi . . . quando disputebat Parisius, nullus disputebat melius eo.'

[34] On the chronicle, which is cited below, see L. Delisle, 'Chronique de Robert de Saint-Marien d'Auxerre', *Histoire littéraire de France*, 32 (1898), pp. 503–35.

[35] É. Chénon, 'L'Hérésie à La Charité-sur-Loire et les débuts de l'inquisition monastique dans la France du Nord au XIIIe siècle', *Nouvelle Revue Historique de Droit Français et Étranger*, 41 (1917), pp. 299–345. See also C H. Haskins, 'Robert le Bougre and the beginnings of Inquisition in Northern France', originally published in the *AHR* in 1902, but cited here from the updated version in his *Studies in Medieval Culture* (Cambridge, MA, 1929), pp. 193–244 (204–7), and Duvernoy, *Histoire*, pp. 141–3.

[36] L. M. Duru, *Bibliothèque historique de l'Yonne*, 2 vols (Auxerre, Paris, 1850–63), 1, p. 431; C. B. Bouchard, *Spirituality and Administration. The Role of the Bishop in Twelfth-Century Auxerre* (Cambridge, MA, 1979), pp. 99, 103–5.

[37] Duru, *Bibliothèque*, 1, p. 445; Robert of Auxerrre, *Chronicon*, 1201, *MGH.SS*, 26, p. 260.

by Hugh, bishop of Auxerre, and many witnesses and items of evidence were produced, leading to Évrard's conviction and sentencing. He was handed over to the count of Nevers, and burnt to death at Nevers, 'in the sight of everyone'. Ten years later Nevers also saw the burning of two brothers of a *bailli* of the count of Nevers, Colin, a knight of Auxerre, both condemned for heresy,[38] but in this case, although there is a presumption of probability that 'heresy' meant Catharism, the sources do not tell us this. A letter from the archbishop of Sens to a later bishop of Auxerre, Henri de Villeneuve, continues to deal with the problem of the Cathars of La Charité, and this around 1221,[39] very close to the date of the writing of the *Summa aurea*.

'The heretic perfect is prepared to suffer all for his false faith', remarked Guillaume, during his discussion of the virtues in book 3,[40] punning on the name of Cathar perfects when pointing out that the imperfect Christian was not prepared to do this. While this may be in part anchored in a point about Cathars undergoing all forms of suffering which had earlier been made by Alexander Nequam[41] and a general northern tradition of comment on this, there is no reason to doubt the obvious, namely Guillaume's knowledge of executions in the diocese of Auxerre. In another passage relating to Cathars the other obvious source of Guillaume's knowledge is explicit.

> They say that the intellectual soul . . . can sin, and when it sins it is inserted into a more ignoble body to suffer there, into the body of a dog or something similar. Thus Master Prévostin, who lived a long time among them and was able to bring back [only] a few to the way of truth, used to recount that he heard them saying, when they saw a dog playing with its tail, 'Its soul will soon be purged and freed.'[42]

Prévostin's own experience of Cathars may have been gained during his period as a scholasticus in Mainz and among Rhineland Cathars –

38 Duvernoy, *Histoire*, pp. 143–4.

39 A. Wilmart, 'Une lettre sur les cathares du Nivernais (V.1221)', *Revue Bénédictine*, 47 (1935), pp. 72–4.

40 *Summa aurea*, III, xliii, 2, *Spicilegium Bonaventurianum*, 18b, p. 825: 'perfectus hereticus paratus est ad omnia pati pro fide falsa.'

41 Alexander Nequam, *Speculum speculationum*, IV, xx, 4, ed. R. Thompson, *ABMA*, 11 (1988), p. 445: 'patiuntur Cathari quoslibet cruciatus'; Thompson comments on the work's influence on Guillaume d'Auxerre, p. xviii. See similar comment by Guillaume d'Auvergne, below and note 97.

42 Translation from *Summa aurea*, II, viii, 1, *Spicilegium Bonaventurianum*, 17, part 1, p. 173.

he refers to Cathars in a sermon from his 'Mainz cycle';[43] this is thrown into uncertainty by the much better-known but questionable attribution to Prévostin of the authorship of a *Summa contra haereticos*, which seems to have an Italian setting.[44] However muddy the question of the Prévostin's source, Guillaume's is clear. He was listening to the Prévostin who was chancellor of Paris between 1206 and 1210: listening in Paris to discussion of Cathar doctrine. If we look through Moneta towards debating Cathar theologians in Lombardy, we look through the *Summa aurea* towards discussion of Cathars' doctrines in Paris and the existence, repression, and reporting of Cathars in the diocese of Auxerre.

One of the dicta used by Cathars of these geographically separate groups, and cited by both Guillaume and Moneta, was *contrariorum contraria sunt principia*. Attributed by Moneta to Aristotle, the dictum seems to be an adaptation of *contrariorum enim cause contrarie* in Aristotle's *On generation*.[45] When and how did Cathars get to know this work? The *On generation* was translated directly from Greek into Latin by an anonymous translator in the twelfth century, about whom nothing else is known apart from the high probability that he was also responsible for an early translation of a fragment of the *Nichomachean Ethics*.[46] The earliest manuscripts of this first Latin translation of the *On generation* suggest early diffusion in northwestern Europe. One is a manuscript from St Albans, while the other is a manuscript from Mont-St-Michel,[47] which is one of a group used in modern study as part of a picture of reception of Aristotle in Normandy and the abbey of Mont-St-Michel in the third quarter of the twelfth century, in particular during the period when the Mont-St-Michel chronicler,

[43] G. Lacombe, *La Vie et les oeuvres de Prévostin* (Le Saulchoir, Kain, 1927), pp. 11–12; an extract from the sermon is given in p. 11, n. 4.

[44] This attribution, stated by Lacombe (*Prévostin*, p. 134), is fragile; see J. N. Garvin and J. A. Corbett, eds, *The Summa contra haereticos ascribed to Praepositinus of Cremona* (Notre Dame, IN, 1958), pp. xiii–xiv and xxvii, n. 26 (observing Lacombe's error in ascribing to one of the manuscripts a title including Prévostin's name). If the attribution goes, so also goes Lacombe's argument (*Prévostin*, pp. 11–12) against years in the Rhineland providing Prévostin with his knowledge of Cathars.

[45] Aristotle, *De generatione et corruptione. Translatio vetus*, ed. J. Judycka, *AL*, 9, i (1986), pp. 74 (lines 19–20) and 75 (lines 8–9).

[46] *AL.Codices. Pars Posterior* (1955), p. 788; L. Minio-Paluello, *Opuscula. The Latin Aristotle* (Amsterdam, 1972), pp. 61, 71–83 passim, and 'Aristotle: tradition and influence', C. C. Gillispie, ed., *Dictionary of Scientific Biography*, 16 vols (New York, 1970–80), 1, p. 271; *De generatione*, ed. Judycka, pp. xxxiv–xxxviii.

[47] *AL. Codices. Pars Prior* (1939), nos. 340 and 408, pp. 398–9 and 437–8.

Robert of Torigny, was displaying knowledge of new translations of Aristotle (1157 × 1169).[48] What is currently known of earliest *use* as well as knowledge of the Latin translation of the *On generation* points to two groups and milieux, on the one hand a few medical authors of the late twelfth and early thirteenth centuries who are linked with Salerno,[49] and on the other hand a broader range of men from the schools of northwestern Europe, the earliest of whom was Daniel of Morley (1175 × 1185).[50] Presence and use in northwestern schools is rendered in some sense a generality or a norm by Alexander Nequam's *Sacerdos ad altare accessurus*, which provided lists of books to be used in various areas of study. Here, '[the person] who wishes to attend to the liberal Arts . . . should also look at the *Metaphysics* of Aristotle, and the same man's book *On generation and corruption* [inter liberales artes invigilare desiderans, [. . .] Inspiciat etiam methafisicam Aristotelis et librum eiusdem de generacione et corrupcione]'.[51] The *Sacerdos* is now dated to the first decade of the thirteenth century,[52] and while Haskins's conjecture was that Nequam's text reflected the practice of Paris, a more cautious conjecture would be that it relates to the practice, or ideal to be aimed at, either in Paris or Oxford, in both of which Nequam was active. One example of something reflecting the ideal from this first decade of the thirteenth century is a treatise which reflected Arts texts and discussion, and more probably in Paris than Oxford. John Blund's *De anima* quoted from the *On generation*, at one point adapting the passage which was also used by the Cathars, in John's case presenting it as 'contrariorum causarum contrarii sunt effectus'.[53]

We have no evidence pressing Cathars towards high medical-natural philosophical milieux in Salerno; a fleeting reference to a bishop of *Francia* in Naples in the late twelfth century[54] reminds us not to dismiss southern possibilities too hastily, given our ignorance of the

48 Minio-Paluello, *Opuscula*, pp. 180, 191, 216–18.

49 D. Jacquart, 'Aristotelean thought in Salerno', in P. Dronke, ed., *A History of Twelfth-Century Philosophy* (Cambridge, 1988), pp. 417–23, 426.

50 *De generatione*, ed. Judycka, pp.xlvii–liv, provides a survey of early users.

51 C. H. Haskins, *Studies in the History of Medieval Science*, 2nd ed. (Cambridge, MA, 1927), p. 373.

52 R. W. Hunt, *The Schools and the Cloister. The Life and Writings of Alexander Nequam (1157–1217)*, revised M. Gibson (Oxford, 1984), p. 30.

53 John Blund, *De anima*, xxi, ed. D. A. Callus and R. W. Hunt, *ABMA*, 2 (1970), p. 77, no. 287.

54 See n. 67 below.

place where *On generation* was translated from Greek into Latin.[55] However, weightier evidence – Guillaume d'Auxerre, other material about the higher learning of Cathars and their strong presence in northern France – does press towards this latter region and one milieu in it: Arts teaching in the schools of northwestern Europe as the most likely setting for Cathars learning of and beginning to use the *On generation.*

We should now turn to the whole range of dicta and their use. 'Une théologie déductive à partir d'axiomes, préalablement définis'[56] is one description of the aim at which twelfth-century theologians were striving, a theology which would be almost Euclidean in its demonstrations on the basis of axioms. Often commented upon, this tendency is associated with the influence of the theological works of Boethius, in particular his *De hebdomadibus*, the examples provided through the diffusion of such aphoristic works as the *Liber de causis* and the *Liber XXIV philosophorum*, and the efforts in particular of Alain de Lille.[57] In his *Regulae caelestis iuris* Alain concentrated specifically on this,[58] in the preface discussing aphorisms and their use. He pronounces the need of each science to have its *regulae*, attends to their varying names,[59] such as *maximae* in dialectic and theorems in geometry, and turns to theology's use of philosophical maxims. He says that theology has the highest need for maxims, and provides examples of those known to the many or to the few – his example of a widely known maxim is 'One being [is] the principle of things [Unum esse rerum principium]'[60] – and the rest of the treatise lists maxims (numbered in some manuscripts) from which theological truths are demonstrated.

What we have, then, in the Cathar statements, as they appear in Guillaume, are examples of a common theological trend, especially one championed in the later decades of the twelfth century. In each case the particular theological proposition is demonstrated by deduction from a general philosophical axiom, which is expressed with elegant brevity. Guillaume's use of words will have been intended to locate

55 Note a parallel, Minio-Paluello's question about southern Italian monasteries as possible sources for the new translations gathered in Mont-Saint-Michel, *Opuscula*, p. 180.

56 M.-D. Chenu, *La Théologie au douzième siècle* (Paris, 1957), p. 151.

57 D'Alverny, *Alain de Lille*, pp. 66–8; Leff, *Medieval Thought*, pp. 132–3.

58 Edited by N. M. Häring, 'Magister Alanus de Insulis. Regulae caelestis iuris', *AHDLMA*, an. 56 (1981), 48 (1982), pp. 97–226.

59 Häring, 'Regulae', p. 121.

60 Ibid., p. 123.

Cathar mode of arguing precisely within the theological style we have been discussing: 'they wish to prove their opinion *with certain maxims*'.

Apart from the quotation from Aristotle, the other maxims put forward by the Cathars have not been identified. Tentatively, I would like to suggest some directions for further conjecture. When looking at Cathar arguments for duality of principles behind Guillaume's report, and behind these arguments Cathar efforts to collect, alongside scriptural authorities, philosophical maxims from which dualist theological propositions seemed ineluctably to flow, we should entertain the possibility of this (a) taking a common literary form of the period, brief collections of *sententiae*, and (b) happening in various stages. Hints of the plausibility of the former suggestion come with the fact that when we turn to the most accessible among the many (about fifty) *florilegia* of authorities from Aristotle,[61] we find it including the *contrariorum contraria* tag,[62] and also a tag from the *Liber de causis* which an Italian Cathar used in the *Liber de duobus principiis*, albeit not with exactly the same wording.[63] If we should see the learning of Italian Cathars as relevant – as I suggest later – then use of a collection of *sententiae* could be an explanation, alongside defective memory, of the imprecision of the quotations in the *Liber de duobus principiis*, in particular its erroneous citation of Aristotle's *Physics*.[64]

Turning to chronology, we can already note some hints of stages in the reports of the maxims. First, in Alain I (around 1160) while the 'immutable cause' maxim is present it is not given an elegantly neat formulation; while the 'constructive or destructive' axiom does have a neat turn, a word for 'destructive', *peremptoria*, is used which does not appear in later reports of the maxim; and the maxim from Aristotle's *On generation* is not yet present. Secondly, in Alain II (around 1185–1200), the 'immutable cause' maxim has now found a neat formulation; Aristotle's maxim is still not present. Thirdly, in Guillaume (1216 × 1222), the maxims are described as *maximae*; all those restated are

[61] On these *florilegia* in general, see the chapter 'Flores et Auctoritates. Aristotelische Exzerptenliteratur' in M. Grabmann, *Methoden und Hilfsmittel des Aristotelesstudiums im Mittelalter*, Sitzungsberichte der Bayerischen Akademie der Wissenschaften, Phil.-Hist. Abt., Heft 5 (1939), pp. 156–88.

[62] J. Hamesse, *Les Auctoritates Aristotelis. Un florilège médiéval. Étude historique et édition critique* (Louvain and Paris, 1974), p. 170, no. 42.

[63] *Auctoritates Aristotelis*, p. 231, no. 5; *Livre des deux principes*, II, 16–18, ed. C. Thouzellier, SC, 198 (Paris, 1973), p. 166.

[64] *Livre des deux principes*, LXIII, 104–6, p. 398; see also p. 47 n. 1, and comment in *Auctoritates Aristotelis*, pp. 13–14, on imprecision in citation of Aristotle.

formulated neatly; and the maxim from Aristotle has appeared. We have little to eke out the pattern we are discerning so far. We must suppose some lapse of time in reporting. There is the impact on northern Cathar theology of conversion to absolute dualism in the mid-1170s, and there is comment by Alexander Nequam, which may be rooted in his experience of Paris (perhaps *c.*1175–82), which seems to link Cathars and the liberal Arts: both points are discussed below. Finally, unless we suppose the Cathars to have been avant-garde, the comments on reception of *On generation* given above suggest the earliest plausible period for Cathar knowledge of it.

THE LEARNING OF THE NORTHERN CATHARS

Thus far, we have been using a microscope on Guillaume, Moneta, and the maxims. In order to reflect further on the significance of what we are seeing, we need to stand a long way back. We need on the one hand a panoramic view of northern Catharism, its priority in the Catharism of the Latin West, the strata in which it flourished and other evidence about its culture, and on the other hand we need an intelligible context for northern and Lombard Cathars using identical maxim-based arguments.

Early Catharism in the Latin West was suddenly made to appear in a new and clear light in a recent article by Bernard Hamilton, 'Wisdom from the East'.[65] Hamilton reflected on three problems, set side by side, the solution of each of which helped the other. There was an historical account of the Cathars written by the inquisitor Anselm of Alessandria, presumably on the basis of Italian Cathar tradition, which decribed the *francigene* (men from *Francia* or northern France) going to Constantinople, and then returning to *Francia*. Associated with the Second Crusade, this posed a problem because of the date – earlier than the second crusade – of the Cathars who appeared in the Rhineland and were described by Eversin of Steinfeld. There was a vision of the Cathars set down by St Hildegard of Bingen, which alluded to the date of their arising. And, finally, there was the problem of the Latin service-books of the western Cathars – deriving from eastern originals which were in use in Greek and old Slavonic, how and where had they been translated from Greek into Latin? In Hamilton's meditative

[65] Biller and Hudson, eds, *Heresy and Literacy*, pp. 38–60.

account these are like jumbled letters which suddenly and with dazzling clarity fall into place to form the only word they can form: the only gloss on Anselm's short but fundamental text which makes sense. Anselm's text refers to the aftermath of the First Crusade, just as St Hildegard's chronology points to Cathar danger arising around 1101, and what he describes as northern French Latins in Constantinople in the wake of the first crusade. There they acquire dualist faith, there they set up the first Cathar Latin Church, there (probably) they translate the service-book from Greek to Latin, and from there they return to *Francia*, setting up the first bishop of *Francia* and multiplying in numbers.

The implications of such a reinterpretation are enormous. In modern secondary works on Catharism (or Catharism within general accounts of heresy), Languedoc has predominated, and secondarily Italy, with the north hardly rating a mention.[66] Regardless of what has contributed to this neglect – the arid inconclusiveness of scholarly polemic on Cathar origins, the extraordinary colour and detail of what can be reconstructed from the Inquisition records of Languedoc, and Occitan monopolization of the modern picture of the Cathar past – it is clear that the north needs resurrection. Following Hamilton, we need to recall the primacy of *Francia* in the historical account given not by a northern Frenchman but an Italian, Anselm of Alessandria. Latin Catharism not only first came to *Francia*, it was spread from *Francia*. It went from *Francia* to the *provinciales* (men of Provence) in the south, and it was a notary from *Francia* who took Catharism into Lombardy, following upon a settlement of Cathars from *Francia* in Lombardy and at a time when the bishop of *Francia* was to be found in Naples.[67] The hammer-blows to northern Catharism seem to have come early, in Flanders in the 1180s, in northern France in the late 1230s – by the time the former Cathar perfect Rainier Sacconi was writing, in 1250, the church of *Francia* had been for some time established in Lombardy, in exile.[68] Its northern history spans the years from around 1100 to

[66] An important exception is Duvernoy, *Histoire*, pp. 107–50.

[67] 'Postea Francigene, qui iverant Constantinopolim, redierunt ad propria et predicaverunt, et multiplicati constituerunt episcopum Francie. . . . . Item provinciales, audientes predicacionem eorum et seducti ab illis de Francia . . . Post longum tempus quidam notarius de Francia venit in Lombardiam . . . Rocavien – et est locus apud Cuneum -, ubi stabant cathari qui venerant de Francia ad habitandum ibi. Et episcopus hereticorum non erat ibi, sed erat Neapoli': Anselm, *Tractatus*, p. 308.

[68] Sacconi, p. 50: 'Ecclesia Francie morantur Verona et in Lombardia, et sunt circiter CL.'

around 1240, and much of the evidence which survives is in brief chronicle entries and papal bulls[69] whose formulaic nature often obscures the precise identity of the heresy in question. The fundamental works on northern heresy are still two articles written by Haskins and Chénon in 1902 and 1918,[70] and although there is other evidence to use (in particular northern anti-Cathar polemics) and some new evidence trickles into view (notably a recently discovered sermon against northern Cathars from Arras around 1200),[71] there is no monograph bringing them together, no *Cathars of Northern Europe*. Two points are being made here, the chronological priority of northern Cathars, and the danger of taking slightness of evidence about them as equivalence of slightness or insignificance of the past phenomenon. In terms of evidence they are the 'dark age' of Catharism, and, like Anglo-Saxon royal government, they deserve their James Campbell to eke out with scholarly resourcefulness what sources there are.

That is not being attempted here, but two points need to be picked out. First, among the few bishops whom we glimpse, in the sequence of the Cathar bishops of *Francia*,[72] one, Robert d'Épernon (which could be the Épernon in Champagne),[73] participated as *episcopus Francie* at the Council of St Félix-de-Caraman (1174 × 1177) together with his *consilium*.[74] There he and Languedocian bishops were addressed by the radical dualist Nicetas, from Constantinople, and provided anew with *consolamentum* and their episcopal order. We may suppose that what took place in the wake of the return to northern France of Robert and his *consilium* was the largest pressure on the learned among northern Cathars: introduction and discussion of absolute dualist doctrine. This

[69] Haskins, 'Inquisition in Northern France', pp. 196–7.

[70] See n. 35 above. B. Despy has re-examined the career of Robert le Bougre in his 'Les Débuts de l'Inquisition dans les anciens Pays-Bas au XIIIe siècle', in G. Cambier, ed., *Problèmes d'histoire de christianisme. Hommage à Jean Hadot* (Brussels, 1980), pp. 71–104, and he has expressed scepticism about the Catharism and heresy of those persecuted as heretics in the north, in his 'Hérétiques ou anticléricaux? Les "cathares" dans nos régions avants 1300', in *Aspects de l'anticléricalisme du moyen age à nos jours. Hommage à Robert Joly, Problèmes d'histoire du christianisme*, 18 (Brussels, 1988), pp. 23–33.

[71] B. Delmaire, 'Un Sermon arrageois inédit sur les "Bougres" du Nord de la France (vers 1200)', *Heresis*, 17 (1991), pp. 1–15.

[72] Borst, *Katharer*, p. 231.

[73] Duvernoy, *Histoire*, p. 147.

[74] B. Hamilton, 'The Cathar Council of Saint-Félix Reconsidered', *AFP*, 48 (1978), pp. 23–53.

backcloth is needed for investigation of stages in their adoption of maxims in their theology, in particular their acquisition at one stage of *contrariorum contraria*, starkly useful for a radical dualist position and based on a text quite recently translated from Greek. The fact that the church of *Francia* described in 1250 as living in exile in Lombardy held to a moderate dualist[75] position suggests controversy and perhaps schisms which our scant evidence does not allow us to follow.

Secondly, Cathars' worldly position is an intelligible context for further examination of their culture. Our sources emphasise the wealth of northern Cathars themselves[76] and their residence in castles and cities, and they portray them as supported by nobles, knights, wool-merchants, and, in Robert of Auxerre's phrase, 'very wealthy men', *viri predivites*.[77] Writing to Gregory IX in 1233 and after describing Cathar presence in the provinces of Bourges, Reims, Rouen, Tours, and Sens, throughout Flanders, and in many other places, particularly those bordering upon the kingdom of France, the inquisitor Robert le Bougre described them not only as 'seducing the simple [simplices seducendo]' but also 'deceiving the clever [astutos decipiendo]'.[78] What more do we know about the culture of 'clever' Cathars?

Through Bernard Hamilton we have a picture of a Cathar service-book in Latin being carried from Constantinople to northern France, and used in Latin among northwestern European and Italian Cathars (unlike those in Languedoc among whom there was further translation into the vernacular). Thus we suppose northern Cathar perfects of Latin culture, but only occasionally do we catch something of the culture of an individual northern Cathar, and even then not always knowing with certainty that we are dealing with a perfect: Gerard, the leader of the mission of German Cathars to England in the early 1160s, who 'seemed *litteratus* [*litteratus videbatur*]';[79] the unnamed notary from *Francia* who carried Catharism into Italy; Adam, a *litteratus* condemned

75 Hamilton, 'Saint-Félix', p. 33.

76 This is the charge of Évrard de Béthune, *Liber antihaeresis*, VII, XX, XXII, ed. J. Gretser and cited here from the reprint in M. de la Bigne, *Bibliotheca patrum et veterum auctorum ecclesiasticorum*, 4, part 1 (Paris [1624], cols 1115, 1153, 1157–60. See note 92 below.

77 *Chronicon* [1198], *MGH.SS*, XXVI, p. 258.

78 Chénon, 'Charité-sur-Loire', p. 330, n. 1.

79 William of Newburgh, *Historia rerum Anglicarum*, in *Councils and Synods with other Documents Relating to the English Church*, I, *A.D. 871–1204*, ed. D. Whitelock, M. Brett, and C. N. L. Brooke, 2 parts (Oxford, 1981), part 2, p. 924. This report is examined in my 'William of Newburgh and the Cathar mission to England', forthcoming in D. Wood, ed., *Life and Thought in the Northern Church, c.1100–c.1700. Essays in Honour of Claire Cross.*

in Arras in 1182;[80] Robert Le Petit or Le Bougre – a perfect before he converted back to the Catholic faith and became a Dominican, like the more famous Rainier Sacconi – who was *competenter litteratus et doctus*.[81] There are some clergymen, to one of whom, a learned canon of Nevers, we shall return. Only once do we glimpse the portable little book, *libellus*, used in the administration of the *consolamentum*. That this is only a fragment of a larger and lost past reality can be seen when we look further at the northern polemicists writing against the Cathars and depicting them as relying on an arsenal of authorities from the Bible, patristic texts, and, as we have seen, some philosophy. Eckbert of Schönau and Alexander Nequam have the Cathars citing and relying on St John Chrysostom and Gregory the Great's *Moralia* on Job,[82] and Eckbert's words – 'they believe the writings of the old fathers attest this' – generalize their reliance on patristic texts.[83]

It is worth considering the currently known sequence of northern writers who turned to look at the Cathars – not so much the remarkable row of English chroniclers from William of Newburgh to Matthew Paris, whose interest in Catharism is part of the northern scene, but the theologians who scrutinized their beliefs. Consider first Eckbert of Schönau. Writing in the 1160s, Eckbert says, 'when I was a canon Bertolph and I often used to dispute with them'.[84] Eckbert's polemic has a vignette of the setting of one such dispute. Eckbert is in his house in Bonn, there is a suspect Cathar present, and Eckbert is pointing out one passage in the Epistles of Paul.[85] We should stand back from this verbal equivalent of a miniature in a manuscript, and remember the sort of man Eckbert was.[86] He came from a high ecclesiastical family, which tended to produce prelates. He was learned – it was probably between 1140 and 1146 that he studied in Paris under Magister Adam of Belsham. He was connected with the most

[80] P. Fredericq, *Corpus documentorum inquisitionis haereticae pravitatis Neerlandicae*, 5 vols (Ghent, 1889–1906), 1, p. 48, no. 48.

[81] Matthew Paris, *CM* [1238], 3, p. 520. See Despy, 'Débuts de l'Inquisition', p. 78 n. 4 for higher praise of Robert, described as *vir doctissimus*, from another contemporary, and see p. 79 for reserve about Robert as a former Cathar.

[82] *Sermones XII contra Catharos*, V, xii, *PL* 195, cols 34–5; *Speculum speculationum*, III, lxii, 1, p. 327.

[83] *Sermo* IX, x, col. 60: 'qui antiquorum Patrum scripta hoc attestari aestimatis.'

[84] *Sermones*, preface, cols 13–14.

[85] *Sermo* XI, viii, col. 88.

[86] The following is based on the article on Eckbert in *Die deutsche Literatur des Mittelalters. Verfasserlexikon*, 2 (Berlin and New York, 1980), pp. 435–40.

important of men, having from his youth been friendly with Rainald Dassel, who was now, when Eckbert was dedicating his anti-Cathar work to him, archbishop of Cologne and chancellor of the Emperor. It was with a man of such status, connections, and learning that Cathars were frequently arguing. As we parade the polemicists we should bear in mind, then, the implications for our view of northern Cathars of the attention they got from learned men, from St Bernard of Clairvaux before Eckbert to a series of scholastic figures after him.

The sequence includes Alain de Lille. There is dispute about the location of the experiences and influences behind Alain de Lille's later and monographic treatise, *De fide*, partly because of its dedication to the count of Montpellier, partly because of the modern tendency to monopolize sources for use on southern Cathars.[87] Setting her face in another direction, d'Alverny has underlined Alain's origin in Lille, a continuing connection probably implied by an obit note of a *magister Alanus* in the cartulary of St-Pierre of Lille, connections with Tournai and the bishop of Noyon (to whom one of Alain's works was dedicated), the appearance in his works of some northern French words, and two writers who place Alain among lists of Paris masters.[88] The treatise cited so far as Alain I, *Quoniam homines* (around 1160), hints at its Parisian milieu, with its allusions to the Seine and Montmartre.[89] In this earlier work Alain seems to look in two directions, patristic and contemporary.[90] On the one hand he addresses the opinion of 'Manicheus', and for one etymology he cites St Hilary of Poitiers' *De synodis*.[91] On the other hand, the word whose etymology he is seeking is *Catari*. He parades statements which, as we have seen, belong to a contemporary cluster of maxim-based theological propositions (some of which are repeated in the first book of Alain's later *De fide*, which is monographically directed against Cathars). And, finally, he justifies arguing against dualism because of its great *contemporary* strength. 'The refutation of this [the opinion of Manicheus] seems extremely useful,

[87] An example of a categorical statement of Alain's contact with Cathars in Languedoc, for which there is no direct evidence, is C. Thouzellier, *Catharisme et valdéisme en Languedoc à la fin du XIIe et au début du XIIIe siècle* (Paris, 1965), p. 82.

[88] M.-T. d'Alverny, 'Maitre Alain – "NOVA ET VETERA"', M. de Gandillac and E. Jeauneau, eds, *Entretiens sur la renaissance du 12e siècle* (Paris and The Hague, 1968), pp. 118–19.

[89] Glorieux, 'Quoniam homines', p. 116.

[90] See also d'Alverny, *Alain de Lille*, p. 157 n.6, for the suggestion of use of Carolingian material in Alain's definition of dualism; in fact the parallel is not close.

[91] Glorieux, 'Quoniam homines', p. 130.

because even now this opinion flourishes among very many people [cuius perutilis videtur infirmatio, quia illa adhuc in plerisque viget opinio].'[92]

Following *Quoniam homines* and *De fide*, there is the extensive, long-known but little studied treatise written against the Cathars by the learned grammarian Évrard of Béthune,[93] probably around 1200. He cannot be certainly associated with Paris, although the place- and river-names mentioned in his works (Rouen, Péronne on the Somme, Seine, Ausonne)[94] firmly place him in an appropriate northern setting.

Next in line is Alexander Nequam, whose treatise *Speculum speculationum* was written in the opening years of the thirteenth century, between 1201 and 1213. Though not monographically directed against the Cathars (whom he only once names as Cathars),[95] their presence and the danger of their opinions were described by him as the reason why he wrote the treatise. 'The old error of the Manichees, now alas renewed, has forced me to write.'[96] Given the far greater evidence around 1200 for Cathars in northern France than in England – where the main direct evidence is references to the execution of a Cathar in London in 1210 and the incursion into England and execution of Cathars in 1211[97] – Alexander's contact with Cathar doctrines is more plausibly rooted in his Paris than his Oxford years, which have been conjectured as around 1175–1182.[98]

We have seen that we then have clear concern in Paris with Guillaume d'Auxerre, and the next in line after him is another of the great men of Paris in this period, Guillaume d'Auvergne. The

[92] Ibid., p. 129; see also his reference to contemporary heretics condemning marriage, p. 130.

[93] On Évrard see K. Lohmeyer, 'Ebrard von Béthune. Eine Untersuchung über den Verfasser des Graecismus und Laborintus', *Romanische Forschungen*, 11 (1901), pp. 412–30, and on Gretser's edition of the *Liber antihaeresis*, C. Thouzellier, *Hérésie et hérétiques: vaudois, cathares, patarins, albigeois* (Rome, 1969), pp. 44–7. In his '"Contra Judaeos" méridionaux au début du XIIIe siècle. Alain de Lille, Évrard de Béthune, Guillaume de Bourges', *CaF*, 12 (1977), pp. 269–93 (at pp. 274–82), M.-H. Vicaire tried unconvincingly to pull this work towards southern France.

[94] Lohmeyer, 'Ebrard', p. 416.

[95] *Speculum speculationum*, IV, xx, 4, p. 445.

[96] Ibid., prologue, p. 5: 'Scribere enim me compellit uetus error Manicheorum, proh dolor diebus nostris innouatus.'

[97] *Cronica maiorum et vicecomitum Londoniarum*, ed. T. Stapleton, *Camden Society*, 34 (1846), p. 3; *MGH.SS*, 27 (1885), p. 357.

[98] Hunt, *Nequam*, p. 4.

earliest chapters of his *De universo* are directed against the Manichees, who were seen by him as one of the greatest of contemporary dangers, and in his *De legibus* he also commented on hearing about (as well as the possibility of seeing) the readiness of heretics to endure fire.[99] Further research might add to this list, and a fuller account of 'concern about Cathars in Paris' could turn to the chancellors of the university of Paris. We have seen that Prévostin, chancellor from 1206 to around 1209, spent a long time among Cathars. Whatever the region in which he got to know them, his talking about Cathars was a Parisian event. Philip the Chancellor (1218–36) was present at the examination of heretics in Châlons.[100] When preaching against heresy his insistence on their avarice and justification of usury closely parallels Évrard, suggesting a shared polemic against northern Cathars.[101] We see a third chancellor, Eudes de Châteauroux (1238–44), commenting on the burning of heretics[102] – referring to the mass execution at Mont-Aimé in 1239? – and once again a figure whose works need to be examined for other traces of concern with heresy. A balanced account would clearly add the much better known theme of northern concern with southern heresy and its repression, and produce a mixture of northern interest in both. On the one hand it is easier to pick out the *Albigenses* in Jean Longère's study of the attention to heresy paid in the sermons of Paris masters in these years,[103] while on the other hand in John Baldwin's study of attention to treatment of heretics among Peter the Chanter, Robert of Courson, and Thomas of Chobham, some at least – Robert – stemmed from the trial in Paris and execution in Nevers of a northern Cathar, Évrard de Chateauneuf.[104]

I would like now to turn to the picture of Cathar learning and culture given by some of the northern authors who wrote about

[99] *De universo*, I, ii, and *De Legibus*, xxi, *Opera omnia*, 2 vols (Paris, 1674), 1, pp. 594 and 57; compare Nequam and Guillaume d'Auxerre on Cathars and execution, above and n. 41.

[100] Haskins, 'Inquisition', p. 230.

[101] R. E. Lerner, *'The Heresy' of the 'Free Spirit' in the Later Middle Ages* (Berkeley, Los Angeles and London, 1972), p. 22.

[102] Haskins, 'Inquisition', p. 237, n. 4.

[103] J. Longère, *Oeuvres oratoires des maîtres parisiens au XIIe siècle. Étude historique et doctrinale*, 2 vols (Paris, 1983), 2, pp. 420–8.

[104] J. W. Baldwin, *Masters, Princes and Merchants. The Social Views of Peter the Chanter and his Circle*, 2 vols (Princeton, NJ, 1970), 1, pp. 189–90, 321–2, 2, pp. 128, 216. Cathar views on sex and marriage also attracted comments from the Chanter and Robert of Courson which John Baldwin cites in his *The Language of Sex. Five Voices from Northern France around 1200* (Chicago, IL, 1994), pp. 4 (and 271 n. 10), 178, 244.

Cathars before Guillaume. Although the commonplace of the heretic as *rusticus* or *illiteratus* is strong in what may be one of the earliest descriptions of northern French Cathars, around 1115, when Guibert de Nogent described heretics found in a village near Soissons, its presence is rather weak in later Catholic polemic. '*Rustici*, return to the same book', Eckbert may exclaim in the 1160s,[105] but at the same time he writes how Cathars present themselves: 'you read and know the Gospels, so you say',[106] and 'you see yourselves as *eruditi* in holy scripture'.[107] The Cathars were 'loquacious [*linguosi*]',[108] and there are, as we have seen, the implications of the fact that the learned Eckbert and a canon dispute with them. When we move on to Évrard de Béthune, we find the Cathars presented as men who put forward propositions based on scriptural authorities which they expound in a certain direction, and against whom Évrard and fellow orthodox expound in a different direction: 'we expound thus [*exponimus sic*]'.[109] They expound several senses of the Bible, as Évrard accuses them of flitting arbitrarily from the letter to allegory.[110] They argue, using *ratio*, and they are seen as presenting their arguments logically: 'Let it be assumed that . . . it will be seen that . . . [*Ponatur quod . . . videbitur quod . . .*]'.[111] Évrard had in fact heard Cathars presenting their views at Douilly, in an area of Cathar concentration near Péronne.[112]

The last figure in the sequence before Guillaume d'Auxerre is Alexander Nequam. At one point his depiction of Cathar culture is straightforward denigration: they are illiterate heretics (*illitterati heretici*).[113] Nequam's contradiction of this in his depiction of the Cathars as people who maintain certain theological positions, on the basis of texts and arguments, shows that this is crude polemical obloquy. Elsewhere in the treatise, another part of Nequam's obloquy, here directed against novelty and error, has the Cathars as 'newfangled commentators of lies [nouelli mendaciorum commentatores]'.[114] Here

[105] *Sermo* V, vii, col. 31: Rustici, redite ad eumdem librum.'

[106] *Sermo* XII, I, col. 94: 'Evangelia legatis et sciatis, sicut dicitis.'

[107] *Sermo* XI, v, col. 86: 'Si estis eruditi de Scripturis sanctis, ut vobis videtur, et vos jactitare soletis.'

[108] *Sermones*, preface, cols 13-1-4.

[109] *Liber antihaeresis*, IX, col. 1128.

[110] Ibid. III, col. 1091.

[111] Ibid., IV, VIII, cols1097, 1121.

[112] Ibid., VIII, col. 1121. On Péronne, see Despy, 'Débuts de l'Inquisition', pp. 97–8.

[113] *Speculum speculationum*, I, i, 1, p. 9.

[114] Ibid., I, ii, 6, p. 21.

the idiosyncratic turn of phrase allows a rather learned picture to peep through the polemic: a picture of Cathars as *commentatores*. Suspiciously precise in polemical denigration of the culture of heretics is Nequam's cry that the Cathars are 'utterly ignorant of the liberal arts and *litteratura* [artium liberalium [. . .] et litterature prorsus ignari]'. A few lines further on Nequam writes that he has 'learned from the truthful claim of credible men that they have seduced some *litteratores* [Virorum fide dignorum assertione veridica didici quosdam litteratores seduxisse]'.[115] *Litteratores* may mean schoolteachers or learned persons, in which case it is a qualification to the point about ignorance of the liberal Arts, or it may mean literalists (in the exposition of scripture),[116] in which case it still carries a concession about Cathar culture. Set within the usual drift of the topos of heretical learning, which was overstatement (even possibly invention) of heretics' ignorance in order polemically to indicate the frail basis of heretical doctrines or heretics' unsuitability for preaching, Nequam's words suggest that the Cathars known to him and his informants could be called 'commentators', that they were making *some* claim (which needed to be rejected) to learning in the liberal arts and *litteratura*, and among their numbers were some *litteratores*.

Even if these jigsaw pieces may be too few to be pieced together without intermediate, missing pieces, they do seem to originate from the same picture. Here is Cathar acquaintance with and use of *On generation*, a text from the Arts in northern schools, especially Paris; here are Cathars, whose learning in liberal Arts is (suspiciously) rejected by an Englishman whose years in Paris were probably *c.*1175–*c.*1182; and here are treatises, two of them clearly from the milieu of Paris, reporting Cathars making use of philosophical maxims. With some hesitation, I would like to raise the possibility that concern about Cathars may have had a minor role in the background of the famous early thirteenth-century preoccupation (1210 and 1215) with heresy and the reading of Aristotle's natural works at Paris.

[115] Ibid., Prologue, p. 5.

[116] Dr D. Howlett has kindly discussed with me Nequam's use of *litterator*, pointing out that Nequam tends to be consistent, and that in two other uses of *litterator* Nequam's sense is 'literalist'.

RELATIONS WITH ITALY AND LANGUEDOC

Northern French Catharism supplied the missionary effort, in the twelfth century, to southern France and Lombardy. Even though most contacts must have been secret, their later continuation looms even in the scant surviving evidence, such as the meeting of Cathars from *Francia*, Lombardy, and Languedoc at the Council of St Félix. Cathars who fled from La Charité, in the diocese of Auxerre, are described as going either to Italy or the Albigenses,[117] while Robert le Bougre seems to have taken a visit to Lombardy, by a northerner convicted of heresy, as grounds of suspicion of relapse into heresy.[118]

Two well-known texts are worth rereading now, against the background of the evidence of northern Cathar learning which we have been examining, continuing contacts, and the priority of northern Catharism. First, after Évrard de Chateauneuf's conviction for Catharism at a council in Paris and his execution in Nevers, his nephew, a canon of Nevers and also a Cathar, seeing that he could hide no longer, fled to the Narbonne area, and served the southern Cathars well, beefing up their strength in open debates with Catholic theologians, while changing his name from 'Guillaume' to 'Thierry'. Peter of Vaux-de-Cernay describes southern Cathar joy at Thierry's arrival, because of his cleverness (he was *acutior*), and because of his origin. 'They gloried in having a companion in their belief from *Francia*, where the fount of knowledge and Christian religion is known to be.'[119] Second is a well-known passage from a letter written by Ivo of Narbonne,[120] a cleric who had fled from Bordeaux and wandered among the Cathars of Lombardy, around 1214/15. Cathars in Como had told him that 'from virtually all the cities in Lombardy and some in Tuscany they [the Cathars] sent suitable scholars to Paris, some to study logical sophistries, others theological discourses [ex omnibus fere civitatibus

[117] In the account of Hugh of Noyers' hammering of the heretics of La Charité: 'alii pertinatiores, in salutis sue dispendium, in Ytaliam vel ad Albigenses, ad sui erroris complices confugerunt', Duru, *Bibliothèque historique de l'Yonne*, 1, p. 431.

[118] Chénon, 'Charité-sur-Loire', p. 336, note 3.

[119] Peter of Vaux-de-Cernay, *Historia albigensis* [1206], ed. P. Guébin and E. Lyon, 3 vols (Paris, 1926–39), 1, pp. 25–26: 'gloriabantur se habuisse de Francia (ubi esse dinoscitur fons scientie et religionis christiane) sue credulitatis socium, sue nequitie defensorem.'

[120] The authenticity of the letter is discussed in P. Segl, *Ketzer in Österreich. Untersuchungen über Häresie und Inquisition im Herzogtum Österreich im 13. und beginnenden 14. Jahrhundert* (Paderborn, Munich, Vienna, and Zurich, 1984), pp. 76–11. Helping to anchor Ivo's experience is his mention of Peter Gallus, bishop of the Cathar church of Vicenza *c.*1210–35.

Lombardiae et quibusdam Tusciae Parisius dociles transmisissent scholares, quosdam logicis cavillationibus, alios etiam theologicis dissertationibus insudantes]'.[121] Like Anselm of Alessandria's account of the origins of the Cathars, these texts are short, and like Anselm's text they have a disproportionately large amount to tell us about the primacy of northern Cathar learning in Latin Catharism as a whole. Southern French Cathars gloried in the accession to their strength of a Cathar from the *fons sciencie* of *Francia*. And in the journeys of Italian Cathar students to Arts and theology in Paris, and their return to Italy, we have our most economical explanation both for the use of identical philosophical maxims by Moneta's Lombard Cathars and those Cathars known to a theologian of Auxerre and Paris, and also of the echoes of Parisian learning (in particular Guillaume d'Auvergne), which Arno Borst detected in the Italian Cathar *Liber de duobus principiis*.[122] Northern Cathars around 1200 played a part in broader northern scholarly trends, the development of maxim-based demonstrative theology and the reception of Aristotle's *On generation*, just as the secret Cathar educational system also played a part in a broader educational trend, in which Lombards and Tuscans journeyed northwards to study in Paris.

University of York

[121] Quoted by Paolini, in Biller and Hudson, eds, *Heresy and Literacy*, p. 96, from Matthew Paris's copy of Ivo's letter.

[122] Borst, *Katharer*, appendix 3, especially pp. 265–79.

APPENDIX

Alain de Lille I	*Alain de Lille II*	*Guillaume d'Auxerre*	*Moneta of Cremona*
		Anima vero utitur corpore tanquam instrumento. Sed instrumento nihil debetur, quia ipsum nihil meretur, sed solum utens instrumento. Ergo cum corpus nihil mereatur, nihil ei debetur; ergo non debetur ei resurrectio[123]	Cathari ... credunt ... quod corpora ısta non sunt nisi organa, id est instrumenta animarum, quae per corpora tanquam per instrumenta, operantur bona, vel mala, ut dicunt. Unde sicut artifex tantum remuneratur, non instrumentum, quo utitur, ita sola anima remunerabitur, non corpus[124]
Item cuius causa est invariabilis et ipsum quoque invariabile. Sed Deus est causa invariabilis et immutabilis; visibilia vero variabilia et mutabilia. Igitur non est causa visibilium[125]	'Si causa immutabilis, effectus immutabilis'; sed constat ista corporalia mutabilia esse, ergo causa eorum mutabilis'[126]	suam opinionem probare volunt quibusdam maximis, quarum prima est: 'Cuius causa invariabilis est, ipsum quoque est invariabile'. Cum ergo Deus benignus sit causa invariabilis, causa non est variabilium[127]	Haer[etici][= Cathari]. Ad idem inducunt quandam propositionem: 'Si causa invaribilis, et effectus ejus'. Cum ergo ista visibilia sint variabilia, non potest esse quod caussa [sic] eorum sit Deus sanctus, et verus, qui invariabilis est[128]

[123] See n. 10 above.
[124] See n. 11 above.
[125] See n. 19 above.
[126] See n. 13 above.
[127] See n. 12 above.
[128] See n. 14 above.

Alain de Lille I	*Alain de Lille II*	*Guillaume d'Auxerre*	*Moneta of Cremona*
Item, Deus est causa constructiva et non peremptoria. Sed malicia pocius ad peremptionem quam ad constructionem pertinet. Ergo mala non sunt a Deo; sed sunt ab aliquo; ergo ab alio[129]		Secunda causa est: 'Non est idem constructivum et destructivum eiusdem'. Cum ergo Deus sit causa malorum hominum, non est causa constructiva eorumdem[130]	
			Praedicti haeretici [= Cathari] . . . Quod enim duo principia sint volunt haberi per hoc dictum
		Tertia: 'Contrariorum contraria sunt principia'. Cum ergo bonum et malum sint contraria, contraria habent principia. Cum ergo Summum Bonum sit causa boni, summum malum erit principium mali[131]	Aristotelis: 'Contrariorum contraria sunt principia'. Cum ergo bonum et malum sint contraria, eorum principia contraria erunt. Cum ergo bonum sit a principio et bono Deo, malum erit a principio, id est Deo malo[132]

[129] See n. 19 above.
[130] See n. 20 above.
[131] See n. 15 above.
[132] See n. 16 above.

PARISIAN THEOLOGIANS AND THE JEWS: PETER LOMBARD AND PETER CANTOR

by JACK WATT

TO honour the scholar whose distinguished contribution to medieval intellectual history has included examination of the early history of Parisian scholarship, I have chosen to examine an aspect of the work of two major teachers and authors in that 'monde scolaire qui préfigure déjà le monde universitaire de demain', the school of Notre Dame.[1] The work of Peter Lombard and Peter Cantor makes clear that in the second half of the twelfth century, Judaism was being placed firmly and permanently on the Parisian theological agenda. Peter Lombard (d. 1160) lectured on the Psalms and the Letters of St Paul. His commentaries on these books came quickly to be received as the standard teaching texts in Paris, the *magna glossatura* replacing, for those books, the *glossa ordinaria* of Anselm of Laon and his associates.[2] Medieval exegetes held these particular books of the Bible in esteem. For Aquinas, articulating common opinion, they contained 'almost the whole of theological doctrine'.[3] And thus, it might well be claimed, almost the whole of theological doctrine about Judaism.

Peter Cantor (d. 1197) was also a scriptural scholar – the first, it has been suggested, to be credited with a commentary on every book of the Bible[4] – but virtually all of this exegesis remains unedited and cannot be considered here. Like the Lombard, he was something more than an exegete. He too was an innovator in the construction of new texts which served both for theology students and for a wider audience anxious to avail itself of the learning of the schools. Two of the

[1] J. Châtillon, 'La Bible dans les écoles du xiie siècle', in *Le moyen âge et la Bible, Bible de tous les temps*, 4 (Paris, 1984), p. 195.

[2] *Magistri Petri Lombardi. Sententiae in IV Libris Distinctae*, t. 1, pars 1, *Prolegomena* (Grottaferrata, 1971), pp. 46–7; stimulating evaluation of the Psalms commentary, Maria L. Colish, 'Psalterium Scholasticorum: Peter Lombard and the development of scholastic Psalms exegesis', *Speculum*, 67 (1992), pp. 531–48 and of Peter's exegesis generally, idem, *Peter Lombard*, 1 (Leiden, 1994), ch. 4, 'Sacra Pagina', pp. 155–225.

[3] '. . . in utraque scriptura fere tota theologiae continetur doctrina': *Prologus in omnes epistolas S. Pauli commentaria. Opera omnia*, t. 13 (Parma, 1862), p. 2.

[4] J. W. Baldwin, *Pierre le Chantre, DSP.* 12 (1985), cols 1533–8, at col. 1535.

Cantor's treatises contain significant material concerning Judaism and attitudes to Jews. The first is his *Summa Abel*, a repertorium of biblical information, arranged encyclopedia-style alphabetically. Peter's collection of biblical *distinctiones* was one of the first and best-known of this new literary genre.[5] The entry *Iudei* effectively constituted, in very compressed form, a short treatise on the subject.[6] The second, his *Summa de sacramentis et animae consiliis*[7] has been hailed as 'the first important collection of medieval casuistry, of, that is, the teaching and dissemination of practical theology through the medium of cases or case-histories from everyday experience'.[8] This treatise of moral theology included a variety of situations involving Christian attitudes to Jews.

The commentary of Peter Lombard on the Psalms and on St Paul's Letters along with the two *Summae* of Peter Cantor offer an excellent opportunity to analyse what was being taught in Paris about Judaism and Christian–Jewish relations in the critical period when Paris was first establishing itself as Christendom's leading centre for the study of theology. This article will concentrate on their treatment of two questions which raised first principles determining the nature of Christian–Jewish relations: Jewish responsibility for the death of Christ and toleration of their presence in Christian society[9] – old questions given fresh airing in a new intellectual environment.

I

The Parisian masters did not of course attempt a *de novo* discussion of these fundamental matters. They necessarily took account of earlier scholarship: not merely to record it for routine transmission but to

[5] On which see P. Delhaye, 'L'organisation scolaire au xiie siècle', *Traditio*, 5 (1945), pp. 211–68 at p. 233; R. and M. Rouse, 'Biblical distinctions in the thirteenth century', *AHDLMA*, 49 (1974), pp. 27–37; J. Châtillon, *La Bible dans les écoles*, pp. 195–6.

[6] G. Dahan, 'L'Article *Iudei* de la *Summa Abel* de Pierre le Chantre', *Revue des études augustiniennes*, 27 (1981), pp. 105–26.

[7] Ed. J. A. Dugauquier, *Analecta mediaevalia Namurcensia* 4, 7, 16, 21 (Louvain and Lille, 1954–63).

[8] L. E. Boyle, 'The interconciliar period 1179–1215 and the beginnings of pastoral manuals' in F. Liotta, ed., *Miscellanea Rolando Bandinelli Papa Alessandro III* (Siena, 1986), pp. 45–56 at p. 53.

[9] Cf. J. Cohen, 'The Jews as killers of Christ in the Latin tradition, from Augustine to the friars', *Traditio*, 39 (1983), pp. 1–27; idem, 'Scholarship and intolerance in the medieval academy: the study and evaluation of Judaism in European Christendom', *AHR*, 91 (1986), pp. 592–613.

select from it intelligently in order to assimilate the most authoritative of previous expositions for presentation in a manner appropriate both for teaching and private study. Thus the *glossa ordinaria* of the Laon exegetes and the *magna glossatura*, which in crucial parts replaced it, are patchworks of tersely summarized renderings of past masters, with clarificatory personal additions playing a secondary though not inevitably an insignificant role.

The mark of one past master was especially strong. Augustine's sermon-commentaries on St John's Gospel, with its lengthy account of the events of Christ's arrest, trial, and death, and on the Psalms where Christ's voice spoke so directly through David as, in the Lombard's view,[10] to make him more an evangelist than a prophet, emerge as a major influence.

In the first of these commentaries, it was a particular concern of Augustine to establish that it was the Jews who were primarily responsible for the crucifixion. How should this be so when it was the Roman soldiers in obedience to Pilate who put Jesus to death? In general terms, in Augustine's argument, by considering the conduct of the Jewish leadership throughout the whole episode: their intentions and purposes, what they plotted, their responsibility for delivering Jesus to Pilate. But especially, in particular terms, because of their outcry which intimidated Pilate into releasing him into their hands for crucifixion (John 19.15–16) – what Augustine called their 'extorquentes clamores'.[11]

Further, in Augustine's reading of St John, the Jews had tried to shuffle off their responsibilities on to the Romans. This they had attempted, Augustine argued, when they refused to accept Jesus for trial according to their own law on the plea, which Augustine clearly thought specious, that it was not lawful for them to put any man to death (John 18.31). It was this particular argument which the *glossa ordinaria* chose to retain, reproducing almost exactly Augustine's words in a text designed to dismiss any case for Jewish innocence. The crime

[10] 'Ea quippe quae alii prophetae obscure et quasi per aenigmata dixerunt de passione et resurrectione Christi, et aeterna genitura et de caeteris mysteriis, David prophetarum excellentissimus ita evidentissime aperuit, ut magis videatur evangelizare quam prophetare': *PL* 191, col. 57.

[11] 'Factum est quod uoluerunt Iudaei: non ipsi, sed milites qui parebant Pilato, iudicante ipso, crucifixerunt Iesum; et tamen si uoluntates, si insidias, si operam, si traditionem, postremo si extorquentes clamores eorum cogitemus, magis utique Iudaei crucifixerunt Iesum': *Tractatus in Iohannem*, CXVIII, Ioh. XIX, 23–24; *CChr.SL*, 36, p. 654.

of the 'Gentiles' or Romans was less than that of the Jews. John has 'demonstrated not Jewish innocence but their madness'.[12]

What Augustine had argued in the context of John's Gospel he found to be powerfully reinforced in the Psalms. The *extorquentes clamores* had been foretold. The Jews had killed Jesus with the *os armatum*; the mouth, the tongue, not the hands bearing weaponry, were the killing instruments.[13] The Lombard's terseness contrasts sharply with Augustine's preaching rhetoric but he grasped the essence of the argument:

> *The sons of men, whose teeth are weapons and arrows, and their tongue a sharp sword* (Ps. 56.5)
> *Sons of men*, that is, the Jews . . . *teeth*, that is, their mockeries *weapons*, what they put forward as advice *and arrows*, what they said. The Jews cannot therefore excuse themselves because though their hands did not hold weapons, the mouth was armed. Hence it is said *and their tongue a sharp sword* while they shout 'Crucify, crucify'. For these shouts of 'Crucify' and the like cause death through provocation, just as does *a sharp sword*.[14]

[12] '. . . ideo Pilatus qui iudex Romanus erat, cum vellet eum reddere Iudaeis, ut secundum legem suam iudicarent eum, noluerunt eum accipere dicentes: *Nobis non licet interficere quemquam*. Ac sic impletus est sermo Iesu, quem de sua morte praedixit, ut eum a Iudaeis traditum interficerent gentes; minore scelere quam Iudaei, qui se isto modo ab eius interfectione uelut alienos facere uoluerunt, non ut eorum innocentia, sed ut dementia monstraretur': *Tr. in Ioh.*, CXIV, 5; *CChr.SL*, 36, p. 643. Cf. *gl. ord.*: 'Cum Pilatus vellet Jesum tradere Iudaeis, ut secundum legem suam iudicarent eum, noluerunt recipere, dicentes: *Nobis non licet interficere quemquam*; et sic impletur sermo Jesu quem de sua morte praedixit, ut eum a Iudaeis traditum gentes interficerent, quasi sic essent alieni a scelere qui magis peccant, in quo non eorum innocentia, sed dementia monstratur': *PL* 113, col. 419.

[13] 'Sed quomodo ipsi occiderunt, qui ferrum non ferebant? Qui gladium non strinxerunt, qui impetum in eum fecerunt ad occidendum, unde occiderunt? *Dentes eorum arma et sagittae, et lingua eorum gladius acutus.* Noli adtendere inermes manus, sed os armatum; inde gladius processit quo Christus occideretur, quomodo et de ore Christi, unde et Iudaei occiderentur. Habet enim ille gladium bis acutum, et resurgens percussit eos, et diuisit ab eis quos faceret fideles suos. Illi malum gladium, ille bonum: illi sagittas malas, ille bonas. Nam habet et ipse sagittas bonas, uerba bona, unde sagittat cor fidele, ut ametur. Ergo aliae istorum sagittae, et alius istorum gladius. *Filii hominum dentes eorum arma et sagittae et lingua eorum machaera acuta.* Lingua filiorum hominum machaera acuta, et dentes eorum arma et sagittae. Quando ergo percusserunt, nisi quando clamauerunt: *Crucifige, crucifige?*': *Enarratio in Ps. LVI, 12, CChr.SL*, 39, p. 702.

[14] The context provides a good example of how the Lombard expanded and clarified the *gl. ord.* Its comment reads: '*Lingua.* Voces illae Crucifige, crucifige, et huiusmodi, etiam fecerunt mortem, ut *gladius acutus*': *Ad Ps. 56.5, PL*, 113. 927. Lombard on the same verse: '*et sagittae* quantum ad verba. Non ergo excusent Iudaei, quia etsi manus inermes, os armatum est. Unde subdit: *Et lingua eorum gladius acutus.* Dum clamant: Crucifige, crucifige. Voces

There was a parallel Psalm text which Augustine had brought into the argument and which the Lombard summarized even more baldly: '*For they have whetted their tongues like a sword* [Ps. 63.4]. In openly calling for death, thus they slew, if not by their hands, by their tongues; and it is Christ who speaks in this text.'[15]

It was not only the respective guilt of Jews and Romans that Augustine considered. He considered too the guilt of the Jewish populace, the led, in relation to that of the leaders. He argued that initially the people at large were so strongly for Christ as to deter their leaders from taking action against him. Augustine had in mind Luke 22.2: 'and the chief priests and scribes sought how to put Jesus to death: but they feared the people'. But later their attitude changed and they connived with their evil and malicious leaders to the extent that fear of the people was no longer a constraint. Thus did the people incur a degree of guilt – not as much as their leaders but certainly a share of culpability and responsibility for the crucifixion.[16] Again the Lombard's summary was brief – in fact, a simple reiteration of the *glossa ordinaria*. Augustine was read as enunciating an ethical principle:

> *Rescue the poor* [Ps. 81.4]. This is said to the less in rank. It is shown here that they were not exempt from guilt for so great a crime

enim illae, scilicet *crucifige*, et huiusmodi citam fecerunt mortem, ut *gladius acutus*': *PL* 191, col. 530.

[15] Augustine: '*Qui exacuerunt tamquam gladium linguas suas. Filii hominum, dentes eorum arma et sagittae, et lingua eorum gladius acutus*, quod dicit et alius psalmus, sic et hic: *Exacuerunt tamquam gladium linguas suas.* Non dicant Iudaei: non occidimus Christum. Etenim propterea eum dederunt iudici Pilato, ut quasi ipsi a morte eius viderentur immunes. Nam cum dixisset eis Pilatus: *Vos eum occidite*, responderunt: *Nobis non licet occidere quemquam* . . . Quod fecit Pilatus, in eo ipso quod fecit, aliquantum particeps fit; sed in comparatione illorum multo ipse innocentior . . . Sed ille dixit in eum sententiam, et iussit eum crucifigi et quasi ipse occidit; et vos, o Iudaei, occidistis. Unde occidistis? Gladio linguae: acuistis enim linguas uestras. Et quando percussistis, nisi quando clamastis: *Crucifige, crucifige?*': *Enarr. in Ps. LXIII*, 4, *CChr.SL*, 39, p. 810. Lombard: '*Quia exacuerunt linguas suas ut gladius.* Aperte in clamando mortem, et ita si non manibus, linguis occiderunt; et loquitur hic Christus.' *PL* 191, col. 577.

[16] 'Sed inuidebunt ei, nec omnino parcent, dicentes: *Hic est heres, uenite, occidamus eum, et nostra erit hereditas* [Matt. 21.38]. *Auferte* ergo *inopem, et pauperem de manu peccatoris eruite* [Ps. 81.4]. Haec dicta sunt, ut sciretur in eo populo in quo natus et occisus est Christus, nec illos fuisse immunes a tanto scelere, qui cum essent tantae multitudinis, ut eos sicut euangelium loquitur, timerent Iudaei, et propterea in Christum manum mittere non auderent [cf. Luke 22.2], postea conniuerunt, eumque interimi a malignis et inuidis Iudaeorum principibus permiserunt; qui si uoluissent, timerentur semper, ut numquam in illum sceleratorum praeualerent manus. De his quippe et alibi dicitur: *Canes muti nescierunt latrare* [Isa. 56.10]. De his etiam ilud: *Ecce quomodo iustus periit, et nemo considerat.* Periit, quantum in ipsis est, qui eum perdere uoluerunt; nam quomodo ille posset perire moriendo, qui eo modo potius quod erat perditum requirebat?': *Enarr. in Ps. LXXI*, 4, *CChr.SL*, 39, p. 1138.

> who allowed their leaders to kill Christ when previously they had feared their great number; they could have freed their leaders from the act and themselves from giving consent to it. For whoever fails to oppose wrongdoing when he is able to, consents to it.[17]

There has been development here. It is appropriate to note at this point that it was not only Parisian theologians who drew an ethical principle from the Augustinian version of Jewish participation in the crucifixion; so too did the Bolognese canonists. Gratian had included in his *Decretum* a text manifestly Augustinian in inspiration in order to establish that he who incites another to commit murder is also a murderer:

> They deceive themselves dangerously who consider that they who kill by their own hand are murderers and they by whose advice and deceit and exhortation men are deprived of life are not. For the Jews did not kill Christ by their own hands, as was written 'It is not lawful for us to put anyone to death.' Yet the death of the Lord is down to them, because they killed him with the tongue, calling 'Crucify, crucify him'. Hence one evangelist states that the Lord was put to death at the third hour, and another, at the sixth hour, because the Jews killed him by tongue at the third hour, the soldiers physically at the sixth. He therefore who delivers a man, he is the one who kills him, as the Lord said 'He has the greater sin who delivered me to you'. Hence the psalm, 'The sons of men, whose teeth are weapons and arrows, and their tongue a sharp sword.' Therefore they by whose advice blood is shed must submit themselves to penance if they wish to merit forgiveness.[18]

[17] *Gl. ord.*: '*Eripite pauperem*. Ostendit, nec illos immunes qui permiserunt principibus Christum, cum prae multitudine timerentur, et possent illos a facto, et se a consensu liberare. Qui enim sinit obviare cum potest, consentit.'*PL* 113, col. 981. Lombard: 'Hoc minoribus dicitur. Per quod ostendit nec illos fuisse immunes a scelere tanto qui permiserunt principibus Christum, cum pro multitudine timerentur, et possent illos a facto et se a consensu liberare. Qui enim desinit obviare cum potest, consentit': *PL* 191, col. 773.

[18] *Decretum, De pen.*, D.1 c. 23. The text is a conflation of citations of Augustine drawn from a number of his books. It was rubricated in the *Decretum*: 'Non solum qui manibus occidunt, sed etiam quorum consilio et fraude alii occidentur, homicidae probantur.' The decretist *glossa ordinaria* shows some influence of the Lombard's commentary: '*dentes* id est, corrosiones et conuitia et *sagittae*, quantum ad consilia *gladius* quantum ad verba *acutus* dum clamarent crucifige, crucifige, etiam voces illae incitativae fecerunt mortem ut *gladius acutus*' (Paris, 1571), col. 1750.

From straight scriptural exegesis, analysis of Jewish responsibility for the death of Christ has entered casuistry. Its permanent place as a case history in moral theology is being established.

II

It was being established especially in that area of moral theology which considered how far guilt for sin was affected or unaffected by ignorance on the part of the one who had committed an immoral act. The role of the Jews in the crucifixion provided an excellent case-study for the analysis of this problem. Jewish responsibility for putting Christ to death might be established by the Augustinian *os armatum* line of argument. But what of the several New Testament texts which apparently proclaimed their ignorance? Texts of the highest authority: from Jesus himself, on the point of death: 'Father, forgive them for they know not what they do' (Luke 23.34); Peter in Acts 3.17: 'And now, brethren, I know that you did it through ignorance: as did also your rulers'; Paul in I Corinthians 2.7–8: 'But we speak the wisdom of God in a mystery, a wisdom which is hidden, which God ordained before the world, unto our glory. Which none of the princes of this world knew. For if they had known it, they would never have crucified the Lord of glory'; and again, Romans 10.2: 'For I bear them witness that they have a zeal for God, but not according to knowledge.' What was the nature of the ignorance of which these texts spoke? Were all the Jews equally ignorant?

The first major contribution in Paris to the discussion was that of Peter Lombard on I Corinthians 2.8. He had already adopted a distinction between the Jewish *maiores*, the educated leadership, the qualified experts in interpreting the scriptures and the *minores*, the populace, the uneducated; leaders and led. The former knew Jesus to be the one promised in the Law, but not that he was God; the latter recognized him as neither:

> *if they had known.* This can be understood as referring to the Jews some of whom recognized who Christ was, while others did not. It was of those who did not that Peter spoke: 'I know, brethren, that you did it through ignorance.' These brethren did not know him to be the one who had been promised in the law. But the rulers, that is, the chief priests, the Scribes and the Pharisees did know him to be the one promised in the Law; but they did not know

> him to be God or the Son of God. So therefore the text can be read of both those who knew and those who did not: both the people (*minores*) who *if they had known* him to be the Messiah promised in the Law and also the rulers, who *if they had known* him to be God or son of God *would never have crucified the Lord of glory* ... For they knew him to be the one promised in the Law, not however the mystery that he was from eternity the Son of God; nor did they know the sacrament of his incarnation, passion and redemption.[19]

This distinction between the *maiores* and others appeared again in the Lombard's comment on Romans 10.2, this time making clear the guilt of the former

> *For I bear them witness that they have a zeal for God but not according to knowledge.* This text speaks of those who delivered Christ in error and not as did the Scribes and Pharisees through envy and malice. It was of those who delivered him in error that Peter spoke: 'I know brethren that you did it in ignorance.'[20]

[19] '*si cognovissent* ... Vel de Iudaeis potest accipi, quorum quidam cognoverunt Christum; alii vero non cognoverunt. De ignorantibus dicit Petrus: *Scio, fratres, quia per ignorantiam id gessistis* [Acts 3.17]. Isti non cognoscebant illum esse qui in lege promissus erat eis. Maiores vero, ut principes sacerdotum, scribae et Pharisaei cognoverunt ipsum esse qui in lege promissus erat; sed Deum esse, vel Filium Dei nescierunt. Et ideo de utrisque sic potest accipi: *si cognovissent*, vel minores illum esse Messiam in lege promissum, vel maiores illum Deum esse, vel Dei filium, *nunquam Dominum gloriae crucifixissent*. Non enim hoc facerent si Deum esse scirent. Si enim daemones Deum factum hominem non intellexerunt, quanto magis homines? Non igitur illum aliter scierunt daemones, quam scierunt principes. Sciebant enim ipsum esse qui promissus in lege, non tamen mysterium eius quod Filius Dei erat, et ab aeterno; neque sciebant sacramentum incarnationis, passionis et redemptionis': *Coll. in ep. I Cor. PL* 192, col. 1549. The gloss incorporates that of the *gl. ord.*: '*Si enim cognovissent.* Vel minores illum esse Messiam in lege promissum, vel maiores Deum esse, vel Filium Dei, *nunquam Dominum gloriae crucifixissent*', *PL* 114, col. 521. Some historians have read this text as meaning that the rulers did know Christ to be God. The meaning, which Peter Lombard followed, is: *If* the *minores* had known Christ to be the Messiah promised in the Law and *if* the *maiores* had known he was God or Son of God, *then* they would not have killed him. It is to be noted that the Lombard drew on the *Quaestiones veteris et novi testamenti*, wrongly attributed to Augustine: 'Si ergo hi sunt principes qui nescientes Dominum maiestatis Christum esse, crucifixerunt, quomodo a daemonibus potuit sciri? Non illum aliter scierunt daemones, quam sciebant principes huius seculi. Sciebant enim ipsum esse qui promissus erat in Lege per signa prophetae: non tamen mysterium eius, quo Filius Dei erat ab aeterno, sciebant, neque sacramentum incarnationis': *PL* 35, col. 2261.

[20] Rom. 10.2 reads: 'For I bear them witness that they have a zeal of God, but not according to knowledge.' Lombard: '*Testimonium enim perhibeo illis quod aemulationem quidem Dei habent; sed non secundum scientiam* ... Et est sensus. Pro dilectione Dei putant se facere, sed veram Dei dilectionem non habent, et ideo necesse est pro eis orare. De his autem hoc dicit qui non invidia et malevolentia, ut Scribae et Pharisaei, sed errore Christum

Did this mean that the erroneously-acting (the *minores*?) were guiltless? Peter Cantor took up the question. He carried the distinction between *maiores* and *minores* from the context of scriptural exposition to that of ethical principle. He was discussing problems concerning the sinfulness of human acts with reference to ignorance, how it extenuated or aggravated guilt for sin. With Romans 10.2 in mind and, no doubt, Peter Lombard's interpretation of it, he argued that both *maiores* and *minores* (or *periti* and *simplices* in his terminology) sinned by acting against their consciences. The former knew Christ was the Messiah promised them in the Law but nevertheless crucified him through envy.[21] A straight-forward violation of the conscience informed by reason (*conscientia sana*). The latter, however, believing themselves to be worshipping God, acted according to an erroneous conscience, a disordered conscience, that is, a conscience making 'an imprudent and foolish assessment'.[22] That this was guilt-worthy Peter argued on an adaptation of Paul's 'For all that is not of faith is sin' (Romans 14.23): 'for all that is against conscience whether erroneous or rational is sin.' It had been Peter Lombard who had explained that 'of faith' meant 'according to conscience'.[23]

But if both *maiores* and *minores* sinned, did they both sin equally? Peter Cantor thought the *minores* sinned the less because it was not expected of them that they should understand that Christ was the promised Messiah, for they were not the experts in reading the

tradiderunt. Quibus Petrus ait: *Scio, fratres, quia per ignorantiam hoc egistis.* Illi ergo aemulationem Dei habentes, sed voluntatem et consilium eius nescientes, contra Deum agebant quem se defendere testabantur': *PL* 191, col. 1472.

[21] 'Queritur ergo utrum equaliter peccarent periti iudei qui ex sola inuidia crucifixerunt Dominum scientes ipsum esse Messiam promissum in lege [I have here preferred the editor's alternative reading from his n. 38] et simplices qui hoc ignorabant et credebant obsequium se prestare Deo. Primi egerunt contra sanam conscientiam. Secundi obediebant conscientie erronee. Et uidetur quod magis peccabant primi quam secundi, quia secundi ex ignorantia hoc fecerunt, et illa ignorantia fuit facti non iuris, quia dicit auctoritas: *Si enim Deum cognouissent, nunquam Dominum glorie crucifixissent.* Ignorantia autem facti excusat saltem a tanto etsi non a toto. Preterea, Dominus rogabat pro illis qui per ignorantiam crucifixerunt eum: *Pater ignosce illis quia nesciunt quid faciunt*, et potest dici quod inuidia fuit quedam circumstantia que aggrauauit peccatum eorum, et ideo magis peccabant': Cantor, *Summa*, III (2b), cap. LX Questiones de actibus humanis et peccato. §365 Utrum ignorantia deformet actionem, pp. 548–9.

[22] '*Erronea conscientia* est indiscreta et fatua estimatio, ut iudeorum qui crucifigentes Christum estimabant se obsequium prestare Deo. *Quicquid ergo fit* contra conscientiam siue erroneam siue sanam, *peccatum est*': Ibid., p. 547.

[23] '*Omne autem quod non est ex fide, peccatum est* [Rom. 14.23] *ex fide*, id est, secundum conscientiam': *PL* 191, col. 1519.

prophecies. It was therefore for them who acted in ignorance that the Lord prayed, 'Father forgive them for they know not what they do', and of whom Paul spoke when he said, 'For if they had known, they would never have crucified the Lord of glory.' Nevertheless they were not totally without sin on the principle that 'ignorance of fact excuses from much though not from all'. For the sin of the *maiores* there were aggravating circumstances making their guilt the more: their envy of Christ was one such circumstance. Another, argued Cantor with perverse ingenuity, was their failure to understand that Christ was God, an omission thought culpable in those expected to understand what was written in the Law about him, and thus aggravating their sin.[24]

This discussion of Jewish ignorance and their responsibility for the death of Christ proved to be the starting-point of debate rather than its conclusion. Of the major Parisian theologians, both Alexander of Hales and Thomas Aquinas made significant contributions.

In his first, somewhat tentative reference to these issues – his commentary on the *Sentences* – Alexander of Hales agreed that both the *maiores* and the *minores* sinned despite ignorance. There was a difference in their ignorance. The former knew Christ to be the Messiah promised in the Law but not that he was God 'because they did not find this stated in the Law'.[25] And as Anselm of Canterbury had argued 'no one could ever knowingly wish to kill God'. The latter did not know that he was either Messiah or God.[26]

[24] 'Erat ibi omissio qua ipsi omittebant intelligere Christum esse Deum, cum magis tenerentur hoc intelligere quia in lege erant periti. Omissio ergo intelligentie eorum que erant scripta in lege de Christo aggrauauit peccatum eorum. Ea enim tenebantur ipsi intelligere, et non simplices quibus suffecit adorare figuras pro rebus. Simplices ergo non omittebant predictam intelligentiam, quia non tenebantur ad hoc': ibid., pp. 549–50.

[25] 'Praeterea in glossa ad Cor. I 2, 8, dicitur quod maiores Iudaei qui ad cognitionem Legis tenebantur, sciverunt quod esset Christus: minores et simplices, qui ad cognitionem Legis non tenebantur, nescierunt. Ergo et daemones et Iudaei sciverunt Christum esse Deum.' This was an argument he rejected: 'Respondeo: et maiores et minores per ignorantiam peccaverunt. Maiores enim ipsum sciverunt esse Messiam, sed non Deum, quia non invenerunt expressum in lege. Minores utroque modo ignorabant': *Glossa in IV Libros Sententiarum Petri Lombardi*, III, dist. XVIII (Quaracchi, 1954), p. 203.

[26] 'Queratur utrum Iudaei sciebant Christum esse Filium Dei. Augustinus super illud: Si cognovissent, I ad Cor. 2,3: "Maiores Iudaei, ut scribae cognoverunt ipsum esse Messiam et in Lege promissum"; et ita sciebant ipsum esse Christum, quoniam talis fuit Christus. Anselm, *Cur Deus homo*, contrarium: "Nullus homo unquam potuit scienter velle occidere vel interficere Deum; et ideo illi qui eum occiderunt, non in illud infinitum peccatum corruerunt, cui nulla alia peccata compari possunt". Dicendum quod nescierunt ipsum esse Deum, sed scierunt ipsum esse Messiam': ibid., III, dist. XX, p. 234. The Augustine reference

In the *Summa* which stands in Alexander's name, however, there was a full discussion of ignorance and sinfulness. The leadership with their knowledge of the prophecies knew Jesus to be the Messiah. Despite their knowledge they had killed him through envy and malice. He cited approvingly Bede's grudgingly restrictive interpretation of Luke 23.34, arguing that Jesus was not praying for the forgiveness of those who had denied and crucified through envy and pride 'the one they knew to be the Son of God'. It would thus appear that his view of the ignorance of the *maiores* either had changed or had been changed by those responsible for the completion of his *Summa*. His view of the ignorance of the *minores* had also hardened in the *Summa* version. It was for them that Jesus was praying for forgiveness, those who acted with 'zeal for God, but not according to knowledge'. Nevertheless it was not a degree of ignorance that excused them totally from guilt. They were in part exonerated because they were not expected to be expert in reading the mysteries of prophecy, but not wholly so, because they had had the opportunity of informing themselves from their own knowledgeable *maiores* and had not availed themselves of it.[27]

is to the *Quaestiones* cited in n. 16 above, which the editors of Alexander attribute to Ambrosiaster.

[27] Two contexts of the *Summa Theologiae* (Quaracchi, 1930) are especially relevant: 'Queritur utrum actus per ignorantiam facti sit peccatum vel non . . . Solutio. Ad quod dicendum quod duplex est ignorantia facti: est enim eius "quod oportuit scire" et est eius "quod non oportuit scire". Si necesse fuit scire, et fuit ignorantia supina, non excusat et est grave peccatum. Si vero fuit eius quod oportuit scire et adhibuit diligentiam, excusatur, etsi non a toto, tamen a tanto. Ad id quod obicitur de Iudaeis qui habent ignorantiam de Christo, qui iam venit, dicendum est quod ignorantia eorum est supina. Possent enim scire tum ex operibus Christi, tum ex collatione Scripturarum propheticarum. Nec est simile de illis Iudaeis qui poenituerunt in primitiva ecclesia, quia nondum plene erat veritas publica quae latebat in Prophetis': *Summa*, t. III, n. 680, p. 661.

'Deinde quaeritur de iis qui per ignorantiam occiderunt Christum, utrum hoc intelligatur de maioribus et de minoribus Iudaeis . . . (Solutio). Dicendum est quod nec maiores Iudaei nec minores immunes a culpa, sed differenter. Maiores enim non erant immunes, eo quod scire poterant ipsum esse qui promissus erat in lege per signa prophetiae; unde per invidiam et malitiam ipsum occiderunt et de iis dicit Beda: "non orat pro eis qui per invidiam et superbiam quem Filium Dei intellexerunt, negant et crucifigunt". Licet ergo in parte non cognoscerent, tamen peccatum eorum non fuit excusabile per ignorantiam. Unde non omnino continebatur sub illa specie peccati quae est per ignorantiam, sed potius sub illa specie peccati quae est per industriam. Et licet esset ignorantia facti, non tamen excusabiles erant, quia fuit ignorantia facti quod oportuit scire et non dederunt operam ad plene sciendum . . . Ad id vero quod obicitur de minoribus Judaeis, dicendum est quod peccaverunt per ignorantiam, "zelum enim Dei habebant, sed non secundum scientiam" (Rom. 10.2) et pro talibus oravit, quia "nescierunt quid fecerunt". Unde pro aliquibus est auditus, et dimissa est culpa ipsis poenitentibus. Non enim fuit illa ignorantia quae reddit hominem immunem a poena et a culpa. Cum enim poterant discere et habebant a quo

This is the type of ignorance, it would seem, which Alexander would categorize as 'gross' (*crassa*): ignorance which should have been remedied, but the neglect of doing so was not willed. It excuses much but not everything. It is less culpable than 'willed' (*affectata*) ignorance, where the neglect of seeking the necessary information was deliberate ('affectum sive desiderium nesciendi'). This sort of ignorance does not excuse at all. This would appear to be the position of the *maiores*, though Alexander did not say so explicitly.[28] But Aquinas was to do so, making it the central argument in his *quaestio*, 'Whether Christ's persecutors knew him?'

Aquinas had already given the problem a preliminary consideration in his commentary on I Corinthians 2.8: had the Jewish leaders known Christ to be God? While apparently registering his agreement with the Lombard's opinion that they had known him to be the one promised in the Law, yet they had not known him to be Son of God, not understanding the mysteries of incarnation and redemption.[29] But then in his final summary he went some way beyond it:

> It must be said therefore that the leaders of the Jews knew for certain Christ to be the one promised in the Law, which the people did not know. That he was the true son of God they did not know for certain but in a way inferred it: but this conjectural knowledge of theirs was obscured by envy and their own greed for glory which they saw to be diminished by the preeminence of Christ.[30]

discerent et operam non dederunt prout oportuit, non omnino excusabantur propter ignorantiam, sed in parte: non enim tenebantur scire mysteria prophetiae ad modum quo maiores tenebantur': *Summa*, t. III, n. 682, pp. 662–3.

[28] 'Quae ignorantia magis excusat et quae minus . . . ignorantia crassa est, quando aliquis negligit scire quod tenetur nec tamen vult se nescire: haec minus excusat quam supra dicta, aliquando tamen excusat non a toto sed a tanto. Ignorantia affectata est, quando aliquis negligit scire ea quae tenetur scire et placet ei nescire, et haec accusat et non excusat': *Summa*, t. III, n. 325, p. 330. 'Alia est facti quod oportuit eum scire sicut ignorantia Iudaeorum, quia quae a Prophetis de Iudaeis fuerant prolata adhuc ignorant esse completa. Prima ignorantia excusat, secunda non. . . . Ignorantia vero affectata privat scientiam et ponit affectum sive desiderium nesciendi et ista maxime accusat ignorantes': *Summa*, IV, pp. 628–9.

[29] 'Solvitur in glossa quod *sciebant*, principes Iudaeorum, *eum esse qui promissus erat in lege, non tamen mysterium eius quod Filius Dei erat, neque sciebant sacramentum incarnationis et redemptionis*.' For this text, cf. nn. 19, 26 above.

[30] 'Dicendum est ergo quod principes Iudaeorum pro certo sciebant eum esse Christum promissum in lege, quod populus ignorabat. Ipsum autem esse verum Filium Dei non pro certo sciebant, sed aliqualiter coniecturabant: sed haec coniecturalis cognitio obscurabatur in

In his *Summa* he was to push the argument further. His discussion remained within the now standard distinction between the *maiores* and the *minores.* He repeated the substance of his earlier view that the *maiores* had known Jesus to be the Messiah since they saw fulfilled in him all that the prophets had foretold. But he did not repeat his view of the inference about his divinity which he had attributed to them. They did not recognize the mystery of his divinity; hatred and envy of Christ had distorted their understanding, to the extent that, though they recognized the manifest signs of his divinity, they did not wish to believe him when he declared himself to be the son of God.[31]

Thus their crime fell into the category of 'willed ignorance'. They were like those of whom Job spoke, people who 'say to God, Depart from us! We do not desire the knowledge of your ways.'[32] The Jewish *maiores* were so intent on sinning that they willed themselves to be ignorant of anything that put them off. Through their *ignorantia affectata*, then, it could be said, 'the Jews sinned in crucifying Christ not only as man but even as God'.[33]

This was not apparently the position of the *minores.* Uninstructed in the scriptures and not therefore recognizing Christ as either Messiah or Son of God, they might have wondered about him from time to time, considering the signs he wrought and the efficacy of his teaching. But they were misled by their leaders and so remained in ignorance. And it was the ignorance of the misled that Peter had acknowledged in Acts 3.17.[34] It is, however, noteworthy that all these

eis ex invidia et ex cupiditate propriae gloriae, quam per excellentiam Christi minui videbant': Ad I Cor. 2.8, *Opera omnia*, t. 13 (Parma, 1862).

[31] 'Sciendum tamen quod eorum ignorantia non eos excusabat a crimine, quia erat quodammodo ignorantia affectata: videbant enim evidentia signa divinitatis ipsius, sed ex odio, et invidia Christi ea pervertebant; et verbis eius, quibus se Dei Filium fatebatur, credere noluerunt': *Summa theologiae*, 3a. 47, 5 (Blackfriars edn, 54, London and New York, 1965), p. 68.

[32] 'Uno modo quia actus voluntatis fertur in ignorantiam; sicut cum aliquis ignorare vult, vel ut excusationem peccati habeat, vel ut non retrahatur a peccando, secundum illud Job, *Scientiam viarum tuarum nolumus* [Job 21.14]; et haec dicitur ignorantia affectata': *Summa theologiae*, Ia IIae 6, 8 edn cit., vol. 17, p. 32.

[33] '. . . ignorantia affectata non excusat a culpa, sed magis videtur culpam aggravare: otendit enim hominem sic vehementes esse affectum ad peccandum, quod vult ignorantiam incurrere, ne peccatum vitet. Et ideo Judaei peccaverunt non solum tamquam hominis Christi, sed etiam tamquam Dei crucifixores': *Summa*, 54, p. 70.

[34] 'Minores vero, id est populares, qui mysteria Scripturae non noverant, non plene cognoverunt ipsum esse nec Christum, nec Filium Dei. Licet enim aliqui eorum in eum crediderint, multitudo tamen non credidit; et si aliquando dubitaverunt an ipse esset Christus, propter signorum multitudinem et efficaciam doctrinae, ut habetur *Jo.*, tamen

extenuating circumstances did nothing to mitigate their punishment. They shared that with their leaders. The concept of corporate guilt remained unexamined in principle and unshaken in acceptance. Aquinas put it briefly in his commentary on Matthew's Passion narrative: Pilate, having washed his hands, handed over Jesus:

> 'Take him you and judge him according to your law' [John 18.31]. Then follows the guilt that binds them to punishment: 'His blood be upon us and upon our children'. And so it comes about that the blood of Christ is demanded of them even to this day and this accords well with 'The blood of thy brother Abel crieth to me from the earth' [Gen. 4.10].[35]

III

Two forces may be identified which stimulated Parisian intellectuals to find reasons why Jews should be allowed to exist in Christian society. One was academic. Just as theologians in twelfth-century Paris refined opinion about Jewish responsibility for the death of Christ, so was there a refining of opinion about toleration of Jews. The other was the impact of events. More Jews were being killed or threatened with death in northern Europe than in any previous period in its history. It seems reasonable to assume that even if there had been no pogroms at times when crusade fervour was at its peak, Parisian theologians would have reappraised and continued the Augustinian tradition of offering reasons why the presence of Judaism was of benefit to Christianity, just as they reappraised the Augustinian analysis of the Jewish role in the crucifixion. But what actually happened on the streets of France, Germany, and England gave a wholly new urgency to the question of Jewish survival, and so to a starker formulation: 'Jews ought to be allowed to live', argued Peter Cantor; 'The reasons why Jews are not to be killed by Christians' was considered by his pupil and colleague

postea decepti fuerunt a suis principibus, ut eum non crederent neque Filium Dei, neque Christum. Unde et Petrus eis dixit: Scio quia per ignorantiam fecistis, sicut et principes vestri, quia scilicet per principes seducti erant': ibid., p. 68.

[35] 'Unde dicitur: "Accipite eum vos, et secundum legem vestram iudicate eum". Tunc sequitur obligato ad poenam: *Sanguis eius super nos, et super filios nostros*. Et ita fiet quod sanguis Christi expetitur ab eis usque hodie: et bene convenit illis quod dictum est Gen. 4.10: "Sanguis fratris tui Abel clamat ad me de terra"': *In Matt. expositio*, cap. XXVII (*Opera omnia*, Parma, t. 10, 1860), p. 265.

Stephen Langton; 'Whether heretics and Jews are to be put to death', asked Thomas of Chobham, another graduate of the Cantor 'school'. Alexander of Hales asked why Jews should not be treated just like those other unbelievers who occupied the Holy Land.

The influence of Augustine on each of these discussions is so pronounced as to demand a preliminary summary. His doctrine on Jewish survival was expressed frequently, appearing in many of his works, and consistently. For present purposes, it suffices to identify its substance as articulated in his sermons on Psalms 40 and 58.

His argument began with the notion of punishment of the Jews. It fitted their crime. They had killed Jesus because they feared that if they did not, 'the Romans will come and take away our place and nation' (John 11.48). But having killed Christ, the Romans did come and they did lose their place (Jerusalem) and kingdom.[36] They also lost their place as Israel: the elder son, Esau, type of the Jewish people, had been rejected in favour of the younger, Jacob. That 'the elder shall serve the younger' (Genesis 25.23; Romans 9.12) was now fulfilled:

> Now, brethren, the Jews serve us, like the slaves who carry their masters' books when they go to study [*capsarii*]. Consider the way they serve us, not without cause. Cain, the elder brother who killed the younger brother received a mark to prevent his being killed, to be interpreted as meaning that the Jewish people should continue in being. With them are the law and the prophets; in which law and in which prophets Christ has been foretold. When we deal with pagans and demonstrate that in Christ's church what was foretold about Christ himself and the head and body of Christ is fulfilled, we put forward the books of the Jews lest the pagans think we have concocted these predictions by arranging them to fit the events. Without doubt the Jews are our enemies and from the enemies' books the adversary is defeated.[37]

[36] 'Occiderunt enim Christum Iudaei, ne perderent locum; illo occiso perdiderunt locum; eradicati a regno, dispersi sunt': *Enarr. in Ps. 40.12*, *CChr.SL*, 38, p. 457.

[37] '*Benedictus Dominus Deus Israel.* Ille est enim Deus Israel, Deus noster, Deus Iacob, Deus minoris filii, Deus minoris populi. Nemo dicat: De Iudaeis hoc dixit, non sum ego Israel. Magis Iudaei non sunt Israel. Maior enim filius, ipse est maior populus reprobatus; minor, populus dilectus. *Maior seruiet minori* modo impletum est; modo, fratres, nobis seruiunt Iudaei, tamquam capsarii nostri sunt, studentibus nobis codices portant. Audite in quo nobis Iudaei seruiunt, et non sine causa. Cain ille frater maior, qui occidit minorem fratrem, accepit signum ne occideretur, id est ut maneat ipse populus. Apud illos sunt prophetae et lex; in qua lege et in quibus prophetis Christus praedicatus est. Quando agimus

This role of service in the conversion of unbelievers was strongly reemphasised in exposition of Psalm 58.12:

> *Scatter them by thy power.* Now this has happened: the Jews are scattered throughout all nations, witnesses of their own iniquity and of our truth. They have the books in which Christ has been prophesied and we hold to Christ. And if on occasion some pagan should be sceptical when we tell him of Christ foretold, the evident nature of which so astonishes him as to cause him to suspect we have made up these testimonies to suit ourselves, we then prove from the books of the Jews how Christ's coming had been foretold. See then how by means of one set of enemies we confound another.[38]

For Augustine, the physical survival of the Jewish people was not the only consideration. It was scarcely less important that their religion should survive. The 'mark' which had been placed on the Jewish people was adherence to Judaism, that unique distinctiveness which they must retain while other nations subject to Roman rule by assimilation have lost their identity.[39] The Jews carry this mark of their religion because it is 'necessary for Christians'. Necessary – as a reminder to them of God's justice and mercy: justice, to the Jews, now pruned as dead branches from the olive; mercy, to Christians, in their

cum paganis, et ostendimus hoc euenire modo in ecclesia Christi, quod ante praedictum est de nomine Christi, de capite et corpore Christi, ne putent nos finxisse illas praedictiones, et ex his rebus quae acciderunt, quasi futurae essent, nos conscripisse, proferimus codices Iudaeorum. Nempe Iudaei inimici nostri sunt, de chartis inimici conuincuntur aduersarius': ibid., p. 459.

[38] '*Disperge eos in uirtute tua.* Iam factum est: per omnes gentes dispersi sunt Iudaei, testes iniquitatis suae et ueritatis nostrae. Ipsi habent codices, de quibus prophetatus est Christus, et nos tenemus Christum. Et si quando forte aliquis paganus dubitauerit, cum ei dixerimus prophetias de Christi, quarum euidentiam obstupescit, et admirans putauerit a nobis esse conscriptas; de codicibus Iudaeorum probamus quia hoc tanto ante praedictum est. Videte quemadmodum de inimicis nostris alios confundimus inimicos': *Enarr. in Ps. 58. 12*, *CChr.SL*, 39, p. 744.

[39] 'Quid de Iudaeis: *Ne occideris eos, nequando obliuiscantur legis tuae*? Istos inimicos meos, ipsos qui me occiderunt, noli tu occidere. Maneat gens Iudaeorum: certe uicta est a Romanis, certe deleta est ciuitas eorum; non admittantur ad ciuitatem suam Iudaei, et tamen Iudaei sunt. Nam omnes istae prouinciae a Romanis subiugatae sunt. Quis iam cognoscit gentes in imperio Romano quae quid erant, quando omnes Romani facti sunt, et omnes Romani dicuntur? Iudaei tamen manent cum signo; nec sic uicti sunt, ut a uictoribus absorberentur. Non sine causa Cain ille est, qui cum fratrem occidisset, posuit in eo Deus signum, ne quis eum occideret. Hoc est signum quod habent Iudaei: tenent omnino reliquias legis suae; circumciduntur, sabbata obseruant, pascha immolant, azyma comedunt': ibid.

being given life through being engrafted in place of the pruned (cf. Romans 11.17–20): 'Look where lie lifeless those who were proud, look where you have been grafted who formerly lay lifeless; and do not you yourselves be proud lest you too come to deserve cutting off.'[40]

Peter Lombard summarized the gist of this Augustinian doctrine. On Psalm 40 he registered the allegory of Esau and Jacob with its message of the elder serving the younger, service the Jews execute as *capsarii*; the supersession of the Old Law, 'We are Israel'; the living witness argument that the Jewish presence with their scriptures proves to pagans that the prophecies about Christ were not Christian forgeries,[41] witness that from the beginning has contributed to the spread of Christianity. For it was by this witness that 'salvation is come to the Gentiles' (Romans 11.11):

> And thus for their crime in rejecting the word of God came the salvation of the Gentiles [cf. Acts 13.46] while because of their sin in killing Christ, the Jews have been devastated by the Romans, scattered throughout the world and wholly uprooted from their country to give witness that the prophecies concerning Christ which the apostles were expounding to the Gentiles were not fictitious.[42]

Augustine's reading of Psalm 58.12 became the text of first recourse in establishing the Jews' right to life whether the case was being made in the schools or in the active condemnation of the murder of Jews when the crusade was being preached. While all agreed with Augustine on the importance of the 'Slay them not', each author gave it an individual slant. Peter Lombard's reading runs:

[40] 'Sunt ergo Iudaei, non sunt occisi, necessarii sunt credentibus gentibus. Quare hoc? *Deus meus demonstrauit mihi in inimicis meis.* In ramis superbia praecisis inserto misericordiam suam demonstrat oleastro. Ecce ubi iacent qui superbi erant, ecce ubi insertus es qui iacebas; et tu noli superbire, ne praecidi merearis': ibid.

[41] 'Nos qui sumus minor filius, id est, minor populus non fide sed tempore, sui servit maior, scil. populus Iudaicus, maior tempore. Iudaei enim sunt capsarii nostri, qui nobis codices portant: nos autem Israel. Aliter putassent pagani ficte quae sunt dicuntur de Christi et de ecclesia, sed vincuntur testimonio inimicorum': *PL* 191, col. 414.

[42] 'Et ita ex eorum delicto quo repulerunt Verbum fuit salus gentium dum Iudaei pro peccata mortis Christi vastati, infelicius a Romanis et divisi per mundum, funditusque a suo regno eradicati in testimonium sunt, non fictas de Christo esse prophetias quas apostoli gentibus de Christo exposuerunt': *PL* 191, col. 1484.

> *Slay them not.* Christ prays that the Jews should not perish completely. They are indeed dispersed, that they might be challenged to conversion. Or, so that the church might have on her behalf the evidence of the old law from her enemies. Therefore he prays *slay them not*, namely those who killed me, but let the Jewish people remain marked with the sign of circumcision, of sabbaths, of paschs, just as Cain bears a sign that no one should kill him. Thus that people, bearing its own mark, is preserved because it is necessary for believers to understand the mercy that has engrafted them in place of the cut-off branches.[43]

Peter Cantor also offered an interpretation of Psalm 58.12. Jewish survival had been prefigured in Cain. As 'our *capsarii* and carriers of our books' and witnesses of the Lord's passion, Jews made a public statement about their service to the Church. They ought not to be allowed to become rich, they should be employed in menial work, such as sweeping the streets.[44]

In the *Summa Abel*, he pursued a somewhat different line of argument. That Jews should be permitted to live had been clearly indicated by God; their survival was part of his providential plan for mankind. Psalm 58 was just one of several such indicators. The Jewish presence manifested God's justice in their punishment of dispersion; it bore witness in the corporate guilt of the Jewish people to the death of Christ, 'his blood be on us and on our children'; it confirmed the Christian faith by giving the evidence of an adversary against other

[43] '*nec occides eos*, hoc specialiter de Iudaeis potest accipi. Hoc est quod Pater ei ostendit, *ne occides eos*. Precatur, ne Iudaei funditus pereant. Dispersi quidem sunt, ut ad conversionem provocentur. Vel ut ecclesia ab inimicis testimonia veteris legis habeat. Ideo pro eis orat, dicens: *ne occides eos*, qui me occiderunt, sed maneat gens Iudaeorum cum signo circumcisionis, sabbati, paschae ut Cain signum habuit, ut eum nemo occideret. Ita et gens illa habens signum suum non est occisa, quia necessaria est credentibus, et in ipsis praecisis ostenditur, etiam quae sit misericordia insertis . . . *disperge* per omnes gentes *illos*, scil. Iudaeos qui portant codices nobis': *PL* 191, col. 546. No doubt Diceto had a similar line of thought in mind when he condemned the infamous attacks on Jews in England by the crusaders of 1190: 'Ubicunque reperti sunt Iudaei manibus peregrinantium percussi sunt, nisi qui municipalium eruebantur auxilio. Necem Iudaeorum tam funestam tam exitialem, viris prudentibus placuisse credendum non est, cum Daviticum illud auribus nostris frequenter occurrat, "Ne occidas eos"': *Ymagines historiarum*, II, *RS*, p. 76.

[44] 'Ipsi enim sunt capsarii nostri et baiuli codicum nostrorum et testes dominice passionis, mundatores platearum. Debent esse non diuites et publici servi Ecclesie, et hoc prefiguratum fuit in Chain, in quo posuit Dominus signum tremoris, ne occideretur.' Text published by G. Dahan, 'L'Article *Iudei* de la *Summa Abel* de Pierre le Chantre', p. 126.

unbelievers, so thus does 'the elder serve the younger'; their final conversion has been promised.[45]

Cain, allegorically representing a wandering, dispersed Jewish people, continued to be a powerful image. Stephen Langton found three aspects of the symbol which argued for Jewish survival:

> *Scatter them O Lord by thy Power.* The Lord has put a mark on them. Their practice of circumcision and literal observance of the law constitutes the mark preserving them from being killed, so therefore they are spared. Or the Lord has marked them with our faith, because through that we discern the passion of the Lord and call it to mind; thus they are witnesses of the Lord's passion. Or the mark denotes the fulfilment of what has been foretold by the prophets; by the reality of their dispersion, predicted so long beforehand, it has been proved that the other prophecies will be fulfilled.[46]

Thomas of Chobham's explanation of why obdurate heretics merited the death penalty but Jews did not, was thoroughly Augustinian with its *capsarii* argument, yet contained the slant of Peter Cantor by arguing that they should be permitted only dishonourable work:

> It has been written of the Jews 'slay them not, lest at any time my people forget'. If they wish to live at peace under the yoke of our servitude and refrain from impugning our faith or attacking our

[45] 'IUDEI seruantur ad uitam: propter iusticiam Dei, ut in eis appareat pena et dispersio, propter mortem Christi, quia dixerunt: *Sanguis eius super nos et super filios nostros*; propter confirmationem uel obsequium, ut scilicet faciant nobis testimonium contra gentiles, quia capsarii nostri sunt. Laudabile enim est testimonium ab aduersario; unde: *Maior seruiet minori*; propter complendam promissionem Dei, qui ait: *Si fuerit numerus filiorum Israel tanquam arena maris, reliquie salue fient* [cf. Is. 10.22; Rom. 9.27]; propter eorum conuersionem que fit per tribulationem; unde: *Imple facies eorum ignominia*' etc. [Ps. 82.17]: ed. Dahan, 'L'Article *Iudei*', p. 106.

[46] '*Allegorice. Capitulum quintum. Causa qua Iudei non interficiantur a Christianis.*
Posuit Deus Chayn signum. Allegorice. Chayn sunt Iudei uagi et dispersi. Unde: *Disperge eos.* Domine, *in uirtute tua.* Posuit in eis Dominus signum. Habent circumcisionem et carnalem observantiam legis in signum ne interficiantur, et ideo parcitur eis. Vel posuit eos Dominus in signum fidei nostre, quia per hoc quod eos uidemus passionem Domini ad memoriam reuocamus, et ita testes sunt passionis Domini. In signum etiam sunt adimpletionis futorum que ante predicta sunt a prophetis; ex quo completa est dispersio in eis, que longe predicta erat, manifestum est quod alia pre predicta sunt a prophetis complebuntur': *Expositio supre Genesim*, ch. iiii, ed. G. Dahan, 'L'exégèse de l'histoire de Cain et Abel du XIIe au XIVe siècle en Occident. Textes', *Recherches de théologie ancienne et médiévale*, 50 (1983), pp. 5–68 at p. 22.

> persons, they are to be preserved among us and allocated work of a base sort so that they cannot exalt themselves over Christians. And so indeed are Jews to be especially sustained among us because they are our *capsarii* and bear the witness of the Law against themselves and for us.[47]

Alexander of Hales put the Jewish survival issue on the formal basis of the *quaestio*: 'whether Jews should be tolerated'.

The case against toleration focused on the Jews as perennial blasphemers – of Christ, of the Blessed Virgin, of the Christian faith generally. Blasphemy, it was argued, was a crime meriting death even in the Old Law (Lev. 24.16).[48] And with a reference to recent sensational events in Paris which, on the instructions of Louis IX, had led to the mass destruction of Talmud books, continued the argument with the notion that just as their blasphemous books should be destroyed, so too should those who held them as authoritative.[49] Further, if Christians lawfully kill those who occupy the Holy Land, how much the more are they deserving of death who commit the worse crime of insulting the Redeemer, as is known to be the Jewish practice in Holy Week.[50]

As against such arguments – their dangerous force when used by bloodthirsty rabble-rousers can be readily appreciated – Alexander offered Peter Lombard's reading of Psalm 58.12: the Lord himself had prayed for the survival of the Jewish people. The living testimony of

[47] 'Utrum interficiendi sint heretici et iudei . . . de [Iudeis] scriptum est: *ne occidas eos ne quando obliviscantur populi mei*. Si volunt esse sub iugo servitutus nostre in pace, neque fidem nostram neque nos impugnare, sustinendi sunt inter nos et deputandi ad aliqua sordida officia, ne possint se extollere super christianos. Verumtamen ideo ita sustinentur precipue iudei quia capsarii nostri sunt et portant testimonium legis contra se pro nobis': *Summa confessorum*, ed. F. Broomfield (Louvain and Paris, 1968), p. 434.

[48] The view that Christ was daily blasphemed in the synagogues was apparently current in Paris. Rigord recorded the conversion of synagogues to churches in 1183: 'Consideravit equidem pia consideratione et honesta, quod ubi nomen Jesu Christi Nazareni, teste Hieronymo super Isaiam, de die in diem blasphemari solebat, a clero et universo populo christiano ibidem lauderetur Deus, qui facit mirabilia magna solus': *Gesta Philippi Augusti*, ed. H. Delaborde, *Oeuvres de Rigord et Guillaume le Breton*, I (Paris, 1882), pp. 30–1.

[49] On the Franco-papal campaign against the Talmud during Alexander's Parisian period, W. C. Jordan, *The French Monarchy and the Jews. From Philip Augustus to the Late Capetians* (Philadelphia, 1989), pp. 137–41. Cf. also R. Chazan, 'The condemnation of the Talmud (1239–1248)', *American Academy for Jewish Research*, 55 (1988), pp. 11–30.

[50] Alexander cited Lateran IV c.68 (= *Decretales* 5.6.15) which, in confining Jews to their homes in Holy Week, assumed a perennial Jewish potential for blasphemous behaviour.

enemies was more potent than any other; the evidence of Moses and the prophets could not be denied. Also the eventual salvation of the Jews had been foretold – which could hardly take place if the whole people had been wiped out. So toleration was to be accepted.[51]

As to their blaspheming ways: they have been punished by dispersion in this life and in the next God will punish them if they do not repent. Lateran IV had instructed all civil authorities to be active against open blasphemy. It was for them too to take action against the Talmud by burning it and bringing criminal charges in their courts against any Jew accused of blasphemy. The argument that the unbelievers who occupied the Holy Land and the Jews should receive similar treatment was to be rejected. The former are attacked as illegally and injuring Christ. Jews are to be allowed to live among Christians because it is from them we accept the Old Testament, because it was of their stock that Christ came and because their salvation has been promised.[52] Any crimes against Christ that they commit are to be tried and punished by legal process. They should no more be spared from punishment for crimes they have committed than should bad Christians.

The Lombard and the Cantor and their successors in the early years of the university of Paris had searched the scriptures, reading them along with patristic, especially Augustinian, opinion to discover the fundamental principles of Christian–Jewish relations. They found two, in tension, pulling in opposite directions. The Jews were and remained enemies of Christ and his Church. Nevertheless their continued

[51] (Against the arguments for non-toleration) 'Contrarium videtur per hoc quod dicitur in psalmo, super illud: *Ne occidas eos*, glossa [Lombardi] "Hoc de Iudaeis specialiter potest accipi; precatur, ne Iudaei funditus pereant: dispersi quidem sunt, ut ad conuersionem provocentur; orat etiam pro eis, dicens: *Ne occidas eos*, qui me occiderunt, sed maneat gens Iudaeorum cum signo circumcisionis". Ergo tolerandi sunt. Item fortius est testimonium quod ab adversariis accipitur; sed ecclesia catholica sumit testimonium a veteri lege, quam observant Iudaei; ad hoc ergo quod ecclesia catholica ab inimicis habet testimonium, tolerandi sunt Iudaei: a lege enim veteri, scilicet a lege Moysi et prophetis, accipitur testimonium de Christo, quod negare non possunt. Item Isai habetur quod *reliquiae Israel salvae fient* et similiter dicit Apostolus [Isa. 10.22; Rom. 9.27]; reliquiae autem salvari non possent nisi semen Iudaeorum maneret; salvandum est ergo semen Iudaeorum; tolerandi ergo sunt Iudaei. Quod concedendum est': *Summa Alexandri*, t. iii, p. 729.

[52] 'Iudaei vero multiplici ratione permittuntur vivere et inter Christianos commorari, tum propter hoc quod a Iudaeis legem veterem accepimus, tum quia de semine illo venit Christus, tum quia facta est promissio salutis eorum, cum *plenitudo gentium intraverit*' (Rom. 11.25]: ibid., p. 730.

presence, in lowly form, was of service to Christianity. They were not new principles but those scholars had done more than most to ensure that they became an ordinary feature of the medieval theological agenda.

THE INSTRUCTIONAL PROGRAMME OF THE MENDICANT CONVENTS AT PARIS IN THE EARLY FOURTEENTH CENTURY

by WILLIAM J. COURTENAY

THE history of teaching and study at the Parisian convents of the mendicant orders has largely been viewed and written as part of the history of the university of Paris. The Parisian doctors of theology at the Dominican, Franciscan, Augustinian, and Carmelite convents , from the time of Bonaventure, Albert, Thomas, and Giles of Rome until the end of the Middle Ages, were regent masters, or professors, at the university, at least for a year or more after inception as masters. And presumably mendicant students sent to Paris for theological study were being sent there for university studies; the brightest of them would be expected to complete the university degree in theology. The connection between the mendicant masters and the intellectual history of the university of Paris in the second half of the thirteenth century is so strong that it is almost impossible to think of these convents except as religious colleges attached to the university of Paris.

In the following remarks I want to suggest a different model of the role of the Paris convents in the educational structure of the mendicant orders. Specifically, I want to focus attention on one important but neglected part of their educational system, namely the lectorate programme, which was numerically the largest part of that system. In doing so I will be presenting a different picture of the relationship of these convents to the university of Paris than the one generally encountered in the literature. And the revised picture has implications for how one should read certain scholastic texts important for the study of medieval philosophy and theology.

First, what is the present picture of mendicant university education, and what implications has it had for our understanding of the normal pattern of a philosophical and theological career? The standard picture was constructed from the constitutions and legislation of the mendicant orders (primarily Dominican and Franciscan) read in light of the curricular and degree requirements of medieval universities (primarily Paris and Oxford). While recognizing that the educational systems of the mendicant orders were developed by the orders for their own instructional and religious purposes and that provincial *studia* and *studia generalia* not located in university towns operated independently of university regulations, it has been assumed that students sent to the university convent were sent there for theological study in which the highest goal was the university doctorate in theology. Training in logic and natural philosophy in one or more *studia* of the order was a necessary prerequisite for the theological programme.[1]

At Paris one attained the doctorate after twelve to fourteen years of theological study, lecturing, and disputing before being licensed and being allowed to incept as a master of theology.[2] Since the religious orders financed the education of their students, so that no one selected to go to Paris was delayed by lack of funds, those who became masters or doctors of theology (the terms were interchangeable by the early fourteenth century), presumably moved through this system, as it was described in the statutes of the order and university, in a smooth and largely uninterrupted sequence, with perhaps a year or two longer at some point because of the novitiate, administrative duties, or health problems, or a year or two shorter at another point because of a papal dispensation. Moreover, it has been assumed that when students were sent to Paris, it was with the expectation that each had an equal opportunity, at least initially, to obtain their degree unless their abilities proved insufficient to the task. Whatever attrition took place along the way was of minor interest to historians, since our attention has focused on those who left philosophical and theological writings, and that group for the mendicants is essentially identical with those who completed the theological doctorate.

Several working assumptions have followed from this depiction of a continuous progression from the beginning to end of theological training for the successful mendicant student. The first is that we are

[1] Rashdall, 1, pp. 371–6; Leff, *Paris and Oxford*, pp. 35–38; W. A. Hinnebusch, *The History of the Dominican Order*, 2 (New York, 1973), pp. 44–9, 58–62; J. Verger, '*Studia* et universités', in *Le Scuole degli ordini mendicanti (secoli XIII–XIV)* (Todi, 1978), pp. 173–203, esp. pp. 189–90: 'Les historiens distinguent habituellement les *studia* Mendiants intégrés dans les universités et ceux qui ne l'étaient pas, coexistant simplement avec l'université dans la même ville et généralement le même quartier. Dans le premier cas, illustré avant tout par Paris et Oxford, les *studia* Mendiants . . . étaient considérés comme des écoles de théologie analogues aux écoles séculières ou canoniales, l'ensemble de ces écoles formant la faculté de théologie.'

[2] Rashdall, *Universities*, 1, pp. 471–86.

looking at *one* programme with *one* principal goal, divided into different stages, much like the sequential pattern of education and professional training in the modern world. Presumably, all beginning students in theology were potentially working towards the doctorate, and the reason why so few made it through the entire programme was that only one student from each religious order was permitted to read the *Sentences* in any one year, and only the most gifted students, in the eyes of their superiors, were chosen to be that one candidate for the baccalaureate at Paris or Oxford and proceed to the doctorate.

A second assumption is that to the extent that academic achievement and merit were the principal criteria in the selection of those permitted to continue to the doctorate, their academic superiors at the Paris convent (those who had observed their early performance in comparison to their student cohort) must have played a primary role in this selection process.

A third assumption is that if one knows the date at which a friar fulfilled one stage in this programme, for example, the date of his promotion to the doctorate or the date at which a friar read (that is, commented on) the *Sentences* of Peter Lombard, one can date approximately the other stages in his earlier career, including an approximate date of birth. Similarly, if one knows the date at which a university friar was ordained to holy office, for example the date at which Ockham was ordained subdeacon, presumably at age 21, one can date the stages of his academic career.

There is one variation to this picture that Eelcko Ypma brought to light some years ago for the educational system of the Augustinian hermits.[3] He stressed the existence of a lectorate programme within the Augustinian order which consisted in five years of theological study at the Paris convent, followed by five to ten years of teaching (i.e., fulfilling the office of *lector*) at the philosophical and theological *studia* of the order, usually in their home province. Only after this period of teaching (and presumably further study) was completed, was one appointed to read the *Sentences* at Paris and proceed to the doctorate. Although Ypma's description of theological training in the Augustinian order was considerably different from descriptions normally presented of Dominican and Franciscan education, his stress was still

[3] E. Ypma, *La Formation des professeurs chez les ermites de Saint-Augustin de 1256 à 1354* (Paris, 1956), pp. 72–3.

on the doctorate as the culmination of one and the same theological programme.[4]

The assumption has been that the Augustinians were unusual in dividing their theological training into a five-year period of initial study at the university of Paris, followed by a eight- to ten-year period of teaching in the *studia generalia et provincialia* of the order, before returning to Paris to complete the degree. Most Franciscans who were destined for the doctorate spent only one or two years lecturing on the *Sentences* at a *studium* of the order before returning to the university to read the *Sentences*.[5] Reading at a lesser *studium* before doing so at a university became a statutory requirement in the reform of the Franciscan educational system under Benedict XII in 1336, but nowhere in that legislation is the timeframe of pre-university study set forth.[6]

Inasmuch as the educational programme of the Augustinian Hermits was modelled in large measure on that of the Dominicans, is it possible that there was a corresponding long period of provincial teaching between the lectorate and baccalaureate for the Dominicans and Franciscans that has simply failed to get the same degree of attention? Has our picture of a twelve- to fourteen-year course of theological study for Dominicans and Franciscans been based too much on university statutes, as if the university doctorate was the goal of their educational system?

The following analysis presents a different picture, one derived from reading mendicant educational legislation on its own terms rather than in light of university statutes, and one that pays more attention to prosopographical evidence. The general lines of the argument are as follows. First, that the educational programme of the older mendicant orders, namely the Dominicans and Franciscans, more closely resembled that of the Augustinians than has been realized. Second, that these orders maintained two related but essentially different theological programmes at their Paris convents, which had two

[4] While Hinnebusch (*History*, 2, p. 59) gave the impression that Dominican students sent to Paris were sent there for the university degree in theology, other Dominican historians (e.g., A. Dondaine, 'Documents pour servir à l'histoire de la province de France: L'appel au concile (1303)', *AFP*, 22 (1952), pp. 381–39) acknowledged that the quota system through which the provinces were obliged to send students to Paris produced a body of students (around 150 by his estimate) far larger than could be accommodated at the level of the baccalaureate.

[5] W. J. Courtenay, *Adam Wodeham* (Leiden, 1978), pp. 45–53, at 48–9.

[6] *CUP*, 2, pp. 469–71, #1006.

different purposes. Third, that the selection of candidates for the baccalaureate and doctorate at Paris was not based solely or perhaps even primarily on academic achievement as evaluated by those under whom they had studied, but rather on a mixture of qualifications within which political and social considerations played an important part. And fourth, that this revised picture calls for some adjustments in the way we reconstruct the biographies of mendicant scholars.

As suggested, the Franciscans and Dominicans ran two distinct but related programmes of theological study at their Parisian convent.[7] One was a lectorate programme, established by each order, whose purpose was to prepare teachers for the convents and schools of each province and to improve the intellectual leadership of the provinces on which the leadership of the order depended. The selection of candidates for the Paris lectorate was entirely in the hands of the leadership of the provinces. It was the programme through which the provinces of an order could send their more accomplished students to complete their training in theology at the Paris convent after they had had many years of preparatory training in philosophy and theology in the convents and *studia* of the home province.[8] The larger student demand in the older orders set the Paris portion of theological study for the Franciscans at four years, and for the Dominicans at three, while the Augustinians allowed up to five years of Parisian study.[9] By

[7] Franciscan legislation regarding the qualifications, quota, and selection process for study at the Parisian convent remained relatively the same from the mid-thirteenth to mid-fourteenth century. For the legislation from the constitutions of 1260 at the general chapter at Narbonne, see F. Ehrle, 'Die ältesten Redaktionen der General-Constitutionen des Franziskanerordens', *Archiv für Literatur und Kirchengeschichte des Mittelalters*, 6 (1892), 1–136, at pp. 33–5. The relevant legislation from the constitution of 1292 appears in *CUP*, 2, pp. 56–9, #580.

While requirements and procedures for study at Cordeliers may have remained relatively stable, the larger Franciscan educational system of which it was a part probably underwent expansion and change between 1280 and 1330. It is difficult to know to what extent the levels and geographical range of the educational programme as described in the constitution 'Redemptor noster' of Benedict XII in 1336 (*CUP*, 2, pp. 469–71, #1006) reflect conditions in 1300. Unfortunately, standard works on the early development of Franciscan education, such as M. Brlek, *De Evolutione iuridica studiorum in ordine minorum* (Dubrovnik, 1942), depend heavily on fourteenth-century evidence, but L. Beaumont-Maillet, *Le Grand Couvent des Cordeliers de Paris* (Paris, 1975), pp. 20–8, is more sensitive to late thirteenth-century conditions. The following description depends primarily on the legislation of 1292.

[8] *CUP*, 2, p. 57: 'Item mittendi Parisius ad studium generale primo exerceantur tribus vel duobus annis post novitiatum in aliquo studio provincie sue vel vicine, nisi adeo litterati fuerint quod post novitiatum continuo possint mitti. Non mittantur tamen nisi de auctoritate ministri cum consilio et assensu Capituli provincialis.'

[9] Although four years of pre-baccalaureate study at Paris for the Franciscan order is

the early fourteenth century, in both the Franciscan and Dominican orders, each province (eighteen provinces for the Dominicans and thirty-four for the Franciscans) was permitted to send two students to Paris, with the possibility of an additional student at the expense of the province.[10] Students in the lectorate programme were generally in their mid to late twenties, and they would be expected to attend the lectures of the regent master and bachelors in the convent. They were probably permitted and may even have been encouraged to attend disputations and perhaps lectures elsewhere in the university community. Yet it is unclear to what extent they were university students. They were studying with a master who was simultaneously a regent master in the faculty of theology, but they were under the supervision of the leaders of the convent, the prior and master of students in the case of the Dominicans and the guardian in the case of the Franciscans, none of whom need have any connection with the theological faculty. Moreover, these students had been sent to Paris to complete an internal course of study at the convent that would give them credentials for teaching in their home province.[11] The opportunity of study at the Paris convent was an important qualitative part of their training, but it was a means to an end that had essentially nothing to do with a university degree.

The other programme was directly linked to the university and the theological faculty. It was this 'programme' which provided candidates for university degrees, specifically the baccalaureate in theology

generally accepted, the text on which this calculation is based seems to apply to the baccalaureate rather than the lectorate. Ibid.: 'Illi autem qui mittuntur Parisius studeant quatuor annis ad minus, nisi adeo provecti fuerint, quod merito judicentur ydonei ad doctoris officium exequendum.' The difference in length of Parisian study among the three major orders may not be accurate, since the statutory language usually expresses minimum requirements rather than fixed terms of residency.

[10] For the Franciscan legislation: *CUP*, 2, p. 57: 'Possit autem quelibet provincia habere duos studentes Parisius sine aliqua provisione, quibus provideatur in libris secundum arbitrium provincialis Capituli et ministri. Quilibet vero studens Parisius de gratia xii libras parisiens. procuret pro conventus ipsius necessitatibus assignari.'

The Dominicans initially permitted three students per province. But when, between 1294 and 1303, the number of Dominican provinces was increased from twelve to eighteen, the number of students sent to Paris from any one province (other than France) at the expense of the order was reduced from three to two. Although Antoine Dondaine interpreted the Dominican rule to mean two or three students per province sent each year, a more reasonable interpretation – one that is supported by the 1303 document referred to earlier – is two students per province in residence at the respective Paris convent at any one time.

[11] The ideal *cursus honorum* is indicated by the language in the margin of the manuscript

(fulfilled by lecturing on Peter Lombard's *Sentences* for one or two years) and the doctorate, or *magisterium*, in theology (fulfilled, after licensing and inception, by a period of one or two years of teaching as regent master).[12] Extensive training in logic, natural philosophy, theology, and lectures on the Bible were required before being admitted to the reading of the *Sentences* at Paris, but those were requirements for admission to the baccalaureate, not stages in the university programme as such.[13] Among the Franciscans, candidates for university degrees – one per year in each category – were chosen by the minister general of the order with the advice and consent of the general chapter. Within a three-year cycle one candidate was to be chosen from the province of France, while in the other two years candidates were selected from the other thirty-three provinces of the order.[14] This policy contrasts with that of the Dominicans, who favoured their French province more heavily by choosing a candidate from that province every other year.[15] And for the Dominicans, the selection of candidates lay with the general chapter more than with the master general. The crucial event in each case was being chosen to read the *Sentences* at Paris, since those who were put forward for licensing and the *magisterium* were chosen from among those who had completed their lectures on the *Sentences* and their required residency as formed bachelors.

In contrast to the lectorate programme, therefore, choosing candidates for the doctorate at Paris was done by the order as a whole, not

of the 1292 Franciscan constitution: ibid., p. 58: 'ad lectoriam, baccallariam, magisterium vel quodcunque Ordinis officium promoveri'.

12 *CUP*, 2, p. 56: 'De fratribus lecturis Sententias et ad magisterium presentandis Parisius minister provideat generalis.'

13 Biblical lectures in the faculty of theology were primarily the responsibility of the regent masters. The earliest university statutes that mention pre-magisterial lectures on the Bible are early fourteenth century, but it is unclear whether they reflect university practice as of 1300: *CUP*, 2, p. 692, #1188 (nn. 9–11). The pre-sentential requirements mentioned in those statutes appear to be more descriptive than prescriptive.

14 *CUP*, 2, p. 56: 'Placet tamen generali Capitulo quod illorum qui Parisius sunt lecturi Sententias vel ad magisterium presentandi tertius semper de provincia Francie, alii vero duo de aliis provinciis Ordinis magis ydonei assumantur, ita tamen quod propter hoc non promoveatur aliquis insufficiens ad officia supradicta, nec potestati generalis ministeri prejudicetur in aliquo quin in provisione hujusmodi libere facere possit et preferre unum alteri sicut Ordini viderit expedire.'

15 The Dominicans had two chairs of theology, one reserved for candidates from the province of France and one for candidates from the other provinces. Since they were not allowed to put forward more than one candidate each year for the baccalaureate, the selection alternated between the two chairs.

by the provinces. Moreover, a closer look at the candidates selected to read the *Sentences* at Paris in the early fourteenth century shows that they were rarely if ever chosen from among those who had just completed the lectorate. They were rather chosen from those who had had several years – usually many years – post-lectorate experience in teaching and administration at the provincial level. Whether it was an official policy or not, almost no student moved directly from the lectorate to the baccalaurate.[16] Among the Franciscans eight to ten years separate the Parisian lectorate and baccalaureate of William of Alnwick, and some twenty years in the case of Anfredus Gonteri. Pierre Auriol was teaching at Toulouse before being chosen to read at Paris; Pastor de Serrescuderio was provincial minister of Provence when he was selected; Arnaud de Clermont had spent many years teaching at Orléans and Angers; and in England Adam Wodeham had lectured at Norwich and probably London (for what length of time we do not actually know) before becoming a bachelor at Oxford.[17]

This is also the case among the Dominicans at Paris. Durand of St Pourçain and James of Lausanne, who were students at Paris in 1303, were not selected to return to Paris until five or six years later in the case of Durand, and ten years later in the case of James, presumably after teaching in the schools of the order. The list of Dominicans who were serving as provincial ministers at the time of their selection to read the *Sentences* at Paris is significant: Guillaume de Laon, Bernard Lombardi, Hugh de Marciaco, and Giovanni Porcari – all sent to Paris for the baccalaureate in the first decades of the fourteenth century.[18] In fact, in every case where we know the location and/or activity of a friar in the year or years before his appointment to read the *Sentences* at Paris we find him in a teaching or administrative position in his home

[16] Admittedly, evidence on the dates and names of friars sent to Paris for the lectorate is all but non-existent. While this makes it impossible to state categorically that no student was promoted directly from the lectorate to the baccalaureate, in every case where we know the pre-baccalaureate status of the candidate he did not come directly from the lectorate 'pool'.

[17] In the case of Alnwick and Gonteri, the Franciscan list of 1303, discussed below, establishes their presence at Paris in the lectorate programme, while the approximate dates of their theological degrees at Paris have been established from manuscripts of theirs and Scotus' works as well as Alnwick's regency at Oxford. The evidence on Auriol, Serrescuderio, and Clermont can be found in *CUP*. The evidence on Wodeham is presented in Courtenay, *Adam Wodeham*.

[18] The date of Durand and James of Lausanne's presence in the lectorate programme at Paris is established by the Dominican list of 1303; cf. Dondaine, 'Documents'. Information on the others listed is taken from documents in *CUP*.

province. And since there was no set rule regarding the number of years that separated the lectorate and the baccalaureate, this period might range anywhere from five to twenty years. This, in turn, makes the mendicant bachelors and regent masters an older group than we have usually thought – probably on the average in their early-to-mid forties rather than their early thirties. Nor is it the case that once sent to Paris for the baccalaureate, one remained at Paris through to regency. In the case of the Dominicans, we find several who were appointed to be promoted to masters who in the previous year or years had been provincial ministers (Berengar of Landorra, John of Luchembergh, and Meister Eckhart), suggesting that a second period of provincial teaching or administrative activity might occur between the baccalaureate and the doctorate.

Thus the programme of theological study laid out in the university statutes and in textbooks, which suggests direct continuity from the initial years of study to admission to read the *Sentences* and continuing on to the doctorate, does not reflect a normal academic progression for mendicant students, including Francisans.[19] Those pursuing the lectorate had been chosen to go to Paris by their province and provincial minister, and it was to their province that they returned. Those chosen to read the *Sentences* at Paris and subsequently be put forward for licensing and inception as master were, among the Franciscans, chosen by the minister general with the advice and consent of the general chapter of the order, and among the Dominicans by the general chapter, perhaps at the recommendation of the master general. With one or two possible exceptions, only those who had been trained in the lectorate at Paris and who had come to the attention of the leadership of the order were viable candidates for selection as *sententiarii*.

The numerical disproportion of the two programmes also argues against the view that the lectorate programme was designed as the beginning stage for university degrees, one programme flowing directly into the other. Those from each order involved in the university degree programme (defined as those sent to Paris to read the *Sentences* up through those completing their magisterial regency)

[19] For the requirements and length of study as defined in the statutes, see W. J. Courtenay, 'Progress of study and genres of scholastic theological production in the fourteenth century' in J. Hamesse, ed., *Manuels, programmes de cours et techniques d'enseignement dans les universités médiévales* (Louvain-la-Neuve, 1994), pp. 325–50.

numbered between eight and ten, while those involved in the lectorate programme for the Dominicans and Franciscans, according to their legislation, would number around 150 each. But mendicant legislation tells us only the number that could be sent to Paris for study by each province, not how many actually went.

The fortuitous survival of a royal document for the Franciscan convent at Paris in 1303, however, gives us the names and home provinces for the students who were actually there at the end of the 1302–3 academic year, and thus provides us precisely with a way of observing the implementation of Franciscan educational policy.[20] Of the 173 friars whose names appear in the document, there were some twenty-five to thirty who were attached to the convent for reasons other than education, or for whom Cordeliers was their home convent, although some of the latter may have been students as well. A second group was composed of those from the custody of Paris (a custody being one of the administrative units into which the province was divided) who were there because it was their custodial (or local) school for philosophy and theology, along with those from the province of France for whom the convent was their provincial *studium* in theology. This was a group of around forty-five to fifty. Third, there were those from outside the province of France who would have been sent there to study theology – a group ranging between eighty and ninety. Finally, there were the eight to ten friars who by academic title or other information are known to have then been involved in the baccalaureate or doctorate category.

The second and third groups, that is, those who were sent to the convent from outside Paris but who had not yet advanced to the baccalaureate, thus numbered close to 140, most of whom would have been studying theology. Since the document groups the non-adhering friars by province, it is easy to see the provincial quota system at work. Each province other than the province of France, which was not bound by the quota, or the provinces of Dalmatia and Syria, which had no students in residence in 1303, exercised its right to send two students

[20] Paris, Archives Nationales, J.488, no. 595; first edited by E. Longpré, 'Le B. Jean Duns Scot: Pour le Saint Siège et contre le gallicanisme (25–28 Juin 1303)', *La France franciscaine*, 11 (1928), pp. 37–62; reedited in W. J. Courtenay, 'The Parisian Franciscan community in 1303', in *Franciscan Studies*, 53 (1993), pp. 155–73. The document and its context are also discussed in Courtenay, 'Between pope and king. The Parisian letters of adhesion of 1303', *Speculum*, 71 (1996), pp. 577–605.

to Paris at the expense of the order, while a few (Ireland, Saxony, Denmark, Milan, and Umbria) with three may have taken advantage of the right to have an additional student at the expense of the province. Only Trevigiana, Tuscany, and England exceeded that number, but some of those 'extra' students were involved in university degrees, for example John Dune Scotus, who was reading the *Sentences* in 1302–3. It may well be that no province exceeded a quota of three for the lectorate programme.

Not only did these two programmes differ in size and selection procedures, but probably also in purpose. From the standpoint of the mendicant orders, at least by the fourteenth century, the purpose of the Parisian doctorate was not ultimately to prepare teachers. The lectorate programme did that. Although the Aristotelian commentaries, the published lectures on the *Sentences*, the *Quodlibetic* debates, and disputed questions may be the product of the Parisian *studium* that allowed us to understand its intellectual activity and concerns, I suspect that in the eyes of the order the purpose of the university-degree programme was to prepare a small group of its members for positions of leadership in the order and in the Church at large.

Newly-minted Parisian masters did not remain at Paris after their regency, which was reduced to one year and in many cases to a few months. Some were sent initially as senior lecturers to other *studia generalia* of the order, as was Scotus who was sent to Cologne; others went into positions of leadership in the order and/or to the papal court at Avignon (for example, Pierre Auriol), where they served on theological commissions and established the connections necessary to be appointed to a bishopric and perhaps later advance to cardinal. Although many considerations beyond academic credentials were necessary for high office in the Church, the mendicant orders realized that for them the Parisian doctorate was an important element. And because those chosen to proceed to the baccalaureate and doctorate were being groomed as much for administration as for learning, I also suspect that social background, diplomatic skills, and contacts within a defined network were important criteria in the selection process.

To the extent it can be reconstructed, the full list of doctors among the mendicant orders in the fourteenth century – not just the great names of philosophy and theology with whom we are familiar – reveals that personal connections and patronage played as large, if not a larger, role in the selection process as intellectual ability. Scotus proceeded to the doctorate at Paris in 1305 soon after the completion of his lectures on the *Sentences* because the newly-elected minister general, Gonsalvus, knew him and liked him, and his appointment to read the *Sentences* may have been facilitated by the tension between Philip the Fair and Boniface VIII, which perhaps inclined the minister general, the Italian Giovanni di Murro, to favour a non French candidate. Francis of Meyronnes was promoted to the doctorate through the patronage of Robert of Anjou, king of Sicily. And the number of Dominican and Franciscan provincial ministers chosen for the baccalaureate or doctorate at Paris suggests that high-level administrative office in the order gave one the needed visibility, contacts, and votes (in the case of the Dominicans) to be selected to return to Paris for a university degree. Therefore, from the majority of Parisian doctors among the mendicants, especially after the 1320s, we should not expect to uncover many lost *Sentences* commentaries or other scholastic works attributable to this group among the anonymous works in manuscript collections. Their pre- and post-university careers were not primarily intellectual in character. And on the other side of the ledger, we will never know how many brilliant philosophical minds were denied an opportunity to be promoted because they did not have the personal connections or the politically correct views (in the case of the Franciscan Spirituals or the Michaelists after 1329) necessary to achieve it.

One must be careful, however, not to make too strong a contrast between an ecclesiastical and an intellectual career as if they were mutually exclusive. The examples of Albertus Magnus and Bonaventure in the thirteenth century or Pierre Auriol and Gregory of Rimini in the fourteenth prove that not to be the case. One must be careful also to note the bias of the evidence on which the foregoing picture was constructed. It is true, as we look at the list of *sententiarii* or at the list of Parisian masters of theology among the Dominicans and Franciscans in the fourteenth century, that the number of individual friars known to be important for intellectual history sharply declines by the second quarter of the century. Among the Dominicans there was an active group of scholars in the opening years of the century: Hervé Noël, James of Metz, John of Parma, Durand of St Pourçain, Pierre de la Palud, and James of Lausanne. Bernard Lombardi, commenting on the *Sentences* in 1327–8, was among the last Dominicans from whom we have scholastic writings at Paris.

The same picture holds for the Franciscans. The history of the early Scotist school is largely dominated by those appointed to read the

Sentences at Paris between 1307 and 1325: James of Esculo, William of Alnwick, Antoine Andreas, Peter Thomas, Francis of Marcia, Francis of Meyronnes, Landulf of Caracciolo, Anfredus Gonteri, and Gerard Odonis. Although not a Scotist, one of the most important Franciscan thinkers of the century, Pierre Auriol, belongs to this early period as well. After 1326 one is hard pressed to find Franciscan authors who left *Sentences* commentaries or disputed questions, or almost any kind of scholastic writing. There was Peter of Aquila whose *Sentences* commentary survived in numerous copies, Pastor de Serrescuderio from whom we have a similar commentary but only in one manuscript, and James of Spinello from whom we have isolated questions. Bernard of Arezzo, about whom we know considerably more today through the work of Zenon Kaluza, left writings largely because of his dispute with Nicholas of Autrecourt.[21]

It must be acknowledged that what we are observing is a drop in the publication of scholastic work, not a drop in fulfilling the academic exercises (lectures and disputations) that were required of candidates for the doctorate. But without written evidence of those activities, we have no way to judge their quality, or depth of preparation, or their intellectual orientation. It is perhaps significant that almost none of these 'non-publishing' mendicants was ever cited even by their closest contemporaries. What requires explanation, therefore, is not necessarily a decline in intellectual rigour but a decline in scholarly productivity, or at least a decline in the dissemination of scholastic work.

Not all the religious orders were affected in this way. The Augustinian hermits remained remarkably active at Paris throughout the fourteenth century. Similarly there were a number of important Cistercian theologians between 1340 and 1380. Something appears to have happened within the educational system of the two mendicant orders – the Dominicans and Franciscans – from whom we would have expected the most scholarly activity, given their history and resources. What would explain this shift in priorities? To what extent was it a result of changes in the educational system of these orders?

Some possible factors can be discounted immediately. It was not a result of insufficient library resources or lack of access to past and contemporary writings, since both St Jacques and Cordeliers were as

[21] Z. Kaluza, *Nicolas d'Autrécourt, ami de la vérité, Histoire littéraire de la France*, 42.1 (Paris, 1995).

well endowed in books in the fourteenth century as in the thirteenth. Nor was it a result of any lack in the means of publishing work, since there was no shortage of scribes, mendicant and secular, and these orders were well-endowed. Nor did the threat of being accused of error or heresy slow academic publication among some seculars and members of other religious orders. Nor is it likely that a decline in the intellectual quality of those recruited into the two oldest mendicant orders could have produced a change in so rapid a time.

The factors that may have caused this shift in priorities – all interrelated – would be a shift in peer expectations, the type of persons chosen to be sent to Paris for promotion to the doctorate, and the place that publication served in career advancement. The Paris doctorate remained in high demand among the mendicant orders, just as it did among secular clerics. But the need to publish as part of that process or in order to gain visibility (let alone because one felt one had something worth saying) seems to have become less important – whether only for the individual friar or for the order as a whole is unclear. Certainly if officials in one's order or potential patrons outside the order were not particularly interested in publication or scholarly reputation beyond the possession of the doctorate, that fact alone would considerably reduce self-motivation to disseminate one's work in written form.

But parallel to that, as suggested above, the Dominicans and Franciscans may have been choosing to send to Paris for the baccalaureate and doctorate those who were being groomed and had been groomed for an administrative career in the order and the Church.[22] In this regard they resembled Benedictine Parisian doctors in the academic generation after Pierre Roger, or secular scholars during almost a century dividing the generation of Henry of Ghent and Godfrey of Fontaines from that of Nicole Oresme, Marsilius of Inghen, and Pierre d'Ailly.[23] To some degree this shift may have resulted from a perception of the type of university doctor that was expected and encouraged by the papal curia, the royal court, and the leadership of the some of the religious orders.

Several observations emerge from the foregoing analysis. The first is

[22] One example among many is Pastor de Serrescuderio, mentioned above; see W. J. Courtenay, 'Pastor de Serrescuderio (d. 1356) and MS Saint-Omer 239', *AHDLMA*, 63 (1996), pp. 325–56.

[23] On the careers of Benedictine masters from Paris see T. Sullivan, *Benedictine Monks at the University of Paris, AD 1229–1500: A Biographical Register* (Leiden, 1995).

the importance of viewing the teaching programme of the Parisian convents as two related but essentially separate programmes. The residence list for the Franciscan convent at Paris in 1303 allows us to go behind the educational legislation of the order to see how the quota system actually worked in reality. It reveals a large lectorate programme, which, given university restrictions, could not be part of one theological programme leading to the baccalaureate and doctorate. In fact, a closer look at the candidates chosen for the doctorate reveals that they were almost invariably chosen from a more senior group of those who had, subsequent to the lectorate, established themselves through teaching and administrative activities in their home province. And this, in turn, means that commentaries on the *Sentences* were not the products of those who had just completed their years of study for the lectorate, but rather of those who had had several years, perhaps many years, of teaching and administrative duties in their home provinces or provincial *studia*.

A second observation is that we can no longer use one fixed point in an academic career, for example the date of the doctorate or of reading the *Sentences*, to reconstruct the biography of a mendicant scholar. We must recognize that there was considerable variation in educational careers and that a longer and interrupted course of study was probably a more frequent pattern than we have realized.

Third, while the Parisian doctorate among the Dominicans and Franciscans in the fourteenth century was generally linked to French candidates (those from the province of France and the other French provinces), the quota system of the lectorate programme, except where affected by the dislocations of warfare, continued to bring young friars to Paris from other regions in Europe, friars who would benefit from Parisian study but who would never be chosen for the baccalaureate. Thus some of the many Franciscan and Dominican scholars in England who lectured on the *Sentences* at Oxford or Cambridge before 1340 must earlier (before 1337) have been sent to Paris for part of their training in theology as part of the lectorate programme. Which ones had that experience, however, it is almost impossible to discern.

There is one final observation that the foregoing study suggests regarding the role of family and patronage. It has long been obvious to social historians of medieval universities that a secular scholar needed the backing of family or a patron (often ecclesiastical) to progress beyond the university into an ecclesiastical career, and even to have his education made financially possible. What is beginning to emerge is that those in religious orders were not oblivious to the advantages of personal connections and patronage outside the order. Prosopographical research on Parisian graduates from the religious orders shows that a large number of them came from prominent, sometimes even aristocratic, families, or had connections with persons of power and privilege. The quest for patrons within the order, the episcopate, and the papal curia, as well as the use of a university degree for personal advancement, was a practice mendicant scholars shared with their secular counterparts. Whatever role beyond intellectual merit these 'political' factors may have played in the selection of those sent to Paris for the lectorate, it appears to have been a factor in the selection of those chosen to proceed to the baccalaureate and doctorate. Thus, if distinguishing oneself at the university produced the visibility important to attract patronage and prepare the way for a subsequent career, it was also patronage and personal contacts that were the means by which many mendicant scholars obtained their chance to become Parisian doctors in the first place.

University of Wisconsin

WILLIAM OF OCKHAM AND THE MICHAELISTS ON ROBERT GROSSETESTE AND DENIS THE AREOPAGITE

by DAVID LUSCOMBE

THE investigation at Avignon of Ockham's suspected errors in the mid 1320s, the canonization by John XXII of Aquinas in July 1323, Ockham's defiance of Pope John XXII for asserting in November 1323, heretically in Ockham's view, that Christ and the apostles had held property and property rights, his association with Michael of Cesena and his followers at Avignon, and then at Pisa and Munich, are some of the well-known circumstances which brought Ockham, from 1327 onwards, to write polemics which have acquired the collective title of *opera politica*.[1] The facility for searching by electronic means the new edition being made of the largest of these works, the *Dialogus*,[2] has revealed a passage that I had not noticed in the edition made in 1614 by Melchior Goldast,[3] nor have I seen any reference to it in modern scholarship. The passage, which is found in Part 1, Book 1, chapter 9, and which is reproduced below in Appendix 1, reads in English as follows:

> Secondly, they principally try to make their assertion known by an example, recounting that, when the commentator on the books of Dionysius, accused, in connection with many articles, by rivals who had bribed the pope and the cardinals with gifts, was forced to reply in consistory, he, although only a philosopher and theologian, and wholly unacquainted with the law, asked the pope for a lawyer. The pope replied, 'No, among all the clergy in this world you are reputed to be more learned; you should not

[1] These polemical writings are the subject of Gordon Leff's chapter on 'Society' in *Ockham*, pp. 614–43.

[2] *William of Ockham, 'Dialogus'. Latin text and English translation*, ed. John Kilcullen and John Scott under the auspices of the Medieval Texts Editorial Committee of the British Academy for the series Auctores Britannici Medii Aevi (*ABMA*), Version 2, March 1996. This is work in progress and further versions, taking various sections of the *Dialogus* to a more advanced stage, are being published on the Internet (http://britac.ac.uk/okdial.html).

[3] *Monarchia S. Romani Imperii*, 3 vols (Frankfurt am Main, 1611–14; reprinted Graz, 1960), 2, pp. 392–957. The continuation of IIus IIIae *Dialogus* iii. 23 was published by R. Scholz in *Unbekannte kirchenpolitischen Streitschriften aus der Zeit Ludwigs des Bayern (1327–1354)*, vol. 2 (Bibliothek des kgl. preuss. hist. Instituts in Rom, 9–10 (1914)), pp. 392–5.

> create difficulty by having someone speak for you in your stead. You should speak for yourself.' Perceiving the malice in this, he took stock of the accusations and was granted a period of three days for deliberation. On the fourth day he gave his reply to all the charges made against him on grounds of civil law, and to very many of those that were based on canon law, on which his adversaries had, irrefutably as they thought, based their case. By theology and by natural reason he showed so clearly how to interpret them in his support that all the laws and rights that had been adduced against him pointed, in the judgement of all men of understanding, plainly and conclusively in his favour. Whence, it is said, the cardinals, who had been opposed to him, later accused his rivals, saying, 'You said that the bishop does not know about laws and rights. He knows the principles, roots and causes of all laws and rights.'
>
> From this they conclude that the theologian, one who is also a great philosopher, interpreted the meaning of laws, of which he had no prior knowledge or memory, more certainly, more deeply and more clearly than those who who had been nurtured in them since infancy but who were ignorant of theology and natural reason.

This story must relate to Robert Grosseteste, Bishop of Lincoln, during his visit to Lyons in 1250. But, before coming to that, I should set the passage in its context in the *Dialogus*. Part I of this work is about heresy and heretics, and it was written by the end of 1334.[4] The first book of Part I establishes whose responsibility it is – that of the theologians or that of the canon lawyers – to decide which assertions, and who, should be regarded as catholic or as heretical. The Master, in dialogue with a Student, explains that it is the theologians who, in the course of teaching, establish what is, and what is not, catholic truth. The pope, in pronouncing which assertions are catholic and which are heretical, should rely chiefly on theology. Furthermore, on purely moral matters contained in the canon law, a theologian or a philosopher has the power to judge more certainly than a canon lawyer. The Student suggests that, on purely positive moral particulars (as distinct from

[4] Cf. Jürgen Miethke, *Ockhams Weg zur Sozialphilosophie* (Berlin, 1969), p. 85; *William of Ockham. A Short Discourse on Tyrannical Government*, ed. Arthur Stephen McGrade, trans. by John Kilcullen. Cambridge Texts in the History of Political Thought (Cambridge, 1992), p. xxxi.

purely moral universals) which are contained in the books of the canonists, the argument that a theologian or a philosopher can judge best lacks probability. The Master counters by offering arguments and an example. One argument is that a higher science can judge more certainly and more deeply with respect to matters subordinate to it in a lower science, and theology and moral philosophy are higher sciences than the canon law. Moreover, particulars are subordinate to universals.[5]

A second argument is that every ecclesiastical constitution and custom is subject to the truth of divine scripture or natural law, and if any constitution or custom is contrary to theology or to true moral philosophy, it should be judged and condemned. As Gratian has written (*dist.* 8, # Dignitate), 'natural law is superior in dignity to custom and constitution alike. For anything which is either accepted as custom or is contained in writing and is opposed to natural law should be considered as void and useless.' Therefore, anything which is found in the canon law to be contrary to theology or to natural law should be condemned by one of those sciences. Ockham now gives the example, in the story reproduced above. It illustrates an instance when a theologian who is also a philosopher as well as a bishop, having been refused the help of a lawyer but using natural reason and theology, judged more certainly of laws of which he had no prior knowledge than did lawyers who were ignorant of theology and natural reason.

Were it not for Ockham's identification of the theologian under attack by cardinals as *commentator librorum Dionysii* and as a bishop we would be reduced to uncertain speculation as to who he was. The commentator can only be Grosseteste. In its details the incident recounted here is uncorroborated, and Ockham does not specify what charges were levelled against the defendant. But the outline of the story was surely drawn from an account of Grossteste's heated clash in the papal curia at Lyons in 1250. On this visit Grosseteste protested in the name of his fellow bishops in England against the large visitation fees demanded by Boniface, the archbishop of Canterbury. He also pursued a wider variety of complaints about the neglect of pastoral

5 'Scientia canonistarum, quantum ad multa moralia particularia et quae valent variationem recipere, est scientia inferior subordinata theologiae, etiam quantum ad multa talia subordinata est morali philosophiae, sicut particularia subordinantur universalibus', *Dialogus*, Part I, bk 1, ch. 9. I cite this passage because the last three words seem out of character in comparison with Ockham's philosophical teaching.

care, and about the misuse of dispensations and provisions and monastic exemptions by the pope, as well as putting forward his fear that Christendom itself was in grave peril. Matthew Paris ensured that a record survived into later times of Grosseteste answering appeals against him at Lyons, at great expense and to no avail, and of Pope Innocent IV railing against him and the English on account of their greed.[6] He reproduced Grosseteste's *optima epistola* which contains the protest he made in 1253 against the grant of a canonry and benefice at Lincoln to the pope's nephew,[7] and he followed this with a story of how Cardinal Gil de Torrres tried to soothe the pope's anger at this protest by extolling Grosseteste's learning and virtue in words which find a parallel in Ockham's version: 'Magnus enim habetur philosophus, Latinis et Graecis literis ad plenum eruditus.'[8] A collection of Grosseteste's writings and speeches, delivered to the Pope and the cardinals at Lyons, was also made by Robert Marsh, the Archdeacon of Oxford who was one of Grosseteste's companions on this visit, and it has come fully to light in this century. These documents were identified by S. Harrison Thomson, surveyed by W. A. Pantin and published by Fr Servus Gieben.[9] The passage in Ockham's *Dialogus* which also bears upon these events is a further witness to the legacy of the conflict.

Of the nine pieces in Marsh's collection, three (numbered *V–VII* in Gieben, *6–8* in Thomson and Pantin) can be aligned with the story told by Ockham. Having presented the complaints of the English clergy

[6] Matthew Paris, *Chronica maiora*, ed. H. R. Luard, 7 vols, *RS* (London, 1872–83), 5, pp. 97–8, 186.

[7] *Chronica maiora*, 5, pp. 389–92. Grosseteste's letter 128 is printed by H. R. Luard, *Roberti Grosseteste . . . Epistolae, RS* (London, 1861), pp. 432–7; Luard also prints the letter of Innocent IV, which occasioned this protest, in a footnote on pp. 432–3. The authenticity of letter 128 is defended by F. M. Powicke, *King Henry III and the Lord Edward. The Community of the Realm in the Thirteenth Century* (Oxford, 1947), 1, p. 285, n. 3, and by Richard Vaughan, who also supports the reliability of Matthew Paris's version of it, *Matthew Paris* (Cambridge, 1958; reissued with supplementary bibliography, 1979), pp. 133–4.

[8] *Chronica maiora*, 5, p. 393.

[9] S. Harrison Thomson, *The Writings of Robert Grosseteste, Bishop of Lincoln 1235–1253* (Cambridge, 1940), pp. 141–7. W. A. Pantin, 'Grosseteste's relations with the papacy and the Crown', in D. A. Callus, ed., *Robert Grosseteste. Scholar and Bishop* (Oxford, 1955), pp. 178–215, especially pp. 209–15. Servus Gieben, 'Robert Grosseteste at the papal curia, Lyons 1250. Edition of the documents', in *Collectanea Franciscana*, 41 (1971), pp. 340–93. See too Powicke, *King Henry III and the Lord Edward*, pp. 282–9, and R. W. Southern, *Robert Grosseteste. The Growth of an English Mind in Medieval Europe* (Oxford, 1986), pp. 272–95; Southern traces in particular the development of Grosseteste's prophetic and global vision of the problem of the papacy and of unsuitable papal provisions.

against the exactions of Boniface in document *III* (the *Conquestio cleri Angliae*), and having told in document *IV* how he himself conducts episcopal visitations in the diocese of Lincoln, Grosseteste in the following three pieces widened the scope of his pleading in order to answer the insistence of cardinals that, according to the common law of the church, a visitor is entitled to procurations. In *V* Grosseteste explores the differing kinds of law – *ius commune, ius divinum* and *ius naturale* – and contrasts the good ruler with the tyrant. In *VI* Grosseteste explains the superiority of *ius divinum* (Scripture) over *ius commune sive positivum*. Marsh introduces this piece with the comment that 'some of the cardinals preferred the positive law and its glosses to the natural and the divine law [quidam cardinalium adhaerebant iuri positivo et eius apparatibus plus quam iuri naturali et divino]'. *VII* is a further, and largely philosophical, account, given orally, of the superiority of *ius naturale* over legal or positive justice. Material is taken in *VI* from the writings of Denis the Areopagite, which Grosseteste knew so well as their translator into Latin and as the writer of commentaries upon them. This material includes a definition of the function of the ecclesiastical hierarchy which exists to save souls, to assimilate and unite them with God. If a hierarch rules his subjects oppressively, this function is not fulfilled.[10]

We do not know whether Ockham ever read this collection; even if he had, it could not have provided him with all the details of his own account of the consistory.[11] None of the known manuscript copies seems to come from south Germany, where Ockham wrote his *Dialogus*.[12] But he may have obtained knowledge of it earlier in his career. It was known that Grosseteste spoke and sought to defend himself in the consistory; like Ockham, Matthew Paris laid emphasis on Grosseteste being forced to defend himself. In his rubric to item *VIII* Marsh relates an incident which arose from Grosseteste's rejection,

[10] Gieben, ed., 'Grosseteste at the papal curia', pp. 382–3.

[11] From the *auctores* indexes given in the volumes of the Franciscan Institute edition of Ockham's *Opera philosophica et theologica*, it can be seen that Ockham made reference infrequently to a number of the writings of Grosseteste. They include, on one occasion, Grosseteste's commentary on the *Celestial Hierarchy*: 'Lincolniensis, *Super Angelicam Hierarchiam*, parte V, cap. 3: Nihil positive dictum potest de Deo et creatura univoce dici', *Scriptum in librum primum Sententiarum Ordinatio, dist.* 2, *q.* 9, *Opera theologica*, 2, ed. Stephanus Brown and Gedeone Gal (St Bonaventure, NY, 1970), p. 326.

[12] The manuscripts used by Gieben for his edition are described in 'Grosseteste at the papal curia' on pp. 344–6; additional manuscripts are listed by Thomson, *Writings of Robert Grosseteste*, pp. 142–7.

on the ground of personal unsuitability, of the claim of a certain Roman noble to be admitted to a prebend in the Lincoln diocese. The prebend had the cure of souls and, it was said, had been conferred by the Pope. Marsh, who sets this event within the proceedings at Lyons,[13] writes that the noble complained to the curia that Grosseteste had called the Pope a slayer of souls and Antichrist, and worse than any sodomite; he copies the text of the speech which Grosseteste made in his own defence and in which he explained that his criticism of bad pastors had been wrongly applied to the Pope.[14] However, this speech is not about the relationship between theology and law. On the other hand, items *V–VIII* in Marsh's collection do concern this relationship which is the main theme in Ockham's account.

The story that Ockham tells is vague in detail and may contain inaccuracies. Ockham does not name Grosseteste or the Pope, nor does he reveal the specific reason for conflict. Moreover, the Pope's allowance to the defendant of three days in which to prepare a defence is not corroborated in other accounts. Nonetheless, Ockham brings together main elements of the drama that had taken place in 1250: the anger of the Pope and the cardinals; the interval of a few days between two appearances before the curia;[15] a great speech; the preparation during proceedings and the oral delivery of a case which was not argued on the basis of canon and civil law but in the light of higher knowledge; the resolute stand taken on the superiority of theology to the canon law; and the stature of the bishop as a man of exceptional learning and as the commentator on the books of Denis the Areopagite. Marsh, who was present in the curia on Friday 13 May 1250, tells us that a statement (the *Memorandum, I*), which was read out to the curia by Cardinal John, had been distributed by Grosseteste in advance to the Pope and to three of the cardinals.[16] His collection of the documents shows also that Grosseteste made his philosophical and theological statements (*V–VII*) a few days later in reply to curial

[13] 'Interim dum praedicta agerentur . . .', Gieben, ed., 'Grosseteste at the papal curia', p. 387.

[14] Gieben, ed., 'Grosseteste at the papal curia', pp. 387–93; cf. Pantin, 'Grosseteste's relations', pp. 214–15. Cf. the *Memorandum*, 7 and 9, Gieben, ed., pp. 354 and 355: 'animarum curae suae commissarum occisores et mortificatores . . . sunt antichristi'; 'Sodomitis peiores et abominabiliores'.

[15] According to Marsh, the speeches in which Grosseteste presented the *Conquestio cleri Angliae* and the account of his own visitations followed the reading of the *Memorandum* by a few days, *paucis elapsis diebus* (Gieben, ed., 'Grosseteste at the papal curia', p. 373).

[16] Gieben, ed., 'Grosseteste at the papal curia', p. 350.

criticisms and also with reference to the teachings of Denis the Areopagite. Ockham also records further declarations which, he writes, were prepared within four days, following a first appearance. This fits very well with Marsh's account of the presentation of the *Memorandum* by Grosseteste and his speeches on the kinds of law, speeches made a few days later when he realized that 'some of the cardinals preferred the positive law and its glosses more than the natural and the divine law'.[17]

In the 1370s John Wyclif was also powerfully impressed by the stand taken by *Lincolniensis*. Wyclif's acknowledged debts to Grosseteste are greater than those of Ockham, but R. W. Southern has singled out especially the connection both saw 'between the vices of the papacy and the decline of pastoral care'.[18] Wyclif's citations show that he knew Grosseteste's works, including his letters, at first hand. In his *De civili dominio*, written in 1376, he cited at length Grosseteste's letter 128, which Matthew Paris and others had reproduced, as well as the letter of Pope Innocent IV, which Matthew Paris had not copied.[19] Southern has suggested that Marsh's collection of the Lyons documents had remained among Grosseteste's papers in the Franciscan library in Oxford, unnoticed and unstudied till the mid-fourteenth century, except for one summary of his main speech which is now in Paris.[20] Wyclif 'studied the documents relating to his visit to the papal court in 1250. They had an explosive effect on his image of Grosseteste'.[21]

[17] Ibid., p. 380.

[18] Southern, *Robert Grosseteste*, pp. 298–307, here p. 306.

[19] Grosseteste's letter 128 (written in 1253 and printed by Luard, *Roberti Grosseteste . . . Epistolae*, pp. 432–7) is copied by Wyclif in his *Tractatus de civili dominio liber primus*, ed. R. L. Poole, WS (London, 1885), cap. xliii, pp. 384–5, 387, 388–9, 389–90; Innocent IV's letter (printed by Luard on pp. 432–3 of his edition of Grosseteste's letters) is copied by Wyclif here on pp. 385–6. On Wyclif's handling of conceptions of hierarchy, in the light of his knowledge of the writings of Grosseteste, see my 'Wyclif and Hierarchy', in Anne Hudson and Michael Wilks, eds, *From Ockham to Wyclif, SCH. S*, 5 (Oxford, 1987), pp. 233–44.

[20] *Robert Grosseteste*, p. 277, n.7. The Paris MS is in the Bibliothèque nationale, lat. 10358; all the other copies listed by Thomson, *Writings of Robert Grosseteste*, pp. 142–7 (and cf. Gieben, 'Grosseteste at the papal curia', pp. 344–6) appear to be English in origin.

[21] *Robert Grosseteste*, p. 300. On one occasion Wyclif, in the course of discussing the notion of heresy, cites Grosseteste's definition from 'a special booklet of his on the subject': 'docet Lyncolniensis in quodam libello speciali istius materie quod "heresis est dogma falsum scripture sacre contrarium, pertinaciter defensatum" . . . Aristoteles primo Ethicorum vocat eleccionem, in qua bonum a malo dividitur, proheresim; et istum sensum dicit Lyncolniensis se extraxisse a Grecorum sentenciis; et concordant Latini catholici', *De civili dominio liber secundus*, ed. Iohann Loserth, 2, WS (London, 1900), cap. 7, pp. 58–9. The quotation and the reference are not taken from the Lyons dossier, and their source remains

But it is also plausible to believe that, after his arrival in Oxford as a student – probably in 1310 when he was twenty-three years old – Ockham was shown the documents in the library of the Franciscan friars.[22] What stories he may have been told about them by older friars we shall never know, but it is altogether likely that, either in Oxford then or later at Avignon, he shared reminiscences about Grosseteste. Well before Wyclif, and some years before Ranulf Higden (who *c.* 1340 cites the opening words of Grosseteste's *Memorandum*),[23] Ockham held some memory of Grosseteste's appearances in the papal court, and, more importantly, he showed a clear understanding of the principles which Grosseteste had expounded there.

* * *

Not only was Ockham little aware, unlike Wyclif, of Grosseteste's writings, but, as de Lagarde once observed, he had not read much of the writings of recent papal publicists.[24] Many theologians and publicists of Ockham's generation and earlier had championed and developed so-called papal hierocratic views, among them James of Viterbo, Giles of Rome, Francis of Meyronnes and Augustinus Triumphus.[25] It is difficult to determine whether Ockham responded

unknown to me. They show, however, a clear similarity with Matthew Paris's report of Grosseteste's last words on his death bed, and thereby offer further support to Southern's rehabilitation of Matthew's reliability. See Matthew Paris, *Chronica maiora*, 5, p. 401, and Southern, *Robert Grosseteste*, pp. 291–3.

22 There was probably at least one other copy of the collection in an Oxford library in the early fourteenth century, Exeter College MS 21 (Gieben, 'Grosseteste at the papal curia', p. 345; Southern, *Robert Grosseteste*, p. 290, n. 31).

23 'Dominus noster Jesus Christus', *Polychronicon Ranulphi Higden monachi Cestrensis*, ed. Joseph Rawson Lumby, 9 vols, *RS* (London, 1865–86), 8, p. 240.

24 *La Naissance de l'esprit laïque au déclin du moyen âge, 4. Guillaume d'Ockham. Défense de l'empire*, new edn (Louvain, 1962), p. 78. Likewise A. S. McGrade, *The Political Thought of William of Ockham* (Cambridge, 1974), p. 82, n. 11: 'I have discovered no clear reference to Egidius in Ockham's political writings', but 'it is more than possible that he was acquainted with the *De Ecclesiastica Potestate*'.

25 See, for James of Viterbo, H. X. Arquillière, *Le plus ancien traité de l'Eglise. Jacques de Viterbe, De Regimine Christiano (1301–1302). Etude des sources et édition critique*. Etudes de théologie historique (Paris, 1926). The Commentary of Giles of Rome on *Unam sanctam* has been edited by P. de Lapparent, 'L'oeuvre politique de François de Meyronnes: ses rapports avec celle de Dante', *AHDLMA*, 15ème-17ème Année, t.13 (1940–42), Appendix, and the *De ecclesiastica potestate* by R. Scholz, *Aegidius Romanus, De ecclesiastica sive summi pontificis potestate* (Weimar, 1929). For François de Meyronnes see de Lapparent, cited in this note, and my 'François de Meyronnes and hierarchy', in Diana Wood, ed., *The Church and Sovereignty c.590–1918. Essays in Honour of Michael Wilks, SCH. S*, 9 (Oxford, 1991), pp. 225–31. For Augustinus Triumphus, and ideas of papal monarchy in general, see Michael Wilks,

specifically to any of these. Ockham too was in support of papal monarchy; with Aristotle he shared the view that monarchy is the best constitution.[26] Its keynote was efficiency.[27] But, unlike the papal publicists, he challenged the papacy in defence of the doctrine of evangelical poverty and he attacked the claim that the pope was the immediate superior of the emperor in temporal as well as in spiritual matters. Ockham's arguments were fundamentally biblical,[28] but included references to a wide range of patristic and canonistic sources. But, whereas the publicists who wrote propaganda in favour of full-blown papal sovereignty often cited in their support the writings of Denis the Areopagite on the ecclesiastical and the celestial hierarchy, Ockham very rarely does so. Why many writers did give Denis their attention while Ockham did not is a puzzle. It cannot be because Ockham was more interested in evangelical poverty and the publicists more interested in questions of sovereignty. The Mendicants had for long referred to Denis in support of their ministry and their role,[29] and Ockham devoted much of his polemical writing to the relationship of the papacy to the empire and to secular monarchy.

One reference to Denis is made by Ockham in the *Dialogus*, Part 2, Tract 1, chapter 10, in the course of lambasting John XXII for heresy, and in particular arguing that the pope could not convincingly plead that what Ockham had taught was heretical. Here Ockham explores the distinction between explicit and implicit belief. No Christian, he writes, can be totally ignorant of the Christian faith, and every Christian must be presumed to have learned and to believe something explicitly. A Catholic will believe that the Scriptures are divine without necessarily knowing the Bible itself. Such belief in the Bible is therefore implicit. Ockham then raises the question what should be explicitly believed and by whom. This leads him to reflect upon the differing levels of knowledge and of understanding achieved by different groups of Christians.

The Problem of Sovereignty in the Later Middle Ages. The Papal Monarchy with Augustinus Triumphus and the Publicists. Cambridge Studies in Medieval Life and Thought, ns, 9 (Cambridge, 1963).

[26] III *Dialogus*, I,ii, 18, pp. 803–4.

[27] McGrade, *Political Thought of William of Ockham*, pp. 158–68, especially pp. 160–1.

[28] On this see Takashi Shogimen, *William Ockham and Spiritual Power* (University of Sheffield, PhD thesis, 1997) and 'Ockham's Vision of the Primitive Church' in R. N. Swanson, ed., *The Church Retrospective*, *SCH*, 33 (Woodbridge, 1997), pp. 163–75.

[29] Yves M.-J. Congar, 'Aspects ecclésiologiques de la querelle entre mendiants et séculiers dans la seconde moitié du XIIIe siècle et le début du XIVe', *AHDLMA*, 28 (1962, 36ème Année, 1961), pp. 35–151.

Prelates, and especially the Pope, should know the Scriptures and the teachings of the Church, and should believe them explicitly. He turns to Aquinas to illustrate the need for those in possession of greater enlightenment to pass this enlightenment on to those who have less knowledge of things divine:

> For the sake of those who follow Thomas's teaching, his words on this matter should be cited. He says in IIa IIae qu.2 art.6: The explanation of the faith to lesser men should be done through superior men. Just as, according to Denis in chapter 12 of the *Celestial Hierarchy*, the higher angels, who enlighten the lower angels, have a fuller knowledge of things divine than lower angels do, so too superior men, whose task it is to instruct others, are required to have a fuller knowledge of matters of faith and to believe them more explicitly.[30]

Aquinas's comment is fully typical of what had already become part of the normal repertoire for the exposition by theologians of the shape and function of the ecclesiastical hierarchy, but Ockham, except in this passage, avoids this theme, and even here he seems to mention it only for the sake of the Thomists.

Ockham and the Franciscan friars, who supported Michael of Cesena in his exile in Germany, ran a propaganda campaign in favour of the Emperor Louis the Bavarian. Their polemical works on imperial and papal power were designed to present what Christians most needed to know. They were appeals to Christians at large, including those who may not understand academic discussions and recitals.[31] The *Allegationes de potestate imperiali* are one such work, a collection of six *articuli* which is generally now thought to have been a cooperative enterprise largely completed by 1338 by the Michaelists rather than one written by William of Ockham.[32] But, as Offler wrote,

[30] 'Propter illos autem, ⟨qui⟩ doctrinae Thomae adhaerent, sunt verba eiusdem de hac materia recitanda, ait itaque secunda secundae quaestio 2. articul. 6. *Explicatio fidei ad inferiores homines, oportet quod perueniat per maiores, & ideo sicut superiores angeli, qui inferiores illuminant, habent pleniorem notitiam de rebus diuinis quam inferiores , vt Dionysius dicit 12. cap. coelestis Hierarchiae: ita superiores homines, ad quos pertinet alios erudire, tenentur habere pleniorem notitiam de credendis & magis explicite credere*', ed. Goldast, *Monarchia*, 2, p. 753.

[31] 'Universis Christi fidelibus praesentem tractatulum inspecturis . . . sine personarum acceptione', *De imperatorum et pontificum potestate*, ed. Hilary Seton Offler, *William Ockham, Opera politica*, 4. *ABMA*, 14 (Oxford, 1997), *Prologus*, pp. 279–80. See further G. Knysh, *Ockham Perspectives* (Winnipeg, 1994). On the Michaelists see Leff, *Heresy* I, pp. 238–55.

[32] H. S. Offler, 'Zum Verfasser der "Allegaciones de potestate imperiali" (1338)', *Deutsches*

Ockham lived with the small group of dissident Franciscans in Munich for twelve years and 'for their extensive literary activity they drew upon and multiplied a common stock of ideas and arguments and materials';[33] 'it is hardly conceivable that he did not share in the deliberations from which the *Allegationes* resulted.'[34]

The *Allegationes* were written in support of the imperial manifesto *Fidem catholicam* which was published at Frankfurt on the Main on 6 August 1338. The manifesto declared the measures taken by the pope against the excommunicated emperor to be null and void, and the *Allegationes* seek to demonstrate in detail why the imperial manifesto is right. They draw heavily upon the accumulations of written quotations excerpted by the friars from patristic and other authoritative sources, and a particular emphasis is placed upon the belief that an emperor is truly emperor by virtue of his election. In one passage Denis is cited, and he is cited so unusually that the reference, as well as the argument which is based upon it, may well be not a contribution made by Ockham to the work but that of another member of the Munich group. But the argument offers a further, if fleeting, example of a lack of sympathy with the current, widespread use made of the writings of Denis in support of papal claims.

To appreciate this, we need to have in mind the general structure of the work. The first of the six articles provides ten proofs that the pope has plenitude of power only in spiritual, and not in temporal, matters. The second article presents four proofs that Christ possessed a two-fold lordship, one according to his uncreated divinity, and a second according to his assumed humanity. The first dominion is God's uncreated omnipotent rule over all creation; this has not been communicated to any creature. The second dominion is itself two-fold, for the dominion Christ held before his passion and death is distinct from that he held after his resurrection. After the resurrection Christ was lord of all physical and spiritual being, the ruler over all men and angels, and this lordship has not been communicated to any successor of Christ. The former dominion, held before Christ suffered and died, has been communicated to Peter, his vicar, and to Peter's successors. But it is a spiritual dominion, not a temporal one, because

Archiv, 42 (1987), pp. 555–619, and also Offler's introduction to his edition of the *Allegationes*, *Opera politica*, 4, pp. 359–61.

33 *Opera politica*, 4, p. ix.

34 Ibid., 4, p. 361.

temporal dominion was incompatible with the poverty, humility, and charity of Christ and the apostles. The third article gives fourteen objections to these proofs as well as replies to these objections. The fourth article provides seven proofs in favour of the view that the pope cannot rest a claim to full temporal power on the basis of man-made law. Both the canon law and the civil law show that papal power and imperial power are both immediately constituted by God and are, respectively, spiritual power and temporal power. The fifth article replies to objections to the fourth. The sixth and final article is a concluding affirmation that papal and imperial power are distinct, and that imperial power is not received from the pope. The quashing by John, the so-called Pope John XXII, of the election of Louis IV as King of the Romans is without effect, and the steps taken by Louis against John are reasonable and just.

It is in the course of the third article that the writer or writers comment upon the *lex divinitatis* derived from Denis's *Celestial Hierarchy*: 'lex divinitatis est infima per media in suprema reducere'. This law, enshrined in *Unam sanctam*, encapsulates the vision of the leading of all creatures back to God by means of hierarchic acts performed by intermediaries.[35] But objection is made to previous interpretations of this 'law' as well as of a passage in Augustine's *De trinitate*.[36] The passage in *De trinitate* contains the observation that, just as in the universe heavier and lowlier bodies are under the sway of subtler and more potent bodies, so too all corporeal beings are ruled by spiritual beings and all creation is ruled by the Creator. So, the argument runs, temporal power is subject to spiritual power. Temporal power is led to its final end by spiritual power and, for this reason, should be subject and subordinate to spiritual power. To this argument the reply is given that, although it is the law of divinity that the lowest beings are brought back to the highest beings by intermediate beings, it does not follow nor is it true that the lowest beings owe their existence to intermediate beings nor do intermediate beings owe their existence to the highest beings.

This may be clearly seen in Denis's writing on the orders of angels: the lowest orders of angels are illuminated and informed by the middle

[35] See my paper on 'The *Lex divinitatis* in the Bull *Unam Sanctam* of Pope Boniface VIII', in Christopher Brooke, David Luscombe, Geoffrey Martin, and Dorothy Owen, eds, *Church and Government in the Middle Ages. Essays presented to C. R. Cheney* (Cambridge, 1976), pp. 205–21.

[36] The relevant passage is printed in Appendix 2 below.

orders as regards their ministry to those outside the angelic hierarchy. But the lowest orders of angels are not brought into existence by the middle orders nor are the middle orders brought into existence by the highest orders. None of the orders of angels owes the nature or the grace or the glory which it has to a higher order of angels. All the orders of angels are constituted by God directly, and all receive their nature, their grace and their glory directly from God, even though, as regards their ministry to those outside the angelic hierarchy, the lowest orders are subject to rule by the middle orders, and the middle orders are subject to rule by the highest orders.

So, likewise, imperial power, although it is subject to papal power in matters which pertain to Catholic faith, is not established by papal power. Nor does imperial law emanate from papal law. These objections are developed in the course of seeking to reply to denials of the proposition that the pope's fullness of power is confined to spiritual matters, and, in particular, to show that kings and emperors owe their authority to election and not to unction and consecration.[37]

This passage in the *Allegationes* is a small but clever pinprick into the vast edifice of arguments in favour of papal monarchy. Unease over the use of the angelic hierarchy as a model for the organization of society in this world had begun to develop in the writings of Aquinas.[38] In particular, Aquinas drove a wedge into the principle of mediation. By and large he accepted the main themes put forward by Denis: God rules lower creatures through higher intermediaries which participate more fully in the divine government of the universe than do inferior creatures. Repeatedly in the *Summa theologiae* Aquinas states that no multitude would be properly organized unless it were arranged into different *ordines* to which are attached differing activities and functions. Not only among angels but also among men, lesser beings are governed by higher beings and are brought back to the highest by intermediaries. And all this is the fixed, unchangeable law of divinity.[39] But qualifications were added to these general affirmations. In his *Summa theologiae* Aquinas writes that the ecclesiastical hierarchy represents the heavenly hierarchy on earth. But, whereas in heaven

[37] *Opera politica*, 4, pp. 416–17 and (on the composition of this work) pp. 359ff.

[38] See my 'Thomas Aquinas and conceptions of hierarchy in the thirteenth century', in Albert Zimmermann, ed., *Miscellanea Mediaevalia. Veröffentlichungen des Thomas-Instituts der Universität zu Köln*, 19: *Thomas von Aquin* (Berlin, 1988), pp. 261–77.

[39] *Summa theologiae*, Ia, q. 90, a. 3; q. 106, a. 3; q. 108, a. 2; q. 112, a. 2. Cf. *Compendium theologiae*, I, c. 124.

an inferior angel cannot enlighten a superior, in the ecclesiastical hierarchy an inferior creature can enlighten superior ones. There are some in the lowest grade in the church who are closer to God, and while they may not be eminently knowledgeable, they can enlighten those above them.[40] The ecclesiastical hierarchy imitates the celestial only to an extent, not perfectly. Aquinas is not cited on this point in the *Allegationes*, but critics of John XXII could sympathize with this conclusion.

Closer to the position of the Michaelists was the view that the ecclesiastical hierarchy does not include temporal authority. John of Paris, on the basis of Denis's treatises, denies in his *De potestate regia et papali* (written in 1302–3) that the ecclesiastical hierarchy can be said to possess temporal power. He rejected the argument, based on Denis's placement of the laity in the lowest grade of the ecclesiastical hierarchy, that kings – being laymen – are subject to the pope even in temporal matters. But he also denied, as the Michaelists did not, that unity under a single temporal monarch is necessary.[41] The writer of *Rex pacificus* argues along similar lines: Denis provides no basis on which to suppose that spiritual power contains within itself temporal power. Control over temporal affairs is not a part of perfection and therefore it is not a responsibility of prelates. Symbolic theology can prove nothing. Men and angels are not the same. In so far as men do resemble angels, the celestial hierarchy provides an exemplar, but, since angels are not corporeal or temporal creatures, their organization into orders does not provide a model for temporal or corporeal organization on earth.[42] The anonymous Gloss on *Unam sanctam* also contains doubts that Denis's writing provides any ground for believing that temporal power is somehow contained within spiritual power like an effect within its cause.[43] This argument – which amounts to a denial that temporal power is caused by spiritual power – is the closest argument I have found so far to the one which is put in the *Allegationes*.

[40] *Summa theologiae*, Ia, q. 106, a. 3; q. 117, a. 2. Many other passages could be cited from Aquinas's writings on these themes. See my 'Thomas Aquinas and conceptions of hierarchy'.

[41] John of Paris, *De Potestate Regia et Papali*, ed. Jean Leclercq, *Jean de Paris et l'ecclésiologie du XIIIe siècle*. L'Eglise et l'état au moyen âge, 5 (Paris, 1942), c. 2, 18, pp. 179, 230 ff. See also Congar, 'Aspects ecclésiologiques', p. 144, and my 'Wyclif and hierarchy', p. 241.

[42] Pierre Dupuy, ed., *Histoire du differend d'entre le Pape Boniface VIII. et Philippe le Bel, Roy de France* (Paris, 1655), pp. 663–83. See also my 'Wyclif and hierarchy', p. 241.

[43] Heinrich Finke, ed., *Aus den Tagen Bonifaz VIII. Funde und Forschungen* (Münster i. W., 1902), pp. c–cxvi. See also Congar, 'Aspects ecclésiologiques', pp. 144–5, and my 'Wyclif and hierarchy', p. 242.

APPENDIX 1

A Defendant in the Papal Court: Grosseteste at Lyons

This is the text of a passage taken from the *Dialogus*, Part 1, Book 1, chapter 9. For the sake of convenience I have omitted all the variant readings collated and shown in the draft edition by Kilcullen and Scott. I am very grateful to Professor Kilcullen for giving me bound copies of a print-out.

Secundo principaliter isti moliuntur suam assertionem exemplo ostendere, referentes quod, cum commentator librorum Dionysii, de multis articulis a suis aemulis qui papam et cardinales muneribus corruperant, accusatus cogeretur in consistorio respondere, ipse, tanquam pure philosophus et theologus, omnino iuris ignarus, a papa petiit advocatum. Cui papa respondit, 'Absit ut tibi, qui inter omnes clericos mundi literatior reputaris, hanc confusionem facias, ut alius pro te loquatur. Pro te ipso loquaris.' Qui cernens malitiam, recepta copia obiectorum, et acceptis ad deliberandum trium dierum induciis, quarta die respondit ad omnium legum civilium et iurium canonicorum quamplurium contra ipsum allegatorum obiecta, quibus adversarii insolubiliter, ut putabant, suam intentionem fundaverant. Per theologiam et rationem naturalem ita patenter pro se intellectum assignans quod, iudicio omnium intelligentium, omnes leges et iura, quae contra ipsum fuerant allegata, pro ipso liquide concludebant. Unde, ut fertur, cardinales sibi contrarii postmodum eius aemulos arguentes dixerunt, 'Vos dixistis istum episcopum nescire leges et iura. Ipse scit principia, radices et causas omnium iurium et legum.'

Ex quibus isti concludunt quod ille theologus, qui est et magnus philosophus, multo certius, profundius et clarius iudicavit de intellectu iurium, quorum antea nullam habuerat scientiam et memoriam, quam theologiae et rationis naturalis ignari, qui tamen ab infantia in illis fuerant enutriti.

APPENDIX 2

The *Allegationes de potestate imperiali* and the Place of the Emperor in the Ecclesiastical Hierarchy

This passage and the supporting notes are taken from pages 416–17 of Offler's edition of the *Allegationes* in *Opera politica*, 4.

Quartodecimo opponitur de eo quod dicit beatus Dionysius in libro Angelicae Hierarchiae iv° capitulo, ubi dicit quod lex divinitatis est infima per media in suprema reducere.[44] Similiter beatus Augustinus iii° libro de Trinitate capitulo iv° dicit: Quemadmodum corpora crassiora et inferiora per subtiliora et potentiora quodam ordine reguntur, ita omnia corpora per spiritum ac universa creatura per creatorem suum.[45] Sed, ut dicitur, potestas temporalis est inferior potestate spirituali; quare reducenda est in ultimum finem per potestatem spiritualem, et per consequens debet illi subdi et subici.

Respondetur quod, licet lex divinitatis sit infima per media in suprema reducere, non tamen sequitur per hoc nec est verum quod semper infima habeant esse per media nec media per suprema, sicut patet expresse in ordinibus angelorum, de quibus ibi loquitur beatus Dionysius. Quia infimi angeli, licet illuminentur et informentur per medios et medii per supremos quantum ad aliqua ministeria exterius numeranda et peragenda, non tamen infimi angeli sunt constituti in esse per medios nec medii per supremos, nec in esse naturae nec in esse gratiae nec in esse gloriae; sed sunt immediate constituti a Deo et quoad esse naturae et quoad esse gratiae et quoad esse gloriae, licet infimi subsint imperio mediorum et medii imperio superiorum quantum ad aliqua ministeria exterius numeranda et peragenda. Consimiliter, licet potestas imperialis in hiis, quae spectant ad religionem fidei catholicae, subsit potestati

[44] 'Lex divinitatis . . . reducere': cited thus by Giles of Rome, *De ecclesiastica potestate*, i. 4, ed. R. Scholz (Weimar, 1929), p. 12; cf. Pope Boniface VIII, *Unam sanctam* = *Extravag. Commun.*, I,8,1, in *Corpus Iuris Canonici*, ed. E. Friedberg (Leipzig, 1879–81), 2, col. 1245. This form of words does not seem to occur in any of the known Latin versions of Denis the Areopagite. But cf. *De caelesti hierarchia*, ed. Ph. Chevallier, *Dionysiaca* (Bruges, 1937), 1, pp. 812–14; Luscombe, 'The *Lex divinitatis* in the Bull *Unam Sanctam*', pp. 205–21.

[45] Augustine, *De Trinitate*, iii. 9. *CChr.SL*, 50, pp. 135–6. Cited in this abbreviated form by Giles of Rome, *De ecclesiastica potestate*, i.5, ed. Scholz, p. 16.

pontificali, non tamen imperialis potestas constituta est a pontificali potestate nec ius imperiale emanavit a iure pontificali, ut superius est ostensum.[46]

The University of Sheffield

[46] Superius: art. ii. 522–74; art. iii. 386–95.

THE MEDIEVAL IDEA OF HERESY: WHAT ARE WE TO MAKE OF IT?

by ARTHUR STEPHEN McGRADE

FOR Thomas Aquinas, writing in a society where there was widespread persecution of heretics, heresy was a species of unbelief (*infidelitas*) worthy of death.[1] In Aquinas unbelief is the genus of vices opposed to the fundamental theological virtue of faith (*fides*). Today, in the liberal West, heresy itself is a more or less serious candidate for theological virtue.[2] What are we to make of this?

In most current scholarship on medieval heresy, ethical categories are replaced by sociological, economic, or political ones. Heresies are understood as social movements or challenges to traditional or emerging power structures, not as individual or organized crime or as spiritual pathology. More about these approaches later. But even among those for whom faith remains explicitly a virtue, heresy seems to have lost much of its character as a vice. The *Declaration on Religious Freedom* of Vatican Council II (1965) asserts that 'the human person has a right to religious freedom', including immunity from persecution by individuals, social groups, or any human power, a right which 'is firmly based on the dignity of the human person as this is known from the revealed word of God and from reason itself'.[3] Karl Rahner, the dean of mid-twentieth-century Roman Catholic theologians, goes further. Writing with Herbert Vorgrimler, Rahner finds a 'possibility that both in doctrine and practice realizations of the nature of Christianity *may* be found within the history of a heresy which potentially, indeed, have always existed in the Catholic . . . and historically legitimate form of Christianity . . . but have not yet been actualized there to the same extent'.[4] In some ways, then, heretics may be better Christians than Catholics.

[1] *Summa theologiae*, IIaIIae, q. 11, art. 3, *resp.*

[2] The prominent Protestant theologian Robert McAfee Brown writes occasionally under the *nom de plume* 'St. Hereticus' (*Writings of St. Hereticus* [Philadelphia, 1979]), and Peter Berger entitles his call for religious affirmation *The Heretical Imperative: Contemporary Possibilities of Religious Affirmation* (Garden City, New York, 1979).

[3] Tanner, *Decrees*, p. 1002.

[4] Karl Rahner and Herbert Vorgrimler, *Theological Dictionary*, ed. Cornelius Ernst, and trans. Richard Strachan (New York, 1965; 3rd impression, 1968), p. 203.

Jaroslav Pelikan, while deeply sympathetic to the emergence of an orthodox consensus in the first six centuries of Christianity, gently entitles his chapter on the major early heresies, 'Outside the Mainstream', and acknowledges Arius's 'act of heroism and honesty' in refusing to sign the creed achieved at Nicaea.[5] Even more sympathy for Arius has been shown by Maurice Wiles as Regius Professor of Divinity at Oxford,[6] while another eminent Anglican theologian, Rowan Williams, who favours Nicaea and Athanasius, holds that the success of orthodoxy depends on its taking adequate account of the sound impulses behind the doctrines it rejects.[7] A similar balance of respect for traditional orthodoxy with rejection of the heresy-hunting mentality of the high Middle Ages is maintained in Brian Tierney's 'Religious rights: an historical perspective'. Tierney finds, however, that 'even in the medieval church there were some developments of Christian thought that might seem favorable to a growth of religious liberty', although 'centuries of cruel experience' were needed to recognize the implications for religious rights in the original sources of religious tradition.[8]

Today, then, religious freedom is affirmed and heresy-hunting abhorred. Religious teachings emerging from times of persecution are available to those freely moved to accept them, but we now understand that no doctrine is to be either imposed or punished by force. This is an attractive position, but there are difficulties. Do 'we' in fact *understand* that choice of religion should be free? It is a commonplace that centuries of cruel experience in the West led to toleration first as political and economic accommodation, only later as moral principle. While most modern Christians accept the morality of toleration and may even have a well founded sense that it is implicit in the original sources of their

[5] Jaroslav Pelikan, *The Emergence of the Catholic Tradition (100–600)*, vol. 1 of *The Christian Tradition* (Chicago, IL, and London, 1971), pp. 68–120, 203.

[6] Maurice F. Wiles, *The Making of Christian Doctrine* (Cambridge, 1967); *Archetypal Heresy: Arianism Through the Centuries* (Oxford and New York, 1996).

[7] Rowan Williams, *Arius: Heresy and Tradition* (London, 1987).

[8] Brian Tierney, 'Religious rights: an historical perspective', in John Witte, Jr and Johan D. van der Vyver, eds, *Religious Human Rights in Global Perspective: Religious Perspectives* (The Hague, Boston, and London, 1996), pp. 17–45, esp. pp. 18–19, 43–45. Tierney has himself been the most effective presenter of medieval developments favourable not only to a growth of religious liberty but to the recognition of natural rights in general. See especially his *Religion, Law, and the Growth of Constitutional Thought, 1150–1650* (Cambridge, 1982) and *The Idea of Natural Rights: Studies on Natural Rights, Natural Law and Church Law, 1150–1625* (Atlanta, GA, 1997).

tradition, how far have these values and perceptions been reconciled, other than pragmatically, with apparently contrary implications in the same sources, implications that led medieval Christians to quite different attitudes? The problem would be serious enough if it were only conceptual and only for Christians, but the worldwide resurgence of movements to integrate religious and political institutions on the basis of uniform religious commitment shows that there is a global 'we' who do not understand the value of religious freedom. To treat heresy as entirely a thing of the past may be an error even for liberals without a religious orientation of their own, for liberal or pluralistic policy with regard to religion may itself be seen as a persecuting orthodoxy when imposed on individuals or communities dedicated to religious uniformity. If liberals find intolerance not only intolerable but unintelligible, if we simply cannot understand why anyone could reasonably think of false *belief* as a crime or regard religious commitment as a political obligation, our treatment of the intolerant as 'fanatics' one and all will begin to resemble the mistreatment of deviance in the supposedly dark ages of the past.[9]

I suggest, therefore, that an attempt to understand medieval heresy may reward the joint attention of historians, philosophers, political theorists, theologians, and others concerned with religion and society in the world today. In this essay I will first present a sampling of material on the medieval idea of heresy and then suggest how engagement with such material might be fruitful for current discussions. Little of the medieval survey that follows will be news to historians of heresy. My intention is to present material that deserves joint exploration by non-medievalists and those who know the period in an attempt to understand phenomena related to heresy, past and present, more adequately than any of us now do.

THE PROBLEM OF DEFINITION

But what is to be discussed? Is there such a thing as 'the' medieval idea of heresy? And is there a deeper ethical conception in terms of which

[9] On the problems involved in finding a place for non-liberal cultures within the framework of liberal political theory see Will Kymlicka, *Liberalism, Community, and Culture* (Oxford, 1989), and *Multicultural Citizenship: A Liberal Theory of Minority Rights* (Oxford, 1995); David Heyd, ed., *Toleration: An Elusive Virtue* (Princeton, NJ, 1996); and John Rawls, *Political Liberalism* (New York, 1993). I am indebted to Erik A. Anderson for these references and for discussion of some of the issues considered in this paper.

we can understand the shift of values from medieval to modern regarding heresy? To judge from the reflections of specialists, it is not easy to reach a clear view of the medieval phenomena. Here are some of the twists and turns that need to be navigated.

In reviewing R. I. Moore's *The Origins of European Dissent*, Jeffrey B. Russell credits Moore with making 'a good stab at the difficult question of determining what constitutes or defines heresy as opposed to orthodoxy' but holds in the end that 'one is obliged to adopt a very practical approach: heresy (at least from about 1050) was doctrine condemned by Rome'.[10] Moore's 'good stab' begins by affirming that for medieval society the 'monster' of heresy 'had being in the form of a concept . . . whose essential unity was not diminished by the diversity of its manifestations'. In attempting to determine whether this concept 'also had reality outside the perceptions of its observers', Moore arrives at a plausible and well argued unitary *sociological* concept which a historian might find helpful in accounting for the diverse medieval applications of the term 'heretic' but which medieval people themselves surely did not have in mind when applying the term.[11] The challenging account of what makes a late medieval heretic given later by Moore in *The Formation of a Persecuting Society* has the same characteristic of proposing a possible *causal* explanation for persecution by reference to underlying motives but not an explanation in terms that the persecutors themselves would have recognized as reasons for their actions.[12] I will indicate later where I think there is a place for non-rational causal explanations even within discussions that aspire to rationality, but it seems appropriate to look first for *reasons*, that is, for conceptions under which our subjects were consciously operating.

With a view to looking for reasons, Russell's practical emphasis on condemnation by Rome has advantages, since holding doctrines condemned by Rome was often given as an explicit and decisive reason for declaring someone a heretic. The problem of taking

[10] Russell's review appeared in *Speculum*, 53.4 (October 1978), pp. 831–3. Russell himself aims at a more theoretical account in *Dissent and Order in the Middle Ages: The Search for Legitimate Authority* (New York, 1992). For a study that succeeds much better than others in getting inside the positions of both heretics and their opponents, see Gordon Leff, *Heresy*.

[11] Moore, *Dissent* (1985), pp. 263–83. 'In seeking a correlation between the incidence of heresy and other phenomena one alone holds. . . . It always flourished where political authority was diffused, and never where its concentration was greatest' (pp. 281–2).

[12] R. I. Moore, *The Formation of a Persecuting Society: Power and Deviance in Western Europe, 950–1250* (Oxford and New York, 1987).

medieval discussion of heresy seriously in its own terms clearly is, to some extent, the problem of understanding how condemnation by Rome was understood to be an event of the gravest kind. But what did Rome think it was doing when it condemned a doctrine or person as heretical? Was something heretical because a pope condemned it, or did the popes condemn certain things because they found them heretical? The practical historian may be happy to accept the first alternative, but we might suppose that the popes attempted to operate on the basis of the second. We might suppose that being a heretic should have been thought of as a condition that might or might not be difficult to identify but which pertained to individuals or did not pertain to them independently of approval or disapproval by others. This does not entirely fit the case of heresy, however, for obedience to authority and solidarity with the Church were widely held to be an intrinsic part of the very concept of orthodoxy. Especially in early Christian centuries, the Greek and Latin terms commonly translated as 'heresy' might equally well be rendered as 'factiousness' or 'divisiveness'. So both alternatives in my earlier question might have a place. A pope acting in good faith would not condemn capriciously, but papal condemnation might nonetheless contribute to the being of heresy.

Yet again, however, matters are not so simple. Medieval canon lawyers and theologians generally acknowledged the possibility of *papal* heresy. This meant that disobedience or factiousness, violation of Christian solidarity, could not simply be defined as disobedience to papal command.[13] The most extensive single discussion of heresy in our period, the massive Part One of Ockham's *Dialogus*, is particularly concerned with papal heresy, a possibility Ockham believed actualized in John XXII's pronouncements denying the complete poverty of Christ and the apostles, the gospel ideal professed by Ockham and his fellow Franciscans.[14] But there is still another twist. Ockham took John

[13] For the canonists see Brian Tierney, *Foundations of the Conciliar Theory* (Cambridge, 1955, repr. 1968). The arch-curialist Augustinus de Ancona, writing in the 1320s, acknowledged the possibility of papal heresy at various places in his *Summa de ecclesiastica potestate* (especially in Question 5, *De depositione papae*) and argued for substantial limits to the obligation of Christians to obey the pope (Question 22, article 1) (Rome, 1584), pp. 129–30.

[14] See my *The Political Thought of William of Ockham: Personal and Institutional Principles* (Cambridge, 1974). Some of Ockham's concerns are expressed in his *Short Discourse on the Tyrannical Government . . . Usurped by Some Who Are Called Highest Pontiffs*, trans. John Kilcullen (Cambridge, 1992) and in the selections from Ockham's major political writings translated by Kilcullen in *A Letter to the Friars Minor and Other Writings* (Cambridge, 1995).

XXII to be a heretic in part because he believed John had contradicted previous *papal* declarations.[15] It is not clear how useful the *Dialogus* would be to practical historians if they gave it more attention than they usually do, but it is undoubtedly a major source for determining what medieval theologians or inquisitors understood themselves to be identifying when they judged a doctrine or person heretical.

In the next few pages I will make a brief attempt of my own to determine what constituted or defined medieval heresy, aiming to pick out some elements in the period's conceptions of faith and infidelity deserving discussion in view of our present situation.[16]

EARLY DEVELOPMENTS

The most widespread persecution of heretics in western Europe occurred in the later Middle Ages, but the rationale and practical means for persecution are generally assumed to have been ready to hand from the early Christian centuries. The Greek *αἵρεσις* from which *haeresis* is derived meant 'choice' (specifically, choice for oneself). It is used classically in the sense of choice of a philosophical school and in the New Testament, sometimes without pejorative implications, for choice of religious affiliation or sect. In Paul the term more often means sect or faction in a bad sense (although Paul averred that, in God's providence, there must *be αἱρέσεις* so that those who are genuine or approved may become manifest [I Corinthians 11.19]). The connection of *αἵρεσις* with harmful *teaching* is clearest, in the New Testament, in

In my introductions to these volumes I argue for Ockham's importance as a proponent, on medieval grounds, of normal but not invariable separation of religious and secular political institutions. Professor Kilcullen's work in progress on a critical edition of the *Dialogus* is on the internet at www.mq.edu.au/pub/hpp/ockham/dialogus/zip.

[15] Brian Tierney thus presents Ockham as an exponent of anti-papal papal infallibility in *Origins of Papal Infallibility, 1150–1350* (Leiden, 1972, 2nd impression with a Postscript 1988).

[16] For a concise presentation of what the early Christian opponents of heresy took themselves to be contending against, see Arland J. Hultgren and Steven A. Haggmark, eds, *The Earliest Christian Heretics: Readings from Their Opponents* (Minneapolis, MN, 1996). Also see Edward Peters, ed., *Heresy and Authority in Medieval Europe: Documents in Translation* (Philadelphia, 1980); R. I. Moore, *The Birth of Popular Heresy* (New York, 1975; repr. Toronto, Buffalo, and London, 1995); Walter L. Wakefield and Austin P. Evans, eds, *Heresies of the High Middle Ages* (New York, 1969, 1991); Lambert, *Heresy*; Bernard Hamilton, *The Medieval Inquisition* (New York, 1981); and the medieval essays in *SCH* 9 and 21. Many of the numerous articles on heretics and heretical movements listed in the Leeds *International Medieval Bibliography* focus on socio-economic and political factors – on causes, that is, rather than reasons – although reasons on one side or another can sometimes be found in them.

II Peter 2.1, and this is taken up in a passage in the first-century martyr Ignatius, bishop of Antioch,[17] and later in influential treatises against a great variety of heresies by authors such as Irenaeus of Lyons, Hippolytus of Rome, and Epiphanius, bishop of Salamis. Augustine made use of Epiphanius, other authors, and his own experience as a religious controversialist in compiling a catalogue of heresies near the end of his life. Augustine's writings cooperated with efforts by church councils to forge a doctrinal consensus regarding God's nature and saving activity in Christ, and provided authoritative texts for later theology and church law relating to heresy. Augustine's eventual willingness to endorse coercion by secular authorities as legitimate for protecting or promoting orthodoxy supported energetic legislative action by emperors such as Theodosius II (401–50) and Justinian I (483–565) to complete an interlocking structure of belief and law on which the enforcement of Christian faith could be based when the need for enforcement was strongly felt centuries later. The need *was* felt strongly only centuries later. No one was executed for heresy in the West between Priscillian in 383 (whose conviction was for sorcery) and fourteen clergy and respectable laity in Orleans in 1022. This picture is accurate enough in outline, but there are complications in each of its parts that could be fruitful for the discussion I have in mind.

The New Testament

If we follow Aquinas in regarding heresy as a vice opposed to the virtue of faith, our understanding of one must be coordinated with an understanding of its opposite. Faith, or believing, is a complex idea in the New Testament. Major aspects include trusting or believing a person or believing *in* a person (where the person trusted, believed, or believed in is God or Jesus Christ) and believing *that* something is the case (holding 'the' faith).[18] The righteous live by faith, according to St Paul (Romans 1.17), but the character of this living may vary with the aspect of faith that is dominant. In particular, even if believing *in* Christ entails a general belief *that* whatever Christ teaches by word or deed is to be accepted, it does not obviously follow that sincere belief

[17] For these earliest uses see Gerhard Kittel and Gerhard Friedrich, eds, *Theological Dictionary of the New Testament*, ed. and trans. Geoffrey Bromley, with an index compiled by Ronald E. Pitkin, 10 vols (Grand Rapids, MI, 1964–76; repr. 1983), 1, pp. 180–4.

[18] See Bultmann's article on πιστεύω in Kittel and Friedrich, *Theological Dictionary of the New Testament*, 6, pp. 205–28.

in Christ entails believing that any particular proposition taught by Christ is true or that any particular practice of Christ is normative. One must also accept that the particular proposition or practice in question is in fact taught by Christ. With perfect knowledge of all of Christ's teachings, believing *in* and believing *that* will go together neatly, but among 'believers in' with imperfect knowledge, there is room for considerable variety in 'beliefs that'. For example, different understandings of Proverbs 8.22–31 and John 1.1–14 in the fourth century led to radically different beliefs about the person of Christ as the wisdom or word of God. A further difficulty with extracting a sharp idea of heresy from the New Testament stems from the common identification of Simon Magus (Acts 8.9–24) with the Simon of Samaria who figures as the father of all heretics in Irenaeus' account. This identification supports an assessment of simony as heresy. Other forms of ecclesiastical corruption besides the purchase of offices could also be brought under the general category of heresy as implicit rejections of Christ's teaching. Actions speak louder than words.

Early heresiographers

At least two of the three major patristic treatises commonly known by the title *Adversus haereses* were not originally so named. Irenaeus, writing against Gnosticism ('knowledgism'), called his work an *Exposé and Overthrow of What Is Falsely Called Knowledge* (ἐλέχου καὶ ἀνατροπῆς τῆς πσευδωνύμου γνώσεως).[19] It is unclear what title Hippolytus intended for his work.[20] Epiphanius's is a *Panarion*, 'which means a medicine chest for those bitten by wild animals'.[21] The idea of

[19] *Against Heresies*, trans. Alexander Roberts and W. H. Rambaut, *The Ante-Nicene Fathers* (henceforth *ANF*), 10 vols (Grand Rapids, MI, 1951–74), 1, pp. 309–567. A new English translation, St Irenaeus of Lyons, *Against the Heresies*, has been begun by Dominic J. Unger for the series *Ancient Christian Writers*. Book 1 appeared in 1992 (New York and Mahwah, NJ). For a critical text with French translation, see SC, 34, 100/1–2, 152–3, 263–4, and 293–4. Also see Dennis Minns, *Irenaeus* (London, 1994).

[20] The best attested title, *Σύνταγμα πρὸς ἁπάσας τάς αἱρέσεις*, can be translated 'A Treatise Against All the Heresies', but *σύνταγμα* has the special connotation of putting things in order, and *πρὸς* is not necessarily adversative (although it is undoubtedly meant to be here). Hippolytus, *Refutatio omnium haeresium*, ed. Paul Wendland, *Die griechischen christlichen Schriftsteller der ersten drei Jahrhunderte*, 26 (Leipzig, 1916), Sig. B*; ed. Miroslav Marcovich (Berlin and New York, 1986). Translated as *The Refutation of All Heresies* by J. H. MacMahon in *ANF*, 5, pp. 9–153.

[21] *The* Panarion *of St. Epiphanius, Bishop of Salamis*: Selected Passages, trans. Philip R. Amidon (New York and Oxford, 1990), p. 5. Epiphanius asks forgiveness from the priests to whom he addresses his work 'if you should ever find [us] speaking in anger or calling certain

heresy as rejection of 'the faith' of 'the Church' is not missing in these works, but it is not as clear or pervasive as the genre title later conferred on them suggests.[22] Although Irenaeus appealed to the traditions of various churches he took to have been apostolically founded, he argued against 'what is falsely called knowledge' primarily on the basis of reason and scripture. Hippolytus (himself a schismatic) is concerned to exhibit the roots of various Christian sects in the errors of Greek philosophy and astrology.[23] Epiphanius includes in his list of eighty heresies such pre-Christian positions or movements as barbarism, Platonism, and Stoicism. Augustine was perhaps the first even to raise the problem of defining what makes a heretic. Factiousness among professing Christians on the basis of false belief was arguably the dominant concern of these authors, but they are far from having a disciplined conception of heresy as deliberate rejection by a Christian of something essential to being a Christian.

Church councils

Concern with heterodox factionalism within the Church became a matter of public interest with the Emperor Constantine's conversion to Christianity in the early fourth century. Although Constantine sought to conciliate pagans and Christians, he was persuaded of the need for unity of faith among the latter. Accordingly he convened and presided at the first ecumenical council, the First Council of Nicaea (325).[24] The

people deceivers or imposters or wretches, even though it is not our custom to ridicule or make fun of people' (p. 6).

[22] Another instance of retroactive sharpening of the opposition between orthodox and heretic is Unger's rendering of the term *Demiourgos* differently in his translation of Irenaeus depending on its presumably distinct meanings for Irenaeus himself and the Gnostics he is concerned to expose and refute. 'Whenever *Demiourgos* refers to the Gnostic creator-god, I translate it *Demiurge*. But when Irenaeus uses it for the true Creator, I translate *Creator* to avoid ambiguity. The Demiurge is the god who made the material world and is the author of wickedness, quite inferior to the supreme deity' (*Against the Heresies*, trans. Unger, 1, note 9 to Pref., p. 127).

[23] On this theme see Gerard Verbeke, 'Philosophy and heresy: some conflicts between reason and faith', in W. Lourdoux and D. Verhelst, eds, *The Concept of Heresy in the Middle Ages (11th–13th C.)*, Mediaevalia Lovaniensia, Series 1, Studia IV (Louvain and The Hague, 1976), pp. 172–97.

[24] Subsequent opinion concerning the need for prompt resolution of the issues raised by Arius about the person of Christ varied. The church historian Socrates Scholasticus (*c.* 380–450) thought that there would have been less controversy if Arius's bishop had been less determined to require immediate agreement with his own position (*Ecclesiastical History*, Book 1, chapter 6; *A Select Library of the Nicene and Post-Nicene Fathers of the Christian Church*, 2nd ser., ed. Philip Schaff and Henry Wace, 14 vols [New York, Oxford, and London, 1890–

first mention and, so to speak, definition of 'heretics' in the councils of the church is found in Decree 6 of the First Council of Constantinople (381), which refuses to allow heretics to bring charges against orthodox bishops in matters of an ecclesiastical kind.

> We call [λέγομεν *dicimus*, 'define as' in the English in Tanner] heretics those who have been previously banned from the church and also those who have been anathematised by ourselves: in addition those who claim to profess a faith that is sound, but who have seceded and hold assemblies in rivalry with the bishops who are in communion with us.

Although heretics may not accuse bishops in ecclesiastical matters, *personal* charges against bishops are to be heard, no matter by whom they are brought. 'It is wholly essential both that the bishop should have a clear conscience, and that the one who alleges that he has been wronged, whatever his religion may be [οἵας ἂν εἴη θρησκείας], should get justice.' The non-pejorative sense of αἵρεσις, in which the term stands for any belief or opinion, is still alive at this point, as in Decree 7 of the same council, which specifies that 'Arians, Macedonians ... those who call themselves Cathars' and certain others will be received again into the Church when they hand in statements and anathematize 'every heresy which is not of the same mind as the holy, catholic and apostolic church of God'.[25] Thus the church council that was most effective in setting forth Trinitarian orthodoxy did not consistently hold that all 'heresies' were bad (some sects were compatible with orthodoxy as the council saw it, and only the incompatible needed rejection). Even condemned heretics were allowed legal rights against the orthodox.

This is in striking contrast with the next significant reference to heretics in Tanner's collection, the ferocious authorization of force by the Third Lateran Council (1179) against the 'loathsome heresy of those whom some call Cathars, others the Patarenes, others the Publicani, and others by different names'.[26] The common elements

1902], 2:5). St Jerome (*c.* 342–420) held that 'Arius was only a spark in Alexandria, but because the spark was not put out at once its flames filled the whole world' (*Commentary on Paul's Epistle to the Galatians* [on 5.9], *PL* 26, col. 403).

[25] Tanner, *Decrees*, pp. 33–5.

[26] Decree 27; Tanner, pp. 224–5. The language of Decree 3 of the Fourth Lateran Council (1215) unleashing the Albigensian Crusade is still harsher (ibid., pp. 233–5). There are only two brief references to heretics between Constantinople I and Lateran III in Tanner's collection.

here are the councils' confidence in their ability to identify heretics and the absence of any formal general definition of heresy or heretic.

Augustine

In Augustine, who has been called the prince and patriarch of persecutors, there are seeds and more than seeds of what is most troubling in the medieval idea of heresy but also material for questioning the same developments. His acceptance of the role of persecutor in relation to the Donatists,[27] combined with his extensive writings against Pelagianism and other positions he deemed erroneous, provided morally authoritative backing for later forceful intolerance.[28] In hindsight his conciliatory initial approach to the Donatists, early reluctance to use coercion against them, and avoidance of the term *heresy* in his early writings against Pelagius only mildly palliate his later attitudes.[29] Augustine's own passage through beliefs that he came to regard as profoundly mistaken does, however, give even his angriest invective against false belief in others a tone of fraternal exasperation rather than self-righteous hatred.

In *On the Advantage of Believing*, his attitude toward some of those in error – followers, not leaders – is genuinely amiable. Addressing the work to a friend from his Manichaean days who had remained a Manichaean, he begins with a distinction essentially of motive. 'The heretic, in my opinion, is one who for some temporal advantage,

[27] In Epistle 185 Augustine replies to the Donatists' denial that a true church can ever persecute by reminding them of their own attempts to bring imperial authority down on the Catholic bishop Caecilian but also by emphasising the need to consider the cause for which persecution is suffered as well as the persecution itself. 'The true martyrs are those who suffer persecution for righteousness' sake, not on account of wickedness or the impious division of Christian unity': *Epistolae*, ed. Al. Goldbacher, *CSEL*, 57, pp. 8–10; *Letters*, trans. Wilfrid Parsons, *The Fathers of the Church* (Washington and New York, 1947–) [henceforth *FOTC*] 30, pp. 149–51. For praise of imperial laws passed against paganism, see Epistle 93, ed. Goldbacher, *CSEL*, 34, pp. 454, 471; trans. Parsons, *FOTC* 18, pp. 65, 82. See W. H. C. Frend, *The Donatist Church* (Oxford, 1952) and, for a survey of research following Frend's book, R. A. Markus, 'Christianity and dissent in Roman North Africa: changing perspectives in recent work', *SCH*, 9, pp. 21–36; repr. as selection 8 in R. A. Markus, *From Augustine to Gregory the Great: History and Christianity in Late Antiquity* (London, 1983).

[28] Augustine is the single most important source on heresy cited in Gratian's *Decretum* (mid-twelfth century), the major point of departure for late medieval canon law. H. G. Walther, 'Häresie und päpstliche Politik', *Concept of Heresy*, pp. 104–43; p. 112.

[29] Peter Brown, 'St. Augustine's attitude to religious coercion', *Journal of Roman Studies*, 54 (1964), pp. 107–16; *Augustine of Hippo* (Berkeley, CA, 1967).

especially for the sake of glory and preeminence, originates or follows false and new opinions.' On the other hand, 'He who believes men of this kind is deceived by a certain image of truth and piety.'[30] (The image of truth that had appealed to Augustine in Manichaeism was the promise of answers to all important questions on the basis of reason alone. After his conversion he self-consciously emphasised the benefit (*utilitas*) of faith, but part of the benefit was that faith allowed access to a kind of understanding of what was believed that satisfied some of the passion for wisdom that had led him into and out of Manichaeism itself.)

At the beginning of his one general treatise on heresies, Augustine avers that 'to grasp in a set definition by rule [regulari quadam definitione comprehendi]' what makes a heretic can be done either not at all or only with the greatest difficulty. . . . If this could be grasped, who does not see how beneficial it would be?' He promises to discuss this later in the work but apparently did not live to do so. It would certainly be difficult to state a defining rule for the eighty-eight heresies Augustine presents in his *De haeresibus*. His one sentence on Coluthus, who denied that God makes or does evils sets Coluthus against scripture (Isaiah 45.7) but does not set him off against Augustine's own celebrated anti-Manichaean thesis that evil is not a reality in its own right but a privation of being. On the other hand, Augustine hereticates a group who always went about barefoot because, he says, they did this on the basis of their understanding of scripture (Exodus 3.5, Joshua 5.16, Isaiah 20.2), not to mortify the flesh.[31] In this work and elsewhere Augustine shows a tendency to

[30] *The Advantage of Believing*, trans. Luanne Meagher in St Augustine, *The Immortality of the Soul, The Magnitude of the Soul, On Music, The Advantage of Believing, On Faith in Things Unseen* (New York, 1947), pp. 391–442, esp. p. 391. Iosephus Zycha, ed., *De utilitate credendi*, *CSEL*, 25.1:1–48; p. 1.

[31] Latin text with English translation by Liguori G. Müller, *The De Haeresibus of Saint Augustine: A Translation with an Introduction and Commentary*, The Catholic University of America Patristic Studies 90 (Washington, 1956). Trans. by Roland J. Teske in Augustine, *Arianism and Other Heresies* (Hyde Park, NY, 1995), pp. 15–77. R. Vander Plaetse and C. Beukers, eds, *De haeresibus ad Quodvultdeum*, *CChr.SL*, 46, pp. 263–358. In correspondence Augustine had observed that two earlier heresiographers had come up with quite different numbers of heresies in the same period. Epiphanius counted 80, Filastrius of Brescia 156. Augustine concluded that 'this would not have happened unless what seemed to be a heresy was different from one to the other of them' (Epistle 222, Teske, p. 26; Vander Plaetse and Beukers, p. 276). He remarks on the value a definition would have and indicates his intention to discuss the question in the preface to *De haeresibus*; the promise is renewed in the epilogue to the work as we have it (Liguori, pp. 61, 129; Teske, pp. 33, 58; Vander Plaetse

regard persistence in schism as heresy.[32] He also recognizes the possibility of wrongful excommunication, however, which seems to imply that persistence in a belief one knew to be orthodox would be obligatory, even at the cost of separation from the main body of believers.[33]

Besides shedding light on the idea of heresy, Augustine is an especially promising source, and not only a 'medieval' one, for responding to liberal perplexity as to how the contrary virtue of faith could be considered the necessary foundation for a genuine society. Three texts in particular deserve attention. Book 19 of *On the City of God against the Pagans* is as concise and effective a presentation of the social benefits of Christian believing as one could wish. The essential argument is that an account of human goods and evils limited in scope to what we know of this life is impoverished. Quite apart from his conviction that the expectations born of faith will be fulfilled in a last judgement followed by eternal punishment or bliss, Augustine holds that it is more reasonable to assess the fragile goods of family, friends, and civic life by reference to the incorruptible goods in which Christians believe than to define happiness and misery by our present experience of them. Any peace or ordered tranquillity that can be hoped for in this world will be pursued more realistically, and hence more effectively, when seen in a broader, more accurate perspective. Even from the standpoint of those whose ultimate commitments reach no further than worldly goods it is good that there are Christians, for Christian interest in maintaining a tolerable life on earth, although it is an instrumental interest, coincides with the reasonable goals of a purely earthly city. Augustine's account of goods and evils in the *City of God* is open to various patterns of life, active or contemplative, powerful or humble, well dressed or scruffy, and so on.

and Beukers, pp. 289, 344–5). For Coluthus and those who always went barefoot, heresies 65 and 68, Liguori, pp. 106–9; Teske, pp. 49–50; Vander Plaetse and Beukers, pp. 330–1.

[32] Joseph de Guibert, 'La notion d'hérésie chez saint Augustin,' *Bulletin de littérature ecclésiastique*, 21 (1920), pp. 368–82, esp. pp. 374–75, 378–79. De Guibert notes (p. 374, n. 5) that the distinction between heresy and schism proposed by the Donatist Cresconius ('a heresy is a sect of those following different [beliefs, i.e., different beliefs from the orthodox], a schism is separation between those holding the same [beliefs]') was often repeated approvingly as being Augustine's (for example, by Thomas Aquinas). Elsewhere Augustine proposed lack of charity as the distinguishing mark of heresy (Sermons 37 and 46; *Contra Cresconium*, II, 15–20 and I, 40; as cited by de Guibert, p. 374). He held in these passages that it was impossible to have charity apart from the Church, from which he presumably did not think it follows that everyone defending the Church's faith does so charitably.

[33] Augustine, *De vera religione*, 6.11; *CChr.SL*, 32, p. 195.

A more liberal-sounding openness presents itself in an earlier work, *On Free Choice of the Will.* Augustine here conceives of wisdom in practical terms, as 'the truth in which the highest good is discerned and acquired'.[34] Different people, however, seek happiness in different lives. Are there many wisdoms, then? No, there is only one. But instead of construing this one wisdom as dictating a single way of life, Augustine presents it as the one light by which the value of *various* personal highest goods may be seen. 'Even supposing that there are many and various goods from which each person chooses what he wants, and that by seeing and pursuing that thing he rightly and truly constitutes it his highest good, it is still possible that the light of wisdom, in which those things can be seen and pursued, is a single thing, common to all the wise.'[35] Attachment to the light source rather than to any particular illuminated goods is what is crucial. 'This is our freedom, when we are subject to the truth; and the truth is God himself, who frees us from death, that is, from the state of sin.'[36] Belief is all important, therefore, because awareness of eternal truth unites one in a liberating, saving relationship with eternal reality. The Truth above the mind and shining down within it *is* God. This is in contrast with modern philosophical views (nicely encapsulated by Richard Rorty as 'the idea idea'), in which a belief is something 'in the mind', ontologically separate from the external object it is about.

In both of the preceding texts Augustine presents the benefits of Christian faith without emphasis on the doctrine most distinctive of late fourth-century orthodoxy, the Trinity. Since the Trinity is probably also the Christian doctrine most difficult for liberals (even Christian liberals) to comprehend as a necessary part of human flourishing, it is fortunate that the one work of Augustine's comparable in depth and influence to the *Confessions* and the *City of God* directly addresses this problem.

Augustine's *On the Trinity*, a preeminent example of faith seeking understanding, operates with a conception of wisdom that initially seems at odds with the practical approach of *On Free Will.* In *On the Trinity* Augustine defines wisdom (*sapientia*) as 'the contemplation of

[34] *On Free Choice of the Will*, Book 2, chapter 9, trans. Thomas Williams (Indianapolis, IN, and Cambridge, MA, 1993), p. 47. Latin text ed. William M. Green, *CSEL*, 74 (Vienna, 1956), p. 61.

[35] Williams, p. 49, and Green, p. 63.

[36] Chapter 13, Williams, p. 57, and Green, p. 73.

eternal things'.[37] This is indeed a shift of sorts, as evidenced by Augustine's need here to set up a practical discipline distinct from wisdom. This is knowledge (*scientia*), which deals with the use of temporal things in the light of wisdom. But the contemplation of eternal things as Augustine develops it also turns out to be extraordinarily useful. This is because the main road leading toward contemplative understanding of the eternal divine Trinity is awareness of ourselves (primarily our minds) as likewise triune, as in this respect made in God's image. The most fully articulated of various created trinities Augustine discerns is that of memory, understanding, and will. Trinitarian contemplation is thus, in effect, also a method for acquiring, maintaining, or extending self-possession. The ideal co-equality or mutual inclusion of the memory, self-consciousness, and affection constituting the human mind would seem to define a distinctive integrity or peace – peace with ourselves that goes beyond acquiring a sufficiency of external goods but is not simply faith in an indeterminate 'something eternal' beyond the present life.[38] A broader appreciation of Augustinian commitment to the Trinity as a teaching articulated for use, not simply credal fiat, would contribute greatly to our understanding of medieval efforts to enforce orthodoxy.[39]

What can we gather about the medieval idea of heresy from its predecessors? A little and a lot. In the early Christian centuries heresy involves choice for oneself, factiousness, and (usually but not always) false belief. Beyond this the concept is unclear. Yet although the phenomenon was not well defined, many authors thought they knew heresy when they saw it, and a number of different ways of responding to it were suggested.

[37] This is in express contrast with Cicero's definition of wisdom as 'the science of things divine and human'. *De Trinitate*, XII.14.22, XII.15.25, XIV.1.3; *CChr.SL*, 50, pp. 375, 379, 423–4. *The Trinity*, trans. Edmund Hill (Brooklyn, NY, 1991), pp. 334, 336, 371–2.

[38] Cf. Edmund Hill, in the introduction to his translation. 'Augustine is proposing the quest for, or the exploration of, the mystery of the Trinity as a complete program for the Christian spiritual life, a program of conversion and renewal and discovery of self in God and God in self': *The Trinity*, p. 19.

[39] On the dogma of the Trinity as a solution to major theological problems in early Christianity, see Pelikan, *Emergence of the Catholic Tradition*, pp. 172–3. For the Trinity in relation to the problems of late classical culture, see Charles Norris Cochrane, *Christianity and Classical Culture* (London, New York, and Toronto, 1957), especially chapter 11, 'Nostra philosophia: The discovery of personality', pp. 399–455. Cochrane argues that the goal of the Augustinian Trinitarian programme is 'the integration of personality' (p. 454).

HERESY AND ENLIGHTENMENT

Using the persecution of heretics as a darkness index for the whole medieval period is not only chronologically erroneous (as mentioned above, there were no executions for heresy in the West from the fifth to the tenth centuries) but is in some respects also a reversal of light and dark. Economically, politically, and culturally, the earlier centuries were the dark ones, while the most intense campaigning against heresy occurred in and around the thirteenth century, an era of renaissance and enlightenment.

When heresy and the persecution of heresy are regarded as signs of something else – something perhaps easier for us to understand, such as stress induced by changing social conditions or a desire to maintain a newly acquired position of power – the attempt to explain the upsurge of heresy and its antagonists in the later Middle Ages naturally proceeds in terms of the something else. Since we here hope to understand the medieval idea of heresy as far as possible in its own terms, we must look for a late medieval increase in factors that heretics and their persecutors themselves regarded as relevant explanations of their behaviour – *reasons* for radical religious dissent on one hand and, on the other hand, *reasons* for regarding such dissent as an evil calling for repression. There were at least three sorts of reasons or ideals at work on a larger scale later rather than earlier, ideals within each of which controversy about faith and heresy took place.[40]

The apostolic ideal

A universally recognized source of energetic religious activity in the later Middle Ages, both heretical and orthodox, was devotion to the ideal of a spiritually exemplary life. The importance of the New Testament as its source justifies calling this 'the apostolic ideal',[41] but centuries of saints' lives and devout monastic practice significantly fleshed out the biblical models. Judging the reasonableness of appeals to such an ideal to justify any particular individual or group's conduct is difficult. A simple life, poor and chaste, more or less critical of

[40] I do not mean to suggest that reasons and non-rational causes operated in separate universes. Some of what I present under the rubric of reasons is part of current research into causes. For example, it was the business of scholastic intellectuals to weigh reasons, but such weighing sometimes influenced the repression or spread of heresy in ways that were arguably other than reasonable.

[41] Gordon Leff, 'Apostolic Ideal'.

worldliness, has seemed commendable to some Christians simply because it was the life led by Christ and the apostles, but varying perceptions of the independent attractiveness of such a life must affect the extent to which readers of the Bible take those models as setting a firm standard. In any case, devotion to the ideal of a spiritually exemplary life may limit tolerance for association on equal spiritual terms with individuals whose lives contradict the ideal. Accordingly, charges of immorality were frequently brought against those accused as heretics. Conversely, corruption among bishops and orthodox clergy was frequently given by the accused as a reason for having nothing to do with their accusers.

In at least one case this last reasoning was applauded at the highest level of the Church. In 1076 one Ramihrdus, after satisfying his bishop and a group of abbots and learned clerics of his doctrinal orthodoxy, refused to receive communion with his examiners 'because they were up to the neck in simony and other avarice'. Thereupon 'certain of the bishop's servants, with many others, led him out and took him – not reluctantly, but without fear, and, they say, prostrate in prayer – to a hut which they set on fire'. When Gregory VII heard of this, he was horrified – and furious with the bishop. 'We have also heard that the people of Cambrai have burnt a certain man because he dared to say that simoniacal and unchaste priests ought not to celebrate mass, and that their offices ought to be avoided. This seems to us a dreadful thing, and if it is true he ought to be avenged with all the rigour of canonical severity.'[42] Ramihrdus had in effect excommunicated his bishop and been posthumously awarded a papal commendation for doing so.[43]

[42] Translated by R. I. Moore from the Chronicle of St André de Castres and the *Registrum* of Gregory VII in *The Birth of Popular Heresy*, pp. 24–5.

[43] More generally, Gregory's opposition to simony and concubinage gave official sanction to bitter popular criticism of clerical shortcomings. '[Gregory's] revolutionizing of the lay masses against married clerks . . . was nothing else but the proclamation of a lay strike: needless to say that the appeal found an immediate response. Upon the sanction of the papal government the masses went to lengths which make us recoil even in our time, hardened as we are in this respect': Walter Ullmann, *Principles of Government and Politics in the Middle Ages* (London, 1961), p. 222. Accordingly, for the early canonists simony was the worst heresy. 'Aufgrund eines Kanons des Dekrets [C. 1, q. 7, c. 27; ed. Friedberg, 1:437–8] hielten sie die simonistische Häresie überhaupt für das grösste Verbrechen.' The seriousness with which it was regarded is reflected in the standard commentaries on the two major parts of the canon law. The *Glossa ordinaria* to the *Decretum* held simony to be worse than heresy. 'Daraus folgerte die *Glossa ordinaria* zum Dekret die Simonie sei ein schlimmeres *crimen* als die Häresie': Othmar Hageneder, 'Der Häresiebegriff bei den Juristen des 12. und 13.

In refusing to receive communion with his bishop, Ramihrdus had apparently not denied that God's grace could be operative in sacraments administered by corrupt priests. Such a denial was made later by many who were condemned for it as heretics. The position is closer to official orthodoxy than is sometimes assumed, however, for the leading theologians of the thirteenth century, Bonaventure and Thomas Aquinas, made similar denials in holding that the sacraments of *heretical* priests were useless, lacking in fruitfulness or effect.[44] When does abhorrence of communion with those with whom one profoundly disagrees about an ostensibly common faith or its associated values become culpably factious? A plausible medieval standard for answering this question is offered by a second ideal.

The communal ideal

If Gregory VII was responsible for raising the moral standards Christians had reason to expect in their clergy, he was equally responsible for asserting the supereminent authority of the papacy. His pontificate begins a period of increasingly effective papal power which extended well into the thirteenth century.[45] Accordingly, there is an increasing tendency in this period to link rejection of papal authority with heresy and to regard correction of heresy, ever more broadly defined, as a work of justice and power rather than love.[46] A

Jahrhunderts', *Concept of Heresy*, pp. 42–103; p. 57. In the *Glossa ordinaria* to the *Decretals* (c. 1241), one who perverts the sacraments of the Church, 'as does a simoniast', begins the list of those who are called heretics (Hageneder, p. 45).

[44] According to Bonaventure, 'Heretics have the sacraments as to truth . . . but not as to benefit [*utilitatem*].' Bonaventure, *In quattuor libros Sententiarum*, Book 4, dist. 6, art. unicus, q. 6; *Opera*, 4, p. 147. 'In manifest heretics sacrament and sacrifice are deprived of all fruit' (ibid., dist. 13, art. 1, q. 1; 4, p. 303). 'One who receives the sacrament from a heretic as a heretic receives nothing' (ibid., dist. 5, art. 3, q. 2; 4, p. 126). Thomas considered the objection that since divine *virtus* prevails over human malice, and since a sacrament contains and causes grace by divine *virtus*, therefore, 'however evil may be the one who gives it – or if he is a heretic – one who receives the sacrament from him attains grace'. He replies that, 'although the sacrament does not lose its *virtus*, it nevertheless does not have an effect in one who comes to it unworthily, acting against obedience to the church'. *In quattuor libros Sententiarum*, Book 4, dist. 3, q. 1, art. 3c, obj. 2 and ad 2; *S. Thomae Aquinatis Opera omnia*, ed. Robertus Busa, 7 vols (Stuttgart-Bad Cannstatt, 1980), 1, p. 492.

[45] See Walter Ullmann, *The Growth of Papal Government in the Middle Ages*, 2nd edn (London, 1962; repr.with minor corrections 1965), pp. 262–309.

[46] On denial of papal primacy as heretical see Hageneder in *Concept of Heresy*, pp. 58–71; and in the same volume Walther, 'Häresie und päpstliche Politik'. Heresy is first declared treasonous, a crime of *laesae maiestatis*, by Innocent III (Walther, p. 134). As curia and canonists came increasingly to regard papal approval as the basis for secular power, love (*caritas*) came to play less of a role in controversy with heretics (p. 137), and there was a

hierocratic papalist conception of authority was given systematic theological expression by a number of writers, notably Giles of Rome, who ascribed to the papacy a status something like the Truth above the mind in Augustine's *On Free Will*.[47] Papal approval of mendicant preaching orders in the early thirteenth century showed a recognition of the need for persuasion and appealing personal example (the apostolic ideal) as weapons against heresy, but the Inquisition, established by the papacy in the same period, was administered primarily by the new orders.[48]

Condemnation by Rome counted as a reason for regarding a person or a proposition as heretical because the papacy had for centuries been acknowledged by western theologians as responsible above all other authorities for preserving the single Christian faith. This was the papacy's primary *raison d'être*, and to the extent that heresy is a matter of factiousness the reasonableness of having a single guarantor of the singleness of faith of the universal Christian community is evident. This evident reasonableness supported the interpretation of certain biblical texts (especially John 21.15–17, Matthew 16.18–19, and Luke 22.32) as warrants for Peter's authority over the other apostles and for the authority of the popes, as Peter's successors, over all Christians. Different ideals of community could also be worked out from scripture and Christian tradition, however. The monastic ethos engendered the classic critique of a papacy too much engaged with worldly affairs.[49] Popes themselves could in some circumstances, from some points of view, be regarded as disruptive. The ardent papalist Augustinus de Ancona held, following Gregory VII, that no one could judge the pope, but Augustinus also held that, 'if he [the pope] clearly [*notabiliter*] commanded things contrary to custom [*inconsueta*] and not

tendency to expand the competence of the papally delegated Inquisition (pp. 140–1). According to the eminent canonist Hostiensis (*d.* 1271), it was heresy not only to contradict the teaching of the Roman Church but even to oppose a papal privilege or command (p. 142). On the tendency for more and more crimes to be brought under the concept of heresy also see Hageneder, pp. 98–100.

47 Giles of Rome, *On Ecclesiastical Power*, trans. R. W. Dyson (Woodbridge, 1986).

48 It must be noted here that medieval canon lawyers, as well as elaborating legal doctrines supporting papal primacy, also made important contributions to the idea of human rights. This aspect of canonist thought is a leading example of Brian Tierney's 'medieval . . . developments of Christian thought that might seem favorable to a growth of religious liberty'. On the canonists and other medieval thinkers involved in this development, see Tierney, *The Idea of Natural Rights*.

49 Bernard of Clairvaux, *Five Books on Consideration*, trans. John D. Anderson and Elizabeth T. Kennan (Kalamazoo, MI, 1976).

in harmony with God's commands and the law of nature, since a pope commanding such things would be an unbeliever, *he would judge himself*, because "Those who do not believe" rightly "have already been judged" (John 3.18)'. Accordingly, Augustinus contended that it was a duty of fraternal charity for every Christian to rebuke a pope who erred against faith or morals.[50]

The faith community from which papal condemnation excluded a heretic or from which a papal heretic excluded himself was that of the universal Church. By the latter part of the thirteenth century intellectual resources for reflecting on the nature of that community had become abundant. The golden age of scholasticism was the work of an intellectual community within the broader community of the Church. Intellectuals both reinforced and challenged the ideals of spirituality and papal-communal authority on the strength of a third ideal inherited from earlier centuries, the ideal of virtue.

The virtuous ideal

Thirteenth- and fourteenth-century scholastics discussed the theological, moral, and intellectual virtues in unparallelled depth and subtlety. The titanic second part of Thomas Aquinas's *Summa theologiae*, for example, is a 'moral consideration of human acts' based on the assumption that human beings properly may and should direct their own acts with a view to their ultimate end. Thomas accordingly organizes his discussion primarily around the virtues and their opposed vices, including the virtue of faith and the vice of heresy. With regard to heresy Thomas draws distinctions that sharpen the concept and support sharper persecution of dissenters. With regard to faith he focuses attention on what may be the central issue for any discussion between liberal pluralism and medieval Christian orthodoxy.

Aquinas separates simony cleanly from heresy, thus leaving anti-clerical dissidents less of a basis for counter-charges. 'Simoniacs', he writes, 'are sometimes *called* heretics by a likeness [*per similitudinem*], because just as a heretic judges [*sentit*] against the faith, so a simoniac

[50] *Summa de ecclesiastica potestate*, q. 22, art. 1, ad 2 (Rome, 1584), p. 130. On the duty to censure an erring pope in Augustinus (*Summa*, question 7), see my 'William of Ockham and Augustinus de Ancona on the righteousness of dissent', in Robert Andrews, ed., *Franciscan Philosophy and Theology: Essays in Honor of Father Gedeon Gál, O. F. M on His Eightieth Birthday*, *FS*, 54 (1994–7), pp. 143–65.

acts *as if* he judged against the faith, when he wants to acquire or give holy things for a price, *as if* he reckoned the gift of the holy spirit to be possessed by money.'[51] Responding to the argument that false belief by itself does not make a heretic unless it is proposed for the sake of some temporal advantage (an argument based on the passage from Augustine's *On the Advantage of Believing* quoted above), Thomas argues that propagation of doctrinal error *necessarily* presupposes evil motivation. 'It is certain [*constat*] that those who make up a heresy *de novo* do expect some advantage, at least a position of leadership, for they want to have followers.'[52] Thus the apparent virtue of, say, a Cathar leader would be only apparent.[53] For Thomas even a heretic's apparent orthodoxy in some articles of the creed is not really a matter of shared faith.

> A heretic does not have the habit [i.e., the theological virtue] of faith if he disbelieves even one article; for by one act of the [sacramentally] infused habit [of faith] the contrary is abolished. For the habit of faith also has this efficacy, that by it the believer's understanding is held back from assenting to things contrary to faith, just as [the virtuous habit of] chastity restrains one from things contrary to chastity.

Hence, 'that a heretic should believe anything beyond what is naturally knowable does not arise from an infused habit – because that habit would direct him equally in all that is to be believed – but from some human reckoning, just as pagans too believe some things about God that are above nature'.[54]

It is the infused habit of faith, lacking in heretics (and culpably lacking, because as baptized Christians they are presumed to have had

[51] *In quattuor libros Sententiarum*, Book 4, dist. 13, q. 2, art. 1, ad 3; ed. Busa, 1, p. 492.

[52] Ibid., ad 9; ed. Busa, 1, p. 493.

[53] Cf. St Bonaventure, who speaks of the fictive joy of heretics in dying for their errors, 'who believe that they are dying in accord with the piety of faith, when they are dying in accord with the impiety of error, and hence they do not feel remorse but rather a certain fictive and vain joy': *In II librum Sententiarum*, dist. 39, art. 2, q. 2; *Opera*, 2, p. 912. Cf. ibid., dist. 28, art. 1, q. 3, ad 4, p. 679, where a similar argument is given to show that heretics exposing themselves to death merit ignominy rather than glory. Would this have satisfied the correspondent who wrote to Bernard of Clairvaux in amazement at the fact that heretics 'entered and endured the torment of the flames not merely courageously but joyfully. I wish I were with you, holy father, to hear you explain how such great fortitude comes to these tools of the devil in their heresy as is seldom found among the truly religious in the faith of Christ'? Quoted by Moore, *Dissent* (1985), p. 2.

[54] *Quaestiones disputatae de veritate*, quest. 14, art. 10, ad 10; ed. Busa, 3, p. 98. Bonaventure to the same effect at *In III Librum Sententiarum*, dist. 23, art. 2, q. 2; *Opera* 3, p. 492.

it at one time and to be responsible for losing it), that poses the most critical issue. St Thomas is best known among philosophers for holding that many truths about God are susceptible of philosophical demonstration, notably God's existence. He also held, however, that Christian faith involves assenting to truths above the capacity of natural reason and that for many believers acceptance even of truths that are in principle demonstrable is a matter of assenting to what the believer takes God in Christ to be teaching by special revelation. Being *able* to accept divine teaching that goes beyond the reach of philosophy and science requires grace – specifically the infused virtue of faith, a grace conferred in the sacrament of baptism. This is to say that the believer has an objectively sufficient basis for believing, but the sufficiency comes from God. Aristotle had held that morally virtuous habits of character, habits acquired through our own actions, involve something like good taste in judging the matters that come under them. Aquinas makes a corresponding point about the divinely infused theological virtue of faith. 'Just as a human being assents to principles by the natural light, so one who is virtuous by the habit of a virtue has a right judgment concerning the things that agree with that virtue. And in this way, too, by the divinely infused light of faith one assents to matters of faith.'[55]

Thomas's account of Christian believing as a venture that both goes beyond what can be demonstrated by philosophy or science and yet is 'sufficiently' grounded agrees with the experience of many believers, as does the explanation offered – that God's action makes it possible for human beings to believe in God. But can the authenticity of this experience – not its sincerity but its objective accuracy – be demonstrated by philosophy or science? Can it be demonstrated 'by natural reason' that the experience of infused faith is what it seems to be, God enabling an individual to believe? The Subtle Doctor Duns Scotus concluded that this cannot be demonstrated.

[55] *Summa theologiae*, IIaIIae, q. 2, art. 3, ad 2. Cf. ibid., art. 9, where Aquinas asks whether the believer has a 'sufficient cause' for believing (obj. 2). He replies that believing is an act of the understanding assenting to divine truth 'from a command of the will moved by God through grace' (body of the article) and that, accordingly, 'the believer has sufficient inducement to believing, being led by the authority of divine teaching confirmed by miracles and, what is more, by the inner impulse of God who invites [*interiori instinctu Dei invitantis*]' (ad 3).

> It is necessary to posit infused faith because of the authority of sacred Scripture and the saints. It cannot be demonstrated to exist in a believer or unbeliever merely from natural reason, unless faith is presupposed – that the believer wants to believe sacred Scripture and the saints – and hence it will never be shown to an unbeliever. Because of this, just as I believe God to be three and one, so by infused faith I believe myself to have infused faith, because I believe this.[56]

If Aquinas's virtue-centered account of human conduct supported in some key respects the institutional Church's repression of heresy, William of Ockham's reading of virtue and vice in the world around him led to the most extensive probing of institutional authority prior to the Reformation. Three points especially merit emphasis.[57]

First, since he was convinced that Pope John XXII had fallen into heresy, Ockham's treatment of the subject cut completely across the grain of normal ecclesiastical procedures for identifying and judging heretics. He did not advocate change in the normal structures of authority, but he argued strenuously that Christians were in some cases obliged to consider the possibility that the supreme earthly authority in the Church had failed grievously. They were further obliged, if such breakdown occurred, to take whatever emergency action was necessary. Ockham thus combines conservative respect for traditional Church structures (particularly, in contrast with Marsilius of Padua, respect for the tradition that regarded papal primacy as scripturally grounded) with the possibility of radical protest against operational failure in those structures.

Ockham himself was automatically considered a heretic for refusing to accept John XXII's pronouncements on the poverty of Christ and the apostles. To gain a hearing for his own contention that John was the heretic, Ockham needed a way of thinking about theological controversy that would to some extent neutralize the disparity in *prima facie* authority between a reigning pope and a rebel friar. He set forth

[56] Duns Scotus, *In III Librum Sententiarum (Reportatio Parisiensia)*, dist. 23, q. unica, 'Utrum ponenda sit fides infusa respectu credibilium?;' *Opera omnia*, 26 vols (Paris, 1891–5), 23, pp. 433–45, at p. 441.

[57] For a general account of Ockham's political thought, see my *Political Thought of Ockham*. On the relation of Ockham's political thought to his earlier theological writings see also the concluding section of 'Natural law and moral omnipotence', my contribution to Paul Vincent Spade, ed., *The Cambridge Companion to Ockham* (Cambridge, forthcoming). Some of the texts most relevant to Ockham's break with John XXII and to other points discussed in these paragraphs are translated in *A Letter to the Friars Minor and Other Writings*.

such a way of thinking in a distinctive conception of 'legitimate' doctrinal correction, the second point in Ockham I want to emphasise. Is an *erring* inferior bound to give up his error at the bare rebuke of an orthodox superior? The position most forcefully argued in the *Dialogus* is that an *errans* is obliged to recant only when clearly shown that his error contradicts the rule of faith. This conception of legitimate correction was not infinitely elastic. It was not up to the *errans* to say whether his error had been clearly and sufficiently shown to him. Nevertheless, the requirement for a clear explanation at least removes the ground for alleging culpable obstinacy whenever any authoritative rebuke is resisted. Conversely, on this view erring superiors who are clearly shown that *they* have erred *are* obliged to give up their errors.[58]

Finally, with regard to Ockham, the attempt to disentangle religious and secular institutions, a major theme in his later works, points to a religiously neutral conception of secular politics. For example, in Part III of the *Dialogus*, when discussing the power laymen may have in spiritual matters, Ockham presents the following distinction:

> By *temporalia* may be understood those things that pertain to human government or [the government of] humankind solely as naturally constituted, without any divine revelation, which things would be observed by those who recognized no law beyond natural law and human positive law and on whom no other law was imposed. By *spiritualia* are understood, however, those things that concern the government of believers insofar as they are instructed by divine revelation.[59]

If, as Scotus and Ockham[60] himself had argued, the reality of infused faith is not accessible to natural reason, it would seem that an

[58] A translation by John Kilcullen of the relevant passages from Book 4 of the *Dialogus* is in preparation for the ethics and political philosophy volume of *Cambridge Translations of Medieval Philosophical Texts*, ed. A. S. McGrade, John Kilcullen, and Matthew Kempshall.

[59] *Dialogus*, Part III, Tract II, Book 2, chapter 4, quoted in *Political Thought of Ockham*, p. 134. Complementing the view that temporal government as such does not rightfully have power in religious affairs is Ockham's conception of ecclesiastical government as normally without power in secular affairs. Ockham's most vehement critique of theories attributing authority over all human affairs to the papacy is his *Short Discourse*. Ockham argued on biblical grounds that papalism or curialism was heretical. Given his clearly positive conception of properly understood papal authority, we have some basis for putting his accusation that papalist views were heretical into the traditional framework: curialism chooses for itself a part of the whole faith and therefore distorts that part in making it serve for the whole.

[60] Ockham, *Quodlibetal Questions*, Quodlibet 3, q. 7; trans. Alfred J. Freddoso and Francis E. Kelley, 2 continuously paged vols (New Haven, CT, and London, 1991), pp. 193–4.

institution concerned with naturally constituted humankind would not be qualified to judge whether a violation of infused faith had or had not occurred. A Christian official in a secular institution might then be in the position of believing, as a Christian, that the spiritual crime of *infidelitas* had been committed by this or that individual while not being officially competent to pass judgement. A 'secular arm' so construed would be unable to punish heretics 'relaxed' to it by even a properly functioning ecclesiastical court.[61]

WAS THERE A MEDIEVAL IDEA OF HERESY?

The task of finding a coherent idea of heresy has two levels. On one level the problem is to find a concept that is coherent in purely medieval terms, that fits the reasons medieval persecutors of heretics thought they had for detesting heresy and acting against it, and reasons the persecuted sometimes gave for regarding their attackers in the same light. At a morally deeper level the problem is to find an ethical conception in terms of which we can understand the differing values placed on heresy in medieval and modern times.

As regards the first-level, medieval problem, much of the material presented above supports something like the following. Heresy was thought of as wilful disruption of a saving awareness of God previously shared with others. It involved choice *for oneself*, hence a departure from the common way, but the choice was *self-deceptive*, a personally motivated choice that was not only uncommon but misdirected. Finally, the communal way abandoned by the heretic was cognitive, an awareness of divine reality that permitted and in some measure constituted a fruitful relationship with that reality. Not everything in the preceding survey fits easily into this conception of heresy. Too simple an equation of heresy with defective cognition is especially problematic. There is also room for disagreement as to how the notions

[61] Ockham argues in his last work that an emperor as such (*imperator, inquantum imperator*) ought not to involve himself in spiritual matters. He holds, however, that if the emperor is a believer, then as such (*inquantum fidelis*) he ought to intervene in many spiritual matters, especially cases touching the faith itself, because such cases pertain to absolutely all Christians. *De imperatorum et pontificum potestate*, ch. 12; ed. R. Scholz, *Unbekannte kirchenpolitische Streitschriften aus der Zeit Ludwigs des Bayern (1327–1354)*, 2 vols (Rome, 1911–14), 2, pp. 453–80, at p. 468. See *Political Thought of Ockham*, pp. 102 and 131–3 for discussion of this and related passages.

of choice, self-deception, community, and awareness of divine reality are best spelled out.

In seeking an ethical conception underlying the shift from medieval to modern, we might begin by asking whether anything in liberal pluralist thought corresponds to the medieval idea of heresy, whether there is some idea that might make it easier for liberals to understand medieval attitudes and perhaps at the same time form a basis for liberals' own horror at the persecution of heretics. The common element between the medieval idea of heresy and the liberal analogue, if there is one, would be the deeper ethical conception in terms of which we could understand and assess the historical shifts.

Liberals (as such) do not habitually speak of saving relationships of any kind, let alone cognitively mediated saving relationships with a divine reality. But is it an exaggeration or too simple to suppose that they are committed to the possibility of mutual human understanding as at least part of a saving relationship with whatever reality there may be? In terms of such a commitment, a plausible candidate for liberal analogue to heresy would be wilful obscurantism (or better, wilfully exclusive obscurantism). When, for example, we require the patient's informed consent to a medical procedure, we do not assume that the patient, or even the doctor, must have a clear vision of all that lies ahead, but we demand that whatever clarity is available to anyone should be available to a responsible patient. Similarly, a liberal need not find all forms of belief or value that contain an element of mystery intolerable, but to obscure the fact of mystery when it is present seems unfaithful to the truth of the human predicament, unfaithful in a way that bears some resemblance to the rejection of truth that troubled medieval thinkers. Is there, then, a usefully discernible common element between the demand for clarity I attribute to liberals and the medieval demand for orthodoxy? This is a question for the sort of discussion this paper aims to encourage.

WHAT ARE WE TO MAKE OF HERESY?

R. I. Moore begins and ends *The Formation of a Persecuting Society* by acknowledging that a persecuting mentality is not the only phenomenon of interest in the later Middle Ages. At the end (p. 153) he gives thanks that historians are not required to determine whether 'the great and positive achievements' of the period 'might have taken place' without the development of persecution in all its forms with which in fact they were inseparably associated. Moore's shying away from the question of what might have taken place is, of course, entirely sensible. Discussion of how heretics would have been treated in the fourteenth century if St Augustine had suffered fools more gladly a millennium earlier can hardly be a serious scholarly enterprise. It certainly cannot be a serious enterprise if the goal is to project an alternative to the historical Middle Ages on a global scale. Yet short of capitulating to a degree of determinism for the actions of medieval people that we cannot readily accept for our own actions, it is reasonable to ask whether particular alternatives to particular choices of expression or particular actions were available that might have lessened persecution without endangering the period's achievements. Were there, at various points, live options available to medieval thinkers within their own frames of reference, 'reasonable' alternatives in the sense of this paper, that might have moved things in a different direction? The present exploration is meant to argue that on this more modest scale something like the question of what 'might have taken place' deserves pursuit, if not by historians as historians, then by historians along with others as citizens who have choices to make in relation to religious (or irreligious) uniformity or pluralism.

Consideration of medieval heresy alongside Tierney's 'developments of [medieval] Christian thought that might seem favourable to a growth of religious liberty' could not only promote a better understanding of the impulse to religious uniformity but also provide a basis for testing the developments favouring liberty in an intellectual context where they were neither taken for granted nor dogmatically rejected. Both for the purpose of taking non-liberal ideas with appropriate seriousness and for the purpose of seeing what can be said for more or less liberal values in a world they do not dominate, we may do well to imagine ourselves as contemporaries with our medieval predecessors, assigned to determine with them whether their great and positive achievements might indeed have taken place without the persecution of heresy which we deplore. With regard to the small sample of material considered in this essay it is evident that conceptions of truth and human well-being supporting the persecution of heretics were at the core of medieval Christian thought but that these conceptions shared that central space with other ideas. In the context of medieval thought Paul's assertion that there must *be* heresies, echoed in various tones through the era, cannot be read as granting merit to dissenters for being the loyal opposition in an amiably cooperative joint search for truth, for such a reading trivializes the issues on which religious disputes arose in the Middle Ages and on which they arise in some quarters today. Nevertheless, Paul's dictum (along with his advice to 'test all things and hold fast that which is good' [I Thessalonians 5.21]) does share some content with the idea of theoretical and moral truth as emerging from the clash of opposing advocacies. Similar observations could be made about other ideas we have considered. The views of early councils and refuters of heresy (and proponents of faith), the apostolic ideal, and the ideals of community and virtue of the later Middle Ages – all of these led naturally enough to persecution, none of them can be imported by defensible direct quotation into a modern liberal ideology, but some of them arguably share content with an intelligent liberalism.

The engagement with medieval ideas about heresy I propose is virtually a liberal's dialogue with the Grand Inquisitor, or with the philosophical theologians and their texts that the Grand Inquisitor could cite to justify his proceedings.[62] Going into such a conversation (that is, going into the close interrogation of such texts as those sampled above) liberals might hope to show their imaginary interlocutors that there never were any heretics – that is, that medieval religious dissent had never been of such a kind as to provide good reasons for persecuting it. In this view heretics would have been something like witches and unicorns, imaginary constructions built on phenomena or reports that did not warrant belief in their real existence or, in the case of dissenters, belief in their real wickedness or their real danger to society. The persecution of heretics would then be seen as contrary not only to the original sources of Christian tradition as those sources are generally now understood in the West but contrary also to the understanding of those sources most defensible even on medieval grounds.[63] The material considered above does not rule out such a result, but neither does it suggest an easy road to it. A different result would be discovery that heresy was not irrational as a category and was

[62] Cf. E. Benz's use of Dostoevsky's famous conversation between Christ and the Grand Inquisitor as a source of epigraphs in *Ecclesia spiritualis: Kirchenidee und Geschichtstheologie der franziskanischen Reformation*, 2nd edn (Stuttgart, 1964). At some point liberal theory would need to address the non-inquisitorial but theologically serious concerns of post-medieval but pre-Vatican II Roman Catholic thinkers. See, for example, the article 'Hérésie, Hérétique' by A. Michel in *DTC*, 6, cols. 2208–57.

[63] In this event the proto-liberal developments in the Middle Ages could be regarded as in some sense the authentic ones, and the research of social historians could be used to explain why what reasonably ought to have happened in fact did not happen.

perhaps not even an empty category but that persecution was not, on balance, a reasonable response even in the clearest cases of the category's being occupied. That persecution of heretics was unjustified does not necessarily entail that medieval thinkers were wrong to regard heresy as a real and calamitous possibility for individuals and communities.

The imaginary dialogue I propose could have a bleaker outcome. It could end in the discovery that good faith efforts to achieve a reconciliation of the disparate elements in medieval thought and culture cannot succeed. If this were only a matter of earnest twentieth-century discussants of medieval texts concluding that nothing anyone could have said to an Augustine or an Aquinas would plausibly have been accepted by these saints as reason to tolerate heretics, the world could well survive such a result. There would, however, be the uncomfortable implication that the original sources of Christian tradition may contain enduringly opposed principles regarding toleration and the need for religious uniformity – and the broader implication that corresponding actual dialogues now going on between liberal and non-liberal cultures in the world today must also fail, that liberals and non-liberals must in the end regard one another as caught each in their own species of infidelity. Before we would be entitled to say that such an impasse had been reached, however, liberalism would at least have been required to search for a deeper grounding for its values than liberal theory currently offers. What is needed is a liberalism equivalent in spiritual depth to the positions it must now contend with.[64] Engagement with medieval thought might help to meet this need if, as we must hope, it is a need that can be met.

University of Connecticut

[64] The welcome hints of a 'spiritual' side to a rights-based political theory in Alan Gewirth's *The Community of Rights* (Chicago, 1996) are to be followed up in a section on 'Spirituality as self-transcendent excellence' in *Self-Fulfillment* (Princeton, in press). Ronald Dworkin in his Rudin lectures on 'Politics, commitment, and faith' delivered at Auburn Theological Seminary in October 1996 argues for a liberalism in which it is a central objective value that things 'turn out well' for every individual in society. The medieval period has much of interest to say about objectively good human outcomes.

FELLOWS AND HELPERS: THE RELIGIOUS IDENTITY OF THE FOLLOWERS OF WYCLIF

by JEREMY CATTO

> [The] persecuted Church though it hath bene of longe season trodden under foote by enemies, neglected in the world, nor regarded in histories, & almost scarce visible or knowne to worldly eyes, yet hathe it bene the true Church onely to God . . . continually stirring up from time to time faithfull Ministers, by whome alwayes hath bene kept some sparkes of his true doctrine and religion.[1]

THESE words of John Foxe sum up the sense of loss experienced by early Protestants, borne along by Luther's scriptural Christianity, in the face of their founding fathers' ahistorical vision of a pure apostolic Church followed by centuries of darkness, ignorance, and corruption. Matthias Flacius Illyricus had already tried to bridge the gap with a chain of true believers in his *Magdeburg Centuries*, a history of the Church Invisible to match the work of Eusebius, Bede, Martinus Polonus on its visible institutions; Foxe strove to demonstrate the continuity of witnesses, the 'secret multitude of true professors' who linked the faith of the apostles with that of the reformers. In his perspective the Lollard martyrs of the century before the Reformation played a vital role in the succession, martyrs on whom he had authentic evidence in the court books of fifteenth-century bishops and record of processes against heretics in episcopal registers. Some of his evidence no longer survives, though what he quotes is consonant with the documentation to be found in the extant originals.

In defiance of the scepticism of James Gairdner in 1908 and of K. B. McFarlane in the 1950s, the work of recent scholars sifting the mass of judicial evidence has tended to confirm the assumptions of Foxe. J. A. F. Thomson was able to map the incidence of Lollard communities in parts of England from the time of Wyclif to that of Cranmer, while

[1] John Foxe, *Acts and Monuments* (London, 1570), fol. iii. On a similar 'historical justification of their opposition to the church' by earlier unorthodox thinkers see Leff, *Heresy*, 1, p. 9. This work is the foundation of modern discussions of the context of medieval heresy.

Anne Hudson, in her magisterial study of Wycliffite texts and their readers, has laid out at least one likely line of succession from the founding fathers to the early sixteenth century.[2] If in the period after 1430 the prominence of the individual preacher had faded, the organizing principle was now the community of believers: at London in 1428, in the district of High Wycombe and Amersham in the 1460s, about Tenterden in Kent, in Bristol, and in Coventry, where bishops' inquiries brought them to light, families and groups of friends who professed beliefs similar to those of the early Lollards were now able to sustain them without the help of the itinerant preacher. Their contact with one another is shown by the names of individuals which recur in different places in the records: William Smith of Bristol or James Wyllis of Henley, who are mentioned below, might serve as examples. They were evidently private teachers working in the houses of believers, rather than preachers; smiths and weavers, they can have had little in common with the early Lollard masters with their theological training, even after allowing for the effects of the latter's popularizing efforts. Some of them had books, with a clandestine circulation, and occasionally the scriptures in English. They were aware of earlier Lollard masters, with whom they identified: Wyclif was revered as a saint by many, and William White's martyrdom was remembered, as were those of Sir John Oldcastle, William Sawtry, and William Taylor. Even if they inhabited a significantly different social and intellectual world from that of their predecessors, their continuity with the Lollard past seems assured.[3]

These differences of circumstance must raise the question, for the historian, of the sense of religious identity of the mid-century Lollards. If this was irrelevant to Foxe, who was content with their role in the stream of martyrs, it has been obscured for his successors by the post-Reformation search for religious allegiances. In the quest for pigeon-holes, it has been too easy to apply the terminology used in ecclesiastical courts, in which terms like 'Lollard' or 'heretic' had a

[2] Thomson, *Lollards*; Hudson, *PR*, pp. 144, 446–56; Rob Lutton, 'Connections between Lollards, townsfolk and gentry in Tenterden in the later fifteenth and early sixteenth centuries', and Andrew Hope, 'The lady and the bailiff: Lollardy among the gentry in Yorkist and early Tudor England', both in *Lollardy and Gentry*. Another more speculative line is traced by Hope from the John or FitzLewis descendants of John Montagu, Earl of Salisbury, to William Sweeting who was burnt in 1511.

[3] C. von Nolcken, 'Another kind of saint: a Lollard perception of John Wyclif', *SCH. S*, 5 (1987), pp. 429–43.

legal meaning, as if the witnesses or persons accused would have understood and accepted them as the modern historian understands them. Though contemporary sources freely termed them a sect, it is clear that they meant by this no more than a body of people holding the same opinion. The Lollards of particular localities evidently did not share the characteristics of the ancient sects of the Christian Near East, the Jacobites, Copts, or Nestorians: they did not form any exclusive body intermarrying only within the group (though Bishop Longland suspected that might happen); they did not profess the same trades, nor inhabit a defined quarter within a town. A community of belief or perhaps only of opinion held them together, sharpened not so much by fear of the authorities as by 'dreed of the people' which persuaded them to outer conformity.[4]

Such beliefs might vary considerably. The eccentric view of William Wakeham of Devizes (1434) that the earth was above the sky, or the opinion of John Woodhull of Hereford (1433) that the worst deed of a man is better that the best deed of a woman were in each case combined with more straightforward Lollard beliefs on the Eucharist and other points.[5] Even if the beliefs only of individuals with numerous associations with other suspects are considered, it is easy to detect variety of opinion and emphasis, the natural effect of private judgement. William Fuer of Gloucester abjured his heresies in 1448; he confessed that he had learnt some of his opinions from William Smith, who had given him a book of unorthodox doctrine. James Wyllis, a Bristol weaver who had migrated to Henley, whence he was taken to be examined in 1462, also confessed that he had been taught by William Smith; he had taught numerous disciples in his turn, instilling unorthodox beliefs in Thomas Skryvener of Amersham, the likely father of William Skryvener who was burnt in 1511. Here if anywhere, then, is the 'scarce visible Church' of Foxe to be glimpsed in the record of Lollard confessions. Yet Fuer recognized a priesthood, which was bound to preach and which should abjure music at mass, while Wyllis denied the power of priests to consecrate the Eucharist or to grant absolution (though he had made his own Lenten confession).[6] Most of the points which appear in abjurations relate to religious practices in

[4] Hudson, *PR*, p. 468.

[5] *Registrum Thome Spofford*, ed. A. T. Bannister (*CYS*, 1919), pp. 153–6; Wiltshire Record Office, *Reg. Neville* (Sarum), ii, fols 52r–v, 57v; Thomson, *Lollards*, pp. 31–3.

[6] Worcestershire Record Office, *Reg. Carpenter*, i, fols 58v–59; Lincolnshire Archives Office, *Reg. Chedworth*, fols.57–63; Thomson, *Lollards*, pp. 34, 68–69.

common use, the cult of the Eucharist, the making of confessions, the worship of images, the practice of going on pilgrimage, and so on. Many of these were rejected absolutely as idolatry, while others, the sacraments in particular, tended to be generalized as capable of being performed by the laity, or of being self-administered. It is arguable whether a sceptical attitude of varying intensity to the practices of every parish needed to be taught as a doctrine when parishioners might participate in, neglect, or denounce them with varying degrees of emphasis. This was not a circumstance calculated to encourage solidarity. Such sense of identity as Fuer or Wyllis felt with the Lollard martyrs and teachers must have been at its strongest in the context of practice rather than belief, particularly within a family circle, or among friends, at a session of Bible study.

This is a long way from the totality of group definition characteristic of Christian sectaries in the great conurbations of Asia, and Lollard consciousness must have had to compete with the neighbourhood loyalties of parish and town, often reinforced by membership of religious guilds or among more prosperous citizens by inclusion among town officers or commissions of government. The preaching of William Thorpe, Richard Wych, William Taylor, and Thomas Drayton would give the faith of the mid-century Lollards whatever coherence it had and would transmit to them the books by which they could sustain it. They in turn looked back to the founders of the band, the radical preachers from Oxford, headed by John Wyclif and staffed originally by Nicholas Hereford, John Aston, Philip Repingdon, and other masters. Their own solidarity, clearly distinct from that of Wyllis and his fellows, is also capable of analysis. How they began to act together is not clear, but Wyclif himself seems to have conceived of them as a band of poor preachers or *simplices sacerdotes*, joined in *operacione voluntaria* to preach to the laity his vision of a purified Church of the predestinate faithful.[7] If this was more than a concept, he may have had in mind something like the contemporary fraternity which came together round Gerard Groote about 1380, the Brethren of the Common Life, who specifically rejected any corporate identity based on a religious rule, but acted together in copying and disseminating spiritual texts.[8] Certainly the Wycliffite masters cooperated in

[7] John Wyclif, *Dialogus*, ed. A. W. Pollard (WS, 1886), p. 54; Hudson, *PR*, p. 63.

[8] See in general T. P. van Zijl, *Gerard Groote, Ascetic and Reformer* (Washington, 1963), and K. Elm, 'Die Bruderschaft vom gemeinsamen Leben: ein geistliche Lebensform

compiling the cycle of 294 English sermons, and other texts which they approved, or occasionally improved, to such an extent that a printed edition of all their works has been calculated to fill twenty-five volumes.[9] This literary and publishing enterprise has now been defined with some precision by careful textual work; the bulk of it must have been achieved in the decade after Wyclif's death in 1384. The resulting Lollard library was put to use at once in the preaching tours of numerous masters, whose work in bringing scattered congregations into contact with its moving spirits constituted the nerve-fibres of early Lollardy. Its musculature was the financial and political support given by a number of courtiers who had been in the service of Edward the Black Prince, the Princess of Wales, or John of Gaunt; their close interrelationship, and patronage of the preachers by some of them at least, have been clearly demonstrated.[10] The language of Richard Wych, addressing another supporter fraternally in 1401, or of William Thorpe recalling his relations with Hereford, Repingdon, and others, with whom he was 'ofte homli, and I comownede with them long tyme and fele' indicates the close personal relations on which their work depended.[11] Everything points to a conscious, persevering, and practical group of masters with a coherent programme of action and missionary zeal comparable to that of the thirteenth-century friars. The active sense of identity of such a body cannot have been the same as that of the loose Lollard communities of the later fifteenth century.

Even in their own terms, however, the Wycliffite founding fathers present a paradox. Among the most curious features of the movement was the early defection of its central core. Philip Repingdon, who had been among its three most prominent leaders in the spring of 1382, had been reconciled to the authorities by November; his submission endured, and he enjoyed a distinguished ecclesiastical career. Robert Alington, who had been one of the unorthodox preachers associated with Hereford and Aston at Odiham in that exhilarating spring, probably submitted at the same time. More dramatic was the defection of Nicholas Hereford himself. Having returned from his Roman prison in 1385, he was once more imprisoned at Nottingham in 1387, where

zwischen Kloster und Welt, Mittelalter und Neuzeit', in *Gert Grote en moderne Devotie*, *Ons Geestelijk Erf*, 59 (1985), pp. 470–96.

9 Hudson, 'Some aspects of Lollard book production' in her *Books*, p. 181.

10 K. B. McFarlane, *Lancastrian Kings and Lollard Knights* (Oxford, 1972), part ii.

11 See F. D. Matthew, 'The trial of Richard Wyche', *EHR*, 5 (1890), p. 531; *The Testimony of William Thorpe*, in *Two Wycliffite Texts*, ed. Hudson (*EETS*, 1993), p. 41.

he remained until 1390. During 1390 he may have written the Latin commentary on the Apocalypse, the *Opus Arduum*, which is notable for its fierce partisanship and somewhat triumphalist tone.[12] Whether he did or not, he must have submitted by the end of the year, as Archbishop Courtenay presented him to the living of St Mary in the Marsh on 22 January 1391.[13] Thereafter he participated in proceedings against Lollards in his own Herefordshire country, where he probably lived from 1394, and was said in 1407 to have 'gretter savoure and more delite to holde agens hem than evere he hadde to holde with hem'.[14] Thorpe included with them two other backsliders, John Purvey and Robert Bowland, whom he associated with Repingdon and Hereford. Purvey and probably Bowland had abjured in 1401, and Purvey had been presented to the rectory of West Hythe; but Thorpe described him as 'neythir with you now here [Archbishop Arundel] . . . neithir he holdith feithfulli with the lore that he taughte and wroot biforehande', and he appeared as a partisan of Oldcastle in depositions following the rising of 1414.[15]

John Aston himself repented of his teaching on his deathbed, according to the much later account of William Mede, a Carthusian of Sheen, who identified him with the Lollard priest mentioned by Walsingham (whose *Historia Anglicana* he quoted) to whom Hereford had denied priestly ministrations. Thorpe however maintained that he had kept the Lollard faith 'right perfyghtli vnto his lyves ende'. Mede may have had Aston's name from Hereford himself, on whose own Carthusian end he had some information; but the last days of the great Lollard preacher must remain uncertain.[16]

Thorpe had no doubt why Hereford and the others had fallen away: 'to resceyuen and to haue and holden temperal beneficis, lyuynge now more worldli and fleischly than thei diden biforehonde'.[17] Modern scholars such as Herbert Workman, for whom the backsliders could all

[12] Hudson, 'A neglected Wycliffite text' in *Books*, pp. 43–66; but see her doubts on this identification in *PR*, p. 266, n.189.

[13] *BRUO*, 2, p. 914.

[14] These words of Arundel's clerk are reported in *Testimony of William Thorpe*, pp. 88–9.

[15] Ibid., p. 40, and see Hudson's note, pp. 109–10; M. Jurkowski, 'New light on John Purvey', *EHR*, 110 (1995), pp. 1180–90.

[16] Bodl. MS Bodley 117, the commonplace book of William Mede, fol. 32r–v; see Thomas Walsingham, *Historia Anglicana*, ed. H. T. Riley (*RS*, 1863–4), 2, pp. 159–60. Mede's collection was made some time after 1449. Thorpe's version is given in his *Testimony*, p. 41.

[17] *Testimony of William Thorpe*, p. 89.

be lumped together as broken reeds, have tended to agree. Such evidence as there is on the opinions of ex-Wycliffites, however, indicates that so easy an explanation is inadequate when religious and even reforming aspirations continued to influence them. While the later views of Purvey and Bowland are beyond recovery, there is some evidence for those of Nicholas Hereford. He participated in the trial of Walter Brut at Hereford in 1391–3, for which he was castigated in a letter from a learned though anonymous Wycliffite. The reply recorded in the register of Bishop Trefnant is attributed at the beginning to Thomas Palmer O. P., but at the end is subscribed *per Magistrum Nicholaum Hereford quem spiritus sanctus ab erroribus revocavit.* As the author replied to his opponent in the first person, it seems clear that the text is really Hereford's. It is not in the least defensive; the tone is that of a tried polemicist enjoying the thrust of academic debate: 'I quite properly reconsidered the errors which I would have committed in thought and deed, following the example of the holy doctors Augustine and Thomas Aquinas, both of whom freely retracted [the errors in] the books they had written.'[18] Hereford seems to have been one of the cathedral canons among whom numerous theological books were passed before being incorporated in the library; he was probably one of the small body of residential canons to whom the establishment of the library in 1412 must be due.[19]

At Lincoln the emergence of an organized library was an instrument for the education of the diocesan clergy, and was linked with the recruitment of a corps of learned preachers. There is no evidence for the latter in the Hereford diocese, though some may have been employed; in any case, even though the chapter may have lacked the powerful reforming spirit of Lincoln or Salisbury, its new library represents some effort in the same direction. Furthermore, Nicholas Hereford's entry into the contemplative life of the Carthusians is an early example of its powerful attraction among the fifteenth-century clergy; he was followed by John Digoun, the rector of St Andrew's, Holborn, John Blacman, founding fellow of Eton and the memorialist

[18] *Reg. Trefnant*, pp. 396–401. In the manuscript register (Herefordshire Record Office, Diocesan Register AL 19/7, fols 128v, 129v), the attributions both to Palmer and to Hereford are in the main text hand, but the text was copied from an original in which Palmer's name (hardly, in the circumstances, Hereford's) may have been added inaccurately.

[19] On the building and stocking of the cathedral library, see R. A. B. Mynors and R. M. Thomson, *Catalogue of the Manuscripts of Hereford Cathedral Library* (Cambridge, 1993), pp. xxi–xxii.

of Henry VI, and Thomas Westhaugh, rector of All Hallows the Great, among many others. The work of the Carthusians included the copying and sometimes the translation of books of spirituality such as the *Imitation of Christ* of Thomas Kempis and Gerard of Zutphen's *De Spiritualibus Ascensionibus*, both transcribed by Digoun.[20] If Hereford in his old age was engaged in the same tasks, he must have recalled the similar work of the scriptorium which translated the scriptures, work in which he had himself probably participated.

Robert Alington was equally explicit, and since he was probably subsisting on the meagre allowances of a college fellow when he wrote, there is no reason to question his motives. His determination on images, *De adoracione ymaginum*, was based on a lecture probably given in Oxford between 1382 and 1395; it is a cool workmanlike exercise based on the standard authorities, which only at the end dismisses the opinion of the *ydiotae* who dissuade people from or disapprove of the practice of burning lights before images of the saints. Neither sympathetic nor bitterly polemical, Alington's tone is dismissive, though he doubtless lectured on images because they were an object of widespread controversy. It was not one of the topics on which he had been accused of preaching errors at Odiham in 1382, but the implication of his lecture, seen from the perspective of his earlier activity, is that he had moved on from youthful exaggeration to a more balanced judgement on the matter.[21]

But the most substantial evidence comes from the career and writings of the formidable ex-Wycliffite master Philip Repingdon. He had submitted to the decrees of the Blackfriars Council before November 1382; thereafter his energies and intelligence were focused on a project which, as Simon Forde has shown conclusively, was as evangelical as the Wycliffite sermons, the production of a model sermon-cycle which would be a standard resource for a reformed, dynamic, but orthodox clergy. Working for at least some of the decade after 1382 in Oxford, and living at Queen's where Wyclif and Hereford had resided and where Alington was still a fellow, he wrote at the request of *fidelium sociorum*, 'as a plain man not for other plain men but for sophisticated minds [*a rudi subtilibus*]',

[20] See Roger Lovatt, 'The *Imitation of Christ* in late mediaeval England', *TRHS*, 5th series, 18 (1968), pp. 101–13; and J. I. Catto, 'Theology after Wycliffism', in *Late Med. Oxford*, p. 274.

[21] Alington's *Determinatio de adoracione ymaginum* is in Merton College, Oxford MS 68, fols 32–40; see Hudson, *PR*, p. 92; Catto, 'Wyclif', p. 227.

presumably indicating or at least including the fellows of Queen's. He drew upon the same well of theological learning as the authors of the Wycliffite glossed gospels. The result was a formidably learned if fairly conventional set of model sermons on the Sunday gospels, organized for use by pastors working in parishes or by clergy appointed to preach. On the evidence of his sermon-cycle, Repingdon plainly continued to share with Wyclif and with his former associates an evangelical fervour and a passion to return the clergy to their primary pastoral function. He differed from them in substituting for their ecclesiastical demonology a practical approach to the recognized duties of the clergy. Tithes were justified to pay for preaching; prelates were responsible for the care of the poor. It was up to bishops to see that bad priests did not administer the sacraments, and stronger measures should be taken to prevent them, prelates coming under vigorous criticism for their laziness and greed.[22]

Proposing specific measures for reform had not been one of Wyclif's strong points; a programme for pastoral care could not have been deduced from his writings. Repingdon on the other hand took his functions as bishop of Lincoln seriously, devising and carrying out a scheme for learned preachers throughout his vast diocese. In his sermon-cycle he deliberately restricted himself to setting out the views of the doctors of the Church, and carefully avoided polemic; but a long excursus on the validity of sacraments conferred by bad priests shows that he had Wycliffite arguments in mind. His response to them, an extended and patient series of metaphors and passages from authorities, was consciously unprovocative; the least gentle of his strictures merely observed that 'if they say that the merits of the church do not suffice without the holiness of the [celebrant] priest, then that is ridiculous'.[23] Like Hereford, but more politely, he implied that his views had evolved from the simple-minded propositions of 1382. From their point of view, cherished Wycliffite opinions on images and the invalidity of bad priests' masses were just youthful radicalism, maintained perhaps in the heady atmosphere of university debate, but on sober reconsideration put aside.

[22] Repingdon, *Sermones dominicales*, Corpus Christi College, Oxford MS 54, fols 1, 135–6v; see S. Forde, 'Writings of a reformer: a look at sermon studies and bible studies through Repyngdon's *Sermones super evangelia Dominica*' (Birmingham Ph.D. thesis, 1985), pp. 311–14, 320–25.

[23] Corpus Christi, Oxford MS 54, fol. 212v.

This implied interpretation of past events by former Wycliffites was of course equally as partial as William Thorpe's. Quite apart from the untouched certitudes of John Wyclif himself, the irreconcilable Marcuse of the Lollards, another group of his Oxford supporters, less prominent perhaps in 1382 than Repingdon and Hereford but increasingly pivotal in later years, showed greater fortitude in the cause. This was the Merton circle of William James (first named in unorthodox company in 1382),Thomas Lucas, Richard Whelpington, and John Gamylgay, who were detected in 1395 as unorthodox itinerant preachers. James evidently remained faithful to the cause and active in it from 1382 until 1420, only abjuring it in old age, while Lucas held on long enough to be arraigned as a supporter of Sir John Oldcastle in 1414. They constituted perhaps the core of support in Oxford for an active Wycliffite programme of preaching, to which, by 1406 at the latest, the younger masters William Taylor and Peter Payne of St Edmund Hall would attach themselves.

Even more impressive is the evidence of constancy of purpose and capacity for common action provided by some Lollard literary productions, among which the great English sermon-cycle of 294 sermons stands out. The work shows signs of composition in stages, which were not completed in one of the constituent sets of sermons, and was probably though not certainly a work of cooperation; its inspiration throughout came from Wyclif. Its authors made no attempt to avoid controversial opinions and repeated or developed some of the strongest opinions of the evangelical doctor. The *Floretum,* a Lollard theological dictionary in which passages of the fathers and Wyclif's writings are topically arranged, was an equally learned and provocative work, useful for embattled preachers, and may well have been put together by the same group of scholars as the sermon-cycle. Both productions were disseminated in an apparently deliberate way, and their copying and distribution seems to imply the operation of some kind of scriptorium.[24] This work could not have been achieved without a high sense of identity with a cause on the part of a nucleus of scholars over ten or fifteen years.

It would be natural to identify the body of scholars by whom the

[24] *English Wycliffite Sermons*, ed. A. Hudson and P. Gradon (Oxford, 1979–96), esp. 4, pp. 33–7; Hudson, 'A Lollard compilation and the dissemination of Wycliffite thought' in *Books*, pp. 13–29; C. von Nolcken, *The Middle English Translation of the Rosarium theologie* (Heidelberg, 1979); Catto, 'Wyclif', pp. 222–3.

sermon-cycle was brought to completion with the Oxford Wycliffite masters whom we know to have remained constant and active as itinerant preachers up to 1395: that is, effectively, the Mertonian circle of which William James was probably the leading light. In the present state of knowledge, that must remain uncertain. Its relation with another and contemporary cooperative project equally inspired by Wyclif, the English translation of the Bible and the associated gloss on the gospels, is also rather elusive. From the early 1380s, perhaps earlier, a group of scholars, *diverse felawis and helperis*, acted together in the intricate process of translation; their text passed through several stages, and there was more than one version of a long and scholarly gloss on the gospels taken from the most orthodox authorities. Completed probably by 1395, the English scriptures were highly influential, and gave their wide readership a chance to interpret the text as seemed right to each individual.[25] Their character however is quite distinct from that of the Wycliffite model sermons. The text in its successive versions is strictly uncontroversial in its renderings, and the glossed gospels are entirely derivative from the *Catena Aurea* of Aquinas, supplemented by passages from Augustine, Ambrose, pseudo-Chrysostom, Gregory, Bede, Bernard of Clairvaux, and Robert Grosseteste. The selection and omission of passages in the glossed gospels, it is true, silently outline many of Wyclif's themes, and the author of the General Prologue gave the scriptures a distinctly Lollard direction; but the Prologue was not circulated with most of the extant manuscript texts, which in its absence must have offered virtually nothing which was unacceptable to orthodox but evangelistic clergy. Furthermore, there is little sign of cross-fertilization between the two enterprises. The English renderings of biblical passages in the sermons were independent of any version of the Wycliffite scriptures; and only one hand, probably amateur, of one text of the sermons is found in a fragment of the later version of the Bible translation.[26] The clearest instance of a polemically Lollard stance among the translators, similar to opinions expressed in the sermons, is probably to be found in the

[25] The most recent detailed survey of current scholarship on the English scriptures is Hudson, *PR*, pp. 231–64. On private interpretation of the text see her '"Springing cockel in our clene corn": Lollard preaching in England around 1400', in S. L. Waugh and P. D. Diehl, eds, *Christendom and its Discontents* (Cambridge, 1996), pp. 132–47, cf. p. 145.

[26] *English Wycliffite Sermons*, 3, xcvi, ii, pp. 81–2 (British Library, MS Harley 2396 of the sermons and Gonville and Caius College, Cambridge MS 179/212 of the gospels). On the character of the glossed gospels, see Hudson, *PR*, pp. 256–8.

General Prologue, whose author makes his role as a translator clear. He asserted, for instance that 'couetouse clerkis ben wode bi symonie, eresie and manie othere synnes, and dispisen and stoppen holi writ as myche as thei moun'.[27] But the Prologue's comparative rarity among texts of the English Bible suggests that it represented the opinion of an individual and was not integral to the project as a whole. Even if some individuals contributed to both of these enterprises, it does not appear that the same group of scholars was responsible for the translation of the scriptures and the compilation of the sermons.

The identity of the translators will probably never be known. They were clearly scholars, and may well have worked in Oxford. Such clues as we have to potential participants and supporters point towards the fellows and resident sojourners of Queen's, which had included Wyclif, Nicholas Hereford, John Trevisa, Philip Repingdon (in 1386–7 if not for longer), and Robert Alington, and would include John Sharpe and Richard Ullerston. Wyclif had undoubtedly provided the original inspiration of the project. Hereford is the only individual mentioned by name as a translator in one of the manuscripts; he is also referred to as *N* in another, though that may only be a subsequent if educated guess. John Trevisa, whether or not he had any part in the translation, was an experienced translator, and reflected on its implications; he defended not only the translation of the scriptures but its revision: 'no sinful man doth so well that it ne might do better, ne make so good a translation that he ne might be better'.[28] Richard Ullerston, a younger fellow of Queen's, defended the translation of the Bible in a determination in 1401.[29]

If these are only fugitive clues to some participants in a project which must have involved many more scholars than were available in a small college, it is clear at least that both the issue and the project of translating the scriptures into English were known and discussed there, evidently with approval. The collegiate aspect is important because there is evidence that about 1400 more than one fellow saw Queen's as

[27] General Prologue cap. 15, ed. Hudson, *English Wycliffite Writings* (Cambridge, 1978), p. 67.

[28] On the Wycliffite scriptures see Hudson, *PR*, pp. 238–47. Trevisa's dialogue on translation is most conveniently read in modernized form in A. W. Pollard, *Fifteenth Century Prose and Verse* (repr. New York, 1964), pp. 203–8; cf. p. 207.

[29] Richard Ullerston's *De translacione sacre scripture in vulgare* is in Österreichische Nationalbibliothek MS 4133, fols 195–207v. See Hudson, 'The debate on Bible translation, Oxford 1401', in *Books*, pp. 67–84.

an institution with a distinct intellectual quality. John Sharpe, later the Provost, in a determination *de oracionibus sanctorum* (given in or after 1396), cited the practice of observing anniversaries at Queen's in defence of praying to the saints.[30] Ullerston went further: 'theology and philosophy among the secular masters would long since have ceased in this university of Oxford had not this puny college been founded', he asserted with loyal exaggeration in his *Defensorium dotacionis ecclesie* of 1401.[31] Sharpe defended the valid priesthood of priests in mortal sin, Ullerston the practical benefits of ecclesiastical endowment.[32] Both points echoed the passages in Repingdon's sermons in which he was most dismissive of Wycliffite teaching. Ullerston however had also defended the translation of the scriptures. It is a reasonable inference that Repingdon in the 1380s, living at least in part in Queen's and engaged in the compilation of his model sermons, was associated with a group of scholars who were familiar with, approved, and some of whom may have participated in, the project of translating the Bible into English.

The opinions expressed by the fellows and sojourners of Queen's must have distanced them progressively, despite their common origin, from the aims and beliefs of the Merton group round William James, which continued to maintain and develop Wyclif's more controversial teaching and to propagate it though the work of itinerant preachers. Both tendencies developed among masters who generally retained their respect for Wyclif's logic and some sympathy with his views on clerical endowments. The surviving notebook of an arts student, compiled about 1400, contains the notes of more than one bachelor of arts of which the common thread is an interest in Wyclif's philosophical realism, and one item of which is a strong refutation of his ideas. Thomas Moston's entries in his notebook about ten years later show that the power of the master's philosophy had not by then diminished. Peter Partridge, Richard Fleming, and Thomas Netter, who in their maturity were active in resisting his partisans, had felt in their youth the attraction of his powerful mind.[33]

[30] John Sharpe, *De oracionibus sanctorum*, Merton College, Oxford MS 175, fols 257–69; cf. fol. 267v.

[31] *Defensorium dotacionis ecclesie*, British Library, Lansdowne MS 409, fols 39–68; cf. fol. 64.

[32] Sharpe in Merton College, Oxford MS 175, fol. 261v; Ullerston throughout his *Defensorium*.

[33] The arts student's notebook is Corpus Christi College, Oxford MS 116; Thomas Moston's is Magdalen College, Oxford MS lat. 92. Cf. J. A. Robson, *Wyclif and the Oxford Schools* (Cambridge, 1961), pp. 224–31; Catto, 'Wyclif', pp. 220, 241, 243–4.

The legacy of Wyclif's ideas on his Oxford associates was, therefore, notably more complex than can be summed up in the notion of a Wycliffite party. His impact on the fellows of Queen's was considerable; they were keen to acquire his works for their library, and quoted him with respect. If they politely and sometimes only implicitly dissociated themselves from some of his ideas, they took up his call for reform of the clergy, and in the hands of Richard Ullerston transformed it into a plan for action which was championed by Robert Hallum, the reforming bishop of Salisbury, and placed before the Council of Pisa. In the concordat of 1418 and more generally during Henry Chichele's rule at Canterbury, the orthodox but reforming programme became the model of good practice in the English church.[34] One item of Ullerston's prescription for evangelical orthodoxy, the vernacular or Wycliffite version of the scriptures, disappeared from his programme after unauthorized translations were prohibited by Archbishop Arundel in 1407 and 1409; but even if Wyclif's name was disparaged increasingly as an heresiarch during the early fifteenth century, his responsibility for the original impulse from which the mainstream reforming ideology of Henry V's bishops derived is difficult to deny.

Behind the preachers, giving them sustenance and support, modern scholarship has discerned a group of 'Lollard knights', courtiers for the most part in the service of the Black Prince, Joan princess of Wales, and Richard II. Their coherence as a group of friends was noticed by Thomas Walsingham and Henry Knighton, and their common experience in war and service has been firmly established by McFarlane. To what extent they shared a religious identity, however, is no clearer than it is for the scholars and thinkers who followed Wyclif. They were clearly identified as a group in the public consciousness, as the two chroniclers witness: the support they gave to the Lollard preachers, as these hostile witnesses alleged, can hardly have been a secret in the 1380s.[35] But the evidence of their backing for

[34] See Catto, 'Wyclif', pp. 238–41, 245–6, 256–60, and 'Religious change under Henry V', in G. L. Harriss, ed., *Henry V: the Practice of Kingship* (Oxford, 1985), pp. 103–6.

[35] See McFarlane, *Lancastrian Kings and Lollard Knights*, pp. 148–9, citing Walsingham, *Historia Anglicana*, 2, pp. 159 and 216 and Knighton, p. 294. Walsingham's more reliable list included Sir Lewis Clifford, Sir Richard Stury, Sir Thomas Latimer, Sir William Neville, Sir John Clanvowe, and Sir John Montagu later earl of Salisbury, with Sir John Cheyne as an afterthought. Closely associated with them were Sir William Beauchamp and Sir Philip de la Vache (*Lancastrian Kings*, p. 171); further research by Charles Knightly has identified other

known Wycliffites, the offence of which the chroniclers complained, is much stronger in the case of some than of others: Sir Thomas Latimer prevented opposition to John Wodard's preaching in 1388 and promoted Robert Hook to a living before 1401; William Neville wrote in support of Nicholas Hereford in 1387, and had him transferred to his own benevolent custody; John Montagu, as we have seen, was entertaining Hereford and perhaps Aston at Shenley, evidently in 1386.[36] Sir Lewis Clifford, further, was reported by Walsingham to have abjured his opinions and informed on his associates in 1402.[37]

Latimer and Montagu were the only knights for whom there is direct evidence of support for Lollard preachers; Sir William Nevill's petition for the custody of Nicholas Hereford, in which he promised to prevent him propagating anything contrary to the Church's faith, is consistent with a more neutral attitude. The mutual association of the others in military and diplomatic business and in their private affairs need not imply that they all shared the same religious standpoint, in an age of independent thinking about and practice of a personal faith. Only two further pieces of positive evidence have been brought forward which might implicate others in a conscious Lollard group: the tract of Sir John Clanvowe, *The Two Ways*, and the language of the wills of Latimer, Clifford, and Sir John Cheyne. It will be argued below that neither the tract nor the wills support that conclusion.

The first piece of evidence is much the weakest for this purpose. *The Two Ways* is a brief moral tract preserved among the collection of moral and meditative works made by William Counter, rector of Pirton and probably a clerk of Clanvowe's friend Sir William Beauchamp, and fragmentarily in the Simeon manuscript, the great library of devotional literature which may have belonged to Joan, countess of Hereford.[38] The author urged his readers to choose the

probable patrons, notably in Herefordshire, who were not chamber knights ('The early Lollards: a survey of popular Lollard activity in England, 1382–1428' [York D. Phil. thesis, 1975], pp. 178–99).

36 McFarlane, *Lancastrian Kings and Lollard Knights*, pp. 168, 193–6, 198–9.

37 Walsingham, *Historia Anglicana*, 2, p. 253.

38 University College, Oxford MS 97, fols. 114r–123v; British Library Additional MS 22283, fol. 116r; ed. V. J. Scattergood, *The Works of Sir John Clanvowe* (Cambridge, 1975), pp. 57–80. On the first manuscript see E. Wilson, 'A critical text with commentary of MS Eng. Th. f.39 in the Bodleian Library' (Oxford B. Litt. thesis, 1968), 2, pp. 30–8. For McFarlane's view see *Lancastrian Kings and Lollard Knights*, pp. 199–206; see also Catto, 'Sir William Beauchamp between chivalry and Lollardy', in *The Ideals and Practice of Mediaeval Knighthood*, 3, ed. C. Harper-Bill and R. Harvey (Woodbridge, 1990), pp. 39–48.

narrow path of God's service, for which they would be reviled by the world. He briefly expounded on the ten commandments, and on the commandments to love God and neighbour with reflections on the nativity and the crucifixion. His hard words for the sins of soldiers, his observation that the world rewarded sinners with the name of *goode felawes*, and perhaps his warning that those who follow the path of righteousness must expect to be called 'lolleris and loselis', might be taken as typical of Lollard sentiment; but the devastation of war might be expected to be on the conscience of any serving knight, while the unpleasantness of being labelled a Lollard, if that is what 'lolleris' implies, was a fate he would share with so orthodox a *dévote* as Margery Kempe. McFarlane implied that the words which follow, 'Recce we neuer though the world scoorne vs or hoolde vs wrecches . . . and, therfore, folewe we [Christ's] traaces and suffre we paciently the scoornes of the world', identified the author with *lolleris*; but it is clear throughout that *we* refers simply to the generality of sinners and not to a select band of true worshippers.[39]

The silent omission of any reference to the Church or the sacraments is a characteristic of the genre, found in other tracts in Counter's collection, including Richard Rolle's eminently orthodox *Form of Living*. There is little in Clanvowe's tract which is more than a fairly conventional personal opinion, according it is true with the sentiments of numerous Lollard tracts, but equally consonant with its companions in Counter's collection, exhortations to a better life by way of private meditation. By itself, it can hardly be used to convict Clanvowe, who died crusading shortly afterwards, of more than a vocal conscience.

The 'Lollard will' has had a distinguished innings since McFarlane identified it, but as an identity card for Lollards it too rests on weak foundations. He found three characteristics shared between the wills of Latimer, Clifford, and Cheyne: extravagant emphasis upon the testator's unworthiness, contemptuous language about their bodies, and strict injunctions against funeral pomp, combined with the use of the English language at an unusually early date.[40] These features are

[39] *Two Ways*, 70, ll.511–12; 72, ll.577, 603; 70, ll.520–1, 525–7; *The Book of Margery Kempe*, ed. S. B. Meech and H. E. Allen (*EETS*, 1940), p. 28.

[40] McFarlane, *Lancastrian Kings and Lollard Knights*, pp. 209–10. Latimer's will is printed in *The Ancestor*, 10 (1904), pp. 19–20; Clifford's in W. Dugdale, *The Baronage of England* (London, 1675–6), 1, pp. 341–2, and see N. H. Nicolas, *Testamenta Vetusta* (London, 1826), 1,

certainly striking. They express within the concise form of a legal instrument a penitential rhetoric which was gradually gathering force in devotional tracts and sermons in the popular or 'ancient' mode. Just for that reason, they are far from characteristic of the Lollards.

The earliest will of this type identified by McFarlane was that of Sir Robert Folkingham, treasurer of Calais, and therefore a former associate of its quondam captain, Sir William Beauchamp. It is dated 6 July 1399, and is preserved in William Counter's collection: Counter was one of the executors. The will is drawn up in English, a fairly new phenomenon: 'I by quethe my wrecchyd synful body to beryen heere in erthe abydyng the dredful doom of God in suche place and manere as it liketh to his wyse endeles purveaunce.' With torches to burn at the elevation of the sacrament and a thousand masses for his soul, there is nothing to indicate that Folkingham was a Lollard sympathizer. But its context in Counter's miscellany of devotional texts helps to explain the origin of its high-flown terminology. Its language is derived wholesale from the tracts which Counter copied for his own devotional use: from the exclamation of the English version of *Speculum Peccatoris*, 'thow proude flesch, thow vile careyne, bee soore a-dred!', described as 'this stynkynge wrecche' in an anonymous meditation, and 'wrecched careyne' in *The Three Arows*.[41] The most obvious explanation is that William Counter himself, apparently the only priest among the executors and probably Folkingham's confessor, drew up the will, using the language of personal repentance in which he was steeped, and preserved the text as a modest effort of his own after the fashion of his devotional library. The language of Richard Rolle and his followers, not that of specifically Lollard literature, is the well from which the extravagant rhetoric of Latimer's, Clifford's, and Cheyne's wills was drawn.

Moreover the 'Lollard will' does not fall into a separable category. Those of the three knights may well imply a spirituality which they had in common; but several characteristic features, as McFarlane noted,

pp. 164–5. Cheyne's is in Lambeth Palace, Reg. Arundel, fol. 203v. On Lollard wills see also J. A. F. Thomson, 'Knightly piety and the margins of Lollardy', in *Lollardy and Gentry*, pp. 95–111, where McFarlane's view of the will as evidence of Lollardy is refined and modified.

[41] Folkingham's will is in University College, Oxford MS 97, fols 170–1; see C. Horstmann, *Yorkshire Writers: Richard Rolle of Hampole and his Followers* (London, 1895–6), 2, pp. 448–9. See also University College, Oxford MS fos 130v, 154, 159v and Horstmann, *Yorkshire Writers*, 2, pp. 439, 443, 446. Cf. McFarlane, *Lancastrian Kings and Lollard Knights*, pp. 213–14.

appear in other wills. The use of the English language is not a reliable guide to radical religious opinions: it was the instrument of perhaps seven London citizens whose wills were proved in the Canterbury Prerogative Court between 1387 and 1413, none of whom showed any other sign of unorthodoxy.[42] It may have accompanied a strong personal religion among the gentry: in 1395 Alice, widow of Sir Thomas West of Hinton, Hampshire directed that she should be buried 'privelich, and with right litel cost' at Christchurch, and left a number of Latin, English, and French books, which may have been devotional, to her daughter (or daughter-in-law) Joan; while Sir Thomas Walwyn of Much Marcle, Herefordshire, left bequests in 1415 to 'helpe nedy men oute of pryson'. His funeral was to be held 'with oute pompe, whyche may not profyt myn soule'.[43] He was the man of business of Sir William Beauchamp, Lord Bergavenny, and was therefore associated with a supposed fellow-traveller of the Lollard knights; but while Beauchamp himself made an English will in 1408, he omitted any of the penitential rhetoric employed by Latimer and Clifford, and directed that he be interred in the Hereford Blackfriars; he had been an early devotee of the cult of the Holy Name.[44] The cases of the elder and the younger Sir Thomas Brooke of Holditch are also instructive. The elder had made a marriage alliance for his son with Sir John Oldcastle, Lord Cobham, in 1410; the son, the younger Sir Thomas, was implicated with Oldcastle in the Lollard rising of 1414, and briefly imprisoned. In the English will of the elder, made in 1415, he referred to his 'wreched unclene soule' and made substantial bequests for the poor, but the repeated motif of threes showed his personal devotion to the Trinity; that of the younger (1439) exhibited many of the same themes, without the trinitarian emphasis.[45]

It follows that neither the use of the English language in wills nor the resort to vivid images of corruption and death can be reliable marks of a Lollard religious identity. The wills of some individuals closely implicated with the knights named by Walsingham lack them;

[42] *The Fifty Earliest English Wills in the Court of Probate, London, 1387–1439*, ed. F. J. Furnivall (*EETS*, lxxviii, 1882), pp. 1–3, 10–17, 21–2.

[43] Ibid., pp. 4–10, 22–6.

[44] Lambeth Palace, Reg. Arundel fol. 155v-156; *Testamenta Vetusta*, 1, p. 171; Catto, 'Sir William Beauchamp', p. 42.

[45] *Fifty Earliest Wills, pp.* 26–8, 129–31; McFarlane, *Lancastrian Kings and Lollard Knights*, p. 216, and *The House of Commons, 1386–1421*, ed. J. S. Roskell, Linda Clark, and Carole Rawcliffe (Stroud, 1992), 2, pp. 375–9 (articles by Roskell, R. W. Dunning and L. S. Woodger).

those of others who had no connection with them have some of the suspect features. It is true, and must be significant, that the three knights with extant wills have all those features, but all it may show is that they or their chaplains had absorbed devotional tracts on the fate of sinners like *The Three Arows*; if William Counter had modelled the will of Robert Folkingham on the examples in his collection, it is likely that Sir Lewis Clifford's 'book of tribulation' as well as Perryne Lady Clanvowe's *Pore Caitif* could provide similar suitable language.[46] Richard Rolle's works or similar literature are the likely inspiration of the terms of Archbishop Arundel's will, which McFarlane found inexplicable: if he shared a contempt of *fetidum et putridum cadaver meum* with Sir John Cheyne, he was at least as well read as the veteran diplomat in its model, the works of Rolle and his followers, which had been disseminated by his circle at York in the 1390s.[47] Some knights at least had championed the Lollard preachers; but the evidence of it refers to the late 1380s. All our later information shows is that they favoured clergy who were suspected by the authorities and who possessed works of Wyclif, that some of them were influenced by well-known devotional tracts, and that one, Clifford, may have repented his unorthodox leanings. The knights' independent spirits may not have professed any particular religious allegiance; friends who shared a cultural milieu, they made their own peace with their consciences without reference either to one another or to any clear and exigent authority. It is not surprising if, on their deathbeds, their personal religion was not very different from that of Alice West, or Thomas Arundel himself.

The notion of religious allegiance, so natural to historians since the division of the Protestant churches, has been the concealed bedrock of debate about who was or was not Lollard in the foregoing centuries. It has only to be uncovered to raise suspicion that it is an anachronism. Some consciousness of belonging to a Wycliffite or Lollard group must be allowed, for instance to William Thorpe, recalling how he 'comowned with' the Wycliffite founding fathers, or to Sir John Oldcastle expressing solidarity with his Bohemian counterparts in

[46] See Dugdale, *Baronage of England*, 1, pp. 341–2; Lady Clanvowe's will is in *Fifty Earliest Wills*, pp. 49–51. Clifford's book might conceivably be *The xii prophetis and avauntegis of tribulacion*, ed. Horstmann, *Yorkshire Writers*, 2, pp. 389–406.

[47] Arundel's will is in *Sede Vacante Wills*, ed. C. E. Woodruff (Kent Archaeological Society, Records Branch v, 1914), pp. 81–2. On Arundel's circle and Rolle see Jonathan Hughes, *Pastors and Visionaries* (Woodbridge, 1988), pp. 203–4.

1410. Like other forms of consciousness it must have fluctuated, and was clearly subject to development; it need not have been continuous. The Lollard movement at its narrowest definition might in 1400 have only consisted of preachers like William James, Richard Wych, and William Thorpe; at its broadest, it might have encompassed all kinds of sympathizers and reformers, including ex-Lollard preachers such as Repingdon, whose continuing social connection with the Latimer family seems to be implied by his appointment as an overseer, with the suspect Lollard priest Robert Hook, of Lady Latimer's will.[48] If, in that sense, the term is effectively meaningless, it might serve to draw attention to the wider consequences for religion in England of Wyclif's call for reform. Among his legitimate heirs, but presumably innocent of any sectarian solidarity, were the former Wycliffites of Queen's, the nursery of the orthodox reformers round Robert Hallum in the years leading up to the Council of Constance; Richard Ullerston, one of the delegates at the Council of Pisa in 1409, drew up a reform programme, the *Petitiones quoad reformationem ecclesie militantis*, more far-reaching than any other proposal before the council; his colleague Robert Stonham brought a copy of Wyclif's *Responsio ad decem questiones* with him.[49] Another obvious legacy was the English Bible, of which upwards of two hundred and thirty manuscripts survive. Some of their owners at least, such as the London Charterhouse (by gift of Henry VI), Syon Abbey, the Shrewsbury Franciscans, and the nuns of Barking Abbey were in the mainstream of orthodox religious practice, and however suspect they might have been in the abstract to the bishops' officers, in practice their unexceptionable text must have stimulated thought and private reflection among the unimpeachably catholic.[50] Even the more obviously polemical and unorthodox English Wycliffite sermons had their effect on the evangelization of the people at large by preachers of independent mind and a more or less orthodox and reforming standpoint; a complex and multiform body of derivative sermons, expurgating, revising, and rewriting material from the sermons is only beginning to be unravelled.[51] The reception of

[48] See *The Ancestor*, 10 (1904), p. 21, dated 13 July 1402.

[49] Ullerston's *Petitiones* are ed. H. von der Hardt, *Magnum Oecumenicum Constantiense Concilium* (Frankfurt and Leipzig, 1697–1700), 1, pp. 1126–71. On Stonham see *BRUO*, 3, pp. 1789–90. I am grateful to Professor Hudson for clarification of the Wyclif text in Stonham's possession.

[50] Hudson, *PR*, pp. 233–4.

[51] See *English Wycliffite Sermons*, 1, pp. 98–123; Helen Spencer, *English Preaching in the late Middle Ages* (Oxford, 1993), pp. 278–310.

Wyclif's ideas, therefore, should no more be constricted within a Wycliffite school than the reception of the thought of Duns Scotus or William of Ockham within a narrow 'Scotism' or 'Ockhamism'; they were absorbed by independent scholars and theologians, and indeed by an educated laity with an increasingly individual religious personality, who developed, modified, misunderstood, and reacted against them in their own way.[52] One version may have passed through preachers and teachers like William White into a 'scarce visible' body of believers, surviving in an enclosed space up to the Reformation; but they also flourished in the fresh air of free discussion, commanding respect in 'a numerous and distinguished company' of reformers on both sides of the channel to whom the task of *reformatio ecclesiae*, in the years after the Schism, would fall.[53]

Oriel College, Oxford

[52] On Scotism and Ockhamism see W. J. Courtenay, *Schools and Scholars in Fourteenth-Century England* (Princeton, NJ, 1987), pp. 178–92.

[53] Leff, *Heresy*, 2, p. 444.

WERE THE LOLLARDS A SECT?*

by MARGARET ASTON

Unde, completo parliamento, Willelmus Cantuariensis firma ecclesiae columna, suos suffraganeos convocavit, . . . ut deliberarent de certis conclusionibus hereticis, quas Wycclyff et illa secta quae dicitur Lollardorum praedicaverant.

Fasciculi Zizaniorum

Ecce novam sectam mittit que plebis in aures
Ad fidei dampnum scandala plura canit.

John Gower, 1396–7

For thre sectis fyghton here agenys cristene mennys secte . . .

Wycliffite sermon[1]

HISTORIANS should not need Wyclif to alert them to the dangers of words. Even if our professional futures are unlikely to be threatened, as his was, by the challenging of accepted terms, the words we use can lead us into false positions, and we sometimes need, like Wyclif, to probe the historical dimension of our terminology. What exactly do we mean when we call Wycliffites or Lollards a 'sect'? How does our word relate to contemporary usage? Do we import alien interpretations by failure to recognize semantic change? If 'sect' is a word that leads us into something of an impasse, this paper does not attempt the impossible of pointing to a way out; my aim is merely to indicate some of the hazards of the linguistic terrain and to suggest that looking at the term may itself tell us something useful about Wycliffites and contemporary attitudes towards them.

Deeper knowledge of Lollardy enlarges our hesitancies. It is easier now than it once was to see the need to beware of post-Reformation prejudice. 'Sect' necessarily carries overtones of Reformation history,

* I am most grateful to Penn Szittya for his helpful comments and suggestions on this paper, and to Barrie Dobson for answering questions and giving advice.

[1] *Fasciculi Zizaniorum*, ed. W. W. Shirley (*RS*, London, 1858), p. 272; *The Complete Works of John Gower*, ed. G. C. Macaulay, 4 vols (Oxford, 1899–1902), 4, p. 347, ll. 30–1; *EWS*, ed. Anne Hudson and Pamela Gradon, 5 vols (Oxford, 1983–96), 2, p. 64.

witness its recent definition as 'a dissenting or breakaway religious body'.[2] Using it, we start with a concept of separation, which is itself prejudicial to understanding a movement the precise nature of whose dissent is the very heart of investigators' interest. During the past generation, historical judgements of Lollardy have undergone considerable alteration. It has come to be recognized that heresy was a malleable concept, subject to changing historical situations, and something about which contemporaries might themselves be unclear. Historians who once saw orthodoxy and heresy more or less in terms of white and black are now more keenly aware of the varying shades of greyness in contemporary religion. John Thomson, who in 1965 wrote 'one must not deny that the Lollards are entitled to be considered as a sect', made clear twenty-five years later the breadth of this grey zone, 'the narrowness of the margin between orthodoxy and dissent'. 'One cannot think of the Lollards adhering to a precise set of sectarian doctrines, comparable to the confessional outlook which developed in the sixteenth century. . . . Even though they are described as a sect in various writings of the 1390s . . . this does not prove that unity of belief existed among all Lollards.' The evidence of textual production shows among the Wycliffites 'a group of dedicated men pursuing a common aim'.[3] That, however, is not necessarily the same as a sect, or even a heresy. Perhaps an examination of contemporary employment of the term 'sect' may itself enable us to think more clearly about what it was that particularly worried opponents of the Wycliffites, and whether there was anything in their behaviour that entitles us to think in terms of 'the sectarian character of the Lollard movement'.[4]

'Sect', *secta*, is a term full of pitfalls which we all fall into, since it has become a word we cannot do without. The problem – simultaneously semantic and historiographic – is recognized and illustrated by Anne Hudson's pages in *The Premature Reformation* on 'Lollardy: a self-conscious sect?' She immediately points to the terminological trap. 'I have tried to avoid terms that assume an answer to the question, using

[2] *Longman Dictionary of the English Language* (new edn, Harlow, 1991), p. 1456.

[3] Thomson, *Lollards*, p. 239; idem, 'Orthodox religion and the origins of Lollardy', *History*, 74 (1989), pp. 39–55, at pp. 41, 48–50; see also p. 53: 'The development of sectarianism was probably a reaction to the increased level of persecution from the accession of Henry IV onwards.' In addition to the above see now the same author's 'Knightly Piety and the Margins of Lollardy', in *Lollardy and Gentry*, pp. 95–111.

[4] I. B. Horst, *The Radical Brethren: Anabaptism and the English Reformation to 1558* (Nieuwkoop, 1972), p. 58.

the neutral word "group" to the exclusion of the more loaded terms "sect", "conventicle", or "congregation".' But (and there is no blame here, for we are all offenders in this respect) the word 'sect' is back in use before this discussion is over.[5] We cannot exclude it from our vocabulary, though Gordon Leff accomplished the feat of writing a whole chapter on the Lollards with only one mention of the word.[6] What we need is some clearer sense of just what the load implied by these terms was at the time.

One thing we can be sure of at the start is that 'sect' carries for us a semantic freight very different from what it bore for Wyclif and his contemporaries. If the word was something of an omnium-gatherum – as a glance at the dictionary, medieval Latin or English, shows – a central aspect of such an enquiry must be to ascertain what it gathered through associations with Lollards. We may do well to listen to David Loades's warning words about the sectarianism of the Reformation, which so indelibly affected the concept – taking it beyond and outside heresy and deviance. 'It seems to me that those scholars who have recently explored the early history of religious dissidence in England have made their own task more difficult by not distinguishing with sufficient clarity between nonconformity, separatism and sectarianism.'[7] Have we not made our task more difficult by thinking in terms that are perhaps not applicable to our period?

In pre-Wycliffite England sect/*secta* was a neutral word, with as many or more secular than religious usages. It did indeed have a context related to religious belief, but this was not one which would have been commonly familiar. Inviting derivation respectively from the Latin verbs 'to follow' or 'to cut',[8] its variousness is reflected in its different applications as 'suit'; suit of court'; suits of clothing; suites of followers. There were the several legal suits of different courts, as well as hue and cry – *secta hutesii*, the following of clamour, outcry.

[5] Hudson, *PR*, pp. 168–73, at pp. 169, 172: 'opponents . . . piled upon the whole sect all the insults they could imagine.'

[6] Leff, *Heresy*, pp. 559–605; p. 590: 'For its part, Lollardy became a clandestine sect, its leaders driven into hiding and its adherents formed into conventicles and small groups.'

[7] David Loades, *Politics, Censorship and the English Reformation* (London and New York, 1991), p. 182. Diarmaid MacCulloch, *The Later Reformation in England 1547–1603* (London, 1990), pp. 154–5, considers how these distinctions apply to Lollardy, pointing out the need to distinguish between non-conformity and Nonconformity.

[8] The word could be seen to be derived either from *sequor*, to follow (whence *sectatores*, followers) or from *seco*, to cut (whence *sectio*, cutting).

Sartorially there were suits of livery, the uniform garments that distinguished ordered groups of people such as archers or foot soldiers, dressed for action by royal command (in *una secta*, or *de una secta vestiti*).[9] More conspicuous suits of this kind were those of courtly fashion, a scandalous example of which, provoking much gossip, was presented in 1348 by the exhibitionist troupes of sexy young women rumoured to be turning up at tournaments wearing party-coloured male dress (hoods and belted tunics) declaratory of their support – one suit for one side and another for the other.[10] Suits and suites here brought together the sartorial and social, for liveried groups of followers posed their own problems and were the subject of legislation. It was not only lordly liveries that could be dangerous. In the context of the rising of 1381, one of the grounds for suspicion of a band of malefactors and disturbers of the peace in Scarborough was the white hoods with red liripipes (tippets) which they wore. It was thought that an illicit confederation bound together those sporting this garb – 'a certain livery of one suit (*de unica secta*)' – but the words used for their suspect association (words with their own history of reproach) were 'conventicles and congregations'.[11]

Though a 'suited' company might sometimes call suits into question, companies of people, or those of a certain category, were called sects without any opprobrium at all. Witness here the wish expressed at the end of Chaucer's *Clerk's Tale* 'for the Wyves love of Bathe – / Whos lyf and al hire secte God mayntene / In heigh maistrie'.[12] A sect in this sense was something more like a set. Elsewhere Chaucer referring to Josephus and the Jews, and Trevisa to Mahomet and the Saracens, employ 'sect' to describe a religion other than the Christian, which was probably the most common religious

[9] T. Rymer, *Foedera, Conventiones, Litterae* (London, 1816–33), 2, pt. 1, pp. 481–2, 2, pt 2, p. 1016.

[10] Knighton, pp. 92–5. I differ from this translation in thinking that the passage, which seems ambiguous, describes different suits for different sides. The episode is reported as hearsay – 'rumor populi'.

[11] A. Réville, *Le Soulèvement des travailleurs d'Angleterre en 1381* (Paris, 1989), p. 257. On conventicles see below at nn. 39–40 and 85–6.

[12] *The Clerk's Tale*, ll. 1170–2; *The Poetical Works of Chaucer*, ed. F. N. Robinson (Cambridge, MA, n.d.), p. 137. For comments on this passage see Ruth Evans and Lesley Johnson, eds., *Feminist Readings in Middle English Literature: The Wife of Bath and All her Sect* (London and New York, 1994), pp. 2–4 and notes 4–5, p. 19. Considerable commentary has become attached to this passage (one of a handful in which Chaucer uses the word 'secte') and the new *OED* has canonized the reading of 'sex', which was not that adopted by the *Middle English Dictionary*.

connotation of this word in the vernacular for most of the fourteenth century.[13]

It is of course in the Latin *secta* that the religious implications of the word must be pursued. If we take the Vulgate as a starting-point, *secta* at once leads to heresy, with which it is synonymous. All examples but one of the word are in the New Testament, and in six out of these seven passages the Latin *secta* is a translation of the Greek *haeresis*.[14] *Haeresis*, as plenty of good sources pointed out, meant simply 'choice', and in classical Latin *secta* held the meaning of the chosen path of a particular school of thought, such as that of the Stoics. This neutrality of the term is still evident in the Theodosian Code. There, the late fourth- and early fifth-century sources relating to heresy apply *secta* equally to those who were hostile to the faith and to the faithful: on one hand to Eunomians, Arians, Donatists, and Manicheans who departed from Catholic faith and observance, and on the other to the *catholica secta* or *orthodoxa secta*, the 'venerable sect of the orthodox'.[15]

A *locus classicus* was in Isidore of Seville's *Etymologies*. The 'choice' of *haeresis* is here related not only to the schools of Peripatetics, Epicureans, and Stoics, but also to Donatists, Arians, Priscillianists, Pelagians, and Nestorians. Sects formed by those following (*sequendo*) and adhering to certain leaders were defined as 'a habit of spirits . . . formed around a discipline or a proposal, holding to which they follow along, holding to different opinions from others in the cult of religion'. This interpretation explained the schismatic nature of those heretics 'who depart from the Church, and are known by the name of their author . . . And while they are not in agreement with one another, being divided by many errors, it is with one name that they conspire against the Church.'[16] In Christian thought choice and the following of

[13] *Polychronicon Ranulphi Higden . . . with the English Translations of John Trevisa*, ed. C. Babington, 9 vols (*RS*, 1865–86), 1, p. 129; *Poetical Works of Chaucer*, ed. Robinson, p. 346, 'The House of Fame', ll. 1432–4.

[14] F. P. Dutripon, *Concordantiae Bibliorum Sacrorum Vulgatae editionis* (Paris, 1844), s.n. *Secta*. Acts 24.5,14; 26.5; 28.22; Gal. 5.20; II Pet. 2.1,10 (the last being the exception in the Greek). In the AV 'sect' appears also in Acts 5.17; 15.5 and I Cor. 11.19 where the Vulgate has *haeresis*.

[15] *Theodosiani Libri XVI cum constitutionibus Sirmondianis*, ed. P. Krüger and T. Mommsen, 2 vols (Berlin, 1905), 1 (2), XVI:5:12, 25, 41–2, 44, 57, 64, 66, 'De Haereticis', pp. 859–60, 863–4, 868–9, 870, 875, 878, 879–80. My thanks to Penn Szittya for directing me to this source.

[16] *Isidori Hispalensis Episcopi Etymologiarum sive Originum*, ed. W. M. Lindsay, 2 vols

individual leaders became more challenging, and implied a turning away from established truths.

Yet later authors, returning as they did to Isidore, concentrated attention not on the separatist tendencies of heretical sects, but on their scriptural infidelity. When Grosseteste said that 'heresy in its Greek etymology means "choice": it is a choice made for human ends, contrary to Holy Scripture, openly declared and stubbornly maintained',[17] he had behind him the authority of Augustine and Isidore of Seville. The latter had made clear the association of heresy with wilful choice, since it was not permitted to believe anything on the basis of individual will, nor to believe what someone else had personally arrived at. Centrally, this meant misinterpreting scripture. Isidore ended the chapter just quoted from with these words: 'But whoever understands scripture in any sense other than that which the Holy Spirit, by whom it was written, requires, even though he may not withdraw from the Church, may nevertheless be called a heretic.'[18] Likewise St Thomas Aquinas, writing on heresy in the *Summa Theologiae* and citing Isidore, identified heresy with sect and centred the definition of heresy on the corruption of Christian faith that resulted from false interpretations of scripture.[19] This meant departing from truth but not necessarily from the Church. Following conventional wisdom, then, calling Lollards a sect would have meant no more nor less than calling them heretics. Infidelity, scriptural infidelity, was at stake rather than separatist tendencies.

When did the word sect begin to be applied to Wycliffites? As observed by John Thomson (above p. 164) it was not until some years after Wyclif's death and the initiation of anti-heretical proceedings that this term enters the public domain. Only in the 1390s does it become noticeable both in official proceedings and unofficial comment. Bishop Trefnant of Hereford, in the wordy preamble to the start of his proceedings against William Swinderby in the summer of 1389,

(Oxford, 1911), 1, Lib. VIII, iii. I have used and somewhat altered the translation of Edward Peters, in *Heresy and Authority in Medieval Europe* (London, 1980), pp. 49–50.

[17] R. W. Southern, *Robert Grosseteste: The Growth of an English Mind in Medieval Europe* (2nd edn, Oxford, 1992), p. 292.

[18] *Isidori . . . Etymologiarum*, ed. Lindsay, 1, Lib. VIII, v; Peters, *Heresy and Authority*, p. 50. St Augustine, *Contra Faustum Manichaeum*, Lib. 20, cap. iii – distinguishing between *secta* and *schisma* ('Secta vero est longe alia opinantem quam caeteri, alio etiam sibi ac longe dissimili ritu divinitatis instituisse culturam'), *PL* 42, col. 369.

[19] *S. Thomae Aquinatis Summa Theologiae*, ed. P. Caramello, 3 vols (Turin, 1962–3), 2, pp. 64–6, II, ii, quest. xi, *De haeresi*, arts 1–2.

applied his rhetoric to those 'preachers or rather prevaricators of the execrable new sect, commonly called Lollards'.[20] A year or so later John Gower, lamenting the fractures in the contemporary Church in his prologue to the *Confessio Amantis*, entered his comment on the emergence of 'This new Secte of Lollardie,/ And also many an heresie/ Among the clerkes in hemselve', which stemmed from taking Bible learning to extremes. And Gower's Latin poem of 1396–7, enumerating the corruptions of the day, headed his list with the 'wiliness of the devil on behalf of Lollardy'; 'Look! He sends a new sect' to pour scandals into the ears of the people to the injury of the faith.[21]

The first conspicuous official proscription of Lollards as a 'sect' is in the papal bull of September 1395, directing Richard II and his archbishops to take action against the 'pestilent and contagious sect' that was threatening the faith in England.[22] After that, the very long petition of the clergy addressed to Henry IV in the Parliament of 1401 (which may have been drafted in the reign of Richard II) was concerned with the dangerous activities 'of a certain new sect', and in the same session the commons petitioned that proper justice should be done on any man or woman imprisoned for Lollardy, 'as an example to others of that evil sect' and to put a stop to their evil preaching.[23] 'Sect' (in both French and Latin) occurs hereafter in secular and ecclesiastical counter-actions: in the parliamentary petition against Lollards of 1406, and in Archbishop Arundel's constitutions of 1407–9.[24]

Does the arrival of the term 'sect' to describe Lollardy mark some

[20] '. . . predicatores videlicet, quia verius prevaricatores execrabilis nove secte, Lollardos vulgariter nuncupatos'; *Reg. Trefnant*, p. 232. The phraseology of Trefnant's long preamble, in which he condemns the preachers of this 'new sect' with fulsome ecclesiastical rhetoric, including the deceptive appearance of their 'simulated guise of sanctity' (on which more below) is of special interest in view of his expertise in canon law. Richard G. Davies, 'The episcopate', in C. H. Clough, ed., *Profession, Vocation, and Culture in Later Medieval England* (Liverpool, 1982), p. 69, and p. 75 on bishops' need to have some understanding of canon law; on Trefnant's large collection of canon law texts (the Decretals, the Sext, the Clementines, Guido de Baysio, among others), see *BRUO*, 3, p. 1901.

[21] *Complete Works of John Gower*, 2, p. 14, ll. 349–51; 4, p. 347 (see epigraph and n. 1 above).

[22] *Reg. Trefnant*, pp. 406–7; *Calendar of Papal Letters, 1362–1404*, pp. 515–16.

[23] *Rotuli Parliamentorum*, 6 vols (London, 1776–77), 3, pp. 466–7, 473–4; A. K. McHardy, '*De Heretico Comburendo*, 1401', in *Lollardy and Gentry*, pp. 115–18.

[24] *Rotuli Parliamentorum*, 3, pp. 583–4; W. Lyndwood, *Provinciale* (Oxford, 1679), end section of Provincial Constitutions, pp. 65–6. See Thomson, 'Orthodox religion', *History*, 74 (1989), p. 47, n. 34 for 'new sect' in a London writ of 1413.

significant shift in perceptions of the danger they presented? What exactly was it that was described by '*new* sect'? It may be instructive to look back to the beginning of these pronouncements. Gregory XI's several bulls of 22 May 1377 – addressed respectively to the university of Oxford, the archbishop of Canterbury and the king – ordering the arrest and imprisonment of Wyclif, were cast in very different terms. There is no mention of 'sect' here. The main concern was with the errors and false conclusions, smacking of heresy, which threatened the polity of Church and state. Though infection of the faith by public preaching was not left out of account, the heart of the matter was the institutional challenge issuing from the university, and the models the Pope cited were those of Marsilius of Padua and John of Jandun.[25] In 1395, by contrast, Boniface IX's concern was centred on popular heresy, and the threat to the faith by those who were barely literate, and who turned their knowledge of letters against holy Church.[26] Public preaching and open writing, even addressing texts to the 'royal parliament' itself, were the activities of those who called themselves 'poor men, treasurers of Christ and his apostles', and whom the world at large called Lollards. The model in this case was the Waldensians, those whose 'hallmark . . . was that they were *ydiote et illiterati*', the heretics who had left their mark as lay people striving to restore apostolic poverty to the church.[27] The self-proclaimed 'poor men' of the 1395 Twelve Conclusions were being written off as comparable to the 'Poor Men of Lyons'.

It is tempting to think that new alarm bells started ringing when the text of the self-proclaimed *pauperes homines*[28] reached Rome. Poor men of this kind, those who sought to revive the actualities of evangelical poverty, had long since left a dent of deep anxiety in the Church. It is impossible to believe it was accidental that the phraseology of the 1395

[25] *Chronicon Angliae*, ed. E. M. Thompson (*RS*, 1874), pp. 174–81; J. H. Dahmus, *The Prosecution of John Wyclyf* (New Haven, CN, and London, 1952), pp. 35–55 on the five bulls, with translations of their texts; Leff, *Dissolution*, pp. 138–41; Leff, *Heresy*, 2, pp. 413–22. On these models and Wyclif's *De civili dominio* see W. R. Thomson, *The Latin Writings of John Wyclyf* (Toronto, 1983), pp. 50, 53–4.

[26] 'Et in tantum hi nempe, ne dicamus viri sed virorum umbre dampnose, cum ex eis sint quam plures propemodum litterati, contra fidem orthodoxam et sacrosanctam Romanam et universalem ecclesiam, in cuius gremio ad eorum et multorum confusionem et eternam dampnacionem litteras didicerunt . . .'; *Reg. Trefnant*, p. 406.

[27] Leff, *Heresy*, 2, p. 484; idem, *Dissolution*, pp. 130–5.

[28] *Rogeri Dymmok Liber Contra XII Errores et Hereses Lollardorum*, ed. H. S. Cronin (WS, London, 1921), p. 25, gives the Latin version of the 'Pretensus stilus lollardorum', which Boniface's bull followed closely; *Reg. Trefnant*, p. 406.

bull harks back to Lucius III's *Ad abolendum* – a key document in the chain of authorities against heresy, which was enshrined in canon law.[29] This was the authoritative text by which the papacy anathematized popular heresies including the Lombard *Humiliati* and Waldensians in the south of France, whose evangelical followings were spread through unauthorized preaching. We can set the 'qui se Humiliatos vel Pauperes de Lugduno falso nomine mentiuntur' of 1184 alongside the 'qui se pauperes homines thesauri Cristi et eius discipulorum nuncupant' of 1395. In both documents the false claims to piety are linked with illicit preaching. 'Et quoniam nonnulli, sub specie pietatis virtutum eius, iuxta quod ait Apostolus, denegantes, auctoritatem sibi vendicant praedicandi' (1184); 'sub pretensis humilitate devocione at abstinencia . . . publice predicare . . . pertinaciter non sunt veriti nec verentur' (1395).[30] The 1184 bull did not use the word *secta*. But if this could be regarded as any kind of lack it had subsequently been more than made good by Bernard Gui, whose inquisitorial manual (*Practica inquisitionis heretice pravitatis*) left no doubt that the Poor Men of Lyons were *secta et heresis*.[31]

The question still remains, of course, as to the precise content of 'sect', and the problem of whether it may have carried different connotations in Latin and in the vernacular. The clergy in Convocation and the commons in Parliament did not necessarily see eye to eye; *nova secta* for churchmen was perhaps not what 'new sect' was for laymen. One might, for instance, discern a contrast between the statute of 1401 (followed by the parliamentary petition of 1406) with its association of 'sect' with conventicles and schools, and the 'sect' in Archbishop Arundel's constitutions of 1407/9. In the clause which regulated preaching about the sacraments, the archbishop prohibited the

[29] 'The first attempt to define the official attitude to manifest dissent'; Brenda Bolton, 'Tradition and temerity: papal attitudes to deviants, 1159–1216', *SCH*, 9 (1972), pp. 79–91, at p. 85.

[30] Friedberg, 2, col. 780, Lib. V, tit. vii, *De Haereticis*, cap. ix; Mansi, 22, cols 476–8; *Reg. Trefnant*, p. 406; Lambert, *Heresy*, pp. 66–8; Moore, *Dissent*, p. 227.

[31] Bernard Gui, *Practica Inquisitionis Heretice Pravitatis*, ed. C. Douais (Paris, 1886), p. 235 and following, on the method of enquiry into and examination of heresy, makes regular use of the word 'sect' for the 'secta Manicheorum' and the 'secta and heresis' of the Valdenses, including (p. 245) the statement that the 'sect' of the Poor Men of Lyons were called Waldensians after their initiator ('secta dicta est seu nominata a quodam nomine Valdesio seu Valdensi actore et inventore primo ipsius secte'); Bernard Gui, *Manuel de l'Inquisiteur*, ed. G. Mollat, 2 vols (Paris, 1926–7), 1, pp. vii, 8, 34–65. For remarks on Gui's 'systematic descriptions of sects', see Peter Biller in P. Biller and A. Hudson, eds, *Heresy and Literacy, 1000–1530* (Cambridge, 1994), pp. 2, 8.

public or private preaching of any 'sectam aut speciem haeresis . . . contra sanam ecclesiae doctrinam'.[32] How should we translate this? *Secta* here, like *species*, is something that can be taught and preached; it describes opinions rather than people. Lyndwood's gloss gives some help here, with notes on both words.[33]

Secta was defined as a cutting off or division. For this there was the authority of Guido de Baysio (Baisieux), whose commentary on the Sext included in the section on heresy; '*secta* is so called from division or cutting, so we speak of sects of philosophers or heretics'.[34] *Species* related to the forms of these divisions, the variety of heretical opinions, which had been numbered at eighty-eight. There was also Hostiensis, whose answer to the question 'What are sects of heretics?' pointed to these four-score deviations from the true sense of scripture as properly interpreted by the holy spirit.[35] If therefore, Arundel's 'sect and species of heresy' dealt with heretical doctrine and opinion, there is small divergence from the 1406 petition, which wanted action against the holding of 'schools of any sect or doctrine'.[36] In other contexts, however, as in the statement of the *Fasciculi Zizaniorum* cited above (p. 163), or in the clerical petition of 1401, 'sect' meant a set of people, a following, like Gui's description of the Waldensians following Valdes. It was possible therefore both to preach a *secta* and for members of a *secta* to preach. Both were consistent with old usages of the word.

[32] Lyndwood, *Provinciale*, last section pp. 65–6 and pp. 295–7 (with some verbal differences). The phrase is repeated: 'si quis contrarium de determinatis per ecclesiam . . . quamcumque sive haeresis speciem, sive sectam publice vel occulte docuerit . . .' These distinctions were important when it came to recidivism and relapse – a matter raised by Arundel in this same chapter. Lyndwood's commentary recites the judgement of the Sext on this important point; namely that someone convicted on one heretical opinion or deviation ('convictus de una specie vel secta haeresis'), who after abjuration embraced another such, was guilty of relapse. Lyndwood, p. 296, note n on *Relapso*: 'qui convictus de una specie vel secta haeresis, . . . postmodum abjurans haeresin simpliciter vel generaliter, extunc in alia haeresis specie sive secta . . . judicandus est ut haereticus relapsus'; Friedburg, 2, col. 1072, Sext, lib. 5, tit. II, cap. viii.

[33] Lyndwood, *Provinciale*, p. 295, notes b and c. Arundel's 'sectam aut speciem' may be compared with the 'falsas opiniones et sectas nostre fidei' which Archbishop Courtenay found Leicester suspects guilty of preaching in 1389. *The Metropolitan Visitations of William Courtenay*, ed. J. H. Dahmus (Urbana, IL, 1950), p. 171.

[34] Lyndwood, *Provinciale*, p. 295, note b, '*Sectam.* Sic dictam, quia sit quasi sectio vel divisio'; Guido de Baysio, *Lectura super sexto* (Milan, 1490), sig. Ovi^{r}, 'Secta; dicta est secta a divisione, quasi sectio, unde secte philosophorum vel hereticorum dicuntur.'

[35] Lyndwood, *Provinciale*, p. 295, note c, '*Speciem heresis.* Cujus species, 88 numerantur'; *Summa Aurea D. Henrici Cardinalis Hostiensis* (Lyons, 1548), bk 5, fol. 238r–v; Southern, *Robert Grosseteste*, pp. 292–3.

[36] 'Ecoles d'ascun secte ou doctrine'; *Rotuli Parliamentorum*, 3, p. 584.

It is a mistake to try to draw a line between Parliament and Convocation in this flow of anti-heretical verbiage. The words, as well as the initiatives, were primarily clerical and traditional. In 1401, as in 1382, the proscriptive phrases were those of churchmen. It is all-important to realize that Lollards were always presented in borrowed garments, in that the phraseology used to condemn them (from which may other descriptions depended) derived from canonical texts, and reverberate with key biblical passages.

Certain phrases constantly recur in official proscriptions of Wycliffites starting in 1382, when the wheels of Church and state first ground into action against them. Conspicuous among these is the stress on specious sanctity which appeared in the 1395 bull. Associated with this is the claim to preach without licence, and the spectre of wolves disguised in sheep's clothing.

Echoing descriptions ring through the condemnations of May 1382: 'sub magnae sanctitatis velamine auctoritatem sibi vendicant praedicandi'; 'en certains habitz souz dissimulacion de grant saintee'; the words appeared respectively in the letters by which Archbishop Courtenay published condemnation of the heresies listed at Blackfriars, and in the related statute by which Parliament authorized new procedures for arresting unlicensed preachers.[37] And, shortly before this, the Archbishop's mandate to the Carmelite Peter Stokes to see that discussion of the twenty-four points was silenced in Oxford refers to wolves dressed in sheep's clothing, and to the canonical sanctions against anyone preaching who had not been sent, which had been openly challenged by false preachers who presented themselves under a cover of great sanctity.[38] Thereafter variants of such descriptions recur, in prose and verse, in official and informal condemnations, whenever the spectacle of unorthodox illicit preaching was seen to threaten Church and society. It would be tedious to labour the point by listing such passages, but some of them must be returned to, because of the weight that has been attributed to them.

[37] Wilkins, *Concilia*, 3, p. 158, mandate for publication of the Blackfriars proceedings; *Rotuli Parliamentorum*, 3, pp. 124–5 refers to these proceedings; H. G. Richardson, 'Heresy and the lay power under Richard II', *EHR*, 51 (1936), p. 7. In my article on 'Heresy and sedition' I listed these repeating phrases without considering the significance of their sources; M. Aston, *Lollards and Reformers* (London, 1984), p. 6, n. 15.

[38] 'Lupos intrinsecus ovium vestimentis indutos . . . licet secundum canonicas sanctiones nemo prohibitus, vel non missus . . . sibi praedicationis officium usurpare debeat . . . sub magnae sanctitatis velamine virtutum ejus abnegantes, auctoritatem sibi vindicant praedicandi'; *Fasciculi Zizaniorum*, pp. 275–82 (cited at p. 275) dated 28 May 1382.

Scripture lay behind these words. Three passages in particular are important. II Timothy 3.5, 'habentes speciem quidem pietatis, virtutem autem eius abnegantes' ('having a form of godliness, but denying the power thereof') comes in a chapter foretelling the perils of the last days, when a variety of evil men and seducers would afflict the godly. Matthew 7 contains, in the sermon on the mount, after Christ's call to keep to the narrow way, avoiding the broad way of destruction, the well-known passage on false prophets. Verse 15 reads, 'Attendite a falsis prophetis, qui veniunt ad vos in vestimentis ovium, intrinsecus autem sunt lupi rapaces' ('Beware of false prophets, which come to you in sheep's clothing, but inwardly they are ravening wolves'). Thirdly, there is Romans 10, another famous passage on the means of access to salvation and the importance of preaching, which included (verse 15) the words 'Quomodo vero praedicabunt nisi mittantur?' ('And how shall they preach, except they be sent?').

All three passages had long since been linked with heresy. I have already quoted from Lucius III's bull of 1184, which used the words of Timothy in condemning the Poor Men of Lyons. We also find there Romans 10.15 cited against these illicit preachers. *Ad abolendum* naturally featured prominently in the canon law exposition of heresy, and this text appeared in Chapter ix of the section *De haereticis* in the Decretals of Gregory IX (of 1234). The bull's coverage of the twelfth-century heretics also included orders about heretics who were meeting in secret conventicles.[39] The dangers of conventicles featured too in the Decretal's citations from Innocent III, who likewise invoked Romans when providing for action against those who usurped the office of preaching. And the problem of separating true religion from the 'cloaked exterior' ('palliata specie') which deceived the simple and even seduced the clever, summoned into papal rhetoric echoes of Matthew and wolves among the sheep ('nec arcere lupos ab ovibus videamur').[40]

If fresh concern about the appearance of heresy led, via canon law,

[39] 'Occulta conventicula celebrantes'; Friedberg, 2, cols 778–90 (Lib. V, tit. vii), at 781; Mansi, 22, cols 476–8; Leff, *Heresy*, 1, p. 37; *conventicula haereticorum* also featured in Isidore of Seville; *Isidori Hispalensis . . . Etymologiarum*, 1, Lib. VIII, i. Also on the term conventicle see below nn. 85–6.

[40] Friedberg, 2, cols. 782, 785, 788. Penn Szittya points out that Lucius and Innocent alike turned back to the Justinian Code, which itself looked back to the Theodosian Code, in both of which *conventicula celebrantes* was the phrase used to describe prohibited religious activities outside the Church.

to a focus on particular biblical passages, the reverse was also the case: looking into certain texts led straight to consideration of heresy. Anyone who turned to the *Glossa Ordinaria* would have known that Matthew's warning to beware of false prophets had, since the time of Tertullian, been seen as a warning against insidious heretics, those false preachers and pseudo-prophets who masqueraded in lambs' fleeces in order to ravage innocent flocks with their vulpine rapacity. *Attendite* ... The resonance of the words came to apply specially to heretics, with their deceitful appearance of piety. Nicholas of Lyra added weight to this association of false prophets with heretical doctors.[41]

At this juncture, however, we must take account of another important context of these scriptural commonplaces. Long before the appearance of Wyclif and Wycliffites they had found widespread usage in the notorious and long-lasting controversy over the rights and wrongs of preaching and mendicancy provoked by the friars. Penn Szittya's exploration of the antifraternal tradition has shown how, from the mid-thirteenth-century writings of William of St Amour, this criticism, bound to a catena of scriptural texts and clarioning of the dangers of the last days before the coming end of the world, became established in England. Key biblical phrases recur like set pieces. They included the passages in Romans, Matthew, and Timothy cited above. Preachers who preached without being sent, false sheep-like prophets who were ravening wolves, men who appeared under a deceptive guise of piety, these were all recognizable attributes of mendicant friars.[42]

Thus far we have mainly been considering official terminology. But it is now time to take a wider view, and to look into the Wycliffites' own writings and the polemical exchanges that took place during Wyclif's lifetime. The term 'sect' was being bandied about well before Wyclif's death. William Rimington for one, writing not long after the 1381 rising for which he put blame on the heretics, referred in no uncertain terms to the poisonous teaching of 'a certain damnable and indiscreet modern sect'.[43] And some Latin verses written against the Lollards, perhaps about the time of the Blackfriars Council, make free

41 *Biblia Sacra cum Glossa Ordinaria*, 6 vols (Antwerp, 1617), 5, cols 149–50.

42 Szittya, *Antifraternal*, pp. 6–7, 22, 45–6, 52, 54, 61, 80, 87. My debt to this work extends far beyond the citations given here and below.

43 Bodleian Library, Oxford, MS Bodl. 158, fols 200v–202r; cited Hudson, *PR*, p. 170; M. Aston, 'Corpus Christi and Corpus Regni: heresy and the Peasants' Revolt', *P&P*, 143 (1994), p. 37.

use of the word *secta* in attacking the heretics.[44] But was belonging to a 'sect' part of Lollard self-imaging, self-naming? And if so, what was understood by it?

Secta and 'sect' both make frequent appearances in Wycliffite writings, specially in and after 1382. Wyclif himself – perhaps particularly when under the threat of prosecution – came to write in terms of 'my followers', 'my following' ('ego cum meis sequacibus, ego cum secta mea') and 'my supporters' ('omnes fautores meos').[45] His use of *secta nostra*, when setting out his eucharistic position in 1381, was closely allied to his sparring with the *secta contraria* of his adversaries, otherwise to be known as the *secta signorum*. Beliefs and those who embraced them, were expounded in antithetical, if not antagonist, terms.[46] Before the end of the fourteenth century Wycliffites were presenting themselves in terms of true 'sect', often taking as a point of departure the counter-models of the New Testament. The characteristics of sects in Acts, Galatians, and II Peter were lying, blasphemy, dissension, and sedition, represented by the Scribes, Essenes, and Pharisees, the last especially being chastized as 'hypocrites' and 'blind guides'.[47] As the Wycliffite tract dubbed 'Of the Leaven of Pharisees' put it, 'yn Cristes tyme there weren thre sectes of ordres founden of mannys ordinaunces, as pharisees, saduces and esseis', the first two of which were 'stronge enemyes to Crist and his lawe', covetous and deceiving the people by hypocrisy. St Paul, who before his conversion to 'the gospel and fredom of Cristes ordre'[48] lived as a Pharisee 'after the most straitest sect of our religion', knew what it meant when he was challenged in Rome to explain his new calling, 'for as concerning this sect, we know that every where it is spoken against'.[49]

[44] *Political Poems and Songs*, ed. T. Wright, 2 vols (*RS*, 1859–61), 1, pp. 233, 235, 241, 243.

[45] *John Wyclif's De Veritate Sacrae Scripturae*, ed. R. Buddensieg, 3 vols, WS (1905–7), 1, pp. 345, 357, cited by M. Wilks, 'Wyclif and the Great Persecution', in *SCH.S*, 10 (1994), pp. 39–63, at p. 58 (an important paper which has contributed much to this one). It seems that Wyclif's concern with 'sects' only emerged, and then as of part of a defence mechanism, after Gregory XI's bulls, with the growth of attacks on the mendicants and controversy over the Eucharist in the 1380s. See W. R. Thomson, *The Latin Writings of John Wyclyf* (Toronto, 1983), pp. 95, 78, 86, 217, 279–302, and pp. 55–6 for late 1377–end 1378 as the date of *De veritate sacre scripture*.

[46] *Fasciculi Zizaniorum*, pp. 125–6; in Wyclif's *Confessio* of 10 May 1381. On this text, which occupied a critical place in the censuring of Wyclif's eucharistic teaching, see Thomson, *Latin Writings*, pp. 69–71; M. Aston, *Faith and Fire* (London, 1993), p. 52.

[47] Matt. 23.13–16; compare Luke 18.9–14; Acts 26.5. *EWS*, 4, on 'The sects', pp. 121–34, at p. 123.

[48] *The English Works of Wyclif Hitherto Unprinted*, ed. F. D. Matthew (*EETS*, 74, 1880), p. 2.

[49] Acts 26.5, 28.22 (AV). See n. 51 for the Wycliffite Bible wording of the latter passage.

The 'sect of Christ', the true following of the true law, emerges in the polarized discourse of true and false religion. The sermon for the Eleventh Sunday after Trinity in the Wycliffite sermon cycle, an address on the respective qualities of Pharisee and publican, equated the Pharisees, Saducees, and Essenes – religious sects of Christ's time – with the contemporary 'new sects' of monks, canons, and friars. All three failed through substituting another rule for the supreme rule of Christ's gospel. True sect was set against false sects. 'I clepe sectis newe mannys ordres, that on seweth anothur as he schulde sewe Crit', as opposed to 'that secte whiche Crist hymself made, that Godis lawe clepyth the secte of Cristen men'. The true following of Christ had in effect existed as long as the gospel and evangelism. True Christian men, following Christ's rule, were members of 'that secte whiche Crist hymself made . . . and . . . this secte is best that any man may have sith Crist, almyghty, al witty, and al willeful, ordeynyd this sect covenable fore eche man'. The untrue sects, on the other hand, made their own rules, believing they could find one better than Christ's.[50]

Wyclif himself had a great deal to say, in this confrontational discourse, of true and false sects. He gives us his own definition of *secta*. In *De fundacione sectarum* (written in 1383 during the author's final retirement at Lutterworth) Wyclif explained the term sect before embarking on this topic.

> First we must see how sect should be defined. It is commonly said that a sect is a collection of men following one patron, accepting one rule. So the sect of Christians ought to include all wayfarers [*viatores*]. What this sect amounts to is clear in Acts 28.22: 'for as concerning this sect, we know that every where it is spoken against'. And since *secta* comes from *sequor* it is evident that all Christians should be of the Christian sect, as is said in Acts 11. The patron of this sect is Jesus Christ, and its rule the catholic faith, that is, the law of the gospel. And it is clear that no sect can be better or more universal than this. For its patron is God and man Jesus Christ, and its rule the law of God, which all men at large should conform with.[51]

[50] *EWS*, 1, pp. 264–7, cited at p. 265.

[51] *John Wiclif's Polemical Works*, ed. R. Buddensieg, 2 vols, WS (London, 1883), 1, pp. 21–2. Acts 28.22 is translated in the earlier Wycliffite Bible: 'forwhi of this secte it is knowun to us, for every where it is agen seid to it'; *The Holy Bible*, ed. J. Forshall and F. Madden, 4 vols (Oxford, 1850), 4, p. 592.

The *secta Christi*, on this showing, was the absolute opposite of any splinter group. It represented the essence of the true Christian church. All variants from this one pure rule were false, and the four orders of friars, 'sects of perdition' (II Peter 2.1), were paradigms of perversion, as false as sects of Mahomet.[52] *De fundacione sectarum* amounted to a demonstration of the scriptural invalidity of the mendicant orders, whose failings matched the worst gospel transgressions. Friars were heretics par excellence, and the many pages penned by Wycliffites against the orders of friars as 'new sects', were premised on the assumption that they were undoing the Church by following rules and patrons other than Christ and his law. 'And byleve techeth us that the state of Cristus secte is moste certeyn and medful to men that wolon arere this towr, for no man may arere it, but yif he be of Cristus ordre.'[53]

This sectarian polemic was, of course, taken up at large in the vernacular. And we find repeated there Wyclif's definition of sect as those following a rule under a patron, the only valid example of which in religious life was that instituted in the gospel. The 'Tractatus de Pseudo-freris', repeating Wyclif's argument, expounded a view of what constituted the newness of 'new sect' on lines that became familiar for another later generation of evangelicals with their own arguments over 'new learning'.

> It were to wite over this what goddis lawe meneth by thise sectis; and it semeth to many men that a secte is a newe ordre bi newe patroun and newe lawe, as was the secte of cristen men, and crist haveth ful autorite to make siche a blissid secte for hym and hise that comen aftir to the ende of the world. Yif a cristen man have a custom that profitith to hym for a tyme, but he haveth non patroun ne rewle but crist and lore that he hath given, he makith not a new secte other then secte of cristen men. And yif benet or dominic or fraunciss or bernard or angel of heevene make a newe secte upon cristis secte, he is herfore worthi to be blamed; and this secte shulde be despisid and cristis secte shulde be holde clene . . .[54]

52 *De fundacione sectarum*, in *Polemical Works*, 1, pp. 30–1.

53 *EWS*, 2, p. 39 (Sermon 62) and 4, p. 245 (note on Sermon 25, the allegory of the tower of virtues necessary to salvation, 'the towr of the gospel', 1, pp. 324–5). Also on *secta Christi* see 4, p. 125.

54 *English Works of Wyclif*, p. 301.

The 'sect of Christ', coming to the fore in the thrust of argument and counter-argument about rights and origins, was integrally related to rivalry with the friars. Accusations of 'newness', as in Reformation exchanges, were rebutted by raising the banner of evangelical news and fidelity to the true faith of antiquity.[55]

The entry on *secte* in the Wycliffite repertory the *Floretum* reflects this context – and perhaps it is significant that this entry did not apparently feature in the English *Rosarium*. After an introductory section based on Isidore of Seville, Bede, and Gregory, dealing with sects as heretics who separated themselves from the unity of the faith, most of this entry is concerned with the contrast between the true and false sects of contemporary times. It is penned in a way which seems to assume knowledge of key aspects.

> The sect of Christ, as true Christians, ought not to proceed contentiously against the four sects newly introduced, but with faith and hope and charity; firstly, seeking and praying God for them to be converted to sound faith in the church and the free following of Jesus Christ; secondly, they should trust in God that, having learned about the easy and just following of Jesus Christ, many of them may be converted to it through the grace of our lord. Thirdly, they ought to hammer home the evidences of scripture so that there is agreement with the sect of Christ.[56]

[55] 'Ego autem teneo fidem antiqui dierum', wrote Wyclif, defending his scriptural understanding of the Eucharist against Rimington in the autumn of 1383; *Johannis Wyclif Opera Minora*, ed. J. Loserth, WS (London, 1913), p. 213; Thomson, *Latin Writings*, pp. 233–4. Predictably, others saw it the opposite way about. Thomas Netter indignantly rejected Wyclif's claim that he stood for gospel antiquity while the religious orders were novelties: 'Numquid sectae Wiclevisticae tanta est antiquitas?' How could Wycliffites claim this, when their detestable novelty was barely fifty years old? Thomas Netter, *Doctrinale Antiquitatum Fidei Catholicae Ecclesiae*, ed. B. Blanchiotti, 3 vols (Venice, 1757–9), 3, cols 573–9 (cited col. 578) (*De sacramentalibus*, cap. 89). On the historical dimension of the appeal to the apostolic ideal embodied in scripture see Leff, 'Apostolic ideal', pp. 58–82. On 'new' carrying the loaded sense of 'non-apostolic', and possibly affecting the C-text of *Piers Plowman*, see Wendy Scase, *Piers Plowman and the New Anticlericalism* (Cambridge, 1989), p. 123, and n. 12, p. 212.

[56] 'Secta Cristi ut fideles Cristiani non debent contra quattuor sectas noviter introductas contenciose procedere, se fide, spe et caritate; primum deum pro ipsis petere et orare ut convertantur ad sinceram fidem ecclesie, et sectam liberam Iesu Cristi. Secundo debent sperare in domino quod doctis illis de secta facili et meritoria domini Iesu Cristi converti possent multi eorum secundum graciam domini ad eandem. Et tercio pulsari debent secundum evidencias fidei scripture ut consenciat secte Cristi': BL, MS Harley 401, fol. 281r. The entry on *Fratres* (fol. 107r–v) ends with an attack on the mendicant orders for the lying pretence that the innovations of *secta novelle* were better than *antiquam religionem Cristi*.

Convert the friars – do not fight them – though the text goes on to describe the errant sects in a way more suggestive of cold-shouldering by the faithful.

If the Wycliffite *secta Christi* belonged to a divided world of contest and persecution, the debate inevitably filtered into the pastoral field. Preachers could not be other than conscious of shouts of trespass – let alone falsity – and they were ready to defend their position. A Lollard sermon on John 1.19 ('the Jews sent priests and Levites from Jerusalem') touched on the problems raised in 'oure Jerusalem', by 'semple prestes that prechen now Goddes lawe faste aboute'. They had to face the argument that the office of preaching was committed only to the orders of friars, and those who took this line were here represented as acting like the Pharisees whose 'gret presumpcioun' about John the Baptist was that 'he wolde be a patron of a new ordre'.[57] No mention of 'sect' here. But if the word was inappropriate for the ears expected to hear this address, the argument was the same.

If it is right to relate this talk about the sect of Christ to the world of rivalry and persecution and anti-fraternal anger, the exchanges between Jack Upland and Friar Daw, initiated (probably between 1390 and 1400) by a series of Wycliffite questions challenging the friars, deserve attention.[58] The validation of the two speakers' respective 'sects' forms part of this debate. 'Frere, of what ordre art thou and who made thin ordre? What been thi rulis and who made thi "cloutid" rulis . . .?' The question Upland puts to Daw is returned in kind: 'But good Jak, your grace, where be you foundid?' 'Sect', as used in this discussion, can describe the following of heresy ('settis of Antecristis sowinge', or 'thi cursed secte'), but the bare word – though either side finds so little to approve of in the other – stands simply for 'order'.[59]

Daw's reply to Jack's question takes pains to justify his Dominican order in the scriptural terms prized by his opponent.

> I am of Cristis ordre, Jak, and Crist made myn ordre –
> Ensaumple in the gospel in many sundry place;

[57] *Lollard Sermons*, ed. Gloria Cigman (*EETS*, 294, 1989), pp. 50–1.

[58] On this dating see Szittya, *Antifraternal*, pp. 196–7.

[59] *Jack Upland, Friar Daw's Reply and Upland's Rejoinder*, ed. P. L. Heyworth (Oxford 1968), pp. 57–8, 100, 108.

following gospel teaching of obedience, chastity, and poverty, so that 'Iff y breke myn ordre, I breke Goddis lawe'. Friars were followers of Christ's own rules, and if heresy was in question it was not they, but Upland's party who were guilty of the division that heresy implied.

> Heresie that is Grw is divisioun on Latyn,
> The whiche in oure langage meneth sunderying and partyng.

Heretics were corrupters of scripture

> And if this sentence be soth, y can noon other seien,
> But thou and thi secte ben heretikes alle.

Upland's reply is predictable. If was Wycliffites, not friars, who were true to Christ and gospel.

> Dawe, thou spekist proudely apechying our prestes,
> But of oon thyng am I certen, thai ben lasse evel than ye.
> For alle if thai synne oft, as it is wel knowen,
> Thit the grounde that thai have is playnly Cristis religion.[60]

What Upland has to say about his own following is interesting, and seems to be rather carefully worded. He appears to be chary of admitting that 'our prestes' are a 'secte'. He is ready to wager £100 on the virtues of his own set of followers of Christ's religion – 'hem that [thou] clepist my secte', and he defends from Daw's malicious charges those 'of thilk Cristis secte that myn [thou] callist'. 'Sect' is a term he accepts only with the qualification that it is Christ's own – the chosen few. 'For to our secte that is Cristis we drawen bot fewe puple', a statement that besides being scriptural should no doubt be attached to antifraternal criticism of the excessive multitude of friars. In rebutting the charge of heresy Upland rebuts the charge of separation, of 'sunderyng and partyng . . . from Crist and his chirche'.[61]

[60] Ibid., pp. 81, 93, 103.

[61] Ibid., pp. 93, 103, 105, 108. Matt. 20.16, 22.14: 'many are called, but few are chosen'. On charges of excessive numbers of friars see Szittya, *Antifraternal*, pp. 143–4, 222–5, and Scase, *New Anticlericalism*, pp. 35–6.

The charged rivalry with the friars which generated such exchanges on the virtues of respective 'sects' also has a direct bearing on reporting of the appearance of Lollard evangelists. This is something that is closely related to historians' judgements of Wyclif as the supposed founder of an order of 'poor priests'.[62] Contemporary commentators, fastening accusations on the early heretics, made much of their barefoot evangelism. This forms part of Walsingham's account of how Wyclif gathered at Oxford and elsewhere a group of companions and allies ('comites atque socios unius sectae') who, as a sign of perfection, wore clothes of russet (the poorest cloth) and went round preaching barefoot.[63] The poem of about 1382 against the Lollards versifies the same point, with the insinuation that this was a deliberate deception.

Villarum in exitibus
Se nudant sotilaribus
   Cum populum ludificant.
Nudis incedunt pedibus,
Cum approprinquant foribus
   Locorum quibus praedicant.[64]

And there is Knighton's tale of William Smith, a leading light among early Lollards, who went barefoot for many years.[65]

[62] H. L. Cannon, 'The poor priests: a study in the rise of English Lollardy', *Annual Report of the American Historical Association for 1899* (Washington, 1900), pp. 451–82, at pp. 470–4; Wilks, 'Wyclif and the Great Persecution', pp. 53–5. It seems legitimate to regard the evidence of an 'order' of poor priests as still an open question. Here too, exploration of the terminology would be useful. For instance, how much can be read into *simplices sacerdotes* (Wilks, p. 53, n. 57), given that this term was already in use? (See for example Innocent III in Friedberg, 2, cols 785, 786.) See also Thomson, *Latin Writings*, pp. 93, 233, 281, 283, including (p.281) 'the ideal of the *secta Christi* . . . small bands of *sacerdotes simplices* . . . must have been, inescapably, another commanding abstraction.'

[63] *Historia Anglicana*, ed. H. T. Riley, 2 vols (*RS*, 1863–4), 1, p. 324, 'incedentes nudis pedibus'; compare *Chronicon Anglie*, p. 395 where Walsingham wrote of 'disciples' living in Oxford, and the word 'sect' is explicitly applied to their clothing: 'Congregavit sibi plures discipulos pravitatis, habitantes simul in Oxonia, indutos longis vestibus de russeto sectae unius, pedibus incedentes' (without the 'nudis'). The idea of some sort of 'uniform' clothing (a poverty costume) 'of one suit' here may be compared with William Ramsbury's matching tunic and cloak ('de una secta'). On these and other passages on the Lollards' appearance see Hudson, *PR*, pp. 144–7; Aston, *Faith and Fire*, pp. 123–4.

[64] *Political Poems and Songs*, 1, p. 233. Note in the preceding lines, p. 232, echoes of the scriptural phrases of condemnation used in 1382: 'Sub sanctitatis specie . . . Sic simplices decipiunt . . . Lupi in agnos saeviunt'.

[65] Knighton, pp. 292–3.

The outward mien of Lollard preachers became a standard method of impugning their sincerity by calling them hypocrites. If eschewing the comfort of riding, to travel the roads on foot, was for adherents a sign of true apostolic life, others damned such behaviour as the self-advertising of false preachers. When Bishop Repingdon caught up with the Leicester Lollard John Belgrave in 1414, he learnt how he had been criticized for not living up to his own earlier example of pedestrian evangelism.[66] Others put firmly on the record the foul deceptions of Lollards who 'go barfoot' and 'openhed', with a wholly misleading appearance of holy living and apostolic life.[67]

Heresy and barefoot preaching had long been associated. Isidore of Seville linked the renunciation of footwear with the choice of false opinions, and Waldensians were described as barefoot missionaries.[68] By the fourteenth century apostolic appearances were in danger of being overshadowed by suspicions of heresy. In the 1370s the sight of men going about 'two and two, bare-foot, clad in sheepskins', and possessing nothing in apostolic fidelity to Christ (as Walter Map described the Waldensians he questioned at the 1179 Lateran Council),[69] could not but seem challenging. There had been too many dangerous outcomes of preachers modelling themselves on those words in Luke and Matthew ('Go your ways: behold, I send you forth as lambs among wolves. Carry neither purse, nor scrip, nor shoes').[70]

The idea of an order of barefoot preachers acquired an alarming dimension in the thirteenth century, through controversies surrounding the teaching of Joachim of Fiore. The potential dynamite of Joachim's concept of a third age of the Holy Spirit burst in the university of Paris in the 1250s, thanks to the extreme doctrines of a fanatical Franciscan, Gerard of Borgo San Donnino. His concept of the

[66] James Crompton, 'Leicestershire Lollards', *Transactions of the Leicestershire Archaeological and Historical Society*, 44 (1968–9), pp. 30, 40; cited Hudson, *PR*, p. 77.

[67] *Three Middle English Sermons*, ed. D. M. Grisdale (Leeds School of English Language, Texts and Monographs, 5, 1939), p. 65; quoted Hudson, *PR*, p. 120.

[68] *Isidori . . . Etymologiarum*, Lib. VIII, v; *Heresy and Authority*, ed. Peters, pp. 50, 179.

[69] Walter Map, *De Nugis Curialium*, ed. M. R. James in *Anecdota Oxoniensa*, Medieval and Modern Series, pt 14 (Oxford, 1914), p. 61 ('the Lord . . . sent them two and two'; Luke 10.1); Lambert, *Heresy*, pp. 63–4; *Heresy and Authority*, p. 145.

[70] Luke 10.3–4; Matt. 10.9–10. Lambert, *Heresy*, p. 42, on the spontaneous following of this model in the twelfth century, describes the clothing of wandering preachers as amounting to 'a special uniform, with bare feet, minimal clothing and the donkey', as signs of the humility of those practising the apostolic life.

third age in which both Old and New Testaments would be superseded by the advent of the Eternal Gospel, whose preaching was to be committed to a new order of a specific kind, caused a tremendous furore.[71] One of the points in Gerard's *Liber Introductorius ad Evangelium Aeternum* condemned as erroneous in 1255 was 'that no-one is plainly suitable to instruct people about spiritual matters except those who go barefoot'.[72] This claim helped to fuel the hostile reactions of the seculars, whose fierce attacks on the mendicants were led by William of St Amour.[73]

Some of Wyclif's contemporaries who, in the century after this Paris scandal, cast censorious eyes over the teaching seeping out of the university of Oxford, were sufficiently well read to be reminded of that earlier event. Henry Knighton (on whom more shortly) was familiar with William of St Amour, who had alluded pointedly to the hypocritical appearance of Pharisees, which included going about unshod.[74] And Thomas Walsingham, too, may have seen a connection. He regarded Wycliffite teaching as particularly threatening to monks and religious orders, and the list of subversive doctrines which follows his report of barefoot preachers (a list which seems to draw on his own knowledge, as well as official proscriptions) emphasized statements

[71] Leff, 'Decline', pp. 36–51, at p. 42; Marjorie Reeves, *The Influence of Prophecy in the Later Middle Ages* (Oxford, 1969), pp. 14, 59–70; idem, *Joachim of Fiore and the Prophetic Future* (London, 1976), pp. 27, 33–4.

[72] 'Quod nullus simpliciter idoneus est ad instruendum homines de spiritualibus, nisi illi qui nudis pedibus incedunt'; Szittya, *Antifraternal*, p. 15, n.14, citing *CUP*, 1, no. 225, pp. 249–50. According to the 1255 list of Gerard's errors, the order to which the Eternal Gospel was to be committed, 'quem ordinem appellat nudipedum', was to be composed of both laymen and clerks. Reeves, *Influence of Prophecy*, p. 188, n. 1. On the text of the *Liber introductorius* see Szittya, p. 28, n. 48.

[73] The fullest account of William of St Amour is M.-M. Dufeil, *Guillaume de Saint-Amour et la Polémique Universitaire Parisienne 1250–1259* (Paris, 1972); see also J. D. Dawson, 'William of Saint-Amour and the Apostolic Tradition', *MS*, 40 (1978), pp. 223–38; Szittya, 'The Antifraternal Tradition in Middle English Literature', *Speculum*, 52 (1977), pp. 287–313.

[74] 'Praetendebant sanctitatis speciem . . . Austeritatem vitae praetendebant in his, quoniam in fimbriis illis ligabant spinas acutas, quibus sive ambularent, sive sederent, pungerentur, quasi sic commoniti retraherentur ad servitium Dei: ex quo apparet, quod ambulabant discalceati: aliter enim ambulando, non pungerentur a spinis' – unless they had been barefoot they would not have been pricked by thorns; O. Gratius, *Fasciculus Rerum Expentendarum et Fugiendarum*, ed. E. Brown, 2 vols (London, 1690), 2, p. 43, from the 1256 sermon *De Pharisao*. On this, and the circulation of St Amour's works in England see Szittya, pp. 17, 39–40, 62–7; Wilks, 'Wyclif and the Great Persecution', p. 44; for Knighton and St Amour's *De periculis* see below. The library of Knighton's house at Leicester had a copy of St Amour; M. R. James, 'Catalogue of the Library of Leicester Abbey', ed. A. H. Thompson, *Transactions of the Leicestershire Archaeological Society*, 19 (1936–7), pp. 111–61, 378–440; 21 (1939–40), pp. 1–88, at p. 137 in the first part; Knighton, p. xxx.

about the sufficiency of the Gospel. 'The Evangel is a sufficient rule in this life for every Christian', and 'all other rules of the saints' regulating the observance of various religious orders 'add no more in the way of perfection to the Evangel than whitewash adds to a wall'.[75] Walsingham, good historian and continuator of Matthew Paris as he was, could have read in Paris's *Chronica Majora* about the *deliramenta* preached in Paris in 1255, when the book called the *Evangelium Aeternum* and other matters 'which it is better not to relate' had caused such consternation. Matthew Paris, discreet in his reporting, entered a full list of the condemned errors of the Eternal Gospel in his *Liber Additamentorum* – the commonplace cum source book which accompanied his History. This list included the statement quoted above about the important role of barefoot preachers.[76]

Knighton and Walsingham, privileged in their learning and literary sources, could relate the apostolic Gospel preachers of their time to past prophetic events. They may not have been alone in this. Vernacular writers too, even if they lacked the learned apparatus, reflect wide familiarity with controversies surrounding the apostolic life and prophesies of the impending last days.[77]

The unflattering stereotype of the deceitful pseudo-apostle, lean, russet-clad, and unshod, which affixed itself to Lollards, was undoubtedly a derivative of mendicant controversy. Robert Henryson was calling on a well-established topos when he gave his Fox the following address to the Wolf-confessor in the fable of *The Fox and the Wolf*.

> Ye ar the lanterne and the sicker way
> Suld gyde sic sempill folk as me to grace;
> Your bair feit and your russet coull off gray,
> Your lene cheik, your paill and pietious face,
> Schawis to me your perfite halines.[78]

[75] *Historia Anglicana*, i, p. 324; *Chronicon Angliae*, p. 396. See also *Eulogium Historiarum*, ed. F. S. Haydon, 3 vols (*RS*, 1858–63), 3, pp. 354–5, for another chronicler (probably Franciscan) who made much of Wycliffite attacks on the religious orders, including mendicants, citing the well-worn text of II Tim. 3.6; 'qui penetrant domos'. On 'Sire *Penetrans Domos*' as a disparagement of friars see Szittya, *Antifraternal*, pp. 3–10; Scase, *New Anticlericalism*, pp. 15–16, 32–9.

[76] Matthew Paris, *CM*, 5, pp. 599–600, 6, pp. 335–9, error seven p. 336. Reeves, *Influence of Prophecy*, p. 62.

[77] Szittya, *Antifraternal*, p. 107 on 'the widespread interest in antifraternal writings among English monks', and p. 207 on poets, distanced from rarefied ecclesiastical debates but understanding 'the value of symbol'.

[78] *The Poems of Robert Henryson*, ed. Denton Fox (Oxford, 1981), p. 30; Szittya,

Some forms of piety betokened hypocrisy more than holiness. Stock behaviour evoked stock responses. According to John Audelay

> Yif ther be a pore prest and spirituale in spiryt,
> And be devoute, with devocion his servyse syng and say,
> Thay likon hym to a lollere and to an epocryte.[79]

It may be instructive, in conclusion, to look at our best account of Lollardy in the light of what has been said about the need for wariness in reading behind the terms and phrases of contemporary descriptions. Henry Knighton is generally accepted as having written the most ambitious and interesting account of early Lollardy, on which much has been built by modern historians.[80] Knighton is unusual in giving an extended narrative account of Wyclif and early Lollardy, spiced with first-hand observations that have added to respect for his words, which include statements about dress and forms of speech. The word 'sect' appears quite often in this chronicling, both when Knighton is describing individual Wycliffites and when he is venturing generalizations. A passage which has proved specially influential is the following, which forms part of a censorious description of Wyclif's disciples ('Wycliffians' or 'Lollards') and their 'sect', sandwiched between the record of Leicester offenders, William Smith, with his ally Richard Waytestathe, and William Swinderby.

> Et licet de novo conversi vel subito et recenter hanc sectam imitantes, unum modum statim loquele et formam concordem sue doctrine mirabiliter habueruent, et doctores evangelice doctrine, tam viri quam mulieres, materno ydiomate subito mutati effecti sunt. Et hoc acsi essent de uno gingnasio educati et doctrinati, ac eciam de unius magistri scola simul referti et nutriti.[81]

Even the newly converted, said Knighton, displayed a remarkable ability to adopt a uniform mode of vernacular speech, men and women alike, as if they had all been trained and nourished together, by one

Antifraternal, pp. 211–12. On the satirical image of the fox dressed in a habit see Scase, *New Anticlericalism*, pp. 120–1.

[79] *Poems of John Audelay*, ed. E. K. Whiting (*EETS*, os 184, 1931), p. 15.

[80] Knighton, pp. xlii–xlvi, lv–lvi; Geoffrey Martin, 'Knighton's Lollards', in *Lollardy and Gentry*, pp. 28–40.

[81] Knighton, p. 302.

master in one school, to become teachers of evangelical doctrine. This uniformity of diction and belief derived from the intoxicating inspiration of their dangerous master, so they became popularly known as Wycliffites.

Knighton gives examples of this shared speech, which Anne Hudson explored in her influential article, 'A Lollard Sect Vocabulary?' There was the disparaging of images of the Virgin as 'witches'. More conspicuous and important was talk about 'Trewe prechours, false prechours'. Knighton harps on this, observing the clamour of this shouted charge at sermons by John Purvey and his followers, and telling of John Aston's praise and reproof of true and false preachers.[82] He makes very clear that this was a significant feature of Wycliffite 'sect' behaviour. And the antithesis was indeed one which is fully vouched for in Wycliffite writings.[83]

However, before we start weighing the significance of Knighton's observations, we ought to be careful to place them in context. Take *gingnasium* (*gignasium*) for a start. Knighton had used this word when describing the goings-on in the chapel of St John outside Leicester. He alleged that Waytestathe and Smith held a school there of evil doctrines and opinions and the communication of heretical error. This statement comes on the heels of the assertion that the two men and others of their *secta* were holding conventicles to communicate their nefarious views.[84] 'Conventicle' is a word that should make us take notice. It came to the fore in legislation against Lollards in 1401, when the making of conventicles and the holding of schools were allied activities, jointly proscribed as essentially covert activities.[85] The term was already well-established in the context of heresy in canon law. Lucius III's 1184 bull called for reporting of *occulta conventicula* celebrated by heretics; and Innocent III's use of the term associated it with illicit instruction in scripture and usurpation of the preacher's office.[86]

[82] Ibid., pp. 286–7, 290–1.

[83] Anne Hudson, 'A Lollard Sect Vocabulary?', in *Books*, pp. 165–80, at 166–7.

[84] Knighton, p. 296.

[85] Hudson, *PR*, p. 178, cites as the first official description of Lollard schools a royal letter to London officials in 1392, in which clandestine scriptural meetings are, significantly, called conventicles (*conventicula*) – not schools. On Lollard 'occulta conventicula', 'prive conventicles or assemblies' for communicating suspect teaching, see Hudson, *Books*, p. 136; *Heresy Trials in the Diocese of Norwich, 1428–31*, ed. N. P. Tanner (Camden 4th ser. 20, 1977), p. 59.

[86] See above, n. 40. Innocent III associated conventicles with lay trespassing on preaching

Knighton's reporting may be graphic but it is also larded with familiar stereotypes. His description of Wyclif's followers is concerned above all to display the hypocrisy of their appearance – the seeming simplicity presented by their wearing of russet clothing; 'quasi simplicitatem cordis . . . speciem sanctitatis sub simplici vestimento pretendentes . . . vestimentum ovium . . . sanctitatis dulcedinem . . .'. The chronicler rings the changes on those scriptural passages anciently applied to such offenders, not forgetting Matthew's 'Attendite a falsis prophetis'.[87]

Knighton knew what he was about. He did not underestimate the dangers that in the 1380s were threatening the whole future, and he had good sources at his finger tips. Central to his understanding of these events was the deep divergence between mendicant friars and Wycliffites. It was against the friars that the repeated charges of 'false preachers' were made. Wycliffites condemned the friars outright and with venomous hostility, poisoning people's minds against them, and ceaselessly attacking them as 'false preachers'. Knighton places the entire topic of heretical activity and development in the context of antifraternal conflict.

> The Wycliffites proclaimed their sect to be the most commendable, and exhorted both men and women everywere to join it, and incited them to reject the doctrines and preaching of all others, and not to attend the sermons of the mendicant friars, whom they labelled false preachers. And they strove against them fervently and unceasingly, in public and in private, calling them false brethren, and asserting themselves to be the true preachers and evangelists, because they had translated the Gospels into the English tongue.[88]

It was this critical aspect of conflict that gave the whole terrible matter a prophetic dimension. We completely miss the tenor of Knighton's interpretation of the Lollards if we fail to read it in the context in which he squarely placed it: the apocalyptic. He surely intended his readers to be in no doubt, setting, as he did at the outset,

and instruction, 'though the wish to understand divine scriptures' and exhortations to study them were in themselves commendable; such conventicles were a means by which lay people usurped the office of preaching, and 'sacerdotum simplicitatem eludunt'. Friedberg, 2, col. 785 (Lib. V, tit. vii, cap. 12).

[87] Knighton, pp. 298–301.

[88] Ibid., pp. 304–5.

Wyclif's publicizing of the Gospel in the context of the Eternal Gospel and Joachimite prophecies of the impending last age. Knighton's opening paragraphs on Wyclif (clearly written well after the master's death) focused on the vernacular translation of scripture which had turned the evangelical jewel into a secular plaything, to the subversion of the church. This was presented as a direct fulfilment of what William of St Amour had written. 'Some there are who labour to change the Gospel of Christ into another which they claim to be more perfect, and better, and more worthy, and which they call the eternal Gospel, or the Gospel of the Holy Spirit.'[89]

These words come from chapter eight of William of St Amour's *De periculis novissimorum temporum* (On the Perils of the Last Times), written in 1255 against Gerard of Borgo San Donnino's work of the previous year. St Amour's counter-attack was that of the outraged secular master of theology, blasting the friars as preeminent pseudo-prophets of the last age before the coming of Antichrist. Knighton turned this prophetic text to fit his own anti-Wycliffite bill. The signs of the approaching end which he summarized seemed convincingly like what he saw and heard around him. 'When the end of the world approaches, those in the church who seem more holy will be censured for false holiness and their presumption. . . . there will arise in the church preachers esteeming themselves . . . [who will] glory in preaching . . . and in the guise of piety they will seduce many.'[90]

After this introduction, the ensuing harping on true and false preachers assumes a special significance. Wycliffites who preached against 'new sects' and advanced the claims of their own true 'sect', were joining in the ongoing battle of the last age. 'He often asserted in his preaching that the people had been deceived these two hundred

[89] Ibid., pp. 244–5; citing St Amour's *De periculis novissimorum temporum.* A more accessible text than that of the *Opera Omnia* ([Paris], 1632) is in Edward Brown's *Fasciculus Rerum Expetendarum*, 2, pp. 18–41, where this passage is on p. 27. On this work see Szittya, *Antifraternal*, ch. 1, and for Knighton's writing with it in front of him, pp. 105–6. See Wilks, 'Wyclif and the Great Persecution', p. 50, for the view that Wyclif 'saw himself as expressing Joachim's Eternal Evangel'. Years before Knighton wrote this passage, in about 1373, the debate between Wyclif and the Carmelite John Kenningham had been concerned with Wyclif's conception of scriptural truth as eternal ('dico quod Novum Testamentum est aeternum'). *Fasciculi Zizaniorum*, pp. 47, 455; B. Smalley, 'The Bible and eternity: John Wyclif's dilemma', in idem, *Studies in Medieval Thought and Learning* (London, 1981), pp. 409–10, 412–13; Catto, 'Wyclif', p. 195.

[90] Knighton, pp. 249–50 (translation altered), signs 5 and 6; *De periculis* in *Fasciculus Rerum Expetendarum*, ed. Brown, 2, p. 28.

years, after these new sects [the order of the friars] appeared, through false flattering preachers, the disciples of Antichrist'; words from the lips of one whom Knighton heard himself, perhaps none other than Philip Repingdon. 'He and supporters of his "sect" often strongly commended those called true preachers, and as often condemned those other preachers, called false preachers'; words attributed to John Aston. And John Purvey, 'like the rest of his followers, always in all his preaching greatly commended them, and always and everywhere disparaged others, above all mendicants . . . praising his own as true preachers and barking at other preachers, mendicants and churchmen alike, as false preachers'.[91]

What had been anti-mendicant became the anti-Lollard charge. If one set of false prophets was as bad as another, the latest breed had a peculiarly menacing role in the imminence of the last days. Knighton was but following where others had led long before. But in his clearly presented interpretation we can see how the scriptural vocabulary used by canonists to characterize heresy had become shot through with all the charge, counter-charge, and innuendo of controversy surrounding the preaching orders. One might go so far as to say that any controversy over a group of false preachers was bound to get caught up somewhere in the antifraternal web. Knighton may have been stating a personal view (and perhaps overstating his case) but it was an interpretation that others would readily have recognized.

So how do these mixed observations affect our view of the Lollards? They show that contemporary observers may have been both helped and hindered by the authorities to which they turned. If they described and acted on what they saw, what they saw was related to their textual dependence. We all see what we expect to see, and we have to talk about our experiences in the terms available. If we give certain words particularly wide currency, we inevitably alter their content. 'Sect' and *secta* were terms that gained larger circulation in the late fourteenth and early fifteenth centuries as the result of the appearance of Lollardy, and to chart their usage is to learn a little bit more about the history of the heresy and its reception.

Archbishop Courtenay, as much as the Augustinian canon Henry Knighton or the Carmelite friar Stephen Patrington, was caught in the flux of interaction between words and events. Canon law defined approaches to heresy and the nature of its falsity. The heretics' own

[91] Knighton, pp. 284–5, 286–7, 290–1. (I have made some changes in the translation.)

actions and writings prompted conclusions about parallels between developments among the mendicants and the behaviour of Lollards. If churchmen began to think about 'sect' as some kind of religious following comparable to a religious order, this surely owed something to the contests of the time, on the page and on the ground, which highlighted the similarities and differences between preaching friars and preaching Wycliffites. Perhaps, as a result, understanding of 'sect' and *secta* inched towards the meaning they would later hold.[92]

Examining the content of key words may not help historians to say more, but it ought to be part of their consciousness. Lacking it we may misinterpret the past as well as mislead the present. Whatever Thomas Netter said, with the benefit of half a century of official proscription, Lollardy was not a church. Maybe it was not a sect either, if we take proper account of this eel of a word, which slips in our hands even as we think we have hold of it. But what else can we call Wyclif's Lollard followers?

[92] See the *Middle English Dictionary*, ed. H. Kurath, S. M. Kuhn *et al.* (Ann Arbor, MI, 1954–) which includes among its definitions of *sect/e*, 2 (d) 'a group within an organized religious body which adheres to doctrines or practices generally regarded by the larger body as unorthodox or heretical; also, the system of beliefs of such a group, a heresy'. Some of the citations relating to Lollardy listed under this heading seem to me to belong more properly under other definitions, and others need to be looked at carefully since (as this paper has been intended to show) this definition, if it arrived at all in the period, did so as the result of the Wycliffites, whose beliefs, or heresies, are debatably described as a 'system'.

CROSS-REFERENCING IN WYCLIF'S LATIN WORKS

by ANNE HUDSON

ONE of the most immediately striking features of all of Wyclif's major writings, whether philosophical, theological, or polemical, is the frequency with which cross-references are found both between different chapters or parts of the same work and between works other than the current one.[1] The frequency of cross-referencing is variable. In the philosophical works and the intermediate tracts traditionally placed before the twelve-part *Summa theologie*, links are not enormously numerous. The first text to show a plethora of them is *De civili dominio*: here on average one instance occurs roughly every other page, more frequently in parts I and III, in other words some 600 in all. This habit continues with slight abatement in *De veritate sacre scripture*, and into *De ecclesia*. Thereafter the remaining parts of the *Summa* show a diminishing number, still further reduced in the *De eucharistia*. Cross-referencing is relatively common in the three long sets of sermons composed after Wyclif's retirement to Lutterworth, and in the *Sermones quadraginta* written *dum stetit in scholis*.[2] The device is obviously in origin an academic one, and it is worth observing that some of the major works which were written

[1] In this study Wyclif's works are quoted from the editions of the Wyclif Society (WS: 1883–1921), with the addition of *De officio pastorali*, ed. G. V. Lechler (Leipzig, 1863); *Trialogus*, ed. G. V. Lechler (Oxford, 1869); *Summa de ente libri primi tractatus primus et secundus*, ed. S. H. Thomson (Oxford, 1930); *De trinitate*, ed. A. du P. Breck (Boulder, 1962); *De universalibus*, ed. I. J. Mueller, with A. Kenny and P. V. Spade, 2 vols (Oxford, 1985). Texts in the WS editions are cited by title, followed if necessary by volume name (*Op. min.* = *Opera minora*, *Pol. Wks* = two volumes of *Polemical Works*). As far as possible, references are given by (volume), page and line number, the last being supplied if necessary, without counting any headings. W. R. Thomson's *The Latin Writings of John Wyclyf: An Annotated Catalog* (Toronto, 1983), though its details need some correction, provides an invaluable catalogue of the manuscripts of the texts; Thomson's numbering of the texts is used here, prefixed with *T*. In references to manuscripts I use 'Vienna' to refer to those in the Österreichische Nationalbibliothek there, 'Prague MK' to refer to the Metropolitan Chapter Library there, and 'Prague UK' to refer to the National, formerly the University, Library there; BL is used for London British Library, TCC for Trinity College Cambridge.

[2] I have considered the implications of those in the *Sermones quadraginta* and *Sermones viginti* in 'Aspects of the "publication" of Wyclif's Latin sermons', in *Middle English Religious Texts and their Transmission: Essays in Honour of A. I. Doyle*, ed. A. J. Minnis (Cambridge, 1993), pp. 121–9.

after Wyclif left Oxford have few if any: in the *Trialogus* the virtually complete absence of internal linkings could be explained as the result of a perception that the orderly organization of the whole obviated the necessity for such an aid, but this explanation does not seem relevant to the final *Opus evangelicum*.[3] Cross-referencing has previously been observed by students of Wyclif, and has traditionally been used in the attempt to order his vast output chronologically, and to put dates to individual works.[4] But this is to jump to conclusions – to assume that the references are authorial and that the works in which they occur were composed as a whole at one time. The discussion here will suggest that there are questions to be answered in regard to the former assumption, and substantial objections to the latter. More modestly, I hope here to use the cross-references to throw light on the ways in which Wyclif's works were written, put together, and 'published'.

Two preliminaries must first be made clear. First, the existing editions of Wyclif quickly proved to offer inadequate documentation for this enquiry. Most simply, more manuscripts of many of the texts edited in the Wyclif Society have come to light; these may offer conflicting or more complete evidence. More worryingly, it also became clear that neither the text, nor the variants cited from those manuscripts known to the editors, were always an accurate record of their witness.[5] In some cases this is probably the result of the editors' reliance on amanuenses, whose work they were either unable or unwilling to check; in others it seems likely that the alteration was deliberately though silently made, to fit in with the editor's understanding of the passage to which reference was intended. These deficiencies in the printed texts have meant that I have felt obliged to check all cross-references across all manuscripts currently known, whether or not they had been quarried by the editors; this has been a slow business, since some thousand or so references scattered through many texts across numerous manuscripts in several countries are

[3] There seems to be only a single internal link in the *Trialogus*: this is the unspecific one in bk ii.14 (123/16) back to *sententia primi libri*.

[4] The most notable examples have been S. Harrison Thomson, 'The order of writing of Wyclif's philosophical works', *Českou Minulostí práce* (Festschrift in honour of V. Novotny), ed. O. Odložilík, J. Prokeš, and R. Urbánek (Prague, 1929), pp. 146–65; I. J. Mueller, 'A "lost" *Summa* of John Wyclif', *SCH.S*, 5 (1987), pp. 179–83. Thomson (*Latin Writings*) draws together the evidence from this source with other scraps of internal and external testimony.

[5] Thus, for instance, the three complete manuscripts of *De ecclesia*, all allegedly used by Loserth, all unambiguously give references to chapter 22 despite the text's 20 at 257/1, and all have 25 as against the text's 27 at 467/29 (no variants given at either place).

involved, and it has not been possible to check all cases for a second time.[6]

The second preliminary concerns terminology. The term 'cross-referencing' can cover a wide variety of linking devices. At its most general, phrases such as *ut patet alibi, ut dictum est in multis locis* can be used; but these are of little interest, since they have no indicative force concerning individual works. They have been ignored in the present study. Much more interesting are those links which offer specific references. The simplest form is a plain specification of work: 'ut patet ex dictis in Trialogo', found in the brief *De fide catholica* (*Op. min.* 116/21), since the title is that of one of Wyclif's final works, offers no problems. But the titles of some of his works are far from being so distinctive as this: 'ut patet in materia de ydeis/de universalibus' may be a reference to two of Wyclif's works *De ydeis* and *De universalibus*, but the nouns are common ones and may not incorporate a title at all. Here some discretion is needed, unless further specification of chapter clarifies the position. The opening 'ex dictis de statu innocencie' in *De quattuor sectis novellis* (*Pol. Wks* i.270/14) leads to the assumption of a reference to Wyclif's brief work of that name, until it is noted that the following words are 'et de statu post finale iudicium', for which no equivalent work is known to survive; the conclusion must be that neither is a cross-reference. It should also be observed at the start that two of the phrases most frequently employed incorporate ambiguity: *ut patet* and *ut dictum est* would normally be translated 'as appears' and 'as is said', but do they imply anything about order or about chronology? Even if both naturally suggest that the material is already available, it is less clear whether any implications of sequence and/or of time should be drawn. The second could equally well be translated 'as has been said', thus more clearly implying chronology but again leaving sequence uncertain. Even the simple verb *est* can apparently be ambiguous in this context: *De potestate pape* specifies at one point 'de istis autem in tractatu *De sacramentis* est sermo lacior' (278/5), and yet a good deal later in the text is found 'sicut dicam, si Deus voluerit, in materia *De sacramentis*' (382/10) – the first must apparently indicate an existing text, though the second looks forward to writing it in the future. The importance of these ambiguities will become clear later.

6 One defect in my first investigations that it has been impossible completely to remedy was my failure to record whether a manuscript had the usual Arabic or less commonly Roman numerals (or spelt out the word); this turned out very occasionally to be of interest. The various editors' usage does not follow that of their base manuscripts.

Turning to the cross-references themselves, usually in Wyclif's works these take the form of the chapter (or sermon) number, together with some indication of work; no lettered subdivisions of chapters or sermons are used, though very rarely words such as *in fine* may give further help in location.[7] When the reference is to another part of the same work, *huius* is usually substituted for any fuller title. The indication of work may take the form of title, or of the number of the part in a longer sequence, or of both. Examples of the first, without the obscurity mentioned above, would be 'ut recitavi in tractatu De *incarnacione*' (T32 *De ecclesia* 126/28 referring to T22 *De benedicta incarnacione*). Examples of the second are 'vide hoc libro 2° tractatu primo capitulo 4to' (T9 *Purgans errores circa veritates in communi* 7/7 referring to T14 *De intelleccione dei*, book II tract 1 of the *De ente*), 'ut ostenditur 25 capitulo libri 5' (T31 *De veritate* ii.216/9 referring to T30 *De civili dominio* iii.71, the fifth book of the *Summa theologie*). The third fashion, as the most cumbersome, is the least common: an example is 'ut tactum est tractatu *De tempore* capitulo 3 et ita libro 6' (T19 *De potencia productiva dei ad extra*, TCC fol.143rb, to T12 *De tempore*, book 6 of the first part of *Summa de ente*). Where reference is to a freestanding work, without numeration in a larger collection, the title has to be the identifying mark. But habit seems to vary somewhat in references to the *Summa de ente* and the *Summa theologie*: to the former either title or book and part might be used, though increasingly the title seems to have been preferred. In the *De civili dominio*, the *De veritate* and the *De ecclesia* references within the *Summa theologie* are almost always by book-number and chapter;[8] but in the fewer indications of the subsequent parts there is an increasing tendency to use titles, and this becomes the invariable method in references to the *De symonia*, *De apostasia*, and *De blasphemia*.

The sections that follow show some of the kinds of evidence produced by these cross-references. Because all sections of the philosophical *Summa de ente* have still not been edited, and a printed source to which recourse can be made is consequently not available, I shall

[7] Lettered subdivisions of chapters or sermons are provided in many but not all of Wyclif's works, but not in all copies; the evidence suggests that this device, necessary for the provision of indexes, was added very soon after Wyclif's own lifetime. For a provisional statement about the device and the indexes see my *PR*, pp. 104–8; a fuller analysis will be published soon.

[8] This numbering implies the twelve-part order, as known from Thomson and the WS editions; for questions about the date when that order was established see below, pp. 207 ff.

largely avoid this area.[9] The sermons will also not be included here: the two short sets, the *Sermones quadraginta* and the *Sermones viginti* have been discussed elsewhere, whilst in the remaining three long groups cross-references form one element in a larger argument about their composition, and will be examined at more length in another paper. The main theological and ecclesiological works, most of them assembled into the twelve sections of the *Summa theologie*, will form the core of the present study.

I

The simplest evidence produced by listing the cross-references in Wyclif's works is a number of titles, apparently of texts by the author himself, that are unfamiliar to the reader of the modern editions. A number of these are identifiable with sections now incorporated into other texts, and seem to point to varying processes of revision. The first example has been recognized since 1977, when a work *De religione* by Wyclif was noted by Eric Doyle from references in William Woodford.[10] Doyle deduced from Woodford's quotations and references that *De religione* consisted of *De civili dominio* iii chapters 1–3, followed by *De apostasia* chapters 1–2. Whether, as Doyle suggests, the *De religione* was originally a section of *De civili dominio* iii (with the two chapters of *De apostasia* replaced after the three of this), or whether it was an independent work subsequently split up by Wyclif between the two now known tracts, does not emerge from Woodford's testimony. But a *De religione* is mentioned within Wyclif's own texts, in *De civili dominio* ii.236/30 and in *De blasphemia* 50/25. These confirm that its opening was incorporated into the opening chapters of *De dominio civili* iii.[11] However, *De blasphemia* also refers to material that was once in the *De religione* under its new home: 'dictum est autem 2° capitulo *De apostasia*' (203/9) is correct for the latter text as we know it, even though it seems originally to have been *De religione* chapter 5.[12] In

[9] Mueller, 'A "lost" *Summa*', and the introduction to his edition of *De universalibus*, pp. xxxiii-xxxviii, covers some of the problems, and suggests the original existence of a third *summa*, of which only parts survive.

[10] E. Doyle, 'William Woodford, O. F. M., and John Wyclif's *De religione*', *Speculum* 52 (1977), pp. 329–36.

[11] The first is to *De civ. dom.* iii.19/36–20/2, the second more vaguely to *De civ. dom.* iii cap. 1; the first involves a reference forward (for which see below pp. 210 ff).

[12] Similarly 'ut patet libro 5° capitulo 3' (*De blasphemia* 203/19) incorporates the book

comparison with the other examples to be considered, it seems fairly certain that it existed as a separate tract and that it was split up by Wyclif himself.

Another text whose existence the cross-references support is *De adnichilacione*: this is referred to in *De benedicta incarnacione* 76/18, 78/30, *De statu innocencie* p. 476/6, and *De eucharistia* 52/11. Dziewicki in his volume for the Wyclif Society entitled *De ente* (1909) included as the final item three chapters, 12–14, of the final tract of the second book of the *Summa de ente*, the *De potencia productiva dei ad extra*, which, he noted, are headed in Trinity College Cambridge B.16.2 (the only manuscript he knew) *De adnichilacione*; in fact that heading covers chapters 12–16.[13] Thomson (p. 35) dismissed the idea that *De adnichilacione* was ever a separate tract, though he seems to think the designation is Wyclif's, not just scribal: he argues that the heading was 'a kind of shorthand tag' for 'a distinctive and recognizable portion of a long and somewhat unwieldy treatise'. There is certainly no sign of any break in the text of *De potencia productiva* in the other manuscript, Prague UK IX. E.6 – but then there are few headings of any description in that copy, even where an undisputed break occurs in Trinity.[14] It seems likely that the indications that an originally separate *De adnichilacione* once existed should be added to the other evidence suggesting that what we now have as the separate thirteen tractates of the *Summa de ente* is a late redaction of earlier material which almost certainly was of different shape and subdivision.[15]

Other allusions are to works hitherto not recognized. First a *De heresi* is mentioned in *De ecclesia* (69/2, 87/25, 298/18). Since all specify it as 'book 6', this must be identified with the final chapter of the *De veritate sacre scripture*. This begins (iii.274/18) 'postremo incidentaliter ad tractatum *De veritate scripture* restat tractare de heresi' (and cf. end iii.309/25), which may suggest that an originally independent tract is

number of *De civili dominio* iii within the *Summa theologie*; 'ut expositum est 2° capitulo *De apostasia*' (220/11) must involve a scribal error in the chapter number (albeit found in all extant copies), since the material in question seems to be chapter 3, p. 31.

13 The title appears as a running title on fols 151r-156r above chapters 12–16, and chapter 12 begins with an illuminated capital of a kind normally found in the manuscript only for a new item.

14 The Prague copy, fols 16r and 51r, does not mark off in any way the start of *De sciencia dei* and *De potencia productiva* respectively.

15 See Mueller, 'A "lost" *Summa*', and intro. to *De universalibus*. It should be noted that a reference in *De trinitate* 166/19 establishes *De ente predicamentali* as the fifth tract of *De ente* book 1, even if this was not its original status.

being incorporated.[16] A *De mendacio* is again mentioned in *De ecclesia* (43/23, 159/30). This may likewise be a part of the *De veritate*, this time chapters 16–20 (ii.1–129); here there is no sign of 'marking off' in the wording; but the subject is certainly right, and the first reference in the *De ecclesia* precedes the title with 'ut patet libro 6' – *De veritate* is the sixth book of the *Summa theologie*. More intriguing is the *De cessacione legalium* found in *De symonia* (51/2 and 76/25), and in *Sermones* ii.259/37. The obvious objection to this as a work by Wyclif is that it alludes to Grosseteste's treatise of this name.[17] That this may not be the right answer is indicated both by the fact that *Lincolniensis* has not been mentioned hitherto in *De symonia* (though he is at 88/20 and 103/8, neither is a reference to the *De cessacione legalium*), and also by the inappropriateness of the subject matter to which this reference is allegedly relevant. In addition to the cross-references, John Bale lists a work of the same title under Wyclif's name, and gives an incipit for it 'Redeundo autem ad propositum de'; this is *not* the incipit of Grosseteste's work, which itself is included by Bale under the latter's name with the right incipit.[18] Bale's evidence provides the essential clue: the incipit he gives is that of the penultimate chapter in the edition of *De veritate sacre scripture*, whose subject is indeed the continued validity of law if the officers imposing it cease to exist. This seems to be a third section of the *De veritate* that may have had independent existence before being incorporated.

A *De privilegiis* is mentioned in *De officio regis* (1/2), and *De ecclesia* (276/14, 304/12, 343/12). These references seem likely to allude to chapters 8–11 (157/25–250/16) of *De ecclesia* itself, as it now stands. Privilege is indeed the subject of those chapters (though chapter 12 continues it). The first reference in *De ecclesia* (cap. 13) is in full '11 capitulo *De privilegiis*',[19] and plainly refers to the citation of Matthew 10 and Luke 10 in chapter 11 (248/2–6); the second 'sicut dixi in

[16] A reference in *De civili dominio* ii.113/12 'considerans dicta de heresi vii capitulo' seems to be to chapter 7, ii.58/8 ff. of the same book, and not to the *De heresi* specified in *De ecclesia*.

[17] Wyclif knew this work, as is evident from *De veritate sacre scripture* iii.104/10–14, 106/12–107/4 and elsewhere.

[18] *Scriptorum Illustrium maioris Brytannie . . . Catalogus* (Basel, 1557–9) i.452, Grosseteste i.306.

[19] *11* appears in Vienna 1294 and Vienna 3929, *20* in Prague UK X. D.11; for a possible cause of the discrepancy in the last see below p. 201. The punctuation given, recognizing a title, is my own, Loserth's being inconsistent; manuscript rubrication can here, as elsewhere, not be regarded as significant because of its frequent omission even with undoubted titles.

materia *De privilegiis*' and the last 'ut patet superius tractatu *De privilegiis*' is less specific, but implies that the tract is part of the current work. Here there is less reason to look to an independent tract, and it may be that the title only refers to a subdivision of a longer work.

Less clear are the remaining references. *De maximo et minimo* appears in *De veritate* (ii.121/7)[20] and in *De ecclesia* (572/5); the most likely candidate for this is chapter 7 of *De logica tractatus tercius*.[21] Other cases, where a philosophical work seems to be in question are: *De continuacione* (*De benedicta incarnacione* 53/18) which could be either chapter 9 of the same work or chapter 20 of *De ente predicamentali* (T13); *De accione* (*De ente* 195/26) which might be an allusion to *De ente predicamentali*, especially chapter 10. The identity of *De anima*, mentioned in *De benedicta incarnacione* (203/19, 230/18) and *De ecclesia* (422/2), is unclear: the obvious answer of *De actibus anime* (T4) seems from the subject matter in question improbable, and the answer may lie in a lost commentary on Aristotle's text of the same name which Mueller, on other grounds, has suggested once existed.[22] Other cases where the nature of the text is less clear are *De perplexitate* (*De dominio divino* 126/21); *De Christo* (*De veritate* iii.118/11).[23]

II

These titles could in some instances (though not in that of *De religione*) point not to modification of earlier plans but simply to subdivision of the work in question. But smaller details of the cross-references make it clear that revision must in some cases be in question. A simple case concerns *De ecclesia*. The organizational problems of *De ecclesia* are obvious to anyone who reads the text attentively: though part of it apparently relates to Wyclif's advice given to the Parliament at Gloucester in 1378 concerning the Shakyl and Haulay sanctuary

[20] With the addition 'et in materia de composicione continui'.

[21] See the opening words of this chapter, p. 129/2.

[22] Mueller, 'A "lost" *Summa*', p. 182; Wyclif's commentary on Aristotle's *Physics* survives in one copy now in Venice (T6 Biblioteca San Marco, Marciana lat. VI.173, fols 1ra–58vb), and his commentary on the *Meteora* once existed in the Prague Carolinum library (list 2, no. F7 in the facsimile in J. Bečka, J. Benda, *Katalogy Knihoven Kolejí Karlovy University* (Prague, 1948).

[23] The context of the first is entirely unhelpful; for the second the editor, R. Buddensieg, suggests tentatively *De benedicta incarnacione* 36/15 ff.

case, it is not clear which section if any was actually presented there and equally the number of opponents to which other sections of the material on this topic were directed is obscure.[24] One oddity in this text is the frequency with which the cross-referenced chapters are incorrectly given in all the available witnesses. The number of surviving manuscripts of this text is not enormous: three complete manuscripts (Vienna 1294 (A), Vienna 3929 (A1), Prague UK X. D.11 (B)), one containing only chapters 1–3, and two containing chapter 7.[25] The situation may be set out as follows: cross-references involving chapter 1–2 are unchanging and correct; a reference to a chapter 10 should be to existing chapter 2 (84/20), two to 12 should be to 3 (177/19, 181/6), one to 14 should be to 5 (388/4), one to chapter 16 should be to 7 (223/12), one to 18 should be to 8 (223/7), one to 20 should be to 11 (276/14), four to 22 should be to 13 (340/26, 343/18, 372/23, 516/27).[26] It is hard to make complete sense of this: it seems certainly to imply that material has been removed between existing chapters 2 and 3, but the number of chapters taken out seems to vary between eight, nine, and ten; assumption of further excisions of chapters later on still cannot produce a single coherent explanation. Unfortunately, there are no useful references to *De ecclesia* in other Wyclif works. Netter, whose quotations from Wyclif's works are usually furnished with identifiable bibliographic details, and are often long enough for checking, seems not to have used this text.[27] But the possibility of intermediate stages, perhaps more than one, in the compilation of the

24 See Thomson, pp. 58–60, and references there given; the historical background to this text, and to other allusions by Wyclif to the case, are being studied by Peter Griffin (Trinity College, Cambridge). The full textual problems cannot be set out here.

25 The sigils are Loserth's, and reflect his belief that the second was a copy of the first. The incomplete versions are respectively Wolfenbüttel Herzog August Bibliothek, Guelf. 1126 fols 46–84v, Trinity College Dublin 242, pp. 398–403 and Florence Biblioteca Laurenziana, Plut. XIX.33 fols 30–32v. Vienna ÖNB 3934, fols 148r–151r contains notes from various Wyclif works including this.

26 These details are those of Loserth's base text without his emendations, Vienna ÖNB 1294; variants to them are as follows: 388/5 all copies, despite Loserth's record, have 14; 223/12 A1 has 6; 276/14 A and A1 have 11 as is correct by the printed text but B has 20; 340/26 A's reading 13 is a marginal correction to 22, A1 has 22, B has 13; 343/18 A's reading is again a correction of 22 to 13, A1 and B have 22; 372/23 A's reading is again 22 corrected to 13, with 13 in the margin, A1 has 22, B 13; 516/27 again A corrects 22 to 13, with 22 and 13 both in the margin, A1 along the line crosses through 22 and writes 13, B has 13.

27 His *De ecclesia et membris eius* is T48, now called the *Supplementum Trialogi*, or *De dotacione ecclesie*; see *Doctrinale Antiquitatum Fidei Catholicae Ecclesiae*, ed. B. Blanciotti, 3 vols (Venice, 1757–9).

text as we know it would seem to be the most probable background to the muddle that remains.

A much more complicated case is the *De veritate sacre scripture*. Here the problem rests not in a discrepancy of references between numbers and actual text, but relates to one divergence between the manuscripts in regard to their inclusion or omission of the section i.151/19–167/8, covering the end of chapter 7 and beginning of chapter 8. Of the twelve manuscripts that contain this part of *De veritate*, six omit this material: Queen's Cambridge 15 (C), BL Royal 7 E.x (R), Prague UK III. B.5 (Q), with a marginal note *hic est magnus defectus*, Prague MK B.53 (K), Prague MK C.38 (S), Olomouc Kapitolni Knihovna C. O.115 (O). The section is present in six: Vienna 1294 (A), but with a marginal note 'vide bene quia aliqui non habent hoc ab isto loco usque ad signum tale' – the sign appears again at i.167/8; Trinity College Dublin 243 (D), but the section was omitted at its proper place by the original hand and was added by another on the opening flyleaves in an odd order;[28] Bodley 924 (B), but with a marginal note (p. 47), 'item cum logica abhinc usque ad hoc + ut 5° folio post non creo' and a corresponding mark at the end of the passage; Peterhouse 223 (P), but marked at either end by marginal pointing hands, and by a new line leaving a blank in the text; Prague UK VIII. C.3 (Z) and Prague MK A.84 (X) in neither of which is there any comment.

At first sight the cause of the problem seems to have been eye-skip: p. 151/18 ends a sentence 'ex intento et institucione et ordinacione legiferi dantis legem sic falsam, ut decipiat', and the omitted section ends 'in casu scripturam sacram et scripturam ut decipiat'. The omission, if such it is, must have arisen very early in the tradition. Scribes of the earlier manuscripts of insular origin seem to have been particularly aware of a difficulty: Vienna 1294, though written by Bohemian scribes, was corrected in Oxford in 1406,[29] and the Bodley, Dublin, and Peterhouse copies all indicate a problem. Only Prague UL III. B.5 of the true continental copies shows awareness of corruption.

This apparent scribal omission has ramifications in the cross-referencing within the *De veritate*. As has been said, it crosses a chapter

[28] On fols 2v–3 appear i.159/1–167/8 with the marginal note *capitulum 8*, then on fols 3–3v pp. 151/19–158/20 with no indication of misplacement; the order perhaps reflects an exemplar two of whose leaves had been reversed from their proper order (the two chunks of material each run to 208 lines in print).

[29] See colophon fol 119vb 'in vigilia Purificacionis Sancte Marie Oxonie per Nicolaum Faulfiss et Georgium de Knyehnicz'.

division, and its inclusion or omission should affect the subsequent numbering of the remaining chapters. No chapter numbers of any kind are found in Prague MK C.38 (itself an incomplete copy ending i.368/18). Numbering that is correct for the inclusion of the passage is found in Vienna 1294, Peterhouse Cambridge 223 and Prague UK VIII. C.3; numbering that is correct for the omission in BL Royal 7 E.x, Queens' Cambridge 15, Prague MK B.53, Prague UK III. B.5, Olomouc and Trinity College Dublin 243 – notwithstanding the subsequent addition of the missing material at the start of the last copy. Prague MK A.84 has only sporadic numbering but, despite the fact that it includes the passage, those numbers that occur after chapter 7 could only be correct for a text without it.[30] It is not clear whether the inconsistencies in Bodley 924's numbering are independent of this particular problem, or whether they too reflect it.[31]

There is, however, a further complication. As with most of Wyclif's major works, an analysis of the text survives in certain copies.[32] For the *De veritate* an analysis up to chapter 21 (according to the numbering of the edited text) survives in four copies: Vienna 1294, Trinity College Dublin 243, Prague UK III. B.5 and Prague MK B.53. The second of these is certainly of English origin; the first, despite the copying of the main text in England, could have been written in Bohemia since the analysis (along with an index by opening) is in a different hand from the main text and in a separable quire.[33] The content of the analysis in all four copies is identical. Significant for the present purpose is that the analysis *of chapter* 7 moves straight from material identifiable with the text at i.148/1 to other material at i.167/14, ignoring all matter in the dubious section. For the two Prague manuscripts this is reasonable, and produces no oddities about the numbering of subsequent chapters since neither copy contains the dubious section – their analysis corresponds with their text. In the Dublin copy the analysis likewise corresponds to the text *as originally written*, with its chapter numbering but without the added material at the start. But the scribe involved in

30 The text ends incomplete in chapter 18 (i.287/8).

31 Chapters 1–11 are correctly marked, allowing for the inclusion of the passage; chapter 12 is again numbered 11, and the remaining chapters are one too low for the text – though sporadically visible plummet notes record the correct form.

32 Whether these analyses were authorial or scribal is not entirely clear, but, as is evident in the present case, the origin of many if not all can be proved to be English, since they are found in both insular and Bohemian copies in identical form.

33 Analysis fols 125va–127rb, index fols 120ra–125rb; the whole forming quire 13 of eight leaves, as opposed to the ten-leaf quires elsewhere.

the analysis in the Vienna manuscript noticed the problem: he continued through the analysis of chapter 7 as that appears in the other copies, but then went back and added *et 8* in the central margin for insertion after 7, continuing then to analyses for what he described as chapters 9–21; these correspond to the edited text 9–21, but to the other analysis copies chapters 8–20. This may suggest only that the analysis was made from a manuscript that lacked the section. The same may be the explanation also for the fact that the index of biblical passages discussed in Wyclif's writing, an index preserved in two Bohemian manuscripts, likewise is only accurate for a copy without the section.[34]

The question of the original state of the text evidently interrelates with the cross-references: this passage should enable decisions to be made also about the authority of the cross-references. If the passage at the end of chapter 7 and beginning of chapter 8 (according to the edited text) were original – as the explanation of eyeskip would imply – then any original cross-references to chapters after 7 should reflect its presence. Conversely, if the cross-references are scribal, then correctly those copies which omit the passage should have numbers one lower than those which contain it in all cross-references involving chapters 8 onwards. But in fact the situation is more complicated and in its complexity provides no help towards the resolution of either the originality of this short passage or the responsibility for the linkings. Two cross-references seem to require inclusion of the passage in *all* manuscripts available: iii.23/2 'ex capitulo vicesimo' refers back to ii.137 chapter 20, but *20* is found without significant variation (ABCDKOQ in which KOQ should have *19*, Z has *secundo* by evident misreading of *20* as *2°*); iii.104/4 'dictum est vicesimo primo huius' refers back to ii.164 chapter 21, but *21* is found in all available manuscripts (ABCDKOQZ in which KOQ should have *20*). So far this would seem to confirm that the omission of pp. 151/19–167/8 was a scribal error, and that the cross-references continued as if no loss had occurred. But more mysteriously in four places lower figures appear, and in those manuscripts that *include* the passage as well as in those that do not: ii.139/30 'sicut in parte tactum est supra capitulo 16', where the reference is to ii.30 chapter 17 (found in ABCDKOPQZ, where

[34] Prague UK IV. G.27 fols 1ra–35vb and Vienna 4522 fols 24–108v; the first is dated 1461, the second is itself undated though another item in the manuscript was copied in 1423.

ABDOPZ should have *17*); ii.140/18 'ut recitatur supra 16 capitulo', where the reference is to ii.44 chapter 17 (found in the same group of manuscripts); ii.154/23 'ut narratur 17' where the reference is to ii.83 chapter 18 (found in the same group of manuscripts); iii.245/18 'ut expositum est 16 huius sexti' to chapter 17 (again in the same group, though P's text stops before this point).[35] These four cases might seem to suggest that the cross-references were inserted after the original composition and to a copy that lacked the original end of chapter 7 and beginning of chapter 8. The only way to explain their presence in manuscripts that *do* have that section would be to assume that the insertion was done on the hyparchetype of the defective copies *prior* to the realization of the eyeskip.

But was it eyeskip? Both *De ecclesia* and *De potestate pape* contain references back to *De veritate*; some of these throw no light on the situation (either because they are too general, are incomplete, or because they refer to material before chapter 7), but all the relevant examples provide a chapter number that is only correct on the assumption that the passage omitted was *not* part of the text as known.[36] Much of the evidence seems to point to a different explanation of the 'missing' passage: that it is not an omission by a careless scribe in a hyparchetype, let alone by a series of careless scribes who coincidentally omitted the same piece, but that it was in fact added to the text at a date subsequent to the completion of the whole and the first 'publication'. Consideration of the content of the passage may confirm this: the opening chapters of the *De veritate* are very largely uncontroversial, concerned with the status and value of scripture, and the need for all Christians to understand it. This subject runs through to the middle of chapter 7 and is continued immediately after the 'missing' section. But the end of chapter 7 and beginning of chapter 8, as edited by Buddensieg, deals with more dangerous topics and in more tendentious terms: the alleged infallibility of the pope, the worldly jurisdiction of the clergy, the identification of heresy, with loaded language such as 'glose sinistre, ut quidam doctor tradicionis

[35] A fifth possible case is at iii.256/9 where 'ut exponitur supra capitulo 18' refers to ii.100 chapter 19; but only B has a number here, whilst ACDKOQZ leave a gap, but B should read *19*.

[36] Thus *De ecclesia* 239/13 refers to chapter 25 (edited text iii.55/11 chapter 26), 257/15 to chapter 24 (iii.12/5 chapter 25), 297/33 to chapter 20 (ii.155 ff. chapter 21); *De potestate pape* 1/7 refers to chapter 14 (i.375 chapter 15); all available manuscripts of each text offer the same number.

humane et mixtim theologus' (153/22), 'corpus ecclesie malignancium' (154/15). Difficult though impressionistic judgements of this kind may be to establish, there seem to be signs of embattled defence in this section which is characteristic enough of much of Wyclif's later writing but not, up to this point and indeed for several chapters beyond, of the *De veritate*.

The implications of this local, but extremely knotty, problem seem to be various. If, as has been suggested, the passage from the end of chapter 7 to beginning of chapter 8 was an authorial addition rather than its absence being the result of a scribal eyeskip, then it must point to revision of the *De veritate*. If this is correct, the revision extended to the modification of some but not all of the existing cross-references within the text. The existence of some copies without the passage would imply that circulation of the text began prior to revision; but the proportion of copies showing awareness of the problematic status of the passage (whether that was of a defect or of addition) suggests a remarkable interest in the authority of the text, and an apparent ability to collate at least parts of an exemplar against another source – 'controlled dissemination' seems not out of the question.

But if a possible explanation is available for *De veritate*, no such solution emerges in the case of another part of the *Summa theologie*. The *De officio regis* (T33) was placed as the eighth book of the *Summa theologie* by the compilers of the Hussite catalogue of Wyclif's works, and has been accepted as such by modern editors and cataloguers.[37] It follows on from *De mandatis*, *De statu innocencie*, the three books of *De civili dominio*, *De veritate sacre scripture*, and *De ecclesia*. Internal evidence of subject matter suggests a date after the Westminster sanctuary case of 1378 discussed in *De ecclesia* (see 157/29 and less explicitly 169/20), and after Urban VI's Bull of November 1378 (see 120/17); but disillusionment with Urban VI has, to judge by his description as 'papa noster' (123/6), not yet set in.[38] The text as a whole is much better organized than the three works that precede it in the *Summa*,

[37] The Hussite catalogues are printed (with some mistakes and the omission of the second half of the last copy) by Buddensieg in *Pol. Wks* i.lix–lxxxiv; the earliest manuscript is dated *c.* 1415. Some consideration of their evidence appears in my article, 'The Hussite Catalogues of Wyclif's Works' in *Husitství, Reformace, Renesance* i (in honour of František Šmahel), ed. J. Pánek, M. Polívka, N. Rejchrtová (Prague, 1994), pp. 401–17.

[38] Arguments against articles of the *abbas de Cartesii* have not yet proved enlightening (98/6 ff., 128/35 ff., 130/18 ff.); John de Usk was Abbot of Chertsey from the 1370s to 1400, but no text by him seems to survive.

with fewer digressions or outbursts. The editors, Alfred Pollard and Charles Sayle, say (p. xxii) 'With chapter VIII there can be no doubt that the *De officio regis* originally came to an end'; but the remaining four chapters deal with four objections mentioned at the start of chapter 9 (217/13, and picked up at the start of the next two chapters 231/2 and 245/26) which are relevant to what precedes and legitimately extend the discussion. The amount of cross-referencing in this text is small in comparison with the three works before it in the *Summa*, but *De mandatis*, *De civili dominio* books i and iii, and *De ecclesia* are mentioned; the reference to 'libro 6 *De pastorali officio*' (163/17) could well be to *De veritate sacre scripture*, the sixth book of the *Summa*, and not to the *De officio pastorali* (T53), though the subject matter would allow either.

But there are in the *De officio regis* half a dozen puzzling references to statements in chapters 33, 34, 36, 38 and two in 39 of another work; one of these last is specified as 'libri proximi'. The 'liber proximus', the *De ecclesia*, has only 23 chapters (and even the assumption of an originally longer work, above p. 201, would not give 39). The only work likely to be relevant that has the requisite number of chapters is *De civili dominio* i. One of the six seems certain to be to this work (231/1 '39 capitulo' to *De civ. dom.* i. 274/9 ff.), and a second seems likely (195/28 '38' to *De civ. dom.* i. 267/7 ff.); but in each case the chapter number in the printed *De civili dominio* is one lower than that in the *De officio regis* reference. Three further references in the latter seem to be to *De civili dominio* ii, but here the numbering is hopelessly discrepant (125/13 'superius 34 capitulo' to *De civ. dom.* ii. 58 ff., chapter 7; 212/1 '39 capitulo' to ii.39/7 ff., chapter 5; 249/29 '33 capitulo' again to ii.39/7 ff., chapter 5). The first instance, 'ex dictis 36 capitulo' (119/3) is difficult to locate. The three known manuscripts of *De officio regis* do not differ in regard to any of these.[39] Unless these references are simply crazy, the implications are bewildering in their ramifications. In terms of their ideas and subject matter, *De officio regis* would make a very reasonable follow-on to *De civili dominio* i. Much of books ii-iii of that latter work is taken up by Wyclif's responses to objections, some of them following on from the 1377 Bull of Gregory XI, to book i; they could thus hardly have been planned from an early

[39] The printed edition is based on Vienna 4514 with correction from Vienna 3933; Prague UK X. D.11, which may be earlier than these, was known to, but not used by, the editors.

stage.[40] *De veritate* and *De ecclesia*, as has been seen, have clear signs of heavy revision, involving the amalgamation of tracts that may well have had independent origins. So *De civili dominio* book i as the 'liber proximus' to *De officio regis* is not impossible. The absence of specification of work from all but one of the six references could suggest that the two works were very closely connected in the author's mind.

There is, however, conflicting evidence. The last suggestion does not begin to deal with the problem of the apparent allusions in *De officio regis* to book ii of *De civili dominio*, allusions which might suggest that some material that we know in that latter book was at the time of the writing of the former in book i. Equally references in *De veritate sacre scripture* specify it as book 6 of the *Summa* (iii.245/18, 301/11, 305/25) and *De civili dominio* iii as book 5 (ii.216/9, 250/13, 21 etc.), a numeration only correct on the now accepted ordering (in which *De officio regis* is part 8). Yet *De civili dominio* iii.447/14 observes 'ut 6 libro propono diffusius exponere' in regard to subject matter involved in any of *De ecclesia*, *De officio regis*, or *De potestate pape*, but not to the subject matter of *De veritate sacre scripture* which is now the sixth book. Certainly the text of *De civili dominio* rests on evidence of extreme fragility, even for Wyclif's case where burning by his opponents has drastically reduced the number of manuscripts: only a single copy of the whole survives (Vienna 1341 for books i-ii, 1340 for book iii), together with an extensive but poor student's copy of about two thirds.[41] But the 1411 Oxford condemnation, which listed forty-four erroneous passages from it, thought the *De civili dominio* had three books, and the cross-references elsewhere in Wyclif's own writings will only work on that assumption.[42]

III

Turning from the detail of individual texts to consider whether any general conclusions can be drawn, the first obviously important

[40] Cf. Catto, 'Wyclif', pp. 206–7.

[41] Paris Bibliothèque nationale lat.15869 contains (*pace* Thomson, *Latin Writings*, pp. 49, 51) book i, book ii caps.1–12 (lacking ii. 110/21–129/1), book iii. 512/21–538/18, 626/19–647/31 somewhat disordered.

[42] Thus *De potestate pape* 9/14 'ut tangitur 21 capitulo 5 libri' to *De civ. dom.* iii. 425, or to *De veritate* in *De officio regis* itself as 'libro 6' (52/29). For the 1411 condemnation see Wilkins, *Concilia*, 3, pp. 339–49; the items from *De civili dominio* are nos. 176–219.

question about all these cross-references is whether they originate from Wyclif's own efforts or whether they were scribal additions. The possibility that they were scribal additions is suggested by the presence of a few marginal cross-references found in the early and (perhaps unjustifiably) prominent manuscript, Trinity College Cambridge B.16.2.[43] It would be readily comprehensible if all the cross-references had started off in such fashion and had been subsequently incorporated into the text. But, though this is a credible hypothesis, there is little or no hard evidence to support it. The references visible in the margins of this manuscript are not replicated at all in other copies of the texts against which they are found, whether marginally or in the text. I have made no systematic search for new cross-references introduced into the margins of Bohemian copies. Some of these manuscripts are very heavily annotated, and such an investigation would take a long time.[44] But were there widespread intrusions of new cross-references from the margins *into the texts themselves*, this would certainly have come to my notice in checking those links printed in the editions; I have not been aware of any cases. Conversely, the presence of cross-references embedded within all texts is entirely stable at the same places through all copies of the texts in question; an almost exhaustive survey of surviving manuscripts has revealed a remarkable uniformity of presence of cross-references at the same places in all extant copies. There are, of course, cases where scribes evidently misread or miscopied numbers – numbers are particularly susceptible to such error; but such cases are few, and in any case do not obscure the intention to provide a cross-reference.[45] This uniformity must, at its lowest, indicate that this means of facilitating access to the texts was provided in the hyparchetype of all copies of the work in question – if

[43] Those I have noted are in the sermons, and are recorded by Loserth in his footnotes to i.309/27, 347/12, 354/6, 362/18, ii.13/11, 107/31, iii.27/29, 110/31, 220/3.

[44] S. H. Thomson, 'A Note on Peter Payne and Wyclyf', *Medievalia et Humanistica*, 16 (1964), pp. 60–3, sought to associate marginalia in seven Vienna manuscripts that he thought to be in a distinctively English hand with Peter Payne, the fugitive Lollard who reached Prague in 1415. Thomson's hypotheses are open to question on a number of fronts.

[45] An instance of visual confusion is *De mandatis* 40/5 where a forward reference to 'tractatu 3 capitulo 10' (i.e. *De civili dominio* i cap. 10) leads to fourteen manuscripts' reading of the chapter as *14*; this probably goes back to an exemplar like Gonville and Caius Cambridge 337/565 which indeed here has Arabic *10* where the second numeral could readily be read as *4*. The forms of certain numerals, notably 5 and 7, in Bohemian script, equally misled several of the Wyclif Society's editors, and produced errors in the printed texts.

the author did not provide them, then a redactor/redactors must have worked with remarkable consistency over a very considerable body of Wyclif's works. With remarkable consistency but not complete uniformity: if a redactor were inserting these references with an eye to 'publication', then one might expect that the same form, of title or of part number, would be used throughout. The sort of fluctuation found is more characteristic of activity over a period of time, an individual scholar's natural tendency to favour one form at one time and another subsequently or to vary by oversight or by stylistic preference even within a single work.

Another piece of evidence that at first sight might point towards scribal origin is the fact that quite a number of these references are in some degree incomplete: most commonly chapter numbers are not entered, as 'patet tractatu *De tempore* capitulo –' (*De dominio divino* 112/7), 'patet ex dictis *De divino dominio* tractatu 1 capitulo –' (*De civili dominio* i.127/4); occasionally the reference is even more defective 'ut exposui capitulo – libri –' (*De officio regis* 7/15, probably referring back to one of the first five books of the *Summa theologie*). But on reflection these deficiencies seem more easily explicable on the hypothesis of authorial origin for the references. Why should a scribe, let alone a redactor charged with providing this means of access to the texts, insert a reference which he could not complete? Perhaps the scribe or redactor hoped to be able to complete the reference subsequently, and failed to do so. But the multiplication of unverifiables does not make this an attractive line of argument.

As may have been noticed from some examples, including one just quoted, references may be explicitly forward as well as backward – explicitly, since they use a future tense in the verb attached or indicate position forwards by an adverb. Thus 'ut posterius dicitur *De sciencia dei*' (*De intelleccione dei* 99/24, the first tract of book 2 of the *De ente*, referring to *De sciencia dei*, itself the second tract of the same book); 'ut patet infra tercio huius capitulo 43' (*De mandatis* 316/32, the first book of the *Summa theologie*, referring to *De civili dominio* i.358, itself the third book); 'ut planius intelligatur tractatus *De symonia*' (*De veritate* iii.310/2, referring forward to a later book of the *Summa*). Some of the references that may be supposed to direct forwards are not marked as such: thus 'vide libro tercio *De humano dominio*' (*De dominio divino* 204/27 referring to *De civili dominio* part i). From the statement at the end of *De statu innocencie* it would appear that Wyclif intended the *De dominio divino* to precede any treatment of human dominion.[46]

The issue of forward allusions seems to form the nub of any debate about the origins of the cross-references. If the origin were editorial (which term I use here to cover both the activities of a scribe and those, presumably more organized, of a redactor), then forward allusions would be as simple to provide as backward ones. If the editor had only the single text on which he was working, then references either way could only be within that text. If he had a range of texts, then the extent of references could be greater and should encompass all available works irrespective of their date or order. Only if the editor had guidance about the date or ordered sequence, could he correctly indicate outside the single work futurity or completion, *posterius* from *superius*, by verb tense, or by adverb. Unambiguous *verbal* indications of future by means of verb tense or adverbs are comparatively rare; as was said at the outset, 'ut patet' or 'ut dictum est' are open to either retrospective or forward interpretation. The number of certain references forward, whether within a single work or between different works, is actually very small – though it does exist – and is far outweighed by the vast number unambiguously, or at least most naturally understood, as alluding backwards. This in itself points against the idea of editorial activity: on simple grounds of probability more forward references would be likely on that hypothesis. There can be no doubt that the presumed aim of the operation, to facilitate access to all Wyclif's texts, would be much better achieved had there been more forward references; such references could also have allowed for the indication that Wyclif had modified a view expressed in his early works in writings from later in his career, and so have reduced the appearance of inconsistency in regard to certain opinions.

Here the question of the origins of these cross-references interlocks with that of date: can a reference within one work to another work provide a chronology of the one text to the other? If, for instance, *De veritate sacre scripture* refers, without clear indication by verbal tense or by adverb, to *De civili dominio* iii (as at ii.216/9 of the former to iii.71 of the latter, cited above p. 208), does this necessarily imply that *De veritate* is the later composition? In view of the evidence adduced above

[46] *De statu innocencie* 524/19–25; it should be noted that all five continental manuscripts of the text end before this point, chapter 10 only existing in the English manuscripts Trinity College Dublin 243 and Gonville and Caius Cambridge 337/565.

concerning the modification of texts, including here both works, I think this must be regarded as dubious – at least in that simple formulation.

Looking in detail at the clear cases, it is striking that the largest number of apparently forward references occur in parts of the *Summa de ente*, the philosophical collection in two books of respectively seven and six parts, whose organization and content has been shown to have been authorially modified in major ways.[47] To summarize the cases that seem proven: I.i *De ente in communi* refers to II.i *De intelleccione dei*; I.ii *De ente primo in communi* refers to II.i *De intelleccione dei*, II.iv *De trinitate* and II.v *De ydeis*; I.iii *Purgans errores circa veritates in communi* refers to I.v *De universalibus*, II.i *De intelleccione dei*, II.iii *De volucione dei*; I.iv *Purgans errores circa universalia in communi* refers to II.v *De ydeis*; I.v *De universalibus* refers to II.iv *De trinitate* (and also to T22 *De benedicta incarnacione*, outside the *Summa*); I.vi *De tempore* refers to a 'tractatu de substancia', probably to be identified with I.vii *De ente predicamentali*;[48] I.vii *De ente predicamentali* refers to II.i *De intelleccione dei*, II.iii *De volucione dei* (with which it has a substantial overlap of two chapters), and II.v *De ydeis*; II.i *De intelleccione dei* refers to II.ii *De sciencia dei*, II.v *De ydeis* (and again to *De benedicta incarnacione*); II.ii *De sciencia dei* alludes to II.iii *De volucione dei*, II.iv *De trinitate* and II.v *De ydeis*; II.iv *De trinitate* in its reference to 'ut patebit in materia *De eucharistia*' (111/3) probably intends a pointer to the section *De anichilacione* which, as previously mentioned, forms a section of II.vi *De potencia productiva dei ad extra*.[49] Such a display is exactly what might be expected if an author worked through previously written material as he assembled it into a single coherent whole.

The contrast with the works of Wyclif's theological and ecclesiological maturity is striking, despite the fact that some texts of that maturity, notably *De civili dominio*, show the densest concentration of cross-referencing. *De dominio divino* contains three allusions, all of

[47] See references above, nn. 4 and 9; for the effects of this reorganization on the availability of exemplars to at least one scribe see my paper 'Trial and error: Wyclif's works in Cambridge, Trinity College MS B.16.2', in *New Science out of Old Books: Studies . . . in Honour of A. I. Doyle*, ed. R. Beadle and A. J. Piper (Aldershot, 1995), pp. 53–80.

[48] Accepting the view of S. H. Thomson, 'Order of writing', p. 161 (c), and his suggestion of chapter 5 of that text.

[49] See above p. 198. For reasons of space full references to the other cases cannot be given; most are deducible from S. H. Thomson and Mueller's articles above n.4 and from W. R. Thomson's observations on his texts T7–19 (though some cases in each that seem to me dubious have been ignored here).

them vague, to a book 'de humano dominio' – should this be italicized, as an alternative title to what became known as *De civili dominio*?[50] *De mandatis*, the first section of what came to be described as the *Summa theologie*, has two more specific allusions to *De civili dominio* i, and two acknowledgements of outline intentions to discuss the power of the pope and simony.[51] Amongst the vast array of the device in *De civili dominio* in book i just six refer to book ii, one to book iii, whilst in book ii two only refer to book iii.[52] Quite apart from the tiny fraction of these forward pointers, two factors are worth observing: that all seven of those in book i derive from four chapters (40–3) and hence might reflect authorial revision of that section. Secondly and more significantly, much of *De civili dominio* ii and iii represent Wyclif's defence of his views in book i against their heretication by Gregory XI's Bull and the ensuing outcry of opposition from William Woodford and other critics – exactly the situation in which forward reference, if entered by a redactor working at a date later than composition, would be most helpful. The remaining examples of forward pointing in the *Summa theologie* are very few and unhelpful; many have already been mentioned in another context.[53] To summarize: the final paragraph in T31 *De veritate sacre scripture* anticipates a 'tractatus *De symonia*' (T35), though T32 *De ecclesia* (342/28) speaks of it as written; T34 *De potestate pape* mentions twice, once in the future, a tract *De sacramentis*, T35 *De symonia* more specifically calls it *De eucharistia*, whilst T37 *De blasphemia* speaks of it as written.[54] The contrast with the *Summa de ente* is striking.

It should be noted that all the early manuscripts contain the references, whether these point backwards or forwards. One of the earliest surviving manuscripts, the extract from *De potestate pape* in Trinity College Dublin 115 probably of 1380, unluckily does not involve a cross-reference.[55] Oriel College 15 of *De benedicta*

[50] See 204/26, 224/12 and 255/20; the first has a future verb, the second and third know that this is a 'third book' and the third that the matter is to be found in chapter 7.

[51] Respectively 40/5 'tractatu 3 capitulo 10', 316/32 'infra tercio huius capitulo 43'; 360/1 'de ista materia cum tangit potestatem pape dicetur inferius', 380/17 'quomodo autem omnes simoniaci sunt heretici est alibi longus sermo' (all manuscripts are unanimous in their witness to the books).

[52] See i.315/17, 330/28, 337/4 (repeated 14, 27) 341/14 (linked to 345/7), 393/5; i.394/5 (repeated at 20), 394/13; ii.209/26, 212/20.

[53] See above pp. 208 ff for details.

[54] Respectively 278/6 and 382/10 (for which see above p. 195); 110/27; 22/31.

[55] The extracts from *Sermones quadraginta* in Exeter College Oxford 6 (for which see J.van Banning, *JThS*, ns, 36 (1985), pp. 338–49) omit the only reference 'ut alias ostendi'.

incarnacione, written by Nicholas Fawkes of Glastonbury Abbey in 1389, has the full panoply of references, as found in the later copies. The two early copies of parts of *De civili dominio*, Durham Dean and Chapter Reg. N of 1391 with chapters 24, 26–7 of book iii, and Paris BN lat.15869, a student copy of not much later than 1381, with two-thirds of the whole, likewise record them (even if curtailed in the latter case by the scribe's abbreviation of parts of the work). There seems to be no stage in the known textual history of any of the writings without these references. After prolonged work with this bulk of evidence, my own conclusion is that the majority derive from authorial insertion: the absence of any significant body of forward references, especially in the *Summa theologie*, seems the strongest evidence for this. But equally traces of authorial revision and recasting are abundant in the philosophical works and in the texts of the *Summa theologie*;[56] the stage at which cross-references were provided cannot be assured, even if they were provided authorially. On their own, it seems, cross-references may be a hazardous means of establishing chronology.

This negative conclusion does not, in my view, end their interest. The evidence of titles and of certain details of cross-referencing seem to make a strong case for the view that the *De veritate sacre scripture* and the *De ecclesia* underwent considerable revision before they reached the state in which modern scholars know them from the Wyclif Society editions. Indeed, those editions give a misleading impression of a settled text in regard to many of Wyclif's works. Scrutiny by Ivan Mueller of the references in the philosophical works pointed to major reorganizations in that area, apparently undertaken at least in part much later than the original writing of the texts. Michael Wilks some years earlier than Mueller drew attention to evidence that Wyclif revised his presumably early *De logica tractatus tercius* (T3) in the 1380s, incorporating into it ideas concerning the eucharist that he certainly had not arrived at in the 1360s.[57] This revision explains why this work, under the title of *De arte sophistica*, was examined by the Oxford investigators before the 1411 condemnation.[58] Wyclif's *Sermones*

56 See Mueller, 'A "lost" *Summa*' and intro. to *De universalibus* for material on the former.

57 M. Wilks, 'The early Oxford Wyclif: papalist or nominalist?', *SCH* 5 (1969), pp. 93–4; it should be noted that the date 1383 (iii.183/39) appears in all four surviving manuscripts (written out as 'mille trecenti octoginta 3' in Assisi Biblioteca Communale 662), and so is unlikely to be a scribal error (as Dziewicki i.vii, knowing only one manuscript, suggested).

58 See Wilkins, *Concilia*, 3, p. 346, and for some of the notes of the investigators Hudson, *PR*, pp. 83–5.

quadraginta certainly underwent reorganization before the 'publication' of the collection, though in this case it is less clear whether either collecting or reorganizing was done by Wyclif himself.[59] Anyone who tries to compare a manuscript of the *Dialogus* (T408) with the printed edition is likely to find that the numbering and order of the later chapters are seriously discrepant.[60] Loose ends, whether of the kind considered here or as evidenced in other ways, abound.[61] None of this, unwilling though Thomson, Wyclif's latest cataloguer, was to recognize revision,[62] should surprise us. Wyclif was a busy man, both as an academic and as a political controversialist, often with many tracts under way simultaneously, answering objections and questions with ferocious energy as soon as they arose. He had every reason himself later to endeavour to tidy up his output, to incorporate the answers to immediate problems into a larger whole, to adjust for afterthoughts, for new arguments and new situations. But, to complicate the situation, his early disciples likewise had every reason to organize their master's output; the provision of indexes to many of the major works, necessitating the prior provision of subdividing letters to each chapter or sermon, seems certainly attributable to their devotion.[63] One conclusion does, however, seem certain: the cautionary one that dating any of Wyclif's texts is even more hazardous than has hitherto been apprehended, and that in particular cross-references should not alone be trusted.

University of Oxford

[59] See 'Aspects of the "publication" of Wyclif's Latin sermons'.

[60] Pollard's edition provides a conflated text with few variants, and used only nine of the twenty-five manuscripts now known.

[61] The Hussite catalogues provide further indications, as I have shown in 'Aspects of the "publication" of Wyclif's Latin sermons'; the evidence provided by the passages duplicated from one work to another will be considered elsewhere. Allusions to Wyclif by near contemporary writers, whether friends such as Hus or foes such as Woodford, are rarely detailed enough for use in this matter; Netter's evidence is an exception to this general rule.

[62] In addition to the examples already given, T391 is another clear instance: this snippet, surviving in only one manuscript, is not a 'letter' (as suggested in Thomson's article 'John Rylands Library MS Eng.86: an unnoticed piece by John Wyclyf', *MS* 43 (1981), pp. 531–6 and repeated in the *Catalog* p. 241) but two extracts from *Sermones quadraginta* (*Sermones* iv.200/27–201/5 plus 233/10–26) strung together with a few words at the beginning and middle.

[63] See *PR*, pp. 104–6 for a preliminary statement.

THE 'MENDICANT PROBLEM' IN THE LATER MIDDLE AGES

by R. N. SWANSON*

ALMOST from their foundation, the mendicant orders proved problematic. Their insistence on poverty, their preaching skills, and their responsiveness to contemporary spirituality challenged the Church at many levels, providing standards against which the secular clergy might be judged and found wanting. Their dependence on papal privileges which limited episcopal oversight, and their claims to a special role as confessors and preachers, threatened the Church's current order, especially in parishes. By undermining the parish priest's authority – jurisdictionally by offering confession and absolution, financially by encouraging burial in their houses – the friars in fact undercut some of the aims of the early thirteenth-century reformers, most notably by disrupting the demands of *Omnis utriusque sexus*, the decree requiring annual confession to the 'proprius sacerdos', issued at the Fourth Lateran Council.[1] The most important resolution of these 'grass root' problems was provided in Boniface VIII's *Super cathedram* of 1300, which by 1326 applied to all four of the main mendicant orders, and formally became part of canon law when enshrined in the Clementines.[2] Unfortunately, *Super cathedram* seemed incompatible with *Omnis utriusque sexus*, and debate on the resulting discrepancy persisted throughout the Middle Ages, despite attempts at resolution such as *Vas electionis* of 1321.[3]

* I am grateful to the British Academy for financial support for the research for this paper.

[1] X 5.38.12; Tanner, *Decrees*, 1, p. 245.

[2] Clem. 3.7.2; Tanner, *Decrees*, 1 , pp. 365–9. For the early history of *Super cathedram*, C. Uyttenbroeck, 'Le droit pénitentiel des religieux de Boniface VIII à Sixte IV', *Études franciscaines*, 47 (1935), pp. 176–85 (see p. 176 n. 5 for its application to individual orders). For later reissues, K. Walsh, *A Fourteenth-Century Scholar and Primate: Richard FitzRalph in Oxford, Avignon and Armagh* (Oxford, 1981), pp. 407, 421. See also R. C. Trexler, 'The bishop's portion: generic pious legacies in the late Middle Ages in Italy', *Traditio*, 28 (1972), pp. 407–11, 415–16. The legal relationship between the mendicants and the secular clergy in the aftermath of Vienne is usefully summarized in H. Lippens, 'Le droit nouveau des mendiants en conflit avec le droit coutumier du clergé séculier, du Concile de Vienne à celui de Trente', *Archivum franciscanum historicum*, 47 (1954), p. 251.

[3] Extrav. comm. 5.3.2.

These issues provided material for canonistic analysis throughout subsequent centuries, ensuring that the debates and doubts did not subside completely.[4]

The practical disputes between seculars and mendicants usually attract less attention than the more exotic conflicts which surrounded the friars (especially the Franciscans) during the thirteenth and early fourteenth centuries. The Franciscans' dabbling with Joachite prophecy, and the likening of the Franciscan Rule to a new gospel, became a theological challenge to the Church with the emergence of the Spiritual Franciscans.[5] At Paris the uproar created by Gerard of Borgo San Donino's *Introduction to the Eternal Gospel* began a lengthy period of discord within the university, as the secular masters exploited the situation to voice their resentment at the mendicants' rise (particularly within the theology faculty), and their unwillingness to be bound by the normal rules of the masters – including a refusal to cease academic exercises when the seculars did. In southern France, the followers of Peter John Olivi developed an extreme Franciscanism which likewise challenged the Church. Finally, the Franciscans were themselves split by factional disputes over the question of apostolic poverty. The ramifications of that dispute impinged on papal authority as the two sides clashed over how far the papacy could alleviate the demands of Francis's Rule and Testament, eventually producing arguments akin to demands for papal infallibility, even while assertions of the apostolic (and gospel) character of the mendicant life undermined the authority and standing of the existing Church. What began as a dispute between Franciscans became a conflict between papacy and Order under Pope John XXII, whose blunt denunciations of the extreme stance on apostolic poverty eventually quashed, but could not quell, the opposition.[6]

[4] On such analysis, Walsh, *Fourteenth-Century Scholar*, pp. 430–1; Uyttenbroeck, 'Droit pénitentiel', pp. 181–2.

[5] For the Franciscans and the Rule, D. Nimmo, *Reform and Division in the Franciscan Order, from St Francis to the Foundation of the Capuchins*, Bibliotheca seraphico-capuccina, 33 (Rome, 1987), pp. 152–8.

[6] Leff, *Heresy*, 1, pp. 51–230; D. L. Douie, *The Nature and Effect of the Heresy of the Fraticelli* (Manchester, 1932); M. D. Lambert, *Franciscan Poverty: the Doctrine of the Absolute Poverty of Christ and the Apostles in the Franciscan Order, 1210–1323* (London, 1961); M.-M. Dufeil, *Guillaume de Saint-Amour et la polémique universitaire parisienne, 1250–1259* (Paris, 1972); J. D. Dawson, 'Richard FitzRalph and the fourteenth-century poverty controversies', *JEH*, 34 (1983), pp. 316–29; Nimmo, *Reform and Division*, pp. 51–138; B. Tierney, *Origins of Papal Infallibility, 1150–1350: a Study on the Concepts of Infallibility, Sovereignty and Tradition in the Middle Ages*, Studies in the History of Christian Thought, 6 (Leiden, 1972).

Discussion of the medieval mendicant problem tends to tail off after the pronouncements of John XXII. The debate over the Beatific Vision in the 1330s, which allowed some of the Franciscans to attack the Pope as a heretic, offers a kind of coda, as does the involvement of individual mendicants as propagandists for Louis of Bavaria in his political struggles with John XXII, and the appointment of the obscure Franciscan Peter of Corbara as antipope in 1327. The storms generated by Richard FitzRalph in the 1350s act as an aftershock; but by shifting the ground from issues of poverty to questions of dominion they also shift the fundamental issue from the mendicants' status to the broader question of ecclesiastical property.[7] The lingering Spiritual tradition in Italy, represented by the *fraticelli*, still caused minor difficulties; but they were only minor.[8] They did, though, ensure that the question of Christ's poverty remained a live issue, providing matter for tractarian controversy well into the fifteenth century.[9]

However, 'the mendicant problem' did not go away; it merely subsided, perhaps changed its emphases, and became a constant irritant within the Church: chronic, intermittently flaring up to attract attention. It is that chronic irritation which is considered here. The continued 'mendicant problem' had extensive ramifications and implications, obviously for the religious orders, but also impacting on the universities, on heresy, and indeed on the Church in general. However, that the 'problem' did not cause fundamental discord also shows how the Church could establish a practical reconciliation of its internal contradictions, in which rival or contradictory 'discourses' co-existed in a manner which, while not always harmonious, was usually reasonably pacific.[10]

[7] Walsh, *Fourteenth-Century Scholar*, pp. 349–447; Dawson, 'Richard FitzRalph', pp. 329–44.

[8] Douie, *Nature and Effect*, pp. 209–47; Nimmo, *Reform and Division*, pp. 252–72; Leff, *Heresy*, 1, pp. 230–55.

[9] E.g. C. Schmitt, 'Le traité du cardinal Jean de Torquemada sur la pauvreté évangélique', *AFP*, 57 (1987), pp. 103–44; D. L. Douie, 'Some treatises against the Fraticelli in the Vatican Library', *FS*, 38 (1978), pp. 16–40, 43–55, 59–78. The debate about poverty also continued in other circumstances; see e.g. A. Williams, '*Protectorium pauperis*: a defense of the begging friars by Richard of Maidstone O. Carm. (d.1396)', and V. Edden, 'The debate between Richard Maidstone and the Lollard Ashwardby', both in P. Fitzgerald-Lombard, ed., *Carmel in Britain: Essays on the Medieval English Carmelite Province*, vol. 2. *Theology and Writing* (Rome, 1992), pp. 35–83, 84–105.

[10] That the disputes were kept within bounds fits them within the structures proposed in R. N. Swanson, 'Unity and diversity, rhetoric and reality: modelling the church', *Journal of Religious History*, 20 (1996), pp. 156–74.

Clearly not all manifestations of 'the mendicant problem' throughout Europe between *c.*1360 and the early sixteenth century can be considered here. The focus is on the relations between the mendicants and the secular clergy. The internal tensions of the orders, especially those linked to the Observant movements, are ignored.[11] The links between the mendicants and the laity are also largely untouched. The concern is primarily with the aftermath of *Super cathedram* and the associated legislation. The geographical focus begins in England, but thereafter turns to continental Europe (and Ireland).

* * *

Late medieval England offers numerous cases of localized conflict over the friars' role and function. There are repeated, if frustratingly obscure, references to conflict, often originating in the traditional issues of confessional powers and the intrusion of mendicants into burial matters. The English bishops apparently adopted a rather idiosyncratic application of *Super cathedram.* Although the Bull was intended to control the confessional activities of friars, by requiring the presentation of suitable individuals to the bishops for licences, England's fourteenth-century bishops apparently used it in other ways as well. Friars were also licensed to preach. The bishops thereby limited the mendicants' role in parochial pastoral care, but this did not eliminate disputes.[12]

The difficulty, not confined to in England, is to assess the relationship between the secular and mendicant clergy with any degree of precision. FitzRalph's diatribes against the friars' undermining of

[11] On the Observant movements, the tensions, and connections with 'laicization', Nimmo, *Reform and Division*, pp. 353–658; P. L. Nyhus, *The Franciscans in South Germany, 1400–1530: Reform and Revolution, Transactions of the American Philosophical Society*, ns 65/viii (Philadelphia, 1975), pp. 10–17; M. Richards, 'The conflict between Observant and Conventual reformed Franciscans in fifteenth-century France and Flanders', *FS*, 50 (1990), pp. 263–81; D. Guttierrez, *The Augustinians in the Middle Ages, 1357–1517* (Villanova, PA, 1983), pp. 73–98; K. Elm, ed., *Reformbemühungen und Observanzbestrebungen im spätmittelalterlichen Ordenswesen*, Berliner historische Studien, 14: Ordensstudien 6 (Berlin, 1989) – esp. articles by R. Manselli, D. B. Nimmo, P. L. Nyhus, J. Smet, and K. Walsh.

[12] B. Z. Kedar, 'Canon law and local practice: the case of mendicant preaching in late medieval England', *Bulletin of Medieval Canon Law*, 2 (1972), pp. 17–26 (for continued control over sermon content even after licensing seemingly lapsed in the fifteenth century, ibid., pp. 26–32); H. L. Spencer, *English Preaching in the Late Middle Ages* (Oxford, 1993), p. 60. The context of the discord in F. Roth, *The English Austin Friars, 1249–1538*, 2: *Sources*, Cassiciacum: Studies in St Augustine and the Augustinian Order, 7 (New York, 1961), pp. 509*–10* is not clear, but may reflect a similar dispute.

episcopal and parochial authority were based primarily on his experiences in Ireland, although they clearly did resonate with audiences in England.

Conflicts were necessarily on very specific issues, often flaring up as individual events which needed a precise remedy. Discord over burial dues had arisen at Ludlow in 1353, leading to the resolution that if someone sought burial in a friary, there should be a preliminary commemoration in the parish church, from which the incumbent would receive the proceeds, before the proper funeral at the friars' house.[13] This was probably a national practice (it was so described in 1404);[14] but disagreement still occurred. In 1402 a local rector accused the Dominicans of Langley of abducting the body of the Duke of York, so depriving him of the burial offerings.[15] Uncertainty about the distribution of offerings from the two ceremonies generated a court case in York in the 1380s.[16] Here, a further problem about the mendicants appeared: although the dispute centred on offerings made at the ceremony in the Dominican friary, the plaintiff incumbent presumably could not cite the friars because of their exemption,[17] and accordingly brought his case against the deceased's executors. The case certainly suggested some collusion to avoid liability to the rector. His claim focused on the lights burnt around the corpse at the funeral; but the executors said that the Dominicans had renounced any right to the lights, and returned them to the executors after the event, thereby invalidating the plaintiff's plea.

While the mendicants might pick off an individual incumbent relatively easily, institutional opponents were a different matter. Conflict here might be between friars and other regulars, as holders of jurisdiction or appropriators. Such was the dispute between the abbey of Bury St Edmunds and the Franciscans of Babwell in 1419, terminated when the bishop of Winchester (as conservator of the friars' privileges) decreed that the friars needed abbatial licences to hear

[13] *Registrum Johannis de Trillek, episcopi Herefordensis, A. D. MCCCXLIV–MCCCLXI*, ed. J. H. Parry, *CYS*, 8 (1912), pp. 195–6.

[14] Lichfield, Joint Record Office [hereafter LJRO], B/A/1/7, fol. 129r. It also appears in a London will of 1462: J. Röhrkasten, 'Londoners and London mendicants in the late middle ages', *JEH*, 47 (1996), p. 468.

[15] M. D. Legge, *Anglo-Norman Letters and Petitions from All Souls MS 182*, Anglo-Norman Texts, 3 (Oxford, 1941), pp. 35–6.

[16] York, Borthwick Institute of Historical Research, CP. E.184.

[17] See the claim for such exemption in Parry, *Registrum Trillek*, p. 170.

confession.[18] As an exempt peculiar, Bury was perhaps in an anomalous position – certainly for the application of *Super cathedram*. Similar jurisdictional concerns, or a fear of claims to exemption in disciplinary matters, presumably lay behind a regulation promulgated in the deanery of the royal free chapel of Bridgnorth in 1510 banning friars from acting as parish priests, chantry priests, or soul priests within the jurisdiction.[19]

Elsewhere, evidence of conflict is spasmodic, and relatively opaque.[20] In the mid-fourteenth century, the priory of Bishop's (now King's) Lynn entered into agreements with mendicant houses in and around the town regarding payments of the canonical quarter in accordance with *Super cathedram*.[21] Despite these, the surviving parochial accounts (the rectory being administered by the priory) offer scattered glimpses of what was presumably a fairly constant process of attrition. In 1429–31 the priory spent slightly over £20 against the friars to maintain its right to the canonical quarter, with two more payments (albeit significantly smaller) within the next five years.[22] The battle was presumably hard fought, certainly costly. Whether it was justified is debatable: between 1431 (the year after the costly battle) and 1477 the parish accounts record the amounts received for the canonical quarter from the friars. These are usually fairly paltry, ranging from 10*s.* 6½*d.* in 1450–1 down to nothing in several other years.[23] Where orders are identified, most payments were made by the Augustinians; none by the Franciscans. Yet the determination to fight – presumably shared by both sides – is significant: status had to be maintained. Yet there is one hint of ambiguity. In a year when 13s. 4d. went towards costs against the friars, the priory also gave the Carmelites 20s. for the expenses of their general chapter.[24] As elsewhere, verbal attacks from the friars also had to be rebutted: the

[18] BL, MS Add. 14848, fol. 26r–v. For later licences, issued to Franciscans and Dominicans, ibid., fols 26v, 79v–80.

[19] Shrewsbury, Public Library, MS 112, fol. 72v.

[20] E.g. Norwich, Norfolk and Norwich Record Office [hereafter NNRO], DCN 2/14/17, the parish account for Great Yarmouth for 1489–90, which records 'expensis contra fratres minores, nihil hoc anno, quia continuatur'. The other relevant entry in these accounts (DCN 2/4/16, for 1485–6) is to a dispute over burials with the Franciscans.

[21] D. M. Owen, *The Making of King's Lynn: a Documentary Survey*, Records of Social and Economic History, ns 9 (London, 1984), no. 87 (Augustinians, in 1361); NNRO, DCN 87/1 (Carmelites, 1371).

[22] NNRO, DCN 2/1/25, 26, 44, 49.

[23] NNRO, DCN 2/1/26–68.

[24] NNRO, DCN 2/1/49.

account for 1445–6 records 56s. 5d. spent 'circa destruccionem oppinionis magistri Johannis Capgrave predicantis, etc.'[25]

Further evidence of the uncertainties of compromise appears in a case from 1403–5, when the rector of Mancetter in Warwickshire challenged the activities of the Austin friars at Atherstone. That house had been established in 1375, and an agreement had been made between the friars and the rector to settle foreseeable difficulties;[26] but thirty years later they were at loggerheads.

The case is first mentioned in a papal bull of June 1403, responding to an appeal from the rector against the friars for alleged breaches of the *Super cathedram* arrangements.[27] The matter was delegated to the bishop of Lichfield, but actually settled by arbitration, duly ratified by the bishop.[28] The rector's claims ranged widely, but primarily centred on burial matters, especially receipt of the canonical portion. He charged that the Augustinians, ignoring the national custom for the '*ultimum vale*' were holding the first post-mortem masses in their house – sometimes with a fictive corpse. The rector also complained about burials of children and *impubes*; about attempts to persuade people to be buried at the friary; and about the anniversaries held there. Jurisdictionally just as significant was the allegation that the Augustinians were usurping the rights of the parish church: they delivered sermons at times which clashed with the parish celebrations, made parochial announcements, distributed holy bread, and had erected 'duas excessivas et vehementes ymagines' of Peter and Paul (the parochial patrons) which detracted from the status of the parish church.[29] The Augustinians responded vigorously to what they perhaps considered a challenge to the mendicants in general – their witnesses included representatives of all four orders.[30] In the event, though, the rector won on most counts, especially those affecting the canonical quarter and burial rights.[31] The provisions here were quite specific: the

25 NNRO, DCN 2/1/39. This dispute perhaps originated during Henry VI's visit to Lynn in 1446: Roth, *Austin Friars*, p. 328*.

26 LJRO, B/A/1/7, fols 133v-134r; Roth, *Austin Friars*, pp. 270*–71*.

27 *CPL*, vol. IV, *A. D. 1396–1404*, pp. 539–40.

28 LJRO, B/A/1/7, fols 128r-137r; Roth, *Austin Friars*, pp. 268*–77*.

29 The rector's claims appear LJRO, B/A/1/7, fols 129r–130r; Roth, *Austin Friars*, pp. 272*–5*.

30 LJRO, B/A/1/7, fol. 131r; Roth, *Austin Friars*, p. 269*. Unfortunately, the testimony is not recorded.

31 The award was delivered in two parts, LJRO, B/A/1/7, fols 131v–133v, 134v–137r; Roth, *Austin Friars*, pp. 269*–70*.

canonical quarter for itinerants buried within the friary was to go to their home parish, but the rector of Mancetter was to have the *ultimum vale*; for vagabonds, however, the rector was to have both the quarter and the *ultimum vale*. Nevertheless, the friars were allowed to celebrate anniversaries for people buried in their cemetery without making any payment to the rector; they retained their image of St Peter (subject to slight restriction). But they were not to interfere in parochial matters (although the arbitrators, while prohibiting distribution of holy bread, tolerated their distribution of blessed but unconsecrated hosts). There were also arrangements for the tithes on properties which the friars had acquired since 1375. The new compromise was to be maintained by bonds and penalties.[32]

While jurisdictional disputes demonstrated the continuity of problems from the thirteenth century, mendicant status and claims caused other difficulties as well. As preachers, the friars had a particular role within the Church – but one which was double-edged. Teaching, while edifying, might also confuse and undermine. Sermons which were too intellectual, or too theological, might disturb faith. The traditional motif that the laity were better off with the sops of basic teaching rather than the meat of theology found expression in fourteenth-century complaints that the laity were being confused by sermons pitched way over their heads. It was against such confusions that Archbishop Thoresby of York directed his *Lay Folks' Cathechism* in 1357; Langland also attacked the complex theology of mendicant sermons which ignored basic instruction about sin.[33]

That the mendicants might use their sermonizing to challenge the received teachings of the Church, to elevate their own status and diminish that of other clerics, appears from scattered cases in fifteenth-century England. In 1425 William Russell, a Franciscan, preached in London against personal tithes, urging that they should be considered free alms rather than obligations, which the laity could direct where they willed – presumably, he hoped, to mendicants.[34] Almost contemporaneously, in York, Thomas Richmond (perhaps significantly

[32] LJRO, B/A/1/7, fols 131v–133v; Roth, *Austin Friars*, pp. 276*–7*.

[33] R. N. Swanson, 'The origins of the *Lay Folks' Catechism*', *Medium Ævum*, 60 (1991), p. 98; *Piers Plowman: the B Version – Will's Visions of Piers Plowman, Do-Well, Do-Better, and Do-Best: an Edition in the Form of Trinity College, Cambridge, MS B.15.17, Corrected and Restored from the Known Evidence, with Variant Readings*, ed. George Kane and E. Talbot Donaldson (London, 1975), passus 15, ll. 70–6, p. 538.

[34] For the case and its context, C. A. Robertson, 'The tithe-heresy of friar William Russell', *Albion*, 8 (1976), pp. 1–13. Similar ideas were allegedly revived among the London

preaching in a chapel run by the city council, and at their invitation) argued that the sacraments of sinful clergy were invalid.[35] In 1464 the London Carmelites reaffirmed the friars' identification with apostolic poverty to increase donations to themselves, so provoking reaction from the seculars.[36] All these cases resulted in heresy trials.

These events may well be the tip of an iceberg: in 1414 there had been another dispute in York, after a Franciscan had spoken injuriously about the clergy; but precisely what he said is not recorded.[37] Such cases suggest that the laity were sometimes receiving 'authoritative' statements from mendicants which were, from the authorities' perspective, unorthodox and threatening. The implications of this are considerable, as they merge into the question of Lollardy in late medieval England. Sermons were clearly a significant means of spreading heretical ideas in pre-Reformation England; but the cases of Richmond and Russell raise questions about the coherence of any heretical movement. Ostensibly, both friars could be considered as 'Lollard', their sermons promulgating material which is condemned in the standard questionnaire used to identify fifteenth-century heretics.[38] Yet it seems equally likely – perhaps certain – that their hearers did not have to be 'Lollards' to receive the message, or to act on it.[39] Radical preaching by mendicants (perhaps, even, a quasi-Spiritual tradition) may have been a significant but hidden element in the context which sustained unorthodoxy in late medieval England.

While conflict and tension were something of a constant, they were normally kept in bounds, and must not be overstated. Indeed, despite

populace in response to Carmelite preaching in 1464: F. R. H. du Boulay, 'The quarrel between the Carmelite friars and the secular clergy of London, 1464–1468', *JEH*, 6 (1955), pp. 161, 173. An early fifteenth-century Doncaster dispute seems analogous, with a Carmelite claiming that offerings on feasts (presumably the compulsory parochial offerings on certain dates) were free offerings which might be given elsewhere than to the parish church – implicitly, to friars: K. Alban, 'The letters of Thomas Netter of Walden', in Fitzgerald-Lombard, *Carmel in Britain*, 2, p. 373.

[35] *The Records of the Northern Convocation*, Surtees Society Publications, 113 (1907), pp. 146–72.

[36] Du Boulay, 'Quarrel', pp. 158–74. This fracas found echoes in contemporary Italian writings on the poverty issue: Douie, 'Some treatises', pp. 14–16, 21, 32.

[37] York, York Minster Library, L2/3a, fol. 78r–v. See also the Doncaster case mentioned in n.34.

[38] Hudson, *Books*, pp. 133, 135. See also idem, *PR*, pp. 152–3, 316–18, 342, and cf. Wilkins, *Concilia*, 3, p. 208.

[39] See the reported reaction to the Carmelite preaching in London in 1464, du Boulay, 'Quarrel', pp. 161, 173.

the antifraternalism of some Middle English literature,[40] more striking is the general lack of hostility to the mendicants – even among the secular clerics. There is no evidence of any deep streak of hostility towards the friars, certainly nothing which would entail their radical uprooting. Even while secular clerics complained of their interference, they were not seeking abolition, but the restoration of the idealized *modus vivendi*, and recognition of their own rights.

* * *

England's experience was matched by events elsewhere; a similar guerilla warfare appears.[41] But in some respects the tensions were different. This may have been partly due to the evolutions within the orders themselves: as the Observant movements arose, so discrepancies between mendicant ideal and reality became painfully obvious. England, for reasons which remain unclear, lacked any indigenous support for such a movement – among all regulars, not just the friars. When the Observant Franciscans were introduced, they were very much an alien import.[42]

The continental context certainly provided opportunities for conflict apparently more insistent than encountered in England. In Germany, for instance, the importance of the towns, and the political power of local ecclesiastical hierarchs meant that conflict could rise to new heights. Here the key element was the mendicants' insistence on their exemption from episcopal authority. In the German towns such exemption had serious implications when bishops or other church authorities were in dispute with the urban governments. The Church's

[40] Szittya, *Antifraternal*, chs 5–7. See also C. Erickson, 'The fourteenth-century Franciscans and their critics', *FS*, 35 (1975), pp. 107–35, 36 (1976), pp. 108–47, which attempts to assess the validity of this material in a broader European context.

[41] For fourteenth-century France, P. Adam, *La vie paroissiale en France au XIVe siècle*, Histoire et sociologie de l'église, 3 (Paris, 1963), pp. 220–45, 307–10; for Brittany, H. Martin, *Les ordres mendiants en Bretagne, vers 1230–vers 1530: pauvreté volontaire et prédication à la fin du Moyen-Age* (Paris, 1975), pp. 140–1, 144–8, 152–4; more generally, Lippens, 'Droit nouveau des mendiants', esp. pp. 266–70, 272–3, 277–84, 288–9.

[42] A. G. Little, 'Introduction of the Observant friars into England', *PBA*, 10 (1921–3), pp. 458–71. For hints of an 'observant' movement among early fifteenth-century English Franciscans, and that the English Franciscans were exceptionally rigorist, D. W. Whitfield, 'Conflicts of personality and principle: the political and religious crisis in the English Franciscan province, 1400–1409', *FS*, ns 17 (1957), pp. 325 (and n.8), 341–2. For a proposed foreign imposition of observance on the English Carmelites, J. Smet, 'Pre-Tridentine reform in the Carmelite Order', in Elm, ed., *Reformbemühungen und Observanzbestrebungen*, pp. 308, 317.

most potent spiritual weapon was the interdict, ending the holding of services and prayers for souls. But the friars' exempt status made such interdicts inapplicable to their churches, and undermined their effects.[43]

While the continental disputes dealt with practicalities, they often appear more intellectual in content than in England. The debate on the friars' confessional powers especially had significant ecclesiological overtones.[44] The stances adopted derived from a dispute of 1317–19 over propositions advanced by Jean de Pouilly; notably his insistence on the binding force of *Omnis utriusque sexus*, and his assertion that priests and bishops held their pastoral office directly from Christ, rather than via the papacy.[45] This stress on the secular clergy's apostolicity gave a new twist to the debates. The apostolic ideal of an historicized Church may be 'the great new ecclesiological fact of the late Middle Ages';[46] but its place in the struggle between seculars and mendicants has been overlooked. By raising the status of the lower clergy it challenged both mendicant apostolicity and papal primacy,[47] posing a latent threat should appropriate circumstances arise. While some of Pouilly's views were condemned in *Vas electionis* in 1321,[48] the ideas continued to circulate, and to be condemned.[49]

The circumstances in which they could become significant arose in 1408, when a quarrel over mendicant powers erupted at Paris, and

[43] D. A. Eltis, 'Tensions between clergy and laity in some western German cities in the later middle ages', *JEH*, 43 (1992), pp. 239–40. For such instances in France, Adam, *Vie paroissiale*, pp. 241–2. The tertiaries sometimes used their links with the mendicants to avoid the penalties of interdicts: Erickson, 'Fourteenth-century Franciscans' (1975), p. 125; (1976), pp. 124–5.

[44] The debate on the confessional powers of the mendicants in the later fourteenth and fifteenth centuries is surveyed in Uyttenbroeck, 'Droit pénitentiel', pp. 306–32.

[45] J. Koch, 'Der Prozess gegen den Magister Johannes de Polliaco und seine Vorgeschichte (1312–1321)', in his *Kleine Schriften*, 2, Storia e letteratura: raccolta di Studi e Testi, 128 (Rome, 1973), pp. 387–422; Uyttenbroeck, 'Droit pénitentiel', pp. 186–8; J. Dunbabin, *A Hound of God: Pierre de la Palud and the Fourteenth-Century Church* (Oxford, 1991), pp. 58–68, 113–19; J. G. Sikes, 'John de Pouilli and Peter de la Palu', *EHR*, 49 (1934), pp. 223–40. For the ecclesiological traditions reflected in this clash, Y. M.-J. Congar, 'Aspects ecclésiologiques de la querelle entre mendiants et séculiers dans la seconde moitié du XIIIe siècle et le début du XIVe', *AHDLMA*, 36 (1961), pp. 52–114.

[46] Leff, 'Apostolic ideal', pp. 71–3, 81–2 (quotation at p. 71).

[47] Koch ('Der Prozess', p. 417) associates it with 'die Demokratie des Weltgeistlichen, der aus jedem Pfarrer einen Papst machen möchte'.

[48] Ibid., pp. 418–20.

[49] Uyttenbroeck, 'Droit pénitentiel', p. 309; Lippens, 'Droit nouveau des mendiants', pp. 260–1, 272.

lasted for some years.[50] Coinciding with debates aimed at ending the Great Schism of the West, and the reform discussions which occupied the Council of Constance, the 'mendicant problem', while remaining very much a debate between seculars and mendicants, became embroiled in wider ecclesiological issues.

Hints of a possible storm at Paris appeared in April 1408, in Jean Gerson's *De visitatione praelatorum*, which called for investigation of the friars' activities at parochial level.[51] He wanted closer checks on their sermons, especially on whether they preached against curates, burial in parish churches, and tithing. He sought examination of how they dealt with sins, and whether they were administering the sacraments contrary to law. He was also concerned that they were allowing excommunicates into their services. This seems, however, to have been an isolated work, provoking little response.

The real conflict began late in 1408, when the Franciscan Jean Gorel issued a series of pro-mendicant conclusions which challenged the status of the seculars. These were considered by the Faculty of Theology, and condemned on 2 January 1409.[52] His reported errors included denial that the clergy had been instituted by Christ; arguing instead that they were founded only under Pope Dionysius (259–68), and accordingly were not entitled to preach, confess, give extreme unction, bury, or receive tithes. In contrast, Gorel asserted that friars were more principally and essentially involved in preaching and hearing confessions than curates, being bound by their rule which was better than the papal statute which governed curates. Moreover, if curates had enough to live off, they should not take tithes.

An imposed retraction required Gorel to reverse his position. He acknowledged that the clergy existed from Christ's institution, and accordingly had all the rights he had denied to them. Moreover, the right to preach and hear confessions pertained *principaliter et essentialiter* to prelates and curates, whereas mendicants enjoyed those rights only accidentally, by privilege, as allowed by their commissions and the good will of the prelates. Gorel also retracted his denials of tithes to the curates, and of the appropriateness of the parish church as the

[50] Outlined in Uyttenbroeck, 'Droit pénitentiel', pp. 311–16; see also D. C. Brown, *Pastor and Laity in the Theology of Jean Gerson* (Cambridge, 1987), pp. 74–8.

[51] *Jean Gerson, oeuvres complètes*, ed. P. Glorieux, 10 vols in 11 (Tournai, 1960–73) [hereafter Glorieux], 8, no. 403.

[52] *CUP*, no. 1864.

place to receive sacraments.[53] Although there was no immediate reaction, suggestions of a gathering storm appeared in mid-year, when Gerson returned to the issues in his *De statu papae et minorum praelatorum*.[54] While limiting papal freedom of action, and asserting episcopal autonomy through apostolic succession to a commission from Christ, Gerson proposed a functional and structural difference between episcopal power and mendicant privileges: the latter could be amended without injury or sin, whereas the status of prelates and curates was unalterable.[55] Curates were equally intrinsic and apostolic, their role being to purge, illume, and perfect their parishioners, giving them the primary right to oversee their subjects' consciences through confession.

In Gerson's view, those enjoying papal privileges (the mendicants) were merely auxiliaries, *coadjutores missos*, although their assistance could only be denied with good grounds. Parishioners were primarily obligated to obey their parish priest, needing his licence to attend services elsewhere. The merely auxiliary function of the privileged limited their scope for action, especially outside their own institutions. Above all, they could act only when permitted by those within the established hierarchy. While the sacramental validity of their actions was not impugned, and a reiterated confession could not be demanded nor confession to the privileged be prohibited, a curate could nevertheless deny the sacraments if uncertain of a confession's reality. The mendicants could also be required to swear to the validity of claimed absolutions if required by the curate, on pain of the denial of the sacraments to those whom they had allegedly absolved. Moreover, Gerson re-asserted the curate's rights to the canonical quarter, and insisted that mendicant preachers should not incite discord.

Perhaps it was this oration which provoked the friars to react, seizing the opportunity presented by the recent election of a Franciscan as Pope Alexander V at the Council of Pisa.[56] On 12 October 1409, the bull *Regnans in excelsis* condemned a list of pro-secular arguments.[57] In the context of the Great Schism, and the flow of conciliarist ideas, the explicit challenge to papal power in the attack on Gorel was just as

[53] Glorieux, 10, no. 494.
[54] Ibid., 9, no. 424.
[55] Ibid., 9, p. 29.
[56] But see below, n.61, for another possible stimulus.
[57] *CUP*, no. 1868.

significant as the rebuff to the mendicants. The Parisian assertion of the parish priest's authority was overruled. Although the secularists had not challenged the sacramental validity of the friars' hearing of confessions and granting of absolution, they had denied their jurisdictional autonomy. Leaving aside a provocative reference to Pope John XXII which rejected *Vas electionis* on the grounds that that pope was a heretic when it was issued,[58] the main thrust of the defenders of the seculars was that confessions to friars had to be repeated to the parish priest, to meet the demands of *Omnis utriusque sexus*, and that parishioners needed licence from their parish priests to go to a friar for confession. Moreover, friars seeking papal privileges to hear confessions and receive burials were to be considered in mortal sin, as were the popes who granted or confirmed such privileges.[59] Finally, the parish priest who licensed mendicants to hear confessions on his behalf to satisfy *Omnis utriusque sexus* was said to give a greater dispensation than that contained in a papal licence to the friars in accordance with *Super cathedram*.[60]

So fundamental an attack on papal and mendicant status was obviously unacceptable to both, and especially to a pope who was also a friar. Alexander V's response was blunt, and extensive. Besides condemning, he banned discussion: any attempt to assert, gloss, defend, hold, or preach the condemned points was forbidden; anyone so doing should be treated as a heretic and *ipso facto* excommunicate, with absolution reserved to the pope except *in articulo mortis*. Moreover, the bull was to be widely published in diocesan gatherings, for proclamation by rectors to enable action to be taken against its opponents and those holding the condemned opinions, any constitutions to the contrary (including *Omnis utriusque sexus*) notwithstanding. The decree was clearly intended as a weapon, and was so used at least by the Irish friars. The Oxford academic John Whitehead (who had certainly written against mendicant begging and confessional activity) appeared before Canterbury Convocation in February 1410, to answer precisely the articles recited in the Bull.[61]

[58] *CUP*, no. 1868, p. 166.

[59] Ibid., no. 1868, p. 167.

[60] Ibid. (*Super cathedram* is cited by its Clementine *incipit*, *Dudum [a Bonifacio]*.)

[61] *Materials for the History of the Franciscan Province of Ireland, A. D. 1230–1450*, ed. F. B. Fitzmaurice and A. G. Little, British Society of Franciscan Studies, 9 (Manchester, 1920), pp. 172–3 (suggesting that the Irish actually procured the Bull); *BRUO*, 3, p. 2037; Wilkins, *Concilia*, 3, pp. 324–5.

The papal ban on discussion and glossing was as unwelcome to the Paris masters as Gorel's original conclusions. Initial reaction was muted, but by March 1410, tensions were rising. Jean Gerson again set the stage, in his *Discours sur le fait des mendiants*, delivered on 23 February 1410.[62] The basic issues were defined, and although Gerson denied that he was attacking the Pope (arguing that Alexander had issued the bull ill-advisedly, and would doubtless retract it when better informed), he delivered a clear attack on papal prerogatives. Essential to Gerson's stand was the assumption that the parish priest's status was established by Christ as part of the overall hierarchy: Christ's commission to the clergy as a whole was no less valid, or binding, than that issued to Peter. The pope could not override that divine institution, which gave those with cure of souls a status intrinsically higher than that of 'simple' religious.[63] Fundamental among the curates' powers were those of preaching – primarily to instruct in the basics of the faith, without confusing – and confessing. The hierarchical structure established by Christ, reinforced by *Omnis utriusque sexus*, confirmed the curates' authority over parishioners, creating a structure in which the role of the religious was strictly limited. Beyond their pastoral rights, curates also had the right to bury their parishioners. Mendicants might enjoy that right by privilege, but only conditionally – and certainly without extracting vows to be buried in their houses.

Much of Gerson's oration defended the curates' right to hear confessions against mendicant interference, they being considered optional extras within the Church. Their powers to confess and preach were held only by commission, and at the goodwill of the prelates – the permission was essential, 'comme accident ne peut naturellement estre sans subget'.[64] Additionally, Gerson answered challenges to the wealth of the secular clergy, notably the claim that they should dispose of surpluses to the poor, and the charge that tithes reduced clerical perfection. Against this last in particular, Gerson replied that to have wealth and use it well was better and more perfect than to beg in poverty. Begging might well produce disorder, and Christ did not beg.[65]

62 Glorieux, 5, no. 387 (pp. 978–92). See also *CUP*, no. 1877.

63 Glorieux, 5, p. 984.

64 Ibid., 5, p. 988.

65 Ibid., 5, pp. 991–2.

The crunch came for the mendicants on 2 March. All four orders were required to state their position. The Dominicans denied knowledge of the bull, and renounced the claims made in it. The Carmelites did likewise, although protesting that they wished to maintain their Order's privileges. The Franciscans and Augustinians were less compliant. They insisted on their rights as defined in the bull, and consequently 'ab universitate reselati sunt' – an exclusion which lasted until November 1417, when both orders capitulated.[66]

Henceforth, two distinct strands merged in these debates. Although largely inseparable, they reflected different issues. One was the bull itself, as an expression of papal power. The other concerned the status of the mendicants in relation to the established local ecclesiastical hierarchies. The conjunction of the strands appears immediately in the condemnation of *Regnans in excelsis* issued by the Paris faculty of theology on 5 March 1410. The bull was declared intolerable, because of the condemnation, the penalties it proclaimed, and its overriding of other constitutions; moreover, it fundamentally disturbed the state of the Church, and could be used as a weapon against prelates, curates, and people, to instill fear. The friars' activities (especially as procurers of the bull) were also condemned, since they disrupted the primitive state of the Church and the ordering of prelates and curates. To make its point about academic freedom, the faculty declared that it would discuss further whether a confession to a friar had to be repeated to the parish priest. Meanwhile, it proposed that the canonical requirement for friars to be licensed to hear confessions should be enforced, and that parishioners should not confess to friars unless they were assured of their status and authority.[67]

The initial campaign against *Regnans in excelsis* proved effective. Despite concerted mendicant efforts to maintain the bull,[68] it was rescinded on 27 June 1410 by the new Pope, John XXIII.[69] The Parisian authorities had carefully exploited divisions within the Orders: a fortnight before issuing *Regnans in excelsis* Alexander V had intervened to end the autonomy of the Observant group among the

[66] *CUP*, nos 1878, 2086; *Auctarium chartularii universitatis Parisiensis*, ed. H. S. Denifle and E. Chatelain, 2 (Paris, 1937), p. 233; *Acta concilii Constanciensis*, ed. H. Finke, 4 vols (Münster, 1898–1928), 2, pp. 572–3.

[67] *CUP*, no. 1879, p. 173.

[68] Ibid., no. 1885; Fitzmaurice and Little, *Materials*, pp. 173–6.

[69] *CUP*, no. 1887.

French Franciscans, which had been encouraged by Benedict XIII. The university had stepped in to defend the rigorists.[70]

Yet the victory was not sweeping enough for the university: in November 1410 both *Regnans in excelsis* and its revocation were condemned – John XXIII had not back-tracked far enough. What the university sought was not just a declaration that the bull would not be enforced, but a formal recognition that it was wrong.[71] In May 1411 a letter to the Pope asked further that the disputed articles be debated at a general council – again an implicit challenge to papal authority.[72] Nothing, however, was actually achieved: while activity continued to secure the bull's negation, it was fairly desultory.[73] Yet the university maintained its stance: in 1413 the rector's oath obliged him to work for the annulment of *Regnans in excelsis* and the determination of the disputed articles at a general council, and to continue the exclusion of the Augustinian and Franciscan friars until that was achieved. Moreover the Franciscans were not to be reconciled until the Observant movement recovered the freedom it had enjoyed under Benedict XIII.[74]

The overall mendicant response to the fracas at Paris is unclear. Individual friars may have taken their message to the people. Certainly in Tournai, possibly as early as 1410, the Austin friar Nicholas Serrurier was proclaiming a range of conclusions, which eventually resulting in heresy charges. His alleged faults included insistence that friars could confess without permission from the parish priest (although he accepted that an episcopal licence was needed), and that a priest could not deny communion to someone who had confessed to a friar. Moreover, he turned to attack the seculars, roundly condemning concubinary priests with a zeal which appears positively Gregorian.[75]

The Parisian dispute was unresolved when the Council of Constance met in November 1414. The dramas of that assembly, and especially the boost to conciliarism provided by the need to

70 Ibid., no. 1886; Nimmo, *Reform and Division*, pp. 538–42.

71 *CUP*, nos 1900, 1915.

72 Ibid., no. 1917.

73 E.g. ibid., nos 1926, 1927.

74 Ibid., no. 1965. The resolution of the Observant issue by *Supplicationibus personarum* of 23 Sept. 1415 (see Nimmo, *Reform and Division*, pp. 549–56) presumably provided grounds for the reconciliation.

75 A. Cauchie, 'Nicole Serrurier, hérétique du XVe siècle', *Analectes pour servir à l'histoire ecclésiastique de la Belgique*, 2nd ser., 8 (1893), pp. 250–2, 289–90.

establish the assembly's credentials in the aftermath of John XXIII's flight in March 1415, provided an ideal context for the reopening of the issues. Indeed, it made them extremely relevant, for the question of papal authority over the Church, the ability to legislate and overturn legislation, was one of the central issues in the university of Paris's challenge to *Regnans in excelsis*. A revised version of the earlier attack on the bull accordingly made much of the papal assault on the structure of the Church, alongside a general statement defending glossing as a way of resolving ambiguities.[76] It was theft and rapine to withdraw rights granted by Christ, yet that was precisely what the papal privileges to the friars amounted to by reducing the authority of prelates and curates. Popes so acting must, therefore, sin gravely. Moreover, the challenge to *Omnis utriusque sexus* had to be addressed: acceptance of papal authority to derogate from the decrees of general councils would undermine any attempt at reform of the Church in head and members, and would fundamentally destabilize the Church by allowing the pope to change things at will. The pope simply could not undermine the hierarchical order as established by Christ. It was for curates to 'hierarchize' (a term clearly linked to Gerson and Dionysius, since 'ierarchizare . . . est purgare, illuminare, et perficere'),[77] and for parishioners to be subject. The pope might grant individual dispensations from confession to the curate, but no blanket privilege. Much was made of clerical apostolicity, that curates held their powers directly from Christ, and therefore could not be challenged. *Regnans in excelsis* had in fact increased discord within the Church, contrary to the aspirations of Augustine, Francis, and Dominic. Paris university sought a direct confrontation with the difficulties created by the existence of the mendicant orders: while not overtly calling for their abolition, they noted that earlier the *chorepiscopi* had been abolished, to prevent a clash of orders and derogation of the system established by Christ.[78] Paris was probably not alone in its assault on the mendicants at the Council: Oxford's reform programme also included clauses seeking clarification of the rules about confessional licences, and other matters.[79]

[76] Finke, *Acta*, 1, pp. 690–8.

[77] Ibid., p. 694. Cf. Brown, *Pastor and Laity*, pp. 38–41, 44–9, esp. 40, 44, 46.

[78] On *chorepiscopi*, E. Valton, 'Évêques: questions théologiques et canoniques', *DTC*, 5/ii (Paris, 1912–13), cols 1706–7.

[79] Wilkins, *Concilia*, 3, pp. 363–4.

The friars could not ignore such a challenge; their reply necessarily defended their own role, and indeed relied on the bull's validity to support the counter-attack. Those seeking its revocation were themselves subject to its penalties, as fautors of error. Denying the threat to hierarchy, the mendicants advanced a different view of the jurisdictional structures: the content of *Regnans in excelsis* did not undermine the status of the council; rather those seeking its revocation challenged the papacy, the Roman Church, and the council.[80]

The friars also defended their record in the Church, with an anonymous preacher in February 1416 turning the traditional anti-mendicant arguments on their heads by asserting that they filled the gaps left by the failings of the secular clergy. Against the seculars' laziness, greed, absenteeism, and neglect of pastoral duties, the friars' mendicancy, building programmes, pastoral care, and religious observance were positive forces within the Church.[81]

Nevertheless, the friars were on the defensive. Reform tracts issued at Constance sought to return the mendicants to their original status: the inconsistencies of their historical development were to be confronted, the original aims were to be restored, with reinforcement by ordinary authority. Thus, one tract proposed that the state of poverty should be reinstated: friars would have no possessions or property, but would live solely from alms, and in common. The bishops would ensure that this happened by removing the office of preaching, the hearing of confessions, and collecting privileges, using canonical censures.[82] The misbehaviour of mendicants in their limitations would be curtailed by abolishing all privileges post-dating *Super cathedram*, and the limits established by that text and the decree *Religiosi* of the Council of Vienne[83] were not to be exceeded. Again, the local ordinary would have oversight with power of enforcement, disregarding any papal privileges current or to be acquired.[84] Moreover, restrictions would be placed on the reception of members of the orders, and on those claiming to be tertiaries, with structural reforms within the orders.[85] Mention of the tertiaries, and the demand that henceforth they live like other honest

80 Finke, *Acta*, 1, p. 699.

81 Ibid., 2, pp. 430–5, esp. 434.

82 *Magnum oecumenicum Constantiense concilium*, ed. H. von der Hardt, 6 vols (Frankfurt and Leipzig, 1697–1700), 1, pp. 713–16.

83 Clem. 5.7.1.

84 Hardt, *Constantiense concilium*, 1, pp. 715–16.

85 Ibid., 1, pp. 715–20.

people,[86] raised another issue affecting mendicant–secular relations. While the tertiaries were usually peripheral to the debate on mendicant practices, their privileges did sometimes cause difficulties when used to undermine the authority of the parish priest.[87] At Cashel in 1353, for instance, the provincial legislation sought to assert the rights of parish clergy over their burials.[88] The tertiaries posed a different problem, being embroiled in the debate about mendicant poverty and sturdy beggars, and often muddled with the beghards and Lollards; but that is a different matter.[89]

The Constance debates proved to be sound and fury. In January 1418, the French were still seeking provisions about mendicant abuses, and hoping to negotiate for a bull to redefine the relationship between friars and parish clergy.[90] The only victory (a relatively hollow victory) came when the case of Nicholas Serrurier was transferred from Tournai to the Council, where he was judged guilty in April 1418 and forced to recant. The articles against him were given a Wycliffite slant, so that he was also forced to distance himself from Wyclif and Hus.[91] This was clearly a significant snub to the friars, but their joint efforts to have the verdict rescinded in a new trial after the Council ended proved unsuccessful.[92]

The ecclesiological debates surrounding *Regnans in excelsis* differ greatly from the legal dispute at Atherstone, yet reflect a similar uncertainty about the friars' status. The fundamental questioning of their privileges – and the associated challenge to papal authority – which appears in the continental debate was, however, more threatening to the friars' position. If the authority which legitimated their existence were undermined, they too would collapse. The inconclusiveness of the Constance debates perhaps also showed that there was no real solution to the tensions which the presence of the mendicant orders created within the Church.

This remained the case in later years, as debates frequently revived

[86] Hardt, *Constantiense concilium*, 1, pp. 715–18.

[87] For relations between seculars and tertiaries in general, Erickson, 'Fourteenth-century Franciscans' (1976), pp. 125–7; see also J.-C. Schmitt, *Mort d'une hérésie: l'église et les clercs face aux béguines et aux béghards du Rhin supérieur du XIVe au XVe siècle*, Civilisations et sociétés, 56 (Paris, 1978), pp. 118–19, 125.

[88] Wilkins, *Concilia*, 3, p. 567 (no. 36).

[89] Schmitt, *Mort d'une hérésie*, pp. 114–30, 155–8, 189–90, 207–12.

[90] Finke, *Acta*, 2, p. 682.

[91] Cauchie, 'Nicole Serrurier', esp. pp. 290, 293.

[92] Ibid., pp. 265–8, 301–2.

over what were essentially the same issues. Parisian academics continued to defend Jean de Pouilly's notions on the derivation of clerical authority from Christ, forcing retractions when alternative views were advanced.[93] Restatements of the condemnations contained in *Regnans in excelsis* (albeit lacking the restrictions on academic freedom) produced fierce responses from the masters, as the issue bubbled throughout the fifteenth century, and beyond.[94] At the Council of Basle, a debate over mendicant privileges lasted some years, inconclusively.[95] As in previous councils, however, stances were affected by political partisanship. The Anglo-Irish Philip Norreys had revived the demand for reiterated confession, for which (as well as for calling them Antichrist and followers of Mohammed) the friars sought action against him from Eugenius IV. Eugenius did act – although Norreys had already declared that he valued the decision of a general council more than that of the pope. Indeed, Norreys threw in his lot with the conciliarists at Basle, although they did not give him the whole-hearted aid which he sought.[96]

In the aftermath of Basle, Nicholas of Cusa, as papal legate in Germany, tried to legislate in local assemblies to ensure that friars received confessional licences from the local authorities.[97] Yet the fifteenth century witnessed not a curtailment but an expansion of the friars' privileges, culminating in 1474 with the so-called *Mare magnum* bull of Sixtus IV, initially issued to the Austin friars but soon extended to the other orders. This effectively ended all the restrictions on their activities, including abolition of the canonical quarter.[98]

* * *

Like previous papal decrees, this was no settlement. Although Sixtus IV inaugurated a mushrooming of mendicant privileges,[99] disputes

93 Uyttenbroeck, 'Droit pénitentiel', p. 317; Lippens, 'Droit nouveau des mendiants', pp. 282–3.

94 Uyttenbroeck, 'Droit pénitentiel', pp. 321–3, 325–6; J. K. Farge, *Orthodoxy and Reform in Early Reformation France: the Faculty of Theology of Paris, 1500–1543*, Studies in Medieval and Reformation Thought, 32 (Leiden, 1985), pp. 122–4, 229.

95 Uyttenbroeck, 'Droit pénitentiel', pp. 317–20.

96 Ibid., pp. 320–1; *Annales Minorum*, ed. L. Wadding, 25 vols (3rd edn, Florence, 1931–4), 11, pp. 121–2.

97 C. J. Hefele and C. de Clercq, *Histoire des conciles*, 11 vols in 22 (Paris, 1902–52), 7/ii, pp. 1209, 1222.

98 Uyttenbroeck, 'Droit pénitentiel', pp. 327–8; Wadding, *Annales Minorum*, 14, pp. 112–27 (canonical portion at p. 122); Lippens, 'Droit nouveau des mendiants', pp. 284–5.

99 Uyttenbroeck, 'Droit pénitentiel', pp. 329–31; Lippens, 'Droit nouveau des mendiants', pp. 286–8.

continued, perhaps changing emphasis from conflict with the parish clergy to challenges to episcopal authority, and perhaps submerging the specific issue of the friars in the general question of regular exemptions from episcopal oversight. At Lateran V, the question of episcopal authority over mendicants and other exempt orders reappeared, with pleas for the restoration of episcopal authority. Although this assault was led by Italian prelates, the silence of others need not indicate lack of sympathy: a Spanish reform proposal produced just before the council met included complaints that the exempt orders did not pay the canonical quarter, and that they preached at the same time as the parish masses were celebrated.[100] On 19 December 1516 a decree on preaching placed controls on friars and all other preachers.[101] On the same day *Dum intra mentis arcana* restricted the friars' pastoral interventions,[102] but still proved unsatisfactory. In England, for instance, there were still occasional disputes over preaching, confession, and burials which crop up even in the 1530s.[103]

Whether the 'mendicant problem' could have been resolved in existing circumstances is debatable. The ecclesiological and practical concerns raised were perhaps too basic, too irreconcilable, to allow real compromise. For three centuries the friars' status had caused dissension within the Church; partisan stances could not easily be eliminated after so long. Even as new forces were stirring which would cause yet greater disruption in the Church, the old sores festered.

University of Birmingham

[100] Hefele and de Clercq, *Histoire des conciles*, 8/i, pp. 311–12; Lippens, 'Droit nouveau des mendiants', p. 290.

[101] For Lateran V, O. de la Brosse, J. Lecler, A. Holstein, and C. Lefebvre, *Latran V et Trente, Histoire des conciles oecumeniques*, 10 (Paris, 1975), pp. 70–4, 109–10. For the preaching decree, Tanner, *Decrees*, 1, pp. 634–8, esp. p. 636.

[102] Ibid., 1, pp. 645–9.

[103] Spencer, *English Preaching*, p. 60 and n.163; Roth, *Austin Friars*, p. 441*. Disputes continued elsewhere to the eve of the Reformation: for e.g. Strasbourg, see F. Rapp, *Réformes et Réformation à Strasbourg: église et société dans le diocèse de Strasbourg (1450–1525)*, Collection de l'institut des hautes études alsaciennes, 23 (Paris, 1974), pp. 215–16.

THE MONASTIC ORDERS IN LATE MEDIEVAL CAMBRIDGE

by BARRIE DOBSON

TOWARDS the end of his long career Abbot John Whethamstede, for many years the most celebrated Benedictine monk in England, took the opportunity of a letter he was writing to the prior of Tynemouth to engage in rhetorical but equally eulogistic praise of the 'extraordinary melodies in praise of the Muses' to be found not only at 'the Cabalinian font which gushes forth in the midst of Oxford' but also from 'the Cirrean stream which runs near the suburbs of Cambridge'.[1] Few historians of England's two medieval universities have found it altogether easy to share the undiscriminating enthusiasm of the venerable abbot of St Albans for both Oxford and Cambridge. Gordon Leff – not of course at all alone in this – has done much to elucidate the intellectual and institutional life of the university of Oxford only to find the medieval history of his own university of Cambridge so much less rewarding that it rarely figures in his published work at all. Quite why, for at least the first two centuries of their existence, the Cambridge schools should have always remained less numerically significant and academically influential than their Oxford counterparts is still perhaps a more difficult question to answer than is usually assumed. Even more difficult to explain are the changing patterns of recruitment, patronage, endowment and intellectual activity which during the course of the mid and later fifteenth century at long last eradicated Cambridge's inferior academic status and established an approximate degree of parity and prestige between the two universities.[2] Without much doubt it was only then, during

[1] *Registra quorundam abbatum monasterii S. Albani*, ed. H. T. Riley (*RS*, 1872–3), 2, pp. 313–14; a reference I owe to J. G. Clark, 'Intellectual life at the Abbey of St Albans, and the nature of monastic learning in England, c. 1350 – c. 1440: the work of Thomas Walsingham in context' (Oxford University D. Phil. thesis, 1997), p. 256.

[2] For the most recent survey, placing particular emphasis on the dramatic increase (from seven to sixteen) in the number of academic college foundations at Cambridge between the creation of God's House in 1439 and of Trinity College in 1546, see Leader, pp. 218–32, 264–91, 341–51: cf. R. Lovatt, 'The triumph of the colleges in late medieval Oxford and Cambridge: the case of Peterhouse', *History of Universities*, 14 (1998), pp. 95–7; J. Taylor, 'The Diocese of York and the university connexion, 1300–1520', *Northern History*, 25 (1989), pp. 39–59.

the century or so before the Reformation, that the historian encounters what Mr Malcolm Underwood has recently diagnosed as perhaps the most remarkable and influential of all 'Cambridge phenomena'.[3] Indeed if one had to choose a particular point in time when that 'phenomenon' must at last have become obvious to all contemporaries, even at Oxford, one might do worse than choose the years between 1505 and 1508, when Lady Margaret Beaufort's transformation of God's House into Christ's College 'took place against the background of an unprecedented number of royal visits'.[4] It was on one of those occasions, almost certainly on 22 April 1506, that Henry VII rode towards Cambridge, where 'within a quarter of a mylle, there stode, first of all the four Ordres of Freres, and after odir Religious, and the King on Horsbacke kyssed the Crosse of everyche of the Religious, and then there stode all along, all the Graduatts, aftir their Degrees, in all their Habbitts, and at the end of them was the Unyversyte Cross'.[5]

The following essay is confined to a highly summary account of some of the many mysterious issues raised by the presence of those 'odir Religious', monks and canons rather than friars, within the University of Cambridge between the mid-thirteenth and the early sixteenth centuries. Obviously enough, no attempt can be made here to consider the profound if often obscurely recorded contribution of its four major mendicant convents to the academic and religious life of medieval Cambridge.[6] In any case, there can be little doubt that whereas the friars who welcomed Henry VII on the road from London in 1506 were by then very considerably fewer and less influential than their predecessors had been one or two centuries earlier, Benedictine monks and Augustinian canons (and to a much lesser extent members of the Cistercian, Premonstratensian, and Gilbertine Orders) had never

[3] M. K. Jones and M. G. Underwood, *The King's Mother: Lady Margaret Beaufort, Countess of Richmond and Derby* (Cambridge, 1992), pp. 227–30.

[4] Ibid., p. 229; M. Underwood, 'John Fisher and the promotion of learning', in B. Bradshaw and E. Duffy, eds, *Humanism, Reform and the Reformation: The Career of Bishop John Fisher* (Cambridge, 1989), p. 43, n. 22.

[5] E. Ashmole, *The Institutions, Laws and Ceremonies of the Noble Order of the Garter* (London, 1672), pp. 558–9; Cooper, *Annals*, 1, p. 281.

[6] For a recent full-scale survey of much of the documentary as well as the architectural and archaeological evidence for the history of the four mendicant houses in Cambridge, see J. L. W. Vinten Mattich, 'Friars and Society in Late Medieval East Anglia' (Cambridge Ph. D. thesis, 1995); cf. J. R. H. Moorman,. *The Grey Friars in Cambridge* (Cambridge, 1952); P. Zutshi and R. Ombres, 'The Dominicans in Cambridge, 1238–1538', *AFP*, 60 (Rome, 1990), pp. 313–73; P. Zutshi, *The Dominicans in Cambridge, 1238–1538: A Catalogue of a Commemorative Exhibition* (Cambridge University Library, 1988).

been so much in evidence at Cambridge before. That the first disciples of St Francis and St Dominic had transformed both the nature of Christian mendicancy and of medieval higher education by the rapidity with which they took advantage of the exhilarating prospects offered by the nascent universities of the early thirteenth century is one of the more familiar commonplaces of medieval religious history. By the beginning of the fourteenth century, at least some of those advantages were also being exploited by various members of the monastic orders, especially Benedictine monks, who increasingly began to frequent the schools of Paris, Oxford, and elsewhere in western Christendom.[7] By contrast, the much smaller groups of monks and canons who studied at Cambridge before the middle of the fifteenth century were clearly less significant for the history of either their university or their own religious houses. Thus of the eighty-five Benedictine monks between 1215 and 1540 selected for inclusion in an 'index of selected biographies' once compiled by the late W. A. Pantin, less than five were Cambridge graduates. Allowances must admittedly be made throughout this paper for the serious evidential distortion created by the acute scarcity of biographical references to monks and canons at Cambridge before the earliest surviving university Grace Book dramatically transforms our knowledge from 1454 onwards.[8] Nevertheless there can be little doubt that it was only in the century before the Reformation – perhaps too late – that English 'university monks' and 'university canons' fully and at last succeeded in seizing the educational opportunities which the university of Cambridge had long presented.

So negative a conclusion would admittedly hardly commend itself to the many scholars and antiquaries who have long tried to trace the vexed origins of the earliest western European universities to the learned interests of major monastic houses already sited in their

[7] Rashdall, *Universities*, 1, pp. 536–9; C. E. Smith, *The University of Toulouse in the Middle Ages: Its Origins and Growth to 1500 AD* (Milwaukee, WI, 1958), pp. 87, 118, 213; Dobson, 'Religious (Oxford)', pp. 542–55. It need hardly be said that this paper is an attempt, perhaps foredoomed to failure, to discover whether the acute shortage of original sources for the history of the monastic orders at medieval Cambridge will always make it impossible to compare and contrast their significance with that of their Oxford counterparts. Without the generous assistance of Professor Christopher Brooke, Mrs Catherine Hall, and Drs Joan Greatrex, Roger Lovatt, Tessa Webber, and Patrick Zutshi, it would be more inadequate still.

[8] Pantin, *Chapters*, 3, pp. 317–24; *Grace Book A*, pp. vii–ix; H. Peek and C. Hall, *The Archives of the University of Cambridge* (Cambridge, 1962), pp. 27–8, 31; *BRUC*, pp. xiii–xv.

immediate vicinity. At Cambridge, the only possible contender for such a role is of course the Augustinian priory of Barnwell, located on the southern bank of the Cam a mile north-east of the town's market place since 1112. In this case too, an obstinately controversial issue still remains at least partly open: the most recent investigation of the beginnings of academic life at Cambridge suggests that the proximity of Barnwell Priory 'was critically important for the development of the University'.[9] Nor can the indirect influence of the priory of Barnwell on the development of medieval Cambridge, above all as the greatest corporate landlord in the town, be denied. However, as in the intriguingly analogous case of the much wealthier Augustinian house of Osney in the western suburbs of medieval Oxford, the surviving evidence suggests that the relationship between Barnwell and the university of Cambridge played a comparatively minor role in the evolution of the latter. That relationship was in any case always likely to be charged with mutual suspicion, if suspicion often mitigated by formal respect. Thus the fact that the two most formidable priors of Barnwell during the thirteenth century, Johan de Thorley (1254–66) and Simon de Asceles (1271–97), were respectively remembered as 'skilled in civil law' and 'a professor of civil law at Cambridge' did not make either of them any the less demanding in pursuing their jurisdictional rights within the town.[10] That the Barnwell prior and chapter should respond favourably to a remarkably early academic initiative by the executors of William of Kilkenny, bishop of Ely (1254–6) – who gave them two hundred marks in order to support in perpetuity two chaplains while they studied theology in the Cambridge schools – is hardly surprising. However, it may be more revealing still that the university chancellor sued the prior of Barnwell for arrears of stipends to these scholar chaplains thirty years later and that such a method of funding Cambridge university students was never to be attempted again.[11]

[9] J. A. Brundage, 'The Cambridge Faculty of Canon Law and the Ecclesiastical Courts of Ely', in P. Zutshi, ed., *Medieval Cambridge: Essays on the Pre-Reformation University* (Woodbridge, Suffolk, 1993), p. 22; cf. C. N. L. Brooke, 'Monk and Canon: Some patterns in the religious life of the twelfth century', in W. J. Sheils, ed., *Monks, Hermits and the Ascetic Tradition*, *SCH*, 22 (1985), pp. 124–5; Rashdall, *Universities*, 3, pp. 274–7.

[10] *Liber Memorandorum Ecclesie de Bernewelle*, ed. J. W. Clark (Cambridge, 1907), pp. 71, 73; *BRUC*, p. 17.

[11] *Liber Memorandorum de Bernewelle*, pp. lvi, 71, 94–5, 146–7; *VCH*, *Cambridge and Isle of Ely*, 2 (1948), pp. 238–9.

In the charter of 1257 whereby they established these two perpetual chaplains, the prior and chapter of Barnwell were prepared to envisage the possibility that in due course of time the university itself might disappear, not too remote a possibility perhaps during a period when the king of England himself 'was not averse to the dissolution of Cambridge'.[12] All in all, it can hardly be said that the canons of Barnwell themselves ever did much to ensure either the university's welfare or indeed its survival. Admittedly, the *priores studentium* of the Augustinian canons studying at Cambridge held their chapters at Barnwell from at least 1371; and it was the judicial verdict of a Barnwell prior, John Chatteris, which finally secured the exemption of the university from episcopal intervention by the terms of the so-called Barnwell Process of 1430. However, the immediate relations between canons and university scholars were more or less continuously prejudiced by a long series of affrays arising from disputes about property and (especially) the conduct of the priory's Midsummer Fair.[13] Even so, it remains surprising that of the fifty or so Augustinian canons now identified as Cambridge university alumni before 1500, only two or three seem to have been from Barnwell; and of these, the single holder of a higher degree was John Asshefeld, already a doctor of theology when in 1396 he became vicar of St John Zachary, one of the five medieval Cambridge parish churches which were at one time or another in the advowson of his convent. Only in the decades immediately before the dissolution of Barnwell Priory in November 1538 is it likely that there were as many as two or three university graduates resident within the ranks of the community.[14] As fewer than ten books from the convent's library have yet been identified, it is therefore by no means easy to reverse the traditional, if still surprising, view that Barnwell 'seems to have contributed little or nothing to learning'.[15]

[12] *Liber Memorandorum de Bernewelle*, p. 94; M. B. Hackett, *The Original Statutes of Cambridge University: The Text and its History* (Cambridge, 1970), p. 64.

[13] *Chapters of the Augustinian Canons*, ed. H. E. Salter, Oxford Historical Society, 74 (1922), p. 69; Cooper, *Annals*, 1, pp. 121, 142, 153, 171–2; *VCH, Cambridge*, 3 (1959), pp. 58–9; Leader, p.15.

[14] *BRUC*, p. 20; C. H. and T. Cooper, *Athenae Cantabrigienses* (2 vols, Cambridge, 1858–61), 1, pp. 28, 51, 82, 109, 219; *VCH, Cambridge*, 2, pp. 243, 247.

[15] G. Baskerville, *English Monks and the Suppression of the Monasteries* (London, 1937), p. 41. Despite the exceptionally detailed regulations for the care of the priory's books recorded in the *Observances in use at the Augustinian Priory of St Giles and St Andrew at Barnwell*, ed. J. W. Clark (Cambridge, 1897), pp. 62–9, only eight of these have been identified: see T. Webber

Even less significant was the contribution to the medieval university made by the only other male monastic community in the immediate environs of medieval Cambridge, the little priory of St Edmund, situated some 300 yards south of Trumpington Gate, where Old Addenbrooke's Hospital now stands.[16] Nothing became the highly mysterious history of this Gilbertine convent more than the circumstances of its foundation in 1290. Appropriately enough perhaps, the first monastic study centre ever founded in medieval Cambridge was the creation of the only completely indigenous religious order in medieval England. Established only a few years after the earliest monastic college in the country (Gloucester Hall at Oxford) and the first secular academic college in Cambridge (Peterhouse), St Edmund's no doubt owed its origins to a wave of late thirteenth-century enthusiasm for the value of university-educated monks and canons in the religious cloister.[17] Accordingly, in September 1290 and on the grounds that 'the Master and brethren of Sempringham had often sent members of their order to study at the *castellum* [*sic*] of Cambridge', Nicholas IV licensed the Gilbertine canons 'to have within their house a discreet and learned doctor of theology to teach those of the brethren who desire to study that science'.[18] Precisely where that house was to be located, neither the pope nor indeed the Gilbertines seem to have been originally at all certain; but that difficult problem was solved at the most opportune moment by a fortunate intervention on the part of Cicely, daughter of William of St Edmund's in Cambridge in 1290. According to the well-informed chronicler of Barnwell Priory, it was

and A. G. Watson, eds, *The Libraries of the Augustinian Canons* (Corpus of British Medieval Library Catalogues, 6; British Academy, 1998), pp. 5–7. In sharp contrast to Osney Abbey near Oxford, no serious consideration was ever given after 1538 to the possibility of adapting the very extensive precincts of Barnwell Priory for alternative educational or religious use.

16 H. P. Stokes, *Outside the Trumpington Gates* (CAS, Octavo Publications, 44 [1908], pp. 57–63; B. Golding, *Gilbert of Sempringham and the Gilbertine Order, c. 1130–c. 1300* (Oxford, 1995), p. 172.

17 The heads of England's major religious houses cannot have been unmindful of the fact that three monastic houses (the Benedictine Collège de Saint-Denis, the Cistercian Collège de St Bernard and the Cluniac Collège de Cluny) had been securely established at the university of Paris by the 1260s: see T. Sullivan, 'The Visitation of the Collège de Cluny, Paris, 1386', *History of Universities*, 11 (1992), p. 2; cf. Dobson, 'Religious (Oxford)', pp. 544–9; idem, 'The Foundation of Gloucester College in 1283', *Worcester College Record* (Oxford, 1985).

18 *CPL*, 1 (1198–1304), p. 516; *VCH*, *Cambridge*, 2, pp. 254–5; Golding, *Gilbert of Sempringham*, pp. 171–3.

on the site of Cicely's family chapel of St Edmund that within the following year (1291) the *canonici de Symplingham* rapidly began to devote themselves to hearing lectures and disputations.[19]

Despite such auspicious beginnings, it can hardly be said that this precocious attempt to found a monastic *studium* at Cambridge proved a positive success in either religious or scholarly terms. In retrospect, as their most recent historian has observed, it might even be that the Gilbertines would have been better advised to lodge their more academically talented canons in secular hostels and colleges within the town, as did all other religious orders before the fifteenth century. The prospects that 'the priory of the chapel of St Edmund', as it was still best known in Cambridge itself until the end of the fifteenth century, might ever develop into a significant centre of advanced learning were in fact doomed by the complete inadequacy of its early endowments.[20] The numerical size of the Gilbertine community at Cambridge, like most aspects of its history, is obscure to a degree; but it seems clear from the very small number of its canons whose ordinations are recorded in the surviving registers of late medieval bishops of Ely that after the mid-fourteenth century there were rarely more than three or four brethren in residence there. Moreover, very few indeed of these Gilbertine canons can actually be proved to have studied in the university schools.[21] Indeed without the small annual contributions or pensions it received from at least twelve Gilbertine houses in the country, it seems hardly possible that the priory could have survived until its suppression in 1539.[22] It is accordingly all the more intriguing that during the fifty years before the Reformation the Gilbertines at last began to show signs of placing an increased emphasis upon the value of a university education in general and of a university degree in particular. Nowhere was this more obvious than at Watton in the East Riding of Yorkshire, much the wealthiest Gilbertine priory in England. James Bolton, for example, was already prior of Watton (1474–97) when he graduated as D.Th. in 1489–90 after many years of study at Cambridge. Forty years later, by what proved to be a not too

[19] *Liber Memorandorum de Bernewelle*, p. 212.

[20] *CPL*, 6 (1404–15), p. 126; Cooper, *Annals*, 1, p. 250; Golding, *Gilbert of Sempringham*, pp. 173–7; *VCH, Cambridge*, 2, pp. 253–6.

[21] See, e.g., *BRUC*, pp. 34, 116, 124, 244, 418, 527. For justifiable doubts as to whether St Edmund's Priory was ever open to students other than Gilbertine canons, see Golding, *Gilbert of Sempringham*, pp. 174–5.

[22] *Valor ecclesiasticus* (Record Commission, 1810–34), 3, p. 506; *VCH, Cambridge*, p. 256.

untypical volte-face on the part of the last generation of medieval university monks and canons, Doctor Robert Holgate, another Cambridge graduate who was later not only a prior of Watton but a future archbishop of York too (1545–55), was to preside over the destruction of the Gilbertine Order itself.[23]

No doubt the handful of Gilbertine canons who studied at late medieval Cambridge can never have been seen by their contemporaries as much more than an intriguing curiosity. However, it was obviously true of the larger monastic orders of western Christendom that they were themselves more likely to observe Benedict XII's reforming constitutions of the 1330s, and to ensure that at least one out of every twenty monks from each major house should study at a university, if they had access to their own exclusive *studium* there.[24] Accordingly the failure of the English religious orders to emulate the example of the Gilbertines at St Edmund's Priory inevitably proved a critical factor in curbing the recruitment of academically promising monks and canons into the Cambridge schools for nearly 150 years. Such a failure was itself understandable enough, perhaps as much the consequence of inadequate monastic financial resources as of the reluctance of increasingly centrifugal religious houses to cooperate in the achievement of a common higher educational objective. Nevertheless these were problems which from the 1290s onwards impaired monastic educational provision at Cambridge even more than at Oxford. It was, after all, to the latter university that the influential superiors of the various English monastic orders most naturally tended to look when their attention turned, like that of the Cistercian abbots of the province of Canterbury in 1398, to the prospects of establishing a permanent university 'mansio studencium nostri ordinis'.[25] Most seriously of all, the very fact that no less than three monastic *studia* for English Black Monks (Gloucester College, Canterbury College, and Durham College) were already in existence at Oxford by the mid-fourteenth century undoubtedly inhibited the creation of a Benedictine counterpart at

[23] *BRUC*, p. 71; A. G. Dickens, *Robert Holgate, Archbishop of York and President of the King's Council in the North*, St Anthony's Hall Publications, York, 8 (1955), pp. 3–10; C. Cross and N. Vickers, *Monks, Friars and Nuns in Sixteenth-Century Yorkshire*, Yorkshire Archaeological Society, Record Series 150 (1995), p.395.

[24] Pantin, *Chapters*, 2, pp. 230–2; *Chapters of Augustinian Canons*, pp. 214–67; Dobson, 'Religious (Oxford)', pp. 544–55.

[25] BL, Royal MS 12 E 14, fols 25v–26; C. H. Talbot, 'The English Cistercians and the Universities', *Studia Monastica*, 4 (1962), p. 212.

Cambridge until Abbot John Litlington of Crowland Abbey took the fateful decision to assume responsibility for a new Benedictine *hospitium religiosum* on the north side of the Cam as late as 1428.[26] That the English Cistercians and Augustinian canons never acquired a Cambridge foundation at all is rather less surprising when one recalls that their monastic colleges of St Bernard and St Mary at Oxford were only established, by 1438 and 1443 respectively, after the most tortuous of negotiations and almost scandalously long delays.[27]

Not however that the lack of properly constituted monastic colleges in Cambridge ever prevented at least some Benedictines, Cistercians, Augustinian canons, Premonstratensians, and even Carthusians from studying in the university's schools. It is clear enough that those learned brethren of English monastic communities who were sent to study at Cambridge – as at Oxford – usually found it by no means difficult to secure comparatively inexpensive accommodation within the colleges and the hostels of the city. Thus both the prior of Selby Abbey in Yorkshire and the prior of St Neots were resident (perhaps only briefly) at Peterhouse in the late 1410s; and the Augustinian canon, Henry Burton, already prior of St Mary Overy, Southwark, rented a room in the new Queens' College in the mid-1460s when he was preparing to incept as a doctor of theology.[28] Not surprisingly, the only religious house with sufficient numbers of monk scholars to warrant the establishment of its own, more or less exclusive, long-term hall of residence seems to have been the cathedral priory of Ely. Before his death in 1341, Prior John de Crauden acquired a hostel on the site of what was to become part of Trinity Hall for that very purpose.[29] Several other major religious houses made arrangements for the accommodation of their student monks at the same Cambridge college or hall for a period of several years. Of these, perhaps the best known

[26] *Cal. Patent Rolls, 1422–29*, p. 475; *Magdalene College*, pp. 4–5.

[27] By 1482 such delays had made the Cistercians 'the centre of gossip for the whole of Oxford': see Talbot, 'English Cistercians', p. 214; Dobson, 'Religious (Oxford)', pp. 552–5.

[28] *Grace Book A*, pp. 51–2; *BRUC*, pp. 110, 503, 517. For evidence that many Augustinian canons studying at Oxford lived in an 'external master's school and/or hall', see S. Forde, 'The educational organization of the Augustinian Canons in England and Wales, and their university life at Oxford, 1325–1448', *History of Universities*, 13 (1994), pp. 33–7.

[29] J. Bentham, *The History and Antiquities of the Conventual and Cathedral Church of Ely* (2nd edn, Norwich, 1812), p. 220; Greatrex, p. 401; C. Crawley, *Trinity Hall: the History of a Cambridge College, 1350–1975* (Cambridge, 1976), p. 28. For the later history of this Ely Hostel, see H. P. Stokes, *The Mediaeval Hostels of the University of Cambridge*, CAS, Octavo Publications, 49 (1924), pp. 9–10.

and best documented example is provided by the comparatively large numbers of Norwich cathedral monks who were pensioners at Gonville Hall during the years immediately before and after 1500. Between 1481 and at least 1505 there can be little doubt that the prior and chapter of Norwich positively preferred to send their Cambridge monk scholars to Gonville Hall rather than to the common Benedictine accommodation by then available in Buckingham College.[30]

However, it is only in very exceptional cases that the places of residence of Cambridge's monks and canons can be known at all; and it may also go without saying that the names of these university religious are always so inadequately recorded (except perhaps in the case of student monks from Ely and Norwich cathedral priories) that any attempt to estimate their numbers at any one point of time is hazardous in the extreme. The evidence painstakingly collected in Emden's *Biographical Register of the University of Cambridge to 1500* therefore provides a much less reliable impression of the total numbers of monks and canons at Cambridge than of their distribution between their respective religious orders.[31] Thus it seems clear that before the late fifteenth century there were hardly any identifiable Cistercian students at the university of Cambridge at all, a not unexpected confirmation of the general truism that 'the general chapter evinced rather more enthusiasm for monastic education than did most monks themselves'.[32] It is hardly less surprising that only six Premonstratensian canons are known to have studied at Cambridge before 1500, probably all of these from houses in East Anglia and Lincolnshire.[33] It therefore follows that until the very late

[30] J. Venn, *et al.*, *Biographical History of Gonville and Caius College, 1349–1897*, 8 vols (Cambridge, 1897–1998), 3, pp. 332–3; T. H. Aston, 'The medieval alumni of the University of Cambridge', *Past and Present*, 86 (1980), pp. 54–5; A. B. Cobban, *The Medieval English Universities: Oxford and Cambridge to c. 1500* (London, 1988), p. 320.

[31] The following estimates are based on an analysis of the biographical information about Cambridge monks and canons available in *BRUC* as well as (for the period between 1500 and 1540) the much less reliable Cooper, *Athenae*, 1, and J. and J. A. Venn, *Alumni Cantabrigienses to 1751*, 4 vols (Cambridge, 1922–7). For Dr Peter Cunich's much more authoritative 'A biographical list of Benedictine monks at Cambridge University from the earliest times until 1540', see Magdalene College Cambridge, MS R. 2. 15.

[32] S. F. Hockey, *Quarr Abbey and its Lands, 1132–1631* (Leicester, 1971), p. 245. Two of the three (only) Cistercian monks who appear in the pages of *BRUC* had previously been scholars of St Bernard's College, Oxford (ibid., pp. 285, 562, 607).

[33] *BRUC*, pp. 22, 422, 460, 634, 655–6; H. M. Colvin, *The White Canons in England* (Oxford, 1951), pp. 321–6. The common assumption that Bishop Richard Redman, much the most celebrated White Canon of late medieval England, studied at Cambridge or

fifteenth century the monastic presence in the university of Cambridge was overwhelmingly dominated by Augustinian canons and Benedictine monks alone. Moreover, of the fifty or so regular canons now securely identified as students at Cambridge in the later Middle Ages, only one was resident there before 1400.[34] All allowances made for the much poorer documentation before that date, it seems highly probable that it was only during the course of the fifteenth century that the larger Augustinian houses seriously began to implement the decree of their Provincial Chapter at Northampton in 1374 which envisaged the dispatch of 'scholars of our order' to the university of Cambridge as well as Oxford.[35]

By contrast, a no doubt small but gradually increasing number of Benedictine monks had begun to study at Cambridge from at least the late thirteenth century onwards. During the 1240s Bury St Edmunds already had links with the canon law faculty there; 'the first of its monks' known for certain to have received a higher degree at Cambridge appears to have been Simon, monk of Walden in Essex, who incepted as D. Cn. L in 1297.[36] It seems inherently likely, however difficult to prove, that from then until the mid-fifteenth century it was usually Black Monks from Bury, Ely, and sometimes Crowland who outnumbered university scholars from any other religious house. Indeed most other Benedictine monasteries, even in East Anglia, could prove remarkably slow to follow their example. Although one member of the Norwich cathedral community is known to have been sent '*versus Cantab.*' as early as 1306–7, he had spent the previous ten years in Oxford; and it was only after the 1440s and 1450s that Norwich university monks were normally to be found in what might have always seemed their local university.[37] Similarly, it was to Oxford rather than Cambridge that the monasteries of Peterborough and

Oxford is shown to be completely without evidence in J. A. Gribbin, 'The Premonstratensian Order in late medieval England' (Cambridge University Ph. D. thesis, 1998), pp. 188, 196.

34 *BRUC*, p. 20.

35 *Chapters of Augustinian Canons*, pp. 70–1.

36 *The Chronicle of Bury St Edmunds, 1212–1301*, ed. A. Gransden (London, 1964), p. 140; Hackett, *Original Statutes*, p. 131, n. 2; *BRUC*, p. 685.

37 J. Greatrex, 'Monk students from Norwich Cathedral Priory at Oxford and Cambridge, c. 1300 to 1530', *EHR*, 106 (1991), pp. 561–2, 579–83. There is no evidence that Cardinal Adam de Easton, the most distinguished of all English university monks by the time of his death in 1397, had any personal connection with Cambridge at all (Greatrex, pp. 502–3).

Spalding were still regularly sending their university students until well after the 1450s.[38] But then it was only in the late fourteenth century, after all, that there is direct evidence that the General Chapters of the Benedictine and Cluniac Orders began to give serious consideration to the possibility that some of their monk scholars might wish to study at Cambridge instead of Oxford.

As far as is known, it was not in fact until 1363 that the Provincial Chapter of the Black Monks, meeting under the sole presidency of Thomas de la Mare, abbot of St Albans (1349–96), rectified an obvious anomaly by creating, as had long been the case in Oxford, the office of *prior studentium*, a senior Benedictine whose duty it was 'to rule and care for the monks studying in Cambridge'. Indeed according to the surviving copy of a letter recently discovered by Dr James Clark, Abbot de la Mare may have been involved in appointing the otherwise unidentifiable G. Peblyngton, a monk of St Mary's Abbey, York, to that very position.[39] Similarly, the first surviving explicit references to the prospect of Cluniac monks studying at Cambridge occur among the proceedings of the two General Chapters of that order which met at Bermondsey in 1392 and 1395. In fact all four of the Cluniac monks so far identified as Cambridge graduates before 1500 were canon lawyers there during the second half of the fifteenth century.[40] It is therefore not too surprising that of the hundred or so late medieval Benedictine monks known to have studied at Cambridge between 1300 and 1500, only thirteen have yet been identified as having done so before their successors moved into the new Benedictine hostel on the site of the future Buckingham College in 1428.[41] Ironically enough, the main argument put forward for the creation of that hostel, namely that Benedictine scholars studying in Cambridge had previously been scattered through the town in the hospices of the laity, itself explains why we will never really know how many such scholars there were.

Perhaps no institution of comparable academic significance in the history of either of England's two universities remains as obstinately

[38] *Visitations of the Religious Houses in the Diocese of Lincoln, 1436–1449*, ed. A. H. Thompson, *CYS*, 24, 33 (1919, 1927), 2, pp. 270, 273, 330; *Account Rolls of the Obedientiaries of Peterborough*, ed. J. Greatrex, Northamptonshire Record Society, 33 (1983), pp. 15, 92, 95, 104, 213, 216, 247.

[39] Cambridge, Corpus Christi College, MS 170, p. 22; Pantin, *Chapters*, 2, p. 76.

[40] R. Graham, 'The English Province of the Order of Cluny in the fifteenth century', in idem, *English Ecclesiastical Studies* (London, 1929), pp. 53–4; *BRUC*, pp. 177, 181, 265, 615.

[41] *Magdalene College*, p. 3; Aston, 'Medieval alumni', pp. 55–6.

mysterious as does the Benedictine hostel – and later college – whose court, however transformed, still overlooks the 'great bridge' which in its original form gave Cambridge its name.[42] However, there can be no serious doubt that the new 'hospicium religiosis competens' of 1428 was the outcome of a fortunate and by no means inevitable conjuncture between the higher educational objectives long discussed in the Provincial Chapters of the English Benedictines and the residential needs of Black Monks already studying in Cambridge. It was two of the latter's *priores studentium*, John de Bardney and John Sudbury respectively, who in turn made an eloquent plea to the successive Provincial Chapters of 1423 and 1426 for the funding of a new Benedictine 'common place' within the university. Such was the only proper remedy, or so they argued, for the dangers and scandals likely to result if the monk students in their charge continued to be lodged in lay hospices.[43] The response of the 1426 Black Monk Chapter itself was immediately favourable; and it may well be that it was the influence of its then president, Prior John Wessington of Durham, himself one of the most celebrated Oxford university monks of the early fifteenth century, which was decisive in securing the support of both Bishop Thomas Langley of Durham and Bishop William Alnwick of Norwich for such a scheme.[44] Within two years (at least by the date of the royal licence they received on 7 July 1428) the two bishops had purchased the messuage now occupied by the First and Second Courts of Magdalene College.

Meanwhile, and even more rapidly, John Litlington, the recently elected abbot of Crowland, had provided the new foundation with its all-important constitutional basis by his assurance that he and his chapter would not only acquire the site but make it available as a common Benedictine student hostel. As a result, this *hospitium religiosorum* – although open to all properly recommended Benedictine

[42] Willis and Clark, 2, pp. 351–66. The following very summary account of Buckingham College is especially indebted to Dr Cunich's recent and much more detailed discussion of its history in *Magdalene College*, pp. 1–30.

[43] Pantin, *Chapters*, 2, pp. 149, 172–3.

[44] *Cal. Patent Rolls, 1422–29*, p. 475. In addition to enjoying particularly warm relations with Bishop Langley, Prior Wesssington – in the company of the then abbot of Crowland – had played a prominent role at the extraordinary assembly of English Black Monks convoked at Westminster by Henry V in May 1421: there is however no evidence that issues relating to university education at Oxford or Cambridge were on the lengthy agenda at that time: R. B. Dobson, *Durham Priory, 1400–1450* (Cambridge, 1973), pp. 223–4, 240–4; Pantin, *Chapters*, 2, pp. 98–134.

students at the university – remained a cell of Crowland until both mother and daughter house were surrendered to the Crown in December 1539.[45] How rapidly Black Monks began to occupy this first of all academic institutions in Cambridge *ultra pontem* is – like most aspects of the history of this new Benedictine university *studium* – obscure to a degree. No attempt can be made here to trace the complexities of that history in any detail; but it seems obvious enough from Dr Cunich's recent important reassessment of the evidence that for many years 'the Hostel called Monkis place' (as it was still being called in 1472) suffered severely from the excessive haste of its foundation and its highly inadequate initial endowments.[46] It is certainly very noticeable that within the long chapter 'de doctoribus, studentibus, et studencium prioribus', as codified in the English Benedictine Statutes of 1444, the monks' hostel at Cambridge is still more or less completely ignored by contrast with the several references to 'our common place at Oxford'.[47] In fact it was probably not until the 1470s and early 1480s that the material and academic welfare of the Benedictine 'common place' at Cambridge was at last placed on a more secure and prosperous footing. The transformation of its name to Buckingham College at this period (the new title is first known to occur in 1483) almost certainly had no constitutional significance at all: its long established counterpart at Oxford, Gloucester College, had certainly never been a college in any strict sense of the word. As a daughter house of Crowland Abbey, it is understandable that Buckingham College never seems to have received its own statutes; but despite its federal structure it remains somewhat surprising that no record survives of its ever being dedicated to a saint.[48]

Much more significant were the material benefits the Cambridge Black Monks apparently secured in the years before 1483 from some member of the family of the Staffords, dukes of Buckingham. Dr

[45] *Magdalene College*, pp. 4–5, 29, 31–3. By at least 1432 the Cambridge borough treasurers had begun to receive an annual payment of 18*d* from the abbot of Crowland for the fishponds or 'pondyards' on the site: see Cambridge Record Office, Treasurers' Accounts, 1432–3, 1435–6, 1436–7; *Cambridge Borough Documents,* 1, ed. W. M. Palmer (Cambridge, 1931), pp. 40, 57.

[46] Cooper, *Annals*, 1, p. 227; *Magdalene College*, pp. 7–9.

[47] Pantin, *Chapters*, 2, pp. 183–220.

[48] Dobson, 'Religious (Oxford)', pp. 546–8; C. N. L. Brooke, 'The dedications of Cambridge colleges and their chapels', in Zutshi, ed., *Medieval Cambridge*, p. 19. The name of Buckingham College was only added to John Rous's well-known list of Cambridge colleges after that list's original compilation *c.* 1450 (Aston, 'Medieval Alumni', p. 15).

Cunich has recently made a powerful case for supposing that their most important benefactor was in fact Anne Neville, the dowager duchess of Buckingham who died in 1480, rather than – as traditionally assumed since the sixteenth century – her grandson, Henry, the second duke of Buckingham, a celebrated victim of Richard III three years later. Of all Dr Cunich's ingenious arguments, perhaps the most persuasive is that in the year of her death, Anne Neville, together with her sister, Cecily Neville, Edward IV's mother, was granted the highly unusual privilege of consorority by the Benedictine provincial chapter.[49] That the first duchess of Buckingham was rich enough to bestow extensive patronage upon the college which thereafter adopted the name of her family is certainly plausible enough; but within the obscure history of that college perhaps nothing is more startlingly obscure than our ignorance of what precisely that patronage may actually have been and why she should have diverted it to Benedictine university monks. It may well be that before the end of her grandson's minority in 1473, Anne Neville was 'perhaps the wealthiest woman in the kingdom'; and it is also worth attention that throughout the 1470s Anne Neville was often resident at Kimbolton Castle near Huntingdon, within an easy day's journey from Cambridge. Such evidence is however highly circumstantial; and it remains remarkable that none of the supposed benefactions to the college of the Cambridge Black Monks by the duchess or any other member of her family are mentioned in either the royal close or patent rolls or the surviving muniments of the Stafford family.[50]

In any case it must have been during Anne Neville's own life-time that there began the ambitious if protracted building campaign at Buckingham College which by the early sixteenth century had resulted in a court 'considerably larger than its sister Benedictine institutions in Oxford'. As is well known, one of the chambers in the south range of the court (the 'Monk's Room' in 'E' staircase) still survives to this day as the best preserved example of late medieval college accommodation in either Cambridge or Oxford university. How often such chambers –

[49] *Magdalene College*, pp. 8–14; Pantin, *Chapters*, 3, p. 116.

[50] B. J. Harris, *Edward Stafford, Third Duke of Buckingham, 1478–1521* (Stanford, CA, 1986), pp. 19–20; C. Rawcliffe, *The Staffords, Earls of Stafford and Dukes of Buckingham, 1394–1521* (Cambridge, 1978), p. 97; Jones and Underwood, *King's Mother*, pp. 142–3; *Magdalene College*, pp. 11–12.

ultimately with sleeping quarters for perhaps as many as forty-eight monks – were ever fully occupied is impossible to say; but clearly the existence of such comparatively plentiful accommodation within a common monastic college was at least partly responsible for the dramatic increase in the number of Black Monks known to have been at Cambridge after the 1470s.[51] Of the 115 or so monks Dr Cunich has been able to identify as inmates of Buckingham College or its predecessor, the great majority studied at the university after the 1470s. It is quite as striking that of the approximately one hundred Benedictine students known to have been resident anywhere in Cambridge before 1500, more or less exactly three-quarters were there between 1470 and the end of the century. This numerical increase became even more remarkable during the thirty-five years before the Dissolution when at least fifty Benedictine scholars are known to have embarked on study at Cambridge, as compared to sixty or so during the previous half-century.[52] However, although it can be fairly confidently assumed that the majority of these Benedictine students were lodged in Buckingham College, it must be emphasised that the availability of so well-appointed and spacious a college was not at all the only reason for the remarkable expansion in the recorded number of university monks at Cambridge during the last two generations of the religious life in medieval England.

Indeed perhaps a more intriguing feature of the history of canons and monks at medieval Cambridge is the increasing presence there from the 1470s onwards of members of religious orders who would previously have rarely been particularly visible at the university at all. Thus, despite the existence of the Augustinian university college of St Mary at Oxford since 1435, at least thirty canons of that order attended the Cambridge schools between 1500 and 1535, many more (as has been seen) than in any previous period. Nor did the requirement of the Cistercian general chapter (in 1482) that all abbeys of the order with twelve monks or more should send one of their brethren to St Bernard's College, Oxford, inhibit at least a handful of White Monks from acquiring Cambridge university degrees during the

[51] R. W. McDowall, 'Buckingham College', *Proceedings of CAS*, 44 (1950), pp. 5–12; Willis and Clark, 2, pp. 359–87; *Magdalene College*, pp. 14–19.

[52] These very approximate estimates are calculated from the entries in *BRUC*, Cooper's *Athenae* and Venn's *Alumni Cantabrigienses*. Cf. Aston, 'Medieval Alumni', p. 19; and *Magdalene College*, pp. 3, 20, 27.

following half-century.[53] More surprisingly still, it was during the closing years of the fifteenth century too that even the brethren of the nine English Carthusian houses, previously highly inimical to university education, began to find their way to the Cambridge as well as the Oxford schools. In this unique case it can often be extremely difficult to distinguish between the several Carthusian monks who studied at a university before they joined the order and those who were sent to Oxford or Cambridge after entering a Charterhouse.[54] This particular problem is complicated even further by the number of Carthusians who joined the order while university students but who managed to acquire, perhaps *in absentia*, a higher university degree after their profession. Thus John Houghton, the most famous of all Carthusian martyrs at the hands of Thomas Cromwell and Henry VIII in 1535, is alleged to have been twenty-five years old when he entered the London Charterhouse, but he became a Cambridge bachelor of civil law some six years later.[55] During the years immediately after its foundation, Christ's College (also attended by Houghton's confessor, William Exmewe) may have become the most popular Cambridge residence of English Carthusian monks. Some other Carthusian university scholars, like John Michel and Henry Eccleston, respectively the last two priors of Witham and Mount Grace, also received their Cambridge degrees several years after entering their convents. By the time of their abrupt departure from the English religious scene between 1537 and 1539, no fewer than five of the nine English Carthusian priors held university degrees.[56]

One of the consequences of the rising numbers of religious in pre-Reformation Cambridge was that the university gradually developed a much stronger appeal, for monastic as well as for secular scholars, outside as well as within East Anglia. Geographical propinquity had rarely in fact been an absolutely decisive factor in determining whether English religious houses would send their most promising scholars to

[53] D. Knowles and R. N. Hadcock, *Medieval Religious Houses: England and Wales* (revised edn, London, 1971), p. 123; Cooper, *Athenae*, 1, pp. 18, 61, 68, 69, 70, 186–7.

[54] C. Rowntree, 'Studies in Carthusian history in later medieval England' (York University D. Phil. thesis, 1981), pp. 147–51.

[55] *Grace Book B*, ii, p. 99; W. St John Hope, *The History of the London Charterhouse* (London, 1925), pp. 150–1; A. R. Wines, 'The London Charterhouse in the later Middle Ages: an institutional history ' (Cambridge University Ph. D. thesis, 1998), pp. 218–19.

[56] *Grace Book B*, ii, pp. 99, 170–1; Venn, *Alumni Cantabrigienses*, 2, pp. 113, 322, 413; 3, p. 182; 4, p. 354; Rowntree, 'Studies in Carthusian history', pp. 148–9. Not one of these Carthusians is known to have been the author of devotional or indeed any other treatises.

Cambridge rather than Oxford. Only in the 1490s (and then not completely) did the monks of Peterborough Abbey, less than forty miles from Cambridge, break with their long tradition of sending their student brethren to Oxford; and on the very eve of the surrender of his monastery, a monk of Ramsey no less, William Ereth, was studying at Gloucester College, Oxford.[57] At Cambridge itself recruitment from eastern England naturally remained the norm; and during the half-century before the Dissolution it was usually brethren from Ely and Norwich cathedral priories, and to an apparently lesser extent from Bury St Edmunds, Crowland, Thorney, Spalding, and St Benet of Hulme who tended to outnumber Benedictine students from elsewhere. Similarly, the Augustinian canons studying at Cambridge were most likely to be brethren from the priory of Walsingham and the abbey of St Osyth in Essex.[58] However, after 1450 Cambridge also attracted an increasing number of university monks and canons from most regions of England except the area immediately around and west of Oxford. Even before that date Cambridge had sometimes become the university of choice for the Yorkshire Black Monks of St Mary's Abbey, York, and of Selby, a development which seems to have reached its climax exactly at the time when there was a sharp acceleration in the number of northern secular clerks who became college fellows there.[59] Perhaps a more significant indication of the gradual rise of monastic respect for the academic and other amenities of Cambridge is that even the abbey of St Albans – despite its traditionally close relationship with Gloucester College, Oxford – began to send several of its monks to study at Cambridge after the 1420s. Some recruits came from even further afield, like Thomas Mynde, who was a very recent Cambridge bachelor of theology when he was elevated to the abbacy of his community at Shrewsbury in 1460, and Thomas Fort, an Augustinian canon from Bodmin in Cornwall,

[57] *Account Rolls of Peterborough*, pp. 88, 92, 95, 97, 104, 106, 240, 247; *The Letter Book of Robert Joseph, monk-scholar of Evesham and Gloucester College, Oxford, 1530–3*, ed. H. Aveling and W. A. Pantin, Oxford Historical Society, ns, 19 (1967), p. 265; *BRUO 1501–1540*, p. 192.

[58] See, e.g., *BRUC*, pp. 115, 220, 298, 424, 443, 520, 534, 609. By the late fifteenth century, if not earlier still, most religious houses seem to have been free to decide to which of the two universities they would send their students (Forde, 'Educational organization of Augustinian Canons', pp. 29–30).

[59] Between 1458 and 1479 at least five St Mary's monks graduated from Cambridge with the degree of either B. Th. or D. Th. (*BRUC*, pp. 316, 374, 503, 587, 616). Cf. Taylor, 'Diocese of York and university connexion', pp. 50–1.

who ended his life as a suffragan bishop as well as a prior of Huntingdon.[60]

Thomas Fort had probably begun his academic career as an arts student at Oxford in the 1480s and is only one example of the twenty or more late medieval monks and canons – many of them future religious superiors – who can be identified as having studied not only at Cambridge but at Oxford too. After 1454, when the first surviving Cambridge *Grace Book* begins to record the practice in detail, no great obstacle was in fact put in the way of monks and other scholars who wished to transfer their academic qualifications from one university to the other. Not only did the practice of incorporation of degrees become particularly common during the thirty years between 1490 and 1520 but (as in the case of secular students at this period) 'the movement was more in the direction of Cambridge' rather than the reverse.[61] The comparative ease with which senior graduates could now have their degrees incorporated at Cambridge clearly brought several senior and academically gifted monks and canons into personal contact with the latter university who would previously have remained exclusively at Oxford. Thus, although he spent nearly all of his monastic life as scholar and then warden of Canterbury College, Oxford, William Chichele, a Christ Church monk, was granted a grace to oppose in theology at Cambridge in 1472–3. A year earlier, and despite the fact that his monastery had long 'preferred Oxford for nearly all its students', Thomas Millyng, the last Westminster monk to become a bishop, had similarly had his Oxford degrees incorporated at Cambridge.[62] Why, with such 'bewildering changefulness', major religious houses like Canterbury Cathedral and Westminster Abbey should have countenanced such incorporation and even broken, if only occasionally, with their long tradition of sending their monk scholars to Oxford must be hard to explain except in terms of the gradually increasing academic prestige of the other university. Few late medieval

[60] Clark, ' Intellectual life at St Albans', pp. 59–60; *BRUC*, pp. 237–8, 418.

[61] Leader, pp. 39, 106. The early history of incorporation at Cambridge is discussed in Hackett, *Original Statutes*, pp. 54, 122–3, 146.

[62] *Grace Book A*, p. 97; *BRUO*, 1, p. 413; 2, pp. 1282–3; B. F. Harvey, 'The monks of Westminster and the University of Oxford', in F. R. H. Du Boulay and C. M. Barron, eds, *The Reign of Richard II: Essays in Honour of May McKisack* (London, 1971), pp. 112, 126, 128. Cf. the career of William Codenham, alias Buntyng, a Bury St Edmunds monk and Oxford B. Th. who then incepted in theology at Cambridge in 1494–5, three years before he became abbot of his monastery (*BRUO*, 1, p. 454).

English monks and canons, it need hardly be said, could contemplate the expense of higher education except in either Cambridge or Oxford. On the limited evidence available, and despite the celebrity of Prior John Selling's expeditions south of the Alps in search of the sources of humanist learning between 1464 and 1470, most of the few members of English religious orders who studied at universities abroad in the fifteenth century seem to have been Augustinian canons in pursuit of a canon law degree at Bologna, like Thomas Legger of Dunstable and John Farewell of Walsingham in 1455 and 1474 respectively. The only English Premonstratensian canon known to have studied in an overseas university was Mathew Mackarall of Cockersand who was incorporated at Cambridge in 1516–17, some years after obtaining a doctorate in theology at Freiburg in Germany. A celebrated preacher who became successively abbot of Alnwick (*c.* 1519–22) and Barlings (*c.* 1529–37), Mackarall was almost alone among the ranks of English university monks and canons in being executed for his alleged involvement in the Pilgrimage of Grace.[63]

At Cambridge, as at Oxford, an increased emphasis upon the value of a higher degree in theology or canon law was itself both a consequence and a cause of the expansion of monastic education during the fifty or so years before the Reformation.[64] On a well known occasion, and with Westminster Abbey particularly in mind, Henry VII once attributed the fact that 'vertue emonges religious men is little used' to the 'lakke of grounded men in the lawes of God. . . .to be the heddes of the same house'; and he went on to express his dissatisfaction on learning that only three Westminster monks currently held a bachelorship or doctorate in theology. In less happy circumstances still, when Dr Richard Layton came to Glastonbury to dissolve the abbey there in 1539, he complained that the house possessed no university doctor and only 'three bachelors of divinity, meanly learned'.[65] It was

[63] *BRUO*, 1, p. 101; 2, p. 1126; Gribbin, 'Premonstratensian Order', p. 187–90. It seems hard to believe that the unusually mobile career of Thomas Mersche, a Gilbertine canon from Lincoln who studied theology at Cambridge and other universities for many years before being appointed apostolic penitentiary at Rome in 1426, can have been anything but highly exceptional (*BRUC*, p. 402).

[64] The late T. H. Aston's numerical analysis ('Medieval Alumni', p. 63) of the higher degrees obtained by members of the various religious orders who studied at late medieval Cambridge almost certainly over-emphasises the gradual decline of theology to a supposed 'modest position'.

[65] *CclR, 1500–09*, p. 139; Harvey, 'Monks of Westminster', pp. 126–7; *Letters and Papers*, 14, pt ii, pp. 60–1.

undoubtedly in response to criticisms of this sort from the Crown, as well as from several early Tudor bishops and the regular assemblies of the Benedictine and Augustinian Chapters, that the most substantial English religious houses began to send more and more of their junior brethren on the arduous path to obtain a higher degree at Cambridge. To take the two best documented examples, eight monks from Norwich cathedral priory secured higher degrees between 1476 and the 1520s (of whom however only one studied at Cambridge); and there were at least eight Ely university monks studying at Cambridge during the twenty-five years before 1535, when their prospects of acquiring a university degree were about to be jeopardized for ever.[66]

It may be even more significant for the closing stages of medieval English monastic history that this was also the period when several of the middle-rank monasteries in the country, which had never previously shown much evidence of observing Benedict XII's constitutions of the 1330s at all seriously, began to send one or two of their brethren to the Cambridge schools. One of many possible instances is John Thetford, an Augustinian canon of Butley Priory in Suffolk, 'the single member of the house to have gained a paragraph in Cooper's *Athenae Cantabrigienses*', who studied nearly ten years at Cambridge before becoming a bachelor of canon law in 1512–13 and later prior of Thetford and Holy Trinity, Ipswich.[67] By the early sixteenth century, as never before, a university degree in theology or canon law had become a highly desirable qualification for the headship of nearly all major Benedictine and Augustinian houses in the country; and it was exactly during this period that 'Cambridge's contribution to the leadership of the religious orders' at last began to surpass that of Oxford.[68] By yet another irony it was only *after* the *ecclesia Anglicana*'s enforced separation from the papacy that Cambridge university monks and canons at last joined their Oxford peers on the English episcopal bench. John Salcot or Capon, perhaps the first bishop of England and Wales to be appointed (in 1534) without papal confirmation, was himself a Colchester monk and a Cambridge doctor of theology; and

[66] Greatrex, pp. 387–465, 478–576; idem, 'Monk students from Norwich', pp. 579–83.

[67] A. G. Dickens, *Late Monasticism and the Reformation* (London, 1994), p. 17; Cooper, *Athenae*, p. 60.

[68] Aston, 'Medieval Alumni', pp. 67–8; *Magdalene College*, pp. 21–2; *VCH, Cambridge*, 2, pp. 216–17 (Thorney Abbey).

of the twenty-five ex-religious who followed him into the ranks of the episcopate more than half were also Cambridge graduates. By the strangest of possible paradoxes the Cambridge-educated monk bishop only came into his own when monasticism itself was no more.[69]

Such enhanced emphasis on the value of a higher university degree (and on the rewards it might bring) not only brought more monks and canons to the Cambridge schools but ensured that by 1500 many of them would be students there for long years at a time. Although members of the religious orders were normally, although not always, exempted from the study of arts at the university, the aspiring doctor of theology or canon law was usually expected to keep terms in Cambridge for at least nine years before he received that degree.[70] Despite the fact that in practice many monastic chapters were reluctant to allow their university students to be continuously resident at Cambridge throughout the whole academic or calendar year, there is no doubt that during the early years of their religious life several monks and canons came to know the streets of Cambridge even better than their own cloisters. Accordingly, some university monks claimed to be positively ignorant of the state of discipline in their mother houses; and it was not unusual for a bishop to require that monks and canons sent to study at a university should only be recalled home with his express permission. After his visitation of the Augustinian priory of Newnham in Bedfordshire in the early 1430s, Bishop William Gray of Lincoln took pains to order that 'your brother, John Litlington, *studium continue exerceat*'.[71] However, although increasingly familiar figures on the Cambridge academic scene, Benedictine monks and Augustinian canons seem to have played a much less significant role in university affairs than their Oxford counterparts. The only monk ever to become chancellor of Cambridge University was an abbot of Colchester, Thomas de Stewkley, D.Cn.L, who had held the office

[69] John Le Neve, *Fasti Ecclesiae Anglicanae. 1300–1541*, revised edn, Institute of Historical Research, London (12 vols, 1962–7), 10, *The Welsh Dioceses*, p. 5; R. B. Dobson, 'English and Welsh monastic bishops at the end of the Middle Ages: the final century, 1433–1533', in *Monasteries and Society in Medieval England*, ed. B. J. Thompson (Proceedings of the Eleventh Harlaxton Symposium, 1994), forthcoming.

[70] For some representative examples of the highly variable (apparently more variable than at Oxford) number of years of study specified by the Cambridge university graces required for admission to a higher degree, see *Grace Book A*, pp. 15, 30, 95; *B*, 1, pp. 134, 144, 145; *Γ*, pp. 54, 65.

[71] *Visitations of Religious Houses in the Diocese of Lincoln, 1420–1436*, ed. A. H. Thompson, *CYS*, 17 (1915), p. 91.

briefly as long ago as 1369.[72] Here again it was no doubt the late date at which the Benedictines acquired their own institutional base at Cambridge which protected them from becoming too heavily engaged in university administration. Only in the early sixteenth century does the increased academic status of Buckingham College seem to have been fully recognized by university and other authorities. In 1514 it was included in the standard proctorial cycle and twenty years later it became one of the Cambridge colleges selected for the radical innovation of two daily public lectures, one in Latin and one in Greek.[73]

Whether the university monks and canons of late medieval Cambridge knew much Greek may well be doubted; but it was in fact as preachers of Latin sermons that they were most likely to appear in public before their academic contemporaries. Proficiency in the delivery of sermons was usually a positive requirement for a higher degree; and accordingly – to take two examples at random – both the abbot of St Benet Hulme (in 1460–1) and the future prior of Buckingham College (in 1499–1500) were each obliged to preach two sermons to complete the form for their admission to the degree of B.Th.[74] Rather more surprising to modern congregations would be the successful petitions of both Thomas Bozoun of Norwich cathedral Priory (in 1474–5) and the Augustinian canon, John Lowth, abbot of Thornton in Lincolnshire (in 1501), to wear a head-covering while preaching because of their liability to headaches, 'propter quandam infirmitatem in capite'.[75] Thanks to the recent painstaking researches of Dr Joan Greatrex, it is now also well established that the preaching of sermons was regarded as one of the most important of all duties of monk scholars, both during and after their university years. In May 1415 no fewer than four Ely monks then studying at Cambridge were licensed to preach in any church appropriated to their cathedral; and in April 1479 Richard Swaffham gave the Palm Sunday sermon at Ely Cathedral despite the fact that he was still a university student and

[72] *BRUC*, p. 556; cf. C. N. L. Brooke, 'Chancellors of the University of Cambridge, *c.* 1415–1535', in Bradshaw and Duffy, eds, *Humanism, Reform and the Reformation*, pp. 233–4.

[73] Cooper, *Annals*, 1, pp. 297, 375; *Magdalene College*, p. 29; *Cambridge Borough Documents*, 1, p. 146.

[74] *Grace Book A*, p. 30; *B* (1), pp. 134, 144–5; *BRUC*, pp. 337, 438.

[75] Whether the protective head covering was to take the form of a hat or a handkerchief seems not entirely certain: *Grace Book A*, p. 107; Greatrex, p. 486; Cooper, *Athenae*, p. 19.

therefore not eligible for payment.[76] Almost all the sermons delivered at assemblies of the Black Monk and Augustinian Provincial Chapters were also preached by Cambridge or Oxford graduates. Thus John de Bardney, *prior studentium* at Cambridge, was required to preach at the Benedictine Chapter meeting at Northampton in 1426; and Richard Vowell, the last prior of Walsingham, preached one of the many sermons which adorned the proceedings at the important General Chapter of the Augustinian Canons held at Leicester in 1518.[77]

Unfortunately for the historian of the religious orders in medieval Cambridge, few reputations – except perhaps those of academic lecturers – are more evanescent than that of the successful preacher. No text of any sermon delivered by a Cambridge university monk or canon seems to survive. Nor, it must reluctantly be said, is there much more direct evidence of literary composition on the part of the monk scholars of late medieval Cambridge than exists for their counterparts at Oxford.[78] Even Robert Mannyng de Brunne's *Handlyng Synne*, intended 'not to lered only but eke to the lewed' and the only work by a Cambridge-educated member of the religious orders ever likely to be widely read today, was quite probably written before rather than after its author joined the Gilbertine order at Sempringham in or about 1302.[79] Considerably more characteristic of the intellectual interests of the last generations of regulars at Cambridge are two works of traditional local *pietas*, a derivative metrical *Historia Sancti Hugonis Martyris* (of Lincoln) and a verse life of Bishop Robert Grosseteste, both written by Richard Bardney of Bardney Abbey, Benedictine *prior studentium* in 1490. One of Richard Bardney's contemporaries at Cambridge, Walter Hothom, a monk from St Mary's Abbey, York, expressed a rather different sort of enthusiasm for the literary achievements of the past by transcribing part of Bishop Richard of Bury's *Philobiblon*.[80] As most of the manuscripts composed or compiled

[76] Greatrex, pp. 423–4, 444, 447, 454, 465. Walter Hothom, a monk of St Mary's Abbey, York, was licensed to preach within the diocese of York in 1478, apparently long before he had completed his theology studies at Cambridge (*Grace Book A*, p. 95; *BRUC*, p. 316).

[77] Pantin, *Chapters*, 2, p. 156; *Letters and Papers*, 2, pt ii, appx, p. 1544; *Chapters of Augustinian Canons*, pp. 131–43.

[78] Dobson, 'Religious (Oxford)', pp. 572–6.

[79] R. Crosby, 'Robert Mannyng of Brunne; a new biography', *Publications of the Modern Language Association of America*, 57 (1942), pp. 15–28. No attempt is made here to assess the influence of a small élite of Cambridge graduates who only joined a religious order after leaving the university.

[80] *BRUC*, pp. 36, 316; cf. N. R. Ker, ed., *Medieval Libraries of Great Britain*, 2nd edn, Royal Historical Society (London, 1964), pp. 228, 321.

by the university monks and canons of late medieval Cambridge are now lost or unidentifiable, it would obviously be hazardous in the extreme to assume that their literary tastes were always so conservative. However, a not dissimilar impression of intense respect for tradition in all forms of intellectual endeavour certainly seems to emerge from the contents of their libraries too.

Indeed it was probably as true five hundred years ago as it is now that the academic and other interests of Cambridge-educated monks and canons have to be assessed – no easy matter – primarily in terms of what they may have read than of what they may have written. That many of the monks and canons studying at late medieval Cambridge acquired their own private book collections, not all the contents of which eventually found their way into their convent's common library, can go without saying. Sometimes such a process was reversed; and there is perhaps no better guide to the works most useful for the student of canon law in a late medieval English university than the list of a dozen books (ranging from a copy of the Bible to several copies of the Decretals) which Alan Kyrketon failed to return to his monastic library at Spalding Priory after his years as a student at Oxford in the mid-1430s.[81] Sufficient evidence also survives to suggest that as purchasers of books, and as sponsors of new forms of book production, the monks and canons of late medieval Cambridge were by no means completely indifferent to non-academic literature, and even to the most recent trends in devotional writing. From the 1470s onwards, printed books were increasingly available to university scholars; and the last abbot of St Albans, himself a university monk, commissioned not only an edition of a breviary of the use of his house but also Lydgate's *Life and Passion of St Alban* from his monastery's own press.[82] More considerable evidence for the impact of university learning on the intellectual tastes of English religious houses sometimes derive from the latter's surviving manuscripts and common library catalogues. Recent research on these previously neglected sources has certainly begun to reveal – as might well be suggested by the enthusiasm for the construction of separate custom-built libraries in so many large fifteenth-century monasteries – that sustained intellectual study within the major English religious houses was by no means as

[81] *Lincoln Visitations, 1436–1449*, p. 330.

[82] Knowles, *Rel. Orders*, 3, p. 26; *BRUC*, pp. 36, 126; cf. Dobson, *Durham Priory*, pp. 371–3.

uncommon as has often been supposed.[83] However, except in the case of most of England's eight cathedral monasteries and a small group of especially well documented other houses, such evidence is hardly plentiful and often ambiguous. Thus it is notoriously the case that comparatively few surviving fifteenth-century monastic manuscripts or library catalogues reveal explicitly where the books in question were actually written or acquired.[84]

Nevertheless, recent intensive study of at least a few of the manuscripts written or compiled in fourteenth and fifteenth-century religious houses, notably at St Albans, is undoubtedly beginning to undermine the traditional view that monastic intellectual endeavour can only be interpreted as 'scanty and stunted literary herbage'.[85] Ironically enough, such study can also have the effect of suggesting that previous historians may have under-estimated the existence of largely self-generating intellectual debate (often about the origins and nature of the religious life itself) within a large monastic cloister. Could it be that the late Dom Ursmer Berlière, Mr W. A. Pantin, and Professor David Knowles, as well as several more recent historians, have over-stated the argument that exposure of their most academically talented monks to university learning and society 'was the greatest single cultural influence on their convents during the last centuries of their existence'?[86] It is certainly noticeable that the surviving manuscripts once owned by Robert Wells, a monk student at Cambridge between 1510 and 1522 before he became the last prior and then the first dean of Ely cathedral, reflect little in the way of scholastic influence at all. Within a collection which was probably not unrepresentative of the eclectic if largely conventional literary interests of the last generation of university monks, the name and armorial insignia of Wells appear in an eleventh-century copy of the works of St Gregory; a twelfth-century *Vitae Sanctorum*; a fifteenth-century copy of Richard Rolle's devotional writing; a copy of the Rule of St Benedict

[83] R. Sharpe, J. P. Carley, R. M. Thompson, and A. G. Watson, eds, *English Benedictine Libraries: the Shorter Catalogues*, Corpus of British Medieval Library Catalogues, 3 (1992); Webber and Watson, *Libraries of Augustinian Canons*. Unfortunately no evidence at all has yet been discovered for either the nature of the library or the books themselves at Buckingham College.

[84] Thus of the three largest library catalogues transcribed in Webber and Watson, *Libraries of Augustinian Canons*, only that for Llanthony (Secunda) provides much evidence of the provenance (often Oxford) of the books catalogued.

[85] Clark, 'Intellectual life at St Albans', passim; Knowles, *Rel. Orders*, 2, p. 264.

[86] Dobson, *Durham Priory*, pp. 342–3.

(dated to 1522); and an early sixteenth-century continuation of the much neglected *Historia Eliensis* which Wells may have himself helped to compile.[87] But then it was not at Norwich cathedral alone that during the years before the Dissolution it was often local patriotism and *pietas* which continued to inform – and often to dominate – reading and writing within monastic cloisters and libraries throughout England.[88]

During the last phase of medieval English monastic history most monks and canons for whom such evidence survives were accordingly still absorbed by the glories of their communities' early history, even if such absorption rarely took the form of a creative rewriting of that history but rather of the copying, revising, and translating into English of chronicle and other material already very familiar to themselves. Thus in 1440, at about the time John Lydgate was writing a vernacular life of St Alban for the latter's Benedictine community, the Premonstratensian Abbot John Wygenhale (himself a Cambridge graduate) commissioned John Capgrave to compose an English *vita* of St Norbert. More significantly still perhaps, Abbot Wygenhale himself once wrote a *historia* (now lost) of his own house of West Dereham.[89] Such obsession with the past, and with the local past of their particular mother houses at that, probably does much to explain why the monks and canons who frequented late medieval Cambridge did less than one might reasonably expect to cultivate the academic or indeed any of the other muses located there by Abbot John Whethamstede in the 1450s. As the preceding pages have revealed, even their most sympathetic historian must admit that the achievements of university monks and canons at late medieval Cambridge and Oxford often call to mind Dr Johnson's celebrated reaction to the experience of listening to women preachers ('not done well; but you are surprised

[87] BL, Harley MS 3721; Greatrex, pp. 457–8.

[88] For an especially well documented example, see A. J. Piper, 'Dr Thomas Swalwell, Monk of Durham, Archivist and Bibliophile (d. 1539)', in J. P. Carley and C. G. C. Tite, eds, *Books and Collectors, 1200–1700: Essays presented to Andrew Watson* (BL, London, 1997), pp. 71–100.

[89] *Registra abbatum S. Albani*, ed. Riley (*RS*, 1872–3), 1, p. 462; *The Life of St Norbert by John Capgrave, OESA (1393–1464)*, ed. C. L. Smetana (Toronto, 1977); Gribbin, 'Premonstratensian Order', pp. 157, 169–79; cf. A. Gransden, *Historical Writing in England, 2: c. 1307 to the Early Sixteenth Century* (London, 1982), pp. 342–424; R. B. Dobson, 'Contrasting chronicles: historical writing at York and Durham in the later Middle Ages', in I. Wood and G. A. Loud, eds, *Church and Chronicle in the Middle Ages: Essays presented to John Taylor* (London, 1991), pp. 205–12.

to find it done at all'). If so, some at least of the other reasons for one's disappointment are not hard to find. With the obvious exception of the Carthusians and Bridgettines, the English religious orders of the fifteenth century were rarely concerned with the 'publication' of their or other written work to a wider world. Indeed for the most accomplished scholar in this highly difficult field, 'by the mid-fifteenth century English monastic book production cannot be considered as operating independently of book production by other hands and outside the monasteries'.[90]

Such acute difficulties of interpretation undoubtedly reflect the even more fundamental – and perennial – ambivalence of monastic attitudes to university learning at all. Despite the high value placed on university study by Benedict XII in the 1330s and by successive Provincial Chapters of the Benedictines and Augustinian canons thereafter, members of the enclosed religious orders at late medieval Cambridge and Oxford could rarely be completely insensitive to the familiar charge that 'a monk out of his cloystre' should be 'likned til a fish that is waterlees'. Indeed within a very few years of the *Benedictina* themselves, the religious of western Christendom were already being castigated by the Franciscan Alvarus Pelagius for their tendency 'to procure university studies and the doctorate in order that they might sit in the first seats and lord it over others, although a monk's duty is not to teach but to mourn'.[91] Late medieval English monastic cloisters were certainly not completely immune from such sentiments: fifteenth-century episcopal visitation records leave no doubt at all of the tensions which might arise between university monks and canons and their less fortunate brethren who were never given the opportunity to study outside their own precincts. Between the 1490s and the 1530s Bishops James Goldwell and Richard Nykke of Norwich were certainly at pains to encourage as many of their cathedral monks to study at Cambridge as possible; but they were not unaware that university education might lead some monks to the sin of pride and disdain for their brethren in their mother house. And as for Roger

[90] A. I. Doyle, 'Publication by members of the religious orders', in J. Griffiths and D. Pearsall, eds, *Book Production and Publishing in Britain, 1375–1475* (Cambridge, 1989), pp. 109–23; idem, 'Book production by the monastic orders in England (c. 1375–1530)', in L. L. Brownrigg, ed., *Medieval Book Production: Assessing the Evidence* (Altos Hills, CA, 1990), pp. 1–19.

[91] Cited from *De planctu ecclesiae* (completed in 1340) in G. G. Coulton, *Five Centuries of Religion (1000–1500)*, 4 vols (Cambridge, 1923–50), 2, p. 545.

Multon of St Benet Hulme, by 1514 he had spent three years at Cambridge and done nothing of value at all ('nihil boni fecit').[92]

But then it is hardly surprising that the young monks and canons who studied at late medieval Cambridge did so – like most university students at most times and in most places – for a wide variety of reasons, not all of them specifically academic. Moreover, nearly all the surviving evidence suggests that the demand for university education within the late medieval cloister was usually much greater than could readily be satisfied. To take only one example, in 1442 the prior of the small Augustinian priory of Canons Ashby in Northamptonshire had to go out of his way to ask his bishop to bridle the 'impetuosam peticionem canonicorum iuvenum' who desired to study at a university.[93] It has been one of the main suggestions of this paper that such impetuous enthusiasm for university study on the part of the religious orders was more likely to be satisfied at Cambridge in the early sixteenth century than ever before. However, even during the two generations before the Dissolution that enthusiasm was often doomed to disappointment. At all times English monks and canons intent on university study were only too likely to discover that there were many practical obstacles in their way. No reader of the records of late medieval English episcopal visitation and of monastic General Chapters can possibly discount the financial difficulties confronting the many abbots and chapters who claimed that they could not actually afford the £10 or more a year which it cost to maintain one of their younger monks at university. Only very occasionally did intellectually talented monks and canons from the smaller English religious houses have a serious prospect of attending university at all. In 1492, for example, the Premonstratensian general chapter permitted Edward Seyton of Sulby Abbey to study at Oxford or Cambridge, but only at the expense of his friends ('*amicorum suorum*').[94] At Cambridge, as of course in most universities throughout Christendom, it was therefore economic stringency rather than hostility to academic study on the abbot's part which usually acted

[92] *Visitations of the Diocese of Norwich, A. D. 1492–1532*, ed. A. Jessopp, Camden Society, ns, 43 (1888), p. 264; J. Venn, *Early Collegiate Life* (Cambridge, 1913), pp. 77–8.

[93] *Lincoln Visitations, 1436–49*, p. 44.

[94] See *Collectanea Anglo-Premonstratensia*, ed. F. A. Gasquet, Camden Society, 3rd ser, 6, 10, 12 (1904–6), 1, pp. 90, 148; 3, p. 626; R. H. Snape, *English Monastic Finances in the Later Middle Ages* (Cambridge, 1926), pp. 105–8; *Lincoln Visitations, 1420–36*, p. 56.

as the most important brake on the numbers and influence of the university monks and canons.[95]

Despite the great wealth of some individual Black Monk houses, the fifteenth-century English monastic orders as a whole therefore seem to have lacked the communal financial resources which underlay the intellectual and spiritual dynamism of the various contemporary and much wealthier 'reforming' Benedictine Congregations of the Rhine Valley, of Swabia and of northern Italy, most notably of all perhaps that of St Giustina of Padua.[96] To evoke so extreme a contrast is of course to raise not only important economic issues but also much more fundamental problems about the nature of late medieval English, as compared to continental, monasticism – so fundamental that they quite transcend the purposes of this essay. The fact is that the intense inherent centrifugalism of the English religious life, and the knowledge that even a university degree might give its holder much status within his community but very little within the lay society outside his precinct walls, always jeopardized the prospects of that *reformatio religionis* which Bishops John Alcock of Ely, Richard Fox of Winchester and many of their contemporaries hoped would precede the *reformatio regni Angliae* itself.[97] Could the remarkable expansion in the numbers of monks and canons at Cambridge during the early sixteenth century have at long last helped to promote so intriguing and desirable a result? Was intense exposure to university education ever likely to be an important, or even necessary, path towards whatever the reform of religion might be taken to mean? For the reasons discussed only too briefly in this paper, there are no easy answers to either of those questions. But then time alas was not allowed to tell. The last generation of medieval Cambridge monks

[95] For the most detailed study of the 'precarious financial substructure' of a monastic college within the university of Paris ('such insecurity was not conducive to intellectual progress'), see J. John, *The College of Prémontré in Mediaeval Paris* (Notre Dame, IN, 1953), pp. 31–43, a reference I owe to Dr Joseph Gribbin.

[96] B. Collett, *Italian Benedictine Scholars and the Reformation: The Congregation of Santa Giustina of Padua* (Oxford, 1985), pp. 1–27; P. Schmitz, *Histoire de l'Ordre de Saint Benoit*, 7 vols (Gemblous, 1943–56), 3, passim; but see the critical comments on such 'piecemeal reforms' in E. Cameron, *The European Reformation* (Oxford, 1991), pp. 41–3.

[97] See, e.g., Bishop John Alcock's *Mons Perfectionis*, printed by Wynkyn de Worde in 1486; Bishop Richard Fox's edition of the *Ruyle of Seynt Benet*, printed by Richard Pynson in 1517; P. G. Caraman, 'An English monastic reformer of the sixteenth century', *Clergy Review*, ns, 28 (1947), pp. 1–16; E. L. Meek, 'Printing and the clergy in the later Middle Ages' (Cambridge University M. Phil. thesis, 1997).

and canons had no alternative but to be accomplices, willing or unwilling, to a *reformatio* which entailed their own – unimaginably abrupt – destruction as well as the final 'dissolution of the medieval outlook' in the university of Cambridge itself.

Christ's College, Oxford

THE ORIGINS AND UNIVERSITY CONNECTIONS OF YORKSHIRE RELIGIOUS, 1480–1540

by CLAIRE CROSS

IN his discussion of the composition of monasteries in the diocese of Lincoln in the early sixteenth century Dom David Knowles wrote 'that recruits came, so to say, in response to advertisement', and then went on to add 'it would seem clear that in the majority of the houses almost all the recruits were local.' With its profusion of abbeys, priories, nunneries, and friaries Yorkshire provides a great deal of evidence for testing his hypothesis. Fairly confident conclusions can be reached about the geographical recruitment of the Cistercians as they continued to adopt toponymics, while the very considerable number of placenames used as surnames by members of other orders may at the very least intimate their origins in the relatively recent past. The social antecedents of the religious pose a more difficult problem but more random sources, particularly wills, give an indication of the levels of society from which they came. To counteract an impression of excessive localism which undue concentration upon this material might produce, details of their university attendance, degrees, and book ownership have also been included. These northerners belonged to a nation as well as to a region, and the intellectual horizons of a sizeable number of Yorkshire monks, canons, and friars, if not perhaps of many nuns, extended well beyond the limits of their county in the last fifty years before the dissolution.[1]

Long before the early Tudor period, monasteries had adjusted their entry policy to accord with economic necessities, and admitted novices only when places became vacant by death. Consequently in most Yorkshire houses numbers do not seem to have fluctuated to any significant extent. St Mary's Abbey, by far the richest monastery in the county, which presented one hundred and twenty-three monks for ordination between 1480 and 1540, contained fifty monks in 1539. With eighty-four ordinations over the same sixty years and a convent of thirty-two at its surrender, Fountains, the wealthiest Yorkshire Cistercian

[1] Knowles, *Rel. Orders*, 3, p. 70.

Ordinations to Yorkshire Monasteries 1480–1540

	Valor[2]	Dissolution numbers[3]	Ordinations 1480–1540[4]
BENEDICTINE			
Monk Bretton	£239 3s. 6d.	14	32
Selby	£719 2s. 6d.	25	64
Whitby	£437 2s. 9d.	22	52
Holy Trinity, York	£169 9s. 10d.	11	31
St Mary's, York	£1650 7s. 0d.	50	123
CISTERCIAN			
Byland	£238 9s. 4d.	25	38
Fountains	£1115 18s. 2d.	32	84
Jervaulx	£234 18s. 5d.	15	59
Kirkstall	no valuation	31	62
Meaux	£298 6s. 4d.	25	55
Rievaulx	£287 10s. 2d.	23	55
Roche	£260 19s. 4d.	18	42
Sawley	£147 3s. 10d.	22	39
CLUNIAC			
Pontefact	£335 12s. 10d.	13	28
CARTHUSIAN			
Hull	£174 18s. 3d.	7	15
Mount Grace	£323 2s. 10d.	20	3
GRANDIMONTINE			
Grosmont	£12 2s. 8d.	5	8
AUGUSTINIAN			
Bolton	£212 3s. 4d.	15	36
Bridlington	£547 6s. 11d.	15	54

[2] J. Caley and J. Hunter, eds, *Valor ecclesiasticus*, 6 vols (London, 1810–34).

[3] Compiled from surrender documents, lists of dispensations, and pension lists printed in C. Cross and N. Vickers, eds, *Monks, Friars and Nuns in Sixteenth Century Yorkshire*, Yorkshire Archaeological Society, Record Series CL (1995).

[4] Compiled from Borthwick Institute, York, Abp. Reg. 23, 25, 26, 27, 28 and Sede Vac. Reg. 5A; the ordinations of religious are printed in Cross and Vickers, eds, *Monks, Friars and Nuns*.

	Valor	Dissolution numbers	Ordinations 1480–1540
Drax	£92 7*s.* 5*d.*	11	28
Guisborough	£628 6*s.* 8*d.*	25	76
Haltemprice	£100 0*s.* 3*d.*	11	25
Healaugh Park	£67 3*s.* 11*d.*	6	15
Kirkham	£269 5*s.* 9*d.*	18	40
Marton	£151 5*s.* 4*d.*	6	20
Newbrugh	£457 13*s.* 5*d.*	18	41
North Ferriby	£60 1*s.* 2*d.*	8	22
Nostell	£492 18*s.* 2*d.*	29	57
Warter	£144 7*s.* 8*d.*	12	34
PREMONSTRATENSIAN			
Coverham	£160 18*s.* 3*d.*	15	49
Easby	£111 17*s.* 11*d.*	14	43
Egglestone	£36 8*s.* 3*d.*	9	31
GILBERTINE			
Ellerton	£62 8*s.* 10*d.*	5	42
Malton	£197 19*s.* 2*d.*	11	80
Watton	£360 16*s.* 10*d.*	9	102
St Andrew's, York	£47 14*s.* 3*d.*	4	38
HOSPITAL			
St Leonard's, York	£309 2*s.* 11*d.*	8	29

abbey, conveys a very similar impression of a community renewing itself over the course of a generation.

The ordination evidence suggests that the situation in almost all the Yorkshire monasteries corresponds with that in St Mary's and Fountains. Over a sixty-year period most admitted two to three times as many monks as the house held at its suppression. Two orders, however, the Carthusians and the Gilbertines, diverge from the norm, the one having many more monks in 1539 than it had dispatched to York for ordination, the other apparently generating eight to ten times more ordination candidates than it had canons at the dissolution. In the case of the Carthusians the discrepancy can quite easily be explained by the fact that the charterhouses tended to attract mature men already in priestly orders. The high numbers being sent for ordination from Ellerton, Malton, Watton, and St Andrew's, however, create greater difficulties, though the answer perhaps partly lies in the mobility of the Gilbertines who may have decided to educate their young canons in the diocese of York. At all events in 1539 about a quarter of the forty-seven canons, including five of the priors, of the seven Lincolnshire Gilbertine houses had been ordained subdeacon, deacon, or priest from one of their four Yorkshire priories, most having gravitated to Malton or Watton, at least one to St Andrew's, York, and another to Ellerton.[5]

In addition to the number of men entering Yorkshire monasteries between 1480 and 1540 the archiepiscopal registers also reveal a considerable amount about the nature of this recruitment. In certain orders it had been usual for the religious to change their surnames on profession, substituting their birthplace or place of residence for their family name. A unique dissolution document proves that in Yorkshire the Cistercians still observed this custom in the sixteenth century. Quite exceptionally the pensions list for Rievaulx gives both the monastic and the secular surnames for almost all of the twenty-three monks in the house in 1538.

Roland Blyton, abbot		100 marks
Thomas Jackson alias Richmond		£6 13*s*. 4*d*.
William Steynson alias Yersley		£5 6*s*. 8*d*.
Robert Smythe alias Stanethorp		£5 6*s*. 8*d*.
Robert Wardale alias Pykerynge		£5 6*s*. 8*d*.
William Storer		£5 6*s*. 8*d*.
Richard Blith alias Scarburgh		£6
Thomas Poulson alias Yarome		£5 6*s*. 8*d*.
Richard Lynge alias Allertone		£5 6*s*. 8*d*.
William Broadleye alias Fayrlington		£5 6*s*. 8*d*.
John Pynder alias Malton	[cancelled	£5 6*s*. 8*d*.]
Roger Watson alias Whitbye		£5 6*s*. 8*d*.
Richard Jenkynson alias Ripon		£6
William Stapleton alias Bedall		£5 6*s*. 8*d*.

[5] Borthwick Abp. Reg. 23, fols 451r, 454v, 462r (Dogilly); Abp. Reg. 26, fols 118r, 119r, 150r (Cartewrighte); Abp. Reg. 26, fol. 111v (Belisby); Abp. Reg. 27, fol. 185v (Bretane); fols 191r, 193r (Hall); fols 205v, 213v (Jacson); fol. 211v (Hudson); *Letters and Papers*, 14, pt I, pp. 598–602.

Richard Halle alias Gyllynge	£5	6*s.* 8*d.*
Henry Cawlton alias Thryske	£6	
William Wordale	£5	
James Fayreweder alias Guisburghe	£5	
Christopher Symondson alias Helmsleye	£5	6*s.* 8*d.*
Oliver Watson alias Broghton	£5	
Matthew Tort alias Ampleforth	£5	
John Altame	£5	
Thomas Caprone alias Skegby	£4[6]	

Apart from the abbot and three others all the monks on this pension list have toponymics from which their origins can be deduced. It is even possible to supply the places where William Storere, John Altam, and William Wordale may have been born: Storere's father died in Hawnby, while Altam can probably be identified with John Preston ordained subdeacon at York on 25 March 1531 and Wordale with William Tanfield ordained priest on 28 February 1533/4. Hawnby lies very near to Rievaulx, Tanfield some twenty miles west of the abbey, and Preston, if it can be assumed to be Preston near Wensley, is under thirty miles away. A visitation of the abbey earlier in the decade accounts for the presence of two outsiders on the list, the abbot himself, Roland Blyton, and Thomas Caprone alias Skegby. In 1533 Cromwell had directed two of his servants to investigate the alleged mismanagement of the abbey; they had persuaded the abbot, Edward Kirkby alias Cowper, to resign and imposed Blyton, then abbot of Rufford, upon the community in his place. When he moved north the new abbot brought with him another Rufford monk, Thomas Caprone who, to judge from his toponymic, came from in Skegby in Nottinghamshire. Except for Robert Smythe alias Stanethorp, who may have been a native of Staindrop just over the border in county Durham, all the other monks bore Yorkshire toponymics. Yearsley, Harome, Farlington, Gilling, Helmsley, and Ampleforth are like Hawnby very close to the abbey, Thirsk, Northallerton, Bedale, Richmond, and Ripon, the latter just in the West Riding, not so very much more distant, with Guisborough and Broughton together with Whitby, Scarborough, Pickering, and Malton at the northern, eastern, and southern extremities of the North Riding.[7]

[6] *Letters and Papers*, 14, pt I, no. 185; P. R. O. E 315/245 fol. 32v.

[7] *Letters and Papers*, 6 (1882), nos. 437, 546, 913, 1408, 1513; W. Brown, ed., *Yorkshire Star Chamber Proceedings*, 1, Yorkshire Archaeological Society, Record Series, XLI (1909),

A more long-term analysis of the surnames of Rievaulx ordinands between 1480 and 1538 concurs well with the information derived from the pensions list. Of the fifty-five monks ordained from the abbey during this period some forty-three have recognizable toponymics, Ampleforth, Gilling, Helmsley, Thirsk, and Beverley all featuring twice. Thirty-one recruits were drawn from townships within a twenty-mile radius of Rievaulx, some of these living very locally indeed, in Ampleforth, Helmsley, Old Byland, Gilling, Marton on the Forest, Harome, Yearsley, Thornton, and Thirsk. A further seventeen originated from Lilling, Farlington, Stillington, Helperby, Bossall, Ebberston, Allerston, Topcliffe, Bedale, Tanfield, Burton, Guisborough, Kirkby in Cleveland, Seamer, Pickering, and Malton, less than twenty miles from the abbey. Another eight had been attracted from somewhat further afield but still from within the North Riding, from Middleham, Preston, Richmond, Brough, Loftus, Broughton, Whitby, and Scarborough. Only four locations lay outside the North Riding: Ripon, Bradford, and Pontefract in the West Riding, and Beverley in the East Riding, and only one outside Yorkshire: Staindrop in the extreme south of County Durham. In at least nine of the places from which the monastic ordinands were drawn, Allerton, Beverley, Great and Little Broughton, Harome, Helmsley, Kirkby in Cleveland, Malton, Pickering, and Bishopthorpe by York, the abbey owned property. On this evidence Rievaulx would seem to have been obtaining its monks in the two generations before the Reformation almost exclusively from north Yorkshire.[8]

Although no other pensions lists give both the monastic and the family surnames of the monks, the disjunction between the surnames of the ordinands, which are virtually all placenames, and the names on the pensions lists intimates that the other Yorkshire Cistercian houses also conferred toponymics on their monks, and from an analysis of their ordinations a very similar pattern of recruitment emerges. Byland sent thirty-eight candidates for ordination between 1480 and 1539, a handful of whom seem to have kept their secular surnames. Of the twenty-eight identifiable toponymics all except one are of Yorkshire provenance, the great majority from the North Riding. Nineteen monks seem to have been natives of villages situated within fifteen

pp. 48–51; Borthwick Prob. Reg. 6, fol. 59v; Sede Vac. Reg. 5A, fol. 669v; Abp. Reg. 28, fol. 193r.

[8] J. Burton, *Monasticon Eboracense* (York, 1758) [hereafter Burton, *Mon. Ebor.*], pp. 358–60.

miles of the monastery. Two apparently originated from Richmond, two from Marton in Cleveland, one from Wensley, and one from Jervaulx. From beyond the North Riding the house seems to have attracted novices from York, from Leathley, Leeds, and Bradford in the West Riding and from Bainton in the East Riding and from outside the county one from Borrowdale in Cumberland. Byland held lands in Thormanby, Farlington, Ampleforth, Thorpe near Ampleforth, Sutton-under-Whitestone-Cliffe, Harome, Kilburn, Thornton, Thirsk, Marton in Cleveland, Baxby, Kirkby Moorside, York, and in Borrowdale, that is in about a third of the places from which the monks took their names.[9]

Jervaulx, the Cistercian house to the west of Byland, similarly appears to have recruited from its own particular hinterland. Of the fifty-nine monks ordained from the house between 1480 and 1537 only two or three seem to have kept their family surnames. Of the forty-four different toponymics shared among the Jervaulx monks, it has proved possible to locate all except four. Many of the monks appear to have been born in Wensleydale and its vicinity. From outside the North Riding monks were drawn from Arncliffe and Wakefield in the West Riding, and from Heslington and Beverley in the East Riding, and three from York. Outside Yorkshire, Penrith in Cumberland supplied two monks and Kendal in Westmorland one. Reinforcing the northern nature of the house yet further, other candidates emanated from Durham and Bishop Auckland, Staindrop, and Hartlepool in County Durham. More than a quarter of the monks ordained at Jervaulx between 1480 and 1536 had apparently once lived in Aysgarth, Newstead Grange, Hornby, Finghall, Gilling, Witton, Thornton Steward, Masham, Brompton on Swale, Richmond, Brough, Lazenby, and Sedbergh where the abbey possessed lands. The monastic community in fact seems very accurately to have mirrored Jervaulx's geographical position in the foothills of the Pennines in the northwestern sector of the North Riding adjoining Cumbria and county Durham.[10]

The sphere of influence of Sawley, a smaller Cistercian house due south from Jervaulx, lay in the west of the West Riding and the east of Lancashire. Even though the house contained at least twenty-two

[9] Ibid., pp. 329–38.
[10] Ibid., pp. 367–72.

monks at its surrender in 1536 it only presented thirty-nine candidates for ordination between 1480 and 1536. Though some monks preserved their family names after profession, twenty-four received identifiable toponymics. Yet again a significant proportion of monks seems to have come from the area very close to the monastery, from Clitheroe in Lancashire, and from Bolton by Bowland, Gisburn, Thornton in Craven, and Sawley itself. One monk had apparently lived in Blackburn in Lancashire and another in Downholme in the south of the North Riding but all the rest seem to have been recruited from somewhat further afield in the West Riding. Nine of the monks came from locations where the house held lands, three monks from Gisburn, and others from Sawley, Bolton, Preston, Bradford, Halton, and York. In the same way as Jervaulx attracted many of its monks from Wensleydale and Cumbria, Sawley drew upon Wharfedale and Craven.[11]

To a certain extent Sawley may have been vying for novices with Kirkstall, which with thirty-one monks at the dissolution was a rather larger and better endowed Cistercian house. A sizeable number of the sixty-two monks ordained from Kirkstall between 1480 and the surrender of the abbey in 1539 retained their family surnames. The thirty-seven identifiable toponymics suggest that Kirkstall limited its recruitment very largely to the West Riding. Once again an analysis of the placenames furnishes a concentration of twenty-two monks from the abbey's near neighbourhood, almost all the rest also being drawn from within thirty-five miles of the house. From outside the West Riding one monk may have been an inhabitant of York before his profession, two of Richmond in the North Riding, one of Hurworth on Tees on the North Riding border, one of Whalley just over the boundary in Lancashire, and one of Nottingham. Of the thirty-seven places from which the monks derived their names, the abbey had property in rather more than a third, that is in Eccup, Leeds, Adel, Horsforth, Lofthouse, Birstall, Shadwell, Newhall, Otley, Kirkstall, Thorpe, Newton, Headingley, and York.[12]

Roche and Meaux, the two Cistercian abbeys situated outside the North and West Ridings, conform to the same model. Roche only contained eighteen monks in 1538 and had generated a mere thirty-six

[11] W. Dugdale, *Monasticon Anglicanum* (new edn, 1846) [hereafter Dugdale, *Mon. Ang.*], 5, pp. 510–11.

[12] Burton, *Mon. Ebor.*, pp. 288–96.

ordinands in the previous half-century. Some of these seem to have kept their secular surnames, but most adopted toponymics of which it has proved possible to identify eighteen. Five townships within a fifteen-mile radius of Roche, Conisbrough, Doncaster, Hampole, and Houghton in Darfield in the West Riding and Haxey in Lincolnshire, account for five of the monks. Most of the rest seem to have originated from somewhat further away in the West Riding, with one from York itself and three from the North Riding. One monk appears to have come from Carlisle in Cumberland and one from Fishburn in County Durham. Of all these locations the abbey certainly owned estates in three: Conisbrough, Houghton and York.[13]

Meaux, the only Cistercian abbey in the East Riding, clearly profited from its isolation. Of the fifty-five candidates ordained from the house between 1480 and 1539 twenty-eight adopted recognizable toponymics, twenty-two of which can be identified with villages in the East Riding, most very near the abbey. From just outside the Riding the house attracted monks from York and from Crambe in the North Riding, from Thorne, Beamsley, Hebden Bridge, and Grafton in the West Riding, and from Sedgefield in county Durham. The abbey held land or appropriations in at least ten of the places, Bainton, Hull, Keyingham, Skipsea, Sutton, Beverley, Burton, Skerne, Wawne, and York, after which these monks were named.[14]

Recruitment at Fountains, the oldest and most important Yorkshire Cistercian abbey, seems to have been rather different from the other seven. This may partly be an optical illusion since over a third of its eighty-four monks ordained between 1480 and the dissolution appear under their family names and this may very well have masked their local origin. Forty toponymics have been identified. Some monks again seem to have come from the vicinity of the monastery, from Sutton Grange, Tanfield, Ripon, Whitcliffe, and Well, but others, though still from the West Riding, from much further afield, from Saxton, Airton, Kippax, Otley, Denton, Norton, Leathley, Barwick, Bradford, Marsden, Horton, Kilnsey, Whalley, Stainburn, Darrington, Crossthwaite, Selby, and Wentbridge, some being as much as forty miles from the abbey. Fountains also attracted recruits from York and nearby Clifton, and Heslington, and from Hayton, Pocklington, Wetwang, and Kirkham in the East Riding, and Thirsk, Melsonby, and Layton in the North

[13] Ibid., pp. 319–23.

[14] Dugdale, *Mon. Ang.*, 5, pp. 398–7.

Riding. From outside the county the abbey drew monks from Durham, from Morpeth in Northumberland, from Ulverston in Lancashire and from Kendal in Westmorland, while no less than three were from Nottinghamshire, from Blyth, Newark, and Ratcliffe. It would seem, therefore, that Fountains was obtaining monks not only from its immediate neighbourhood, but from throughout much of the rest of the north of England, governed to some extent by the location of its very extensive estates. Of the forty places from which the monks had taken their names the abbey held land in just under half, that is in Sutton, Tanfield, Marsden, Airton, Norton Moor, Ripon, Thirsk, Kilnsey in Craven, Melsonby, Otley, Stainburn, Horton, Crossthwaite, Well, Clifton, and York.[15]

Apart from the Cistercians, no other monastic order in Yorkshire in the late Middle Ages seems to have substituted toponymics for secular surnames. Recent historians have emphasised that Benedictine monks normally retained their family names and have warned against inferring origins from surnames derived from placenames. Professor Dobson found no obvious correlation between monastic surnames and the places where Durham priory held property. Evidence for Yorkshire Benedictine monasteries seems rather less ambiguous. Selby abbey owned lands in Selby, Snaith, Barwick in Elmet, York, Thorpe iuxta York and Thorpe iuxta Selby, Acaster Selby, Barley, and Wistow. All but twelve of the sixty-four monks ordained from the abbey between 1480 and 1540 had placenames for surnames. Four of these placenames have not been located, but the remaining forty-eight relate to forty different townships, grouped predominately in the Selby area, in the east of the West Riding and the west of the East Riding. It is suggestive, to put it no more highly, that the abbey possessed estates in approaching a quarter of the places from which its members derived their names.[16]

A very similar situation seems to have pertained at Monk Bretton, a much smaller Benedictine house, which owned lands in Bretton, Rotherham, Bolton upon Derne, Pontefract, and Woolley. About two thirds of the thirty-two ordinands from the priory in the later fifteenth and early sixteenth century had placenames as surnames, in this instance the townships being almost exclusively in the West

[15] Burton, *Mon. Ebor.*, pp. 148–209.

[16] R. B. Dobson, *Durham Priory 1400–1450* (Cambridge, 1973), pp. 56–7; Burton, *Mon. Ebor.*, pp. 388–404.

Riding, some very close to the priory such as Bretton itself, South Kirkby, Silkston, Bolton on Dearne, Royston, and Woolley.[17]

The concurrence between monks' surnames and land ownership does not emerge so clearly at two other Yorkshire Benedictine monasteries, Whitby, and St Mary's in York. At Whitby less than half the fifty-two monks ordained between 1480 and 1539 had identifiable placenames as surnames. A cluster of nine monks bore the surnames of Whitby, Leatham, Thorpe, Ellerby, Saxby, Sneaton, Aislaby, and Lythe, all settlements very near to the house. The abbey had land and property in Whitby, Pickering Lythe, Thorpe, Sneaton, Saxby, Wilton, and York.[18]

Partly because of its size St Mary's abbey presents a more complex picture. Of the one hundred and twenty-three monks ordained from the abbey in the sixty years before the dissolution fifty-three took their surnames from placenames. The house had a cell at St Bees and extensive possessions in Kirkby Lonsdale, Kendal, Allonby, and Cockermouth as well as in Thornton, Sheriff Hutton, Bedale, Grimston, Burton Agnes, Richmond, Middleton, Gilling, Kirby Misperton, Rudston, Dalton, Hornsea, Bootham, Clifton, and York. Once again all these placenames appear at least once as surnames of St Mary's monks.[19]

The two Yorkshire Cluniac and Grandimontine houses conform to this Benedictine model. Two thirds of the twenty-eight religious ordained from Pontefract between 1480 and 1538 had placenames as surnames, with twelve monks taking their names from Kellington, Brayton, Selby, Mexborough, Sherburn, Barnsley, Womersley, Ledston, Emley, Bretton, Ackworth, and Pontefract itself, all within a radius of ten miles of the house. The priory owned property in Pontefract, Middlethorpe and Bishopthorpe, York, Barnsley, and Ledston and each of these places appears as a monastic surname during the period. By far the poorest of all the Yorkshire monasteries, Grosmont only presented eight monks for ordination between 1480 and 1539, but most of these had placenames as surnames. The priory's meagre property lay in Eskdale, Egton, and Grosmont: two of the monks were named Grosmont, one Egton, and two others Seamer and Skelton.[20]

17 Burton, *Mon. Ebor.*, pp. 92–8.
18 Ibid., pp. 70–8.
19 Dugdale, *Mon. Ang.*, 3, pp. 530–7.
20 Ibid., 5, pp. 129–30; 6, pt II, p. 1025.

Cumulatively this surname evidence suggests that the Yorkshire Benedictines, Cluniacs, and Grandimontines like the Cistercians recruited their members locally and partly from the areas where they had estates. Interestingly the Carthusians and the Augustinian, Gilbertine, and Premonstratensian canons appear far less frequently in the ordination lists with placenames as surnames and consequently a study of their surnames provides few indications of their origins, though sporadic evidence from wills once again implies that their recruitment was similarly local.

Whereas it seems relatively clear from which geographical areas Yorkshire monasteries recruited their members between 1480 and 1540, information concerning the social origins of these religious is much less readily available, a fact which may in itself be significant. The sources do not permit a systematic analysis of the backgrounds of the approximately one thousand monks, canons, friars, and nuns expelled at the dissolution, but the wills of the relatives and of some of the former religious themselves, together with their secular surnames taken from the pensions lists, can at least give an impression of the kind of families from which they came.[21]

Few of the more than eight hundred monks and friars in Yorkshire in the early sixteenth century seem to have been of gentry status. Richard Vavasour, a Cluniac from Pontefract, may have descended from the ancient gentry family of that name. William Vavasour, the last warden of the York Franciscans, certainly did, in his will of 1544 making numerous bequests to his relatives in Copmanthorpe. The last prior of the Hull Charterhouse, Ralph Maleverer, was the son of James Maleverer of Seamer and cousin of Sir William Maleverer of Woodsome, an equally old Yorkshire gentry family. His predecessor at Hull, Ralph Smith, also had gentry connections. Smith's brother-in-law, John Swift, possessed lands in Easington, while his nephew, another John Swift, on his death in 1529, in addition to requesting burial in the Hull charterhouse, left £10 both to pay for a priest to sing for his soul and his parents' souls in Easington church and to relieve poor scholars. William Bedale alias Stapleton, the Rievaulx monk, could perhaps have been related to the Stapleton family of Carleton by Snaith or Wighill. Similarly the Bolton Augustinian, Lawrence

[21] The figures of monks, canons, friars, and nuns have been compiled from the pensions lists, augmented by the lists of dispensations to hold secular livings granted to monks and friars who did not qualify for pensions, in Cross and Vickers, eds, *Monks, Friars and Nuns.*

Plumpton, may have been a member of the Plumpton family of Plumpton. The three former Yorkshire religious who became bishops after the dissolution also derived from gentry backgrounds. Robert Holgate, the last Master of the Gilbertine order and prior of Watton, appointed archbishop of York in 1545, belonged to a minor gentry family of Hemsworth. Robert Ferrar, prior of Nostell, and after its surrender the Edwardian bishop of Llandaff, came from a lesser gentry family in Halifax. The last prior of Guisborough, Robert Pursglove alias Sylvester, suffragan bishop of Hull from 1538, was born into a landed family in Tideswell in Derbyshire.[22]

Many more northern nuns than monks and friars appear to have been from gentry families. Although there were only about two hundred and thirty nuns and sisters in Yorkshire at the dissolution compared with slightly over six hundred monks and canons and around two hundred friars, scarcely any of the twenty-four Yorkshire nunneries failed to attract their complement of gentlewomen. The double house of Watton contained in 1539 both Anne and Agnes Ellerker, Dorothy Vavasour, Margaret Evers, Joan Roos, Eleanor Constable, and Joan Hurtsky. Anne Ellerker seems to have been either the sister or aunt of Sir Ralph Ellerker of Risby, knight, who made his will in 1559. Though of lower status, Joan Hurtsky's father held lands in Watton. In addition, in 1535 William Hungate, gentleman, of North Dalton intended that his daughter, Lucy, should be made a nun at Watton, but, perhaps because of the uncertainty of the times, she appears never to have been professed. The last prioress of Clementhorpe, Isabel Ward, may have been related to the Elleker family to whom she left several bequests. In addition to Joan Slingsby, almost certainly of gentle birth, Nun Monkton had received at least one other gentlewoman, Margaret Vavasour. Christabel Cowper, the prioress who surrendered Marrick to the crown, seems to have been the aunt of Christopher Thormanby of Thormanby, gentleman, while one of her nuns, Marjory Conyers, was the daughter of Christopher Conyers and sister of Sir Christopher Conyers of Sockburn in County Durham.[23]

22 York Minster Library D & C Prob. Reg. 5, fols 6r–7r (Vavasour); Borthwick Prob. Reg. 9, fols 440r–v (Swift); A. G. Dickens, *Lollards and Protestants in the Diocese of York, 1509–1558* (London, 1959), pp. 148–51, 151–3.

23 Borthwick Prob. Reg. 11, pt I, fol. 186r (Hungate); pt II, fol. 573v (Hurtsky); Prob. Reg. 15, pt I, fol. 68r–v; Prob. Reg. 17, pt I, fol. 91r (Elleker); Prob. Reg. 18, fol. 152v (Ward); J. W. Clay, ed., *Testamenta Eboracensia*, 6, Surtees Society, CVI (1902), p. 256 (Conyers).

A member of the Wilberfoss community until its surrender, Isabel Craike was the daughter of Robert Craike, esquire, and of Isabel Craike who both chose to be buried in Beverley Minster. On the death of her grandfather, William Lutton, Elizabeth Lutton, professed a nun at Yedingham early in the reign of Henry VIII, inherited a claim to the manors of Knapton and West Lutton. The prioress of Handale, Anne Lutton, may also have been a member of the same family. Agnes Aslaby, a nun of the very small priory of Ellerton in Swaledale until its dissolution, received £6 13*s.* 4*d.* and goods in the will of her father, Richard Aslaby of Whitwell, gentleman, in 1542. The former nuns of Hampole included Elizabeth Arthington, bequeathed a considerable amount of goods in 1557 by her mother Elizabeth Arthington of Adwick le Street, Agnes Frobysher, probably the daughter of John Frobysher, left an equal share with her brothers in her father's estate in 1542, and Jane Gascoigne sister of Humphrey Gascoigne, clerk, master of Greetham and parson of Barnbrough, who arranged to have his image and the arms of his father and mother set up in the glass of his parish church after his death. In 1539 George Norman of Thirkleby decided that his daughter, Isabel, then a nun at Handale, should have her share of his goods if her house fell to the crown.[24]

The last prioress of Nun Appleton, Eleanor Normavale, was the sister of William Normavale, esquire, of Kildwick by Watton. Sinningthwaite, where the penultimate prioress had been Alice Goldsborough, in 1536 also contained Joan Goldsborough, apparently related to Thomas Goldsborough of Goldsborough who died in 1566, Margaret Dodsworth, daughter of John Dodsworth of Sinningthwaite and Jane Fairfax, daughter of Robert Fairfax of Acaster Malbis. At Swine, the best endowed of the Yorkshire nunneries, Elizabeth Clifton seems to have been the daughter of Hezekiah Clifton of Burton Agnes and sister of Walter Clifton of Gray's Inn. The last prioress of Wykeham, Katherine Nandyke, who numbered Elizabeth Percy among her nuns, in her will of 1541 acknowledged the favours she had received from the countess of Northumberland. In addition to Elizabeth Vavasour, Arthington in 1539 housed Effam Ratcliffe,

[24] Borthwick Prob. Reg. 11, pt I, fol. 363v (Norman); II, fol. 647r (Aslaby); Prob. Reg. 13, fol. 460r (Craike); Prob. Reg. 15, pt II, fol. 185v (Arthington); Abp. Reg. 28, fols 182v–83v (Gascoigne); Brown, ed., *Yorkshire Star Chamber Proceedings*, 1, pp. 186–8 (Lutton); Clay, *Testamenta Eboracensia*, 6, pp. 164–5.

probably the daughter and, in 1542, the executrix of Effam Ratcliffe, of Drax, widow.[25]

At Durham priory in the first half of the fifteenth century most monks apparently came from the middling ranks of urban and rural society below the gentry and a hundred years later the same seems to have been true for their Yorkshire counterparts. William Storer of Rievaulx was the son of John Storer of Hawnby who commissioned a trental of masses from his son on his death in 1506. In 1522 William Christalow of Coxwold made his brother, Marmaduke, a monk of Byland, the supervisor of his will. Christopher Stainforth of Sawley abbey may have been the son of James Car of Giggleswick who left him 10*s*. in 1528. The last prior of the York Dominicans, Brian Godson, in 1541 referred to his brother John Godson, yeoman, of Leeds. Once a Cistercian at Kirkstall, Thomas Kirkstall alias Pepper, in 1548 inherited lands in Bramley from his father John Pepper, also described as a yeoman.[26]

Interestingly these monastic recruits from the middle ranks of society derived from urban as well as rural backgrounds. William Kildale, monk of Whitby abbey, was one of the nine children of John Kildale of Whitby, while Richard Speght alias Hudson, the last prior of Holy Trinity, York, was the son of Henry and Margaret Speght of St Nicholas, Micklegate. Alice Perte, widow, of Thirsk in 1529 appointed her son William Thirsk alias Perte, abbot of Fountains, as the supervisor of her will. Another Fountains monk, Roger Hardy, seems to have been a native of Ripon where his mother, Marion, was living until her death in 1520. In 1529 Robert Cawton of Thirsk, the brother of Henry Thirsk alias Cawton, a monk of Rievaulx, asked to be buried in Thirsk parish church. The Kirkstall monk, Paul Mason, was the son of Thomas Mason, a substantial glover of St Martin's, Micklegate. The former Rievaulx monk Richard Scarborough alias Blythe had a brother, Thomas, a secular priest, who in 1545 asked to

25 Borthwick Prob. Reg. 9, fol. 133v (Normavale); fol. 136v (Dodsworth); fos 412r–v (Fairfax); Prob. Reg. 11, pt II fos 559v–560r (Nandike); fol. 671r (Ratcliffe); Clay, *Testamenta Eboracensia*, 6, pp. 301–2 (Goldsborough); pp. 121–2, 173–4 (Clifton).

26 Dobson, *Durham Priory 1400–1450*, p. 58; H. Aveling, 'The Rievaulx Community after the Dissolution', *Ampleforth Journal*, LVII (1952), p. 106 (Storer); G. W. O. Woodward, *The Dissolution of the Monasteries* (London, 1966), pp. 149–152 (Pepper); Borthwick Prob. Reg. 9, fol. 250v (Christalow); fol. 403v (Car); York Minister Library D/C Prob. Reg. 2, fos 198v–199r (Godson).

be buried alongside their parents in the Corpus Christi aisle in Scarborough parish church.[27]

The Augustinian and Gilbertine canons in particular seem to have attracted urban recruits. Thomas Paiteson, a Bridlington Augustinian canon, in 1521 inherited £10 in the will of his mother, Alice Paiteson, widow of Bridlington. John Grayson, clerk, who transferred to St Leonard's Hospital in York after the suppression of Drax in 1536, was the son of William Grayson, wiredrawer, of York and brother of Thomas Grayson, canon of Newburgh. Lawrence Richardson, draper, of New Malton, in 1528 definitely had one son, William, and possibly a second, Dom George, at Malton priory. The sons of at least two other Malton families joined the same house. In 1528 Agnes Kellet, widow of New Malton, bequeathed her son John, canon of the order of St Gilbert, a silver spoon, bedding and 20*s.* for a trental, and in the same year the Gilbertine William Marshall received 20*s.* in the will of his father, William Marshall of New Malton. The very much smaller Gilbertine priory of St Andrew's in York at the dissolution contained Leonard Sharpe, probably the son of Janet Grenewell of All Saints, Pavement.[28]

The Yorkshire nunneries also drew some of their recruits from urban backgrounds. The last prioress of Wilberfoss, Elizabeth Lord, daughter of Robert Lord of Kendal, not only had a brother, Brian Lord, a merchant in St Michael's, Ousebridge, but a sister, Mary, married to George Gale, goldsmith and twice lord mayor of York. After the surrender of her priory she made her home in the city with her sister and brother-in-law, dying in 1551 a very wealthy woman with a massive amount of gold and silver plate. Before the dissolution Elizabeth Lord had her niece, Alice Mabell, with her as a nun at Wilberfoss. In the will he made in 1527 John Lawton of Thirsk mentioned a daughter who was professed at Arden. In 1534 Isabel Whitfield, a York alderman's widow, left £3 6*s.* 8*d.* to her daughter, Margaret, a nun of Swine.[29]

[27] Borthwick Prob. Reg. 9, fol. 115r–v (Hardy); fol. 444r (Thirsk); fol. 457r (Cawton); Prob. Reg. 11, pt I, fol. 37r–v (Speght); fos 313v–314r (Mason); Prob. Reg. 13, pt. I fol. 118r (Blythe); fol. 186v (Kildale).

[28] Borthwick Prob. Reg. 9, fol. 216r (Paiteson); fol. 396v (Marshall); fol. 400r (Richardson); fol. 402v (Kellet); Prob. Reg. 11, pt I fol. 523r (Grenewell); F. Collins, ed., *Register of the Freemen of the City of York*, Surtees Society, XCVI (1897), pp. 267–8 (Grayson).

[29] Borthwick Prob. Reg. 9, fol. 368v (Lord); fol. 374v (Lawton); Prob. Reg. 13, pt I fol. 105r–v (Whitfield); pt II fol. 705r–v (Lord).

Drawn from rural and urban elites in the hinterland of their monasteries, the Yorkshire religious formed an integral part of local society. The cost of this assimilation might have been intellectual stagnation, a fate which in the sixteenth century the nunneries and some of the smaller monasteries had probably not escaped, but participation in higher education in particular safeguarded the better endowed monasteries and the friaries from isolation from the main trends of national life. About a third of the monks sent to the university in the later Middle Ages by the cathedral priories of Norwich and Worcester remained there sufficiently long to take a degree. At least thirty Yorkshire monks and friars are known to have graduated from a university between 1480 and 1540 and, by analogy with cathedral monks, it could well be that approaching a hundred spent some time at Oxford or Cambridge. The chance survival of a compotus roll demonstrates that St Mary's abbey, in compliance with the decrees of the Benedictine General Chapter of 1277, was still regularly supporting some of its young monks at the university in the early sixteenth century; in 1531, in an attempt to regain St Romburgh's cell previously surrendered to Wolsey for his educational foundation at Ipswich, the abbot undertook to set aside the revenues from Lincoln to keep three monks there in the future. Other Benedictine, Cistercian, Augustian, and Gilbertine houses were certainly also maintaining the same practice.[30]

At some of the more important Yorkshire houses, indeed, a degree seems to have been well on the way to being a requirement for high office. Around 1512 William Perte alias Thirsk went from Fountains to St Bernard's College at Oxford where in 1521 after nine years of study he proceeded to the degree of Bachelor of Theology. Deemed 'well learned, and of good experience and gravity', he was elected abbot on the death of Marmaduke Huby in 1525. Another Cistercian, Richard Stopes, received the degree of B.D. at Oxford in 1521 after ten years away from his community; only two years later he became abbot of Meaux. Similarly Edward Kirkby alias Cowper, B.D., was chosen as abbot of Rievaulx within five years of his return from more

[30] J. Greatrex, 'Monk students from Norwich Cathedral Priory at Oxford and Cambridge c. 1300–1530', *EHR*, CVI (1991), p. 564; J. Greatrex, 'Benedictine monk scholars as teachers and preachers in the later Middle Ages: evidence from Worcester Cathedral Priory', *Monastic Studies*, II (Bangor, 1991), p. 5; C. Wellbeloved, 'The Compotus . . . of Thomas Syngleton, monk . . . of the Monastery of St Mary, York', *Proceedings of the Yorkshire Philosophical Society*, I (1855), p. 129; *Letters and Papers*, 5, no. 313.

than a decade at Oxford. James Cockerell, D.D., apparently from Oxford, served as prior of the Augustine house of Guisborough from 1519 to 1536, while at St Mary's abbey John Elmer or Amler seemed destined for a similar role. When he failed to be elected abbot in 1530, no less a patron than Anne Boleyn intervened to procure his release from administration and return to Cambridge, where he took the degree of D.D. in 1536.[31]

Even more closely associated with the universities than the monasteries, the Yorkshire friaries also actively cultivated their ties with Oxford and Cambridge in the two generations before the dissolution. John Pickering, ordained acolyte from the York Dominican friary in 1510 and priest six years later, proceeded B.D. at Cambridge in 1525 and ended his career as prior of the York house, being executed in 1537 for his support of the rebels at the time of the Pilgrimage of Grace. His successor as prior, Brian Godson, another local man, had been in Oxford in 1505 and may have studied at the university but not stayed long enough to take a degree. From the Franciscans William Vavasour, after his ordination as acolyte, subdeacon, and deacon at York between 1484 and 1487, migrated to the Oxford convent before the turn of the century where he incepted as doctor of divinity in 1500. He moved north again to become warden of the York friary in about 1514 and remained in the city until the surrender of his house in 1538. Simon Clarkson, prior of the York Carmelites at the dissolution, may also have been a northerner, being ordained acolyte from the York convent in 1522. After nine years of study he took the degree of B. Th. at Oxford in 1533, winning the approval of the conservative bishop of Lincoln for his participation at a heresy trial in 1538. Clarkson later went on to support religious reform, and married in Edward VI's reign, and another friar, the Franciscan Gilbert Berkley, B.D. from Oxford in 1538, followed a similar path. Although most reluctant initially to abandon his habit, he preferred exile to conformity in the Marian period, before returning on the Catholic queen's death to take office as the first Elizabethan bishop of Bath and Wells.[32]

[31] *BRUO 1501–1540* (Oxford, 1974) pp. 335, 543–4, 567, 669; J. and J. A. Venn, *Alumni Cantabrigienses* (Cambridge, 1922–7), pt I, 2, p. 99; M. Dowling, *Humanism in the Age of Henry VIII* (London, 1986), p.90.

[32] *BRUO*, 3, p. 1843; *BRUO 1501–40*, pp. 123, 236; Venn, *Alumni Cantabrigienses*, pt I, 3, p. 359; *DNB*, 4, pp. 359–60; Dickens, *Lollards and Protestants*, pp. 145–7; *Letters and Papers*, 13,

In addition to giving Yorkshire friars access to the south, the mendicants' peripatetic way of life also provided a means of introducing southerners into the north. Preeminent among such unsettling presences in the last years of monasticism was John Bale. Born in Suffolk in 1495, he entered the Norwich Carmelite friary and then proceeded to Jesus College, Cambridge, from where he took the degree of B.D. in 1529. Having served for a time as prior of the Ipswich Carmelites, in about 1530 he arrived in Doncaster to be prior of his order's convent. There he began preaching reformist beliefs, opposed in the pulpit by the prior of the Doncaster Franciscans, Thomas Kirkham (or Kirkby), D.D. The archbishop soon took measures to silence him, with the result that he retreated south to Suffolk where he was again accused of spreading 'erroneous opinions' in 1536; he fled into exile after the death of his patron, Thomas Cromwell.[33]

Most of the native Yorkshire religious, however, who attended a university and subsequently returned to the county of their birth remained loyal to Catholicism. William Swynborn or Gwynborne, ordained from the York Franciscan convent, acolyte in 1497 and priest in 1501, and admitted Doctor of Divinity at Cambridge in 1517, was dispatched to London from the Beverley friary in 1534 on a charge of having written against the king's divorce. A Meaux Cistercian, Robert Robinson, who had lived in St Nicholas hostel when he was studying in Cambridge but had apparently not taken a degree, established himself as a teacher in Beverley after the dissolution. Accounting him 'a papist' in the reign of Edward VI, certain townspeople warned local boys against enrolling at his school. Robert Pursglove, S.T.P., who joined the Augustinians when a student at Corpus Christi College at Oxford, retained throughout his life the interest in humanism he had learnt there. Cromwell's candidate as prior of Guisborough on the enforced resignation of James Cockerell in 1536, after the surrender of his house he went on to become, among much else, suffragan bishop of Hull and to found grammar schools in both Guisborough and Tideswell, but lost all his preferments on his refusal to conform under Elizabeth.[34]

pt I, no. 1434; Borthwick Abp. Reg. 23, fols 390r, 394v, 409r; Abp. Reg. 26, fol. 109r; Abp. Reg. 27, fol. 174r.

33 *DNB*, 3, pp. 41–2; Dickens, *Lollards and Protestants*, pp. 140–3; *BRUO 1501–40*, p. 336.

34 Venn, *Alumni Cantabrigienses*, pt I, 4, p. 193; *Letters and Papers*, 7, no. 953; 12, pt I, no. 201 (pp. 98–100); Borthwick Ord. 1554 1/11; *BRUO 1501–40*, pp. 467–7, 735; H. Aveling, *Northern Catholics: The Catholic Recusants of the North Riding of Yorkshire 1558–1790* (London, 1966), pp. 37–8.

Other northern religious advanced by Cromwell unlike Pursglove moved from humanism to adopting 'the new learning'. A fellow Augustinian, Robert Ferrar, was ordained acolyte, subdeacon, and deacon from Nostell in 1524 before going to study at both Oxford and then Cambridge, where he graduated B.D. in 1533 after twelve years of study. On his proselytizing visits to Oxford Thomas Garret introduced him to Lutheranism. As Cromwell's nominee Ferrar in 1538 was elected prior of Nostell, which he aspired to transform into a college for the 'advancement of the lively Word of God'. Too radical in religion to hold office in the Henrician church, he obtained the bishopric of St David's soon after Edward VI's accession, dying for his faith at Carmarthen in 1555.[35]

Though reconciled to Catholicism in his last years, Robert Holgate throughout most of his career in the secular church proved almost as active a propagator of Protestantism as Ferrar. A Gilbertine, he had studied at the order's house in Cambridge, taking the degree of B.D. in 1537. Through Cromwell's agency elected both Master of Sempringham and prior of Watton, he oversaw the surrender of all the houses of his order in 1539. Having been appointed in 1537 President of the Council in the North and bishop of Llandaff in 1545 he succeeded Edward Lee as archbishop of York, in Edward's reign proving a determined advocate of Protestantism throughout his diocese. He founded no fewer than three grammar schools at York, Malton, and Hemsworth.[36]

Whether radical or conservative in religion, a devotion to learning formed a common bond among these graduate religious. When he died in 1544, William Vavasour left his library to be distributed among various York priests including a former member of his convent, Ralph Clayton. Though he does not seem to have had a degree, Clayton was said to be 'well learned' in 1548 and to have spoken Latin 'very often in his [last] sickness'. A former Benedictine of Monk Bretton, Robert Scolay alias Kirkby, from his vicarage of Brodsworth kept in contact for decades after the dissolution with a remarkable circle of former Monk Bretton monks: Thomas Forbisher, Thomas Wilkinson, and Richard Hinchcliff, who under the direction of their one time prior,

[35] Venn, *Alumni Cantabrigienses*, pt I, 2, p. 134; *BRUO 1501–40*, pp. 202–3; Dickens, *Lollards and Protestants*, p. 149; Borthwick Abp. Reg. 27, fols 203r (*bis*), 204r.

[36] Venn, *Alumni Cantabrigienses*, pt I, 2, p. 391; A. G. Dickens, *Robert Holgate, Archbishop of York and President of the Council in the North*, Borthwick Paper no. 8 (York, 1955).

William Browne, recovered some one hundred and fifty books which had once belonged to Monk Bretton library and which Browne intended should be restored to the monastery if it should ever be re-founded. Edward Heptonstall, a former Kirkstall monk, engaged in a similar undertaking, bequeathing to John Heptonstall's son a chest of Kirkstall books on the understanding that his executors would deliver them back to the abbey 'if it go up in their times'. The collection of a hundred and fifty books preserved by his namesake and successor as vicar of Driffield in 1581 may just possibly have been carried away from Byland abbey by its last prior, Robert Barker.[37]

These religious, by no means all graduates, felt a real concern for their books in the sixteenth century. Most monks and canons may have come from families living in the near neighbourhood of their houses, but after their profession education literally and metaphorically helped to broaden their horizons, a minority leaving their communities for as much as a decade to study at the university, many more at the very least gaining a respect for book learning inside the cloister. Provincial they may well have been in origin, but the contacts which the larger monasteries and friaries maintained with the universities ensured that at least some Yorkshire monks and friars had access to a wider intellectual world in the last fifty years before the dissolution.

University of York

[37] York Minster Library D/C Prob. Reg. 3, fols 6r–7r; Borthwick CP G 3441; Prob. Reg. 15, pt III, fol. 59v (Heptonstall); Peculiar Wills Driffield 1581 (Barker); J. W. Walker, ed., *Chartularies of the Priory of Monk Bretton*, Yorkshire Archaeological Society, Record Series LXVI (1924), pp. 5–7.

HOLY WAR, ROMAN POPES, AND CHRISTIAN SOLDIERS: SOME EARLY MODERN VIEWS ON MEDIEVAL CHRISTENDOM

by CHRISTOPHER TYERMAN

SOME time in 1608, there arrived at Corpus Christi College, Cambridge a distinguished foreign visitor who, through the good offices of the Chancellor of the University, Robert Cecil, earl of Salisbury, and of Merlin Higden, a Fellow of Corpus, had been given permission to examine a manuscript in the college library. The visiting scholar had secured access to the library through a network of contacts that included his friend, a naturalized Frenchman and diplomat working for Cecil, Sir Stephen Lesieur, and a Chiswick clergyman, William Walter. What makes this apparently unremarkable (and hitherto unremarked) incident of more than trivial interest is that the industrious researcher was Jacques Bongars, veteran roving French ambassador in Germany and staunch Calvinist, and that his text was William of Tyre's *Historia Ierosolymitana*.[1]

That Bongars produced, in 1611, the first printed edition of this, and other, major texts on what we now call the crusades, and what sixteenth-century scholars tended to describe as the 'holy wars', may, at first sight, appear surprising. Yet he was one of a group of Lutheran and Calvinist scholars who were among the first to engage in the scholarly editing of manuscripts of crusading history. Their interest was not without ulterior polemic purpose. However, in addition to exposing how the papacy corrupted and misled both the Church and the faithful, there was a clear desire to extract positive lessons, to embrace as well as confront the medieval past. Across Christendom the religious changes of the sixteenth century led to fresh scrutiny of the European Christian inheritance, on all sides of the confessional divides. Especially, perhaps, for those who claimed to be representing or

[1] MS letter of William Walter, *minister* of Chiswick, pasted into the Bodleian Library, Oxford copy of the *Gesta Dei Per Francos* E.2.8. Art. Seld. after fol. 6; cf. *Gesta Dei Per Francos* (Hanau, 1611), Contents item 11 where Bongars thanks Higden and Lesieur, although not Walter. For Lesieur's contacts with Cecil, *Historical Manuscripts Commission*, Third Report (London, 1872), pp. 172, 175 (letters of 1607 and 1609); there are numerous other examples of the Lesieur correspondence in the Cecil papers.

creating a pure form of religion, there was a search for continuity as much as condemnation. The literary career of Archbishop Matthew Parker exemplifies this quest for justification in the past in Elizabethan England. Appropriately, it was one of Parker's own manuscripts that Bongars consulted at Corpus.[2]

Given their prominence in papal apologetics and continued relevance in political conflict, it is unsurprising that the crusades attracted the attention of intellectuals, Protestant and Catholic, or that their study was a significant feature of in a process of re-interpreting the past to suit and legitimize the present. The re-creation of the crusades was nothing new, responses to the holy wars had been consistently remoulded to suit current fashion. For Protestant scholars, the assimilation of crusade history into their fresh perspectives on the past signalled an important integration of tradition into the new world of reformed religion and national identity. No less intriguing is the extent to which the sixteenth-century re-examination of crusading was in tune with ideas current from the thirteenth and fourteenth centuries. In addition to fuelling contemporary anti-papal polemic and a growing market for antiquarianism, Protestant study of the crusades appears as part of a tradition of criticism reaching back centuries, evidence of certain continuities in attitudes as much as of a parting of ways of thought and belief. What appears ostensibly as Protestant critique of the Middle Ages has clear Catholic ancestry. Why and how else would Parker collect the xenophobic Matthew Paris or Bongars edit the nationalist Pierre Dubois?

The crusade appeared to sixteenth century *savants* in a number of guises, at once a subject of contemporary political concern and of religious controversy. With the Ottoman advance threatening central Europe and the western Mediterranean, traditional means of funding, recruiting, and justifying international warfare against the infidel could not be ignored by those living near the front line, such as Germany. Neither, for church reformers of any persuasion, could a religious exercise dependent upon papal authority and indulgences remitting sin be regarded with indifference. So far from being a matter of merely antiquarian or, in the hands of a Tasso, romantic interest, crusading touched upon two of the most engrossing problems of sixteenth-

[2] Cambridge, Corpus Christi College MS 95; M. R. James, *Descriptive Catalogue of the Manuscripts in the Library of Corpus Christi College, Cambridge* (Cambridge, 1911–12), pp. xxxiv, 182–3.

century Europe: the apparatus of papal legal and penitential authority, and the Ottoman threat to Christendom itself.[3] Responses to one could be modified by the imperatives of the other. Both Luther and Calvin trimmed initial condemnation of holy war against the Turks when faced with the reality of Suleiman the Magnificent.[4]

Under the pressure of religious dispute and political reality, perceptions of resistance to Islam shifted from wars of religion to wars of territory. Traditional epithets and mentalities wore thin. In the fifteenth century, while humanists such as Benedetto Accolti fashioned a literary revival of crusading, some suggested a new role for the Holy Roman Emperor as defender of Europe as much as of the Faith.[5] The secularization of war against the infidel, in an academic context at least, is evident in Juan de Segovia's critique of holy war, where he rejected the legitimacy of war fought for religious motives while accepting the legitimacy of secular resistance to Moslem aggression, essentially the line later adopted by Luther after 1521.[6] Leaving aside the tenaciously academic opposition to holy war by Erasmus, whose intellectual pose *de haut en bas* allowed for such principled stances, acceptance of the traditional appeal of crusading became attenuated. At Rome successive popes attempted to break the ideological stranglehold of tradition and Habsburg self-interest over indulgences, crusade or otherwise.[7] Even Leo X, at the Fifth Lateran Council, had distanced himself from the

[3] In general, K. Setton, *The Papacy and the Levant*, 4 vols (Philadelphia, 1976–84), 2–4; N. Housley, *The Later Crusades* (Oxford, 1992), esp. ch. 4; R. Schwoebel, *The Shadow of the Crescent: The Renaissance Image of the Turk* (Nieukoop, 1967).

[4] A. Fischer-Galati, *Ottoman Imperialism and German Protestantism* (Harvard, 1959), pp. 17–18; Housley, *Later Crusades*, p. 380; J. W. Bohnstedt, *The Infidel Scourge of God: The Turkish Menace as seen by pamphleteers of the Reformation Era*, Transactions of the American Philosophical Society (Philadelphia, 1978), pp. 12, 14, 20, 32, 46–51; M. J. Heath, *Crusading Commonplaces: La Noue, Lucinge and Rhetoric* (Geneva, 1986), p. 15. Cf. Luther's original stance attacked in the papal bull *Exurge Domine* (1520) with his later thoughts, *Vom Kriege widder die Turken* (1529) and the *Exhortation* (1541); on the impact of these changes, M. J. Heath, 'Erasmus and war against the Turks', *Acta Conventus neo-Latini Turonensis*, ed. J.-C. Margolin (Paris, 1980), pp. 991–9. J. Pannier, 'Calvin et les Turcs', *RH*, 180 (1937), pp. 268–72.

[5] Housley, *Later Crusades*, esp. pp. 99–100, 380, 383–8, 390–1, 393, 398, 409; R. Black, *Benedetto Accolti and the Florentine Renaissance* (Cambridge, 1985), esp. pp. 226–40; idem, '*La storica della Prime Crociata* di Benedetto Accolti', *ASI*, 131 (1973), pp. 2–25; see also the general books cited in n. 4 above and A. S. Atiya, *The Crusade in the Later Middle Ages* (London, 1938), chs 9, 11 and 19.

[6] Schwoebel, *Shadow of the Crescent*, p. 223.

[7] Setton, *Papacy and Levant*, 3 & 4, chs 12, 13 and 18; Housley, *Later Crusades*, pp. 312–15, 410–20.

rhetoric and legal forms of previous conciliar decrees on the crusade.[8] Protestants could not claim a monopoly on reforming ideas of the holy war. In 1532, in a sermon delivered at Mossburg, a Catholic preacher, Matthias Kretz, whose recorded utterances suggest close knowledge of crusade history, condemned as 'Turkish' motives for a Christian warrior such as honour, glory, material gain, anger, or vengeance, that is, in most instances, precisely the incentives lauded by St Bernard of Clairvaux and three centuries of subsequent crusade propaganda.[9]

Thus rejection of some of the characteristics of the crusade emphasized by papal apologists then and since was not confined to anti-catholic dialectic or experience. At the Council of Trent, Paul III attempted to restrict the use of bulls granting indulgences, which were only finally abolished in 1567.[10] Even before that, indulgences were given minimal space in Catholic tracts on fighting the Turks, such as the German *Turkenbuchlein* of the 1510s to 1540s. By the 1580s, when the Savoyard Catholic crusade enthusiast Réné de Lucinge was urging the overthrow of the Ottomans, the indulgence and much of the scriptural justification had been abandoned.[11]

Such developments were by no means orderly, progressive or universal. Numerous popes continued to employ the rhetoric and mechanisms of traditional crusading. However, in doing so they exposed a feature of crusading apparent since the thirteenth century. After Innocent III (1198–1216) the ideology of holy war, crusading polemic, and apologia, except where applied to the conquests in the Atlantic and the Americas, had become sclerotic. Foundations of patristic not scriptural authority looked increasingly awkward ranged against biblical fundamentalists. More generally, crusading's emphasis on external demonstrations of communally ordained and executed spiritual exercises – vow, taking the cross, fighting, purchasing indulgences, giving alms – appeared at odds with the increasing concentration on inner piety, common to Catholic as well as Protestant reformers. Neither politics nor intellectual fashion assisted traditional perceptions, as the Most Christian kings of France, let alone the heretic

[8] Tanner, *Decrees*, pp. 609–14 (*Postquam ad universalis* of 1514), 651–4 (*Constitutio iuxta verbum* of 1517). K. Setton, 'Leo X and the Turkish peril', *Proceedings of the American Philosophical Society*, 113 (1969), pp. 367–424.

[9] Bohnstedt, *Infidel Scourge*, pp. 14, 34–5, 41–6.

[10] R. Naz, ed., *Dictionnaire de droit canonique*, 4 (Paris, 1949), col. 781, and note 7 above.

[11] Bohnstedt, *Infidel Scourge*, pp. 43–4, where Kretz talked of martyrdom but not indulgences; Heath, *Crusading Commonplaces*, pp. 10, 24, 88.,

Queen of England, entered into political and commercial alliances with the Turks, and theorists such as Gentili and Grotius, in elaborating theories of secular international laws of war, discounted religion as sufficient just cause.[12] Although carefully describing current and past ideas of religious wars, as well as criticisms of them, in his *Advertisement Touching on holy Warre* (1622), Francis Bacon summed up the new consensus in 1624: 'offensive wars for religion are seldom to be approved, or never, except there be some mixture of civil titles.'[13] Prudence and law, not faith and religion, now appeared the touch-stones.

The secularization of holy war in the sixteenth century was a prime cause of the disintegration of crusading as an ideal and religious institution. It also provided a bridge over which empathy for the inspiration and enthusiasm which underpinned such wars was conveyed to those otherwise confessionally hostile to them, from the German Lutheran Ulrich von Hutten in the 1520s to the Huguenot François de la Noue in the 1580s.[14] In 1585, the Calvinist-trained James VI of Scotland published a poem in praise of the victory of Lepanto which, as he later admitted, some regarded as 'far contrary to my degree and religion' appearing as it did as 'praise of a forraine Papist bastard' (i.e. Don John of Austria, the Christian commander).[15] As king of England, James retained a sentimental ambition to lead a united Christian league against the Ottomans. Such enthusiasm was possible within the increasingly popular ecumenical concept of Europe, a non-denominational sense of a common Christendom which led to the virulently anti-Catholic Bishop Jewell of Salisbury, among other English diocesans, authorizing prayers for the survival of Malta in 1565, and provoked a service of thanksgiving at St Paul's, bonfires, and dancing in the streets of London on news of Lepanto in 1571, in the words of Raphael Holinshed, 'for a victorie of so great importance unto the whole state of Christian commonwealth'.[16]

[12] Cf. Heath, *Crusading Commonplaces*, pp. 21–2.

[13] J. Spedding *et al.*, eds, *The Works of Francis Bacon*, 7 (London, 1859), p. 4.

[14] Schwoebel, *Shadow of the Crescent*, p. 217; Setton, *Papacy and Levant*, 3, pp. 179, n. 28, 89–90, n. 72; Fischer-Galati, *Ottoman Imperialism*, esp. pp. 9–10; Heath, *Crusading Commonplaces*.

[15] *Lepanto*, J. Craigie, ed., *The Poems of James VI of Scotland*, 1 (Edinburgh, 1955), pp. 198 and, in full, 197–257.

[16] F. L. Baumer, 'England, the Turk and the Common Corps of Christendom', *AHR*, 50 (1944–5), pp. 26–48, esp. 31, 36–8, 43–7; C. J. Tyerman, *England and the Crusades 1095–1588* (Chicago, 1988), pp. 348–50.

Yet such superficial ecumenism, while helping to provide a general circumstance within which interest in crusading could be sustained in varying religious traditions, was initially less significant than religious dispute in provoking the first academic studies of medieval crusade texts and history. Only at the very end of the sixteenth century were the crusades beginning to be examined outside a precise religious context, contemporary or historical. Whereas until the 1520s, crusading formed part of a lively and accepted political, literary, and intellectual culture, thereafter, on both sides of the theological divide, it was observed from fractured perspectives. Loyola, it has been argued, borrowed aspects of crusade spirituality for his own ideals of internal purification and external 'reconquest' of Protestants.[17] For obvious reasons, crusading, and thus crusade texts, appealed to those eager to identify the Reformers with Turks. A fairly typical example was François Moschus who, in his edition of Jacques de Vitry's *Historia Orientalis* (1587), compared the wars against Islam with those against 'Lutherans and other Evangelical pseudo-prophets', equating the teaching of Luther with that of Mohammed. Moschus was more than a pamphleteer, having searched widely for manuscripts of his thirteenth-century text.[18] This harnessing of scholarship to the chariot of controversy was, however, to be especially the preserve of Moschus's confessional opponents.

The dismissal by Protestant scholars of the legal and theological framework of crusading did not mean they necessarily followed Erasmus in rejecting the concept of armed resistance to the Infidel. In his *History of the Turks* (1566), the English martyrologist, John Foxe (1516–87) agreed that Moslems were 'the enemies of Christ'. He praised the defence of Rhodes by the Hospitallers in 1522 and was clear that much effort, courage, and preparation had gone in to the holy 'viages'. One of his explanations for the failures of the crusade was traditionally medieval, *ratione peccati*: evil-living Christians did not merit God's support. The other was predictably polemic, 'the impure idolatry and profanations' of the Roman Church. 'We war against the Turk with our works, masses, traditions and ceremonies,: but we fight

[17] H. Wolter, 'Elements of Crusade spirituality in St. Ignatius', *Ignatius of Loyola: His Personality and Spiritual Heritage*, ed. F. Wulf (St Louis, MO, 1977), pp. 97–134; N. P. Tanner, 'Medieval Crusade decrees and Ignatus's Meditation on the Kingdom', *Heythrop Journal*, 31 (1990), pp. 505–15.

[18] Jacques de Vitry, *Historia Orientalis*, ed. F. Moschus (Douai, 1597), Preface to Reader.

not against him with Christ.' Foxe's diatribe encapsulated the standard Protestant critique: the laudable desire to fight the Infidel had been corrupted by Rome.[19]

This theme was taken up by Foxe's younger contemporary, Matthew Dresser (1536–1607). A Lutheran, Dresser held a number of chairs of classical language, rhetoric, and history in northern Germany, as well as being official historiographer to the elector of Saxony and protégé of the duke of Brunswick. In his academic circle, the editing of classical and medieval texts and the writing of history of remote periods of the past was flourishing. One of Dresser's acquaintances, the editor, historian, and antiquarian Reinier Reineck (1541–95), persuaded him to write a commentary on the causes of the holy war for an edition of an anonymous compendium of crusade texts, *Chronicon Hierosolymitanum*, which Reineck published at Helmstadt in 1584.[20]

Dresser's approach was subtler than Foxe's. 'This war had a double cause: one by the Roman popes, the other by Christian soldiers.'[21] This distinction allowed him to explain the failure of what was ostensibly a good cause. Throughout he insisted on the selflessness and piety of the crusaders, while condemning the papacy and church for poisoning the truth and justice of their ambition with superstition. Thus Dresser was able to point out that Frederick Barbarossa's drowning on crusade in 1190 was no reason to doubt his pious intent. Lack of settlers and high mortality rates may, Dresser argued, have assisted in the loss of Christian Outremer, but the enterprise was fatally undermined by the papal greed and lust for temporal power, a theme he pursued with much erudition. While the First Crusaders were likened to the Argonauts, he insisted that Urban II's promotion of the First Crusade had more to do with his campaign against Henry IV of Germany than any genuine desire for defending Christendom or spiritual renewal (an idea which, had Dresser but know it, had occurred to William of Malmesbury four and a half centuries earlier). Consistently popes placed their trust in earthly not heavenly Jerusalem. The crusaders'

[19] J. Foxe, *Acts and Monuments*, ed. S. R. Cattley (London, 1837–41), 4, pp. 18–21, 27–8, 33–4, 38, 52–4, 69, 113, 120–1.

[20] Reinerius Reineccius Steinhemius, *Chronicon Hierosolymitanum* (Helmstadt, 1584) (Part 2 [1585] contains Dresser's Commentary); idem, *Liber Epistolarum Historicarum*, pp. 44, 60 for correspondence between Dresser and Reineck in 1583.

[21] *Chronicon Hierosolymitanum*, 2, fol. 2v.

fault was to have been obedient to duplicitous popes and profane monks.[22]

The suggestion that crusaders were pious but ignorant and misled rather than themselves mischievous became and remains a familiar convention of crusade historiography, one that had its parallels in the Middle Ages. Such an interpretation permitted Dresser to conclude that the only thing wrong with sixteenth-century resistance to the Turks was papal and episcopal interference, to which he attributed the collapse of Hungary in the 1520s.[23] By implication, an army free from clerical direction and composed of faithful, honest, and virtuous soldiers (i.e. Protestant ones) would attract divine approval and the good fortune that had so palpably eluded the crusades.. Here, too, Dresser was clinging to a basic set of assumptions about popular religion that would not have seemed out of place in earlier centuries.

Dresser's commentary was also a form of dialogue with the medieval past, part of scholarly effort to understand, even identify with it. This effort was to a large degree carried forward through the editing of medieval texts, in which endeavour Reinier Reineck was prominent. Reineck, who conducted a wide correspondence with fellow scholars, himself wrote mainly about ancient history. However, as an editor he specialized in German medieval history, publishing editions of the *Annals* of Charlemagne, Helmold's *Chronica Slavorum*, as well as chronicles by Thietmar of Merseberg and Widukind of Corvey. Apart from the *Chronicon Hierosolymitanum*, he edited a number of other texts linked to the crusade, including Hayton's *Flowers of the History of the East*, a perennial favourite found widely in the sixteenth century, a collection known as the *Historia Orientalis*, and Albert of Aachen's account of the First Crusade. Reineck was a conscientious editor, claiming to have collated and compared the *Chronicon Hierosolymitanum* with William of Tyre and Robert of Rheims, as well as referring to a number of Greek sources and to Otto of Freising. Here was a man steeping himself in medieval history for a purpose beyond providing ammunition for religious debate. This purpose is evident both in the nature of the texts he edited and by his own comments in his introduction to the *Chronicon*. As he declares to his patron the duke, the First Crusade brought glory to the house of Brunswick.[24] The

22 *Chronicon Hierosolymitanum*, 2, fols. 1r–7v.

23 Ibid., 2, fol. 7r.

24 Ibid., 1, Introduction; his main publishing activities of texts date from the last fifteen

German bias throughout is unmistakable, as it was in Dresser's commentary.

Thus the crusade was employed to support a sense of national identity or pride, explicitly derived from the pre-Reformation past and deliberately non-confessional. Dresser and Reineck were rescuing German crusading heroes and a significant part of German history for Protestant Germany, just as Archbishop Parker rescued many of his medieval predecessors from the condescension and disapproval of the new Anglicans. This desire to reconcile the present with a possibly controversial past was similarly evident in the work of Jacques Bongars (1554–1612), one of the greatest of all editors of crusade texts. As with his German colleagues, Bongars was intent on using the past to inform and interpret the present. Although only a part of his scholarly output, he appropriated the crusade to support an abiding myth of French nationhood and monarchy.

Bongars was a career diplomat working for Henry of Navarre, later Henry IV, from 1585. Between 1593 and 1610, as resident ambassador in the Holy Roman Empire, he acted as Henry's agent to the Lutheran princes of Germany, including the duke of Brunswick, patron of Dresser and Reineck.[25] Bongars was also an indefatigable bibliophile and historian, interests which he pursued with an energy and passion that impressed itself on his acquaintances. At his death he left a collection of between five and six hundred manuscripts and over three thousand printed books.[26] In his twenties he had worked in the Vatican Library and had begun publishing texts in 1581. Fluent in Latin, French, German, and English, he travelled widely throughout Europe, from Constantinople (in 1585–6, when he called himself a 'peregrinator') to England (at least twice). Although not a violent sectarian, he did not follow his master in converting to Rome, retaining his Calvinist beliefs as well as a loathing of 'la superstition papistique' which he described in a letter of 1602 as 'contre la crainte et le service de Dieu, l'amour du roi et de la patrie'.[27]

years of his life, while he had made his reputation as a scholar of, in particular, Ancient Greece at Wittenberg and Leipzig in the 1570s.

25 G. E. Lothholz, *Commentatio de Bongarsio Singulisque eius aequalibus* (Leipzig, 1857), pp. 4–14; L. Anquez, *Henri IV et l'Allemagne* (Paris, 1887), pp. xiii–lxxxvi, 'Jacques Bongars', for the biographical details and academic influences based on Bongars' extensive correspondence.

26 Anquez, *Henri IV et l'Allemagne*, pp. xli–xlii.

27 Ibid., p. xv, in a letter to the Landgrave of Hesse; p. xx for his description of himself in 1587 as a pilgrim to Constantinople.

Bongars' link with the German Lutheran scholars was direct. He had studied at Jena shortly before Dresser had taken the chair of rhetoric and history there. At various times he had helped Reineck with his researches.[28] When Bongars came to compile his collection of crusade texts the only chronicle he was content to reprint rather than edit afresh was Reineck's Albert of Aachen.[29] Wherever he went, Bongars searched archives and libraries and met fellow scholars, such as, in England in 1608, the prominent English antiquarian Sir Henry Savile.[30]

The great edition Bongars published in 1611 was significantly published under the title *Gesta Dei Per Francos*. It was a Herculean achievement, the two parts comprising over 1,500 closely printed pages, containing almost a million words. In scope, originality, and detail of scholarship, the *Gesta Dei Per Francos* was stupendous. Based on scrutiny of variant manuscripts wherever he could get access to them, from Rome to Cambridge, the work stands as the most significant single contribution to the editing of crusade texts before the nineteenth century. Among the sources edited are the main narratives of the First Crusade: the anonymous *Gesta Francorum*; Robert of Rheims; Baldric of Dol; Raymond of Aguilers; Albert of Aachen; Fulcher of Chartres, and Guibert of Nogent (from whom Bongars took his title). In addition he included not only William of Tyre's *Historia*, but also that of Jacques de Vitry, and Oliver of Paderborn's account of the Fifth Crusade. In all, in Part One, there were thirteen separate chronicles or fragments, many, such as William of Tyre, Fulcher of Chartres, and the *Gesta Francorum*, published for the first time, as well as a selection of thirteenth-century papal bulls, a number of letters written by or about crusaders and, tellingly, documents on the canonization of Louis IX in 1297. In the second part were edited, from a bewildering array of manuscripts, the *Secreta Fidelium Crucis* (final redaction 1321), a work of crusade advice and history by the Venetian Marino Sanudo Torsello, as well as the *De recuperatione Terrae Sanctae* (1306/7) of the anti-papal Norman *légiste* Pierre Dubois, and a collection of Sanudo's correspondence and maps (these last from a Vatican manuscript).[31]

[28] Anquez, *Henri IV et l'Allemagne*, p. xxi; Lothholz, *Commentatio*, pp. 4–5.
[29] See the introduction to the table of contents of *Gesta Dei Per Francos*, I.
[30] Anquez, *Henri IV et l'Allemagne*, p. lxv, according to a letter dated 21 March 1611.
[31] Vatican Codex Reginae Cristinae 548.

Bongars' *Gesta Dei Per Francos* is, in effect, a complete history of the holy wars to capture and hold the Holy Land from the first expedition in the 1090s to the abortive schemes of the early fourteenth century. On one level the motive was academic. In the words of William Walter, one of Bongars' intermediaries in England in 1608, the aim was to produce 'the most correct' editions.[32] On another, there are traces of the diplomat. The dedication of the second part to the Senate of Venice not only dwells on the city's historic role in maintaining the crusaders in Outremer and in conquering Constantinople, but also praises the Republic's contemporary independence and the assistance she gave Henry IV against the Habsburgs.[33]

The most striking feature, however, is the sight of a Calvinist devoting such energy to studying events inspired by doctrines he rejected yet describing them as 'most dangerous and most glorious'.[34] Bongars was aware of the incongruity. In the preface to Book One, he acknowledged that readers would find details of impiety, superstition, and shame. Yet, unlike Dresser, much of whose critique of motive and value he adopted, Bongars avoided cheap anti-Catholic or even anti-papal polemic, commenting simply that such things are the common experience of mankind and that history 'is a mirror of human life'.[35] Calvin himself had rejected a thorough pacifist response to the Turkish problem, arguing that there was a difference between resistance organized to suit papal self-interest and legitimate opposition in the hands of divinely ordained lay magistrates.[36] As already noted, this approach, which equated service of God and love of ruler and country, appealed to Bongars. His position is clear from the title, the prayer with which he concluded his introduction, and the dedication. The title proclaimed that the crusades were God's deeds performed by Frenchmen, hardly original as it followed a misleading tradition that had begun as early as the 1100s. The prayer looked to princes to implement God's commands as being next to Him in power. The dedication of Book One was to the young Louis XIII, 'the Most Christian' king, descended from St Louis, heir to the royal line which, of all princely

32 Walter's letter at fol. 6, Bodleian Library copy of *Gesta Dei Per Francos*, E.2.8. Art. Seld.

33 Dedication to *Gesta Dei Per Francos*, 2.

34 'Periculosissimis ita gloriosissimis expeditionibus', from the dedicatory Preface to Part 1.

35 In the author's Preface to Part 1.

36 Pannier, 'Calvin et les Turcs', pp. 278–86.

families, had the crusade as their especial concern. Bongars was chauvinist and royalist. In a new secular cult of kingship the Calvinist was reconciled to crusading.

Bongars was not alone either in his interest in crusading nor its association with the French monarchy. Two panegyrists of Henry IV, Jean-Aimes de Chavigny and Jean Godard, both published works concerning the crusade and the eastern question, as had a relative of Bongars' wife, François de la Noue in 1587.[37] Bongars, however, goes further than his contemporaries in implicitly attempting to defuse or divert a potentially divisive aspect of this piece of French history. One problem with any discussion of the holy war was whether or not religious opponents were legitimate targets for crusading. In France where, under Henry IV, religious accommodation was government policy, this was an especially sensitive issue. Catholic writers in France at the end of the Religious Wars, such as the Celestine Pierre Crespet or the Savoyard diplomat Réné de Lucinge, equated Protestants with the Turks, as did Florimond de Raemond in works published in 1597 and 1605.[38] Bongars' purpose was to render crusading as a national achievement, therefore ecumenical, free from the stultifying grasp of contemporary theological debate. Thus could the old world be recruited to the aid of the new.

This did not mean that Bongars saw the crusaders as teaching lessons that were politically neutral. Citing William of Tyre as tutor to King Baldwin IV of Jerusalem, Bongars regarded history as a good teacher. His choice of texts reveals something of what he wished to be learnt. This is especially obvious in the case of Pierre Dubois's *De recuperatione Terrae Sanctae*, published for the first time by Bongars. Dubois was a fierce French nationalist, in the context of his time. In Part I of the *De recuperatione*, he advocated a general attack on the East, embracing Constantinople as well as Syria, an idea current in late sixteenth-century French. He suggested, as a prerequisite to a successful crusade, radical reform within Christendom, including disendowment of the Church, educational reform, and an end to clerical celibacy.[39] Just as English reformers in the 1530s had sought medieval

[37] Heath, *Crusading Commonplaces*, pp. 10, 53, 84, 103–4; for the family relationship, Anquez, *Henri IV et l'Allemagne*, p. xliv.

[38] Heath, *Crusading Commonplaces*, pp. 13, 39, 49, 66, 74.

[39] For the most comprehensive study, Pierre Dubois, *The Recovery of the Holy Land*, trans. W. I. Brandt, Introduction, pp. 3–65; pp. 69–198 for the text.

precedents for the creation of an erastian church, including a tract, *Disputacio inter clericum et militem* once attributed to Dubois, so Bongars had hit upon a crusade writer whose attitudes paralleled his own.[40] Dubois was not only an advocate of ecclesiastical administrative reform, he was also a vivid exponent of royal power, a theme which permeates Part II of the *De recuperatione*, where it is proposed that the king of France should dominate Europe by, among other things, administering the temporalities of the pope and controlling the Empire.[41]

In such points of contact and reference, scholars such as Bongars or Dresser are found to be the intellectual heirs of those medieval authors whose works they edited. Discussion and debate as to the legitimacy and nature of crusading was not a creation of the sixteenth century. It had existed from the start. The themes of sin and abuse were apparent in the histories of William of Tyre, Jacques de Vitry, and Sanudo, as well as Dubois and other fourteenth-century critics.[42] The spectacle of Christian faith overcoming great obstacles was a *leitmotif* of all crusade narratives. The threat of Islam was a common experience. By separating crusading from religious polemic and accepting that there was good in a holy war even where corrupted by papal dogma, the Reformed Church could demonstrate itself to be a lineal successor to its medieval predecessor. This process was immensely assisted by the association of crusading with national identity, by Reineck in Germany or Bongars in France. Bongars' national bias was considered and self-conscious, as in private, if his correspondence is to be believed, he saw himself almost as a naturalized German. That his message was popular or fashionable, if not influential (its bulk perhaps precluding that for many of those likely to own a copy), is witnessed by the large numbers of copies of the 1611 edition that survive in libraries all across Europe, public, academic, aristocratic, collegiate, and private. It seems as

[40] A. G. Dickens, *The English Reformation*, 2nd edn (London, 1989), p. 317.

[41] Dubois, *The Recovery*, trans. Brandt, pp. 167–98; M. della Piane, *Vecchio e Nuovo nelle idee politiche di Pietro Dubois* (Florence, 1959), pp. 106–43.

[42] On fourteenth-century critics, E. Siberry, 'Criticism of crusading in fourteenth-century England' and C. J. Tyerman, 'The Holy Land and the Crusades of the thirteenth and fourteenth centuries', *Crusade and Settlement*, ed. P. W. Edbury (Cardiff, 1985), pp. 127–34 and 105–12; A. Luttrell, 'Chaucer's Knight and the Mediterranean', *Library of Mediterranean History*, 1 (1994), pp. 127–60; C. J. Tyerman, *The Invention of the Crusades* (London, 1998).

though few major libraries of western Europe can have been without a copy.[43]

Not all responses to the crusades in Bongars' generation were so solemn. Torquato Tasso's popular and much translated *Gerusalemme Liberata* (1580) reinvented the First Crusade as a romantic story of chivalry, love, and magic. Others, such as Pierre de Bourdeille, seigneur de Brantôme (*c.*1540–1614), regarded the age of crusading as hopelessly distant and quaint, a fund of good stories, not moral, political, or religious instruction.[44] In the 1620s, Francis Bacon could examine the holy war dispassionately, as an exercise in dialectic and antiquarianism, even, in places, as a joke, like the Philosopher's Stone a '*rendez-vous* of cracked brains that wore their feather in their head instead of their hat'.[45]

However, the academic heroics of scholars such as Bongars and Reineck opened the way to a fundamental transformation in attitudes to the crusades ironically precisely because, unlike Moschus for instance, they lacked the confessional acceptance of the religious dogma attached to it. Some might argue that this prevented them from understanding or empathizing with their subject. In fact, avoidance of knee-jerk condemnation (or approval) liberated the history of the crusades, if not the surviving phenomenon itself. In a long-standing medieval tradition, the faith of the Christian soldiers was admired by these Protestant observers even if the leadership of the pope was excoriated. With many thirteenth- and fourteenth-century critics, the Protestant crusade historians were outraged by holy wars against Christians. Yet instead of treating the past as an alien land of monsters and freaks, these scholars integrated their vision of the past into the interpretation of their own times. In this small way, at least, the veil of the Temple was not rent. The past remained alive, of more than literary or anecdotal concern. By neither rejecting the past nor being condescending to it, these editors ensured the survival of the crusades as a model as well as a warning, a familiar, perhaps the most familiar, aspect of the Middle Ages in the mentality of modern European culture. In Gordon Leff's words, 'the crusades were part of a

[43] On a personal, tiny, and random sample there exist or existed until recently two copies in the Bodleian Library, Oxford, and copies in the college libraries of New College, Queen's and All Souls'; there was also a copy at Castle Howard.

[44] Pierre de Bourdeille, seigneur de Brantôme, *Oeuvres complètes*, ed. L. Lalanne, 9 (Paris, 1876), pp. 433–4, 450.

[45] *Works of Francis Bacon*, 7, p. 24 and, generally, pp. 1–36 for the *Advertisement*.

European movement under papal direction'.[46] The Protestant scholars of the late sixteenth century dug new channels for the reception of the history of that movement which allowed it to fructify or astonish observers of all religious persuasions and to form part of a continuing secular, non-denominational European consciousness.

Hertford College, Oxford

[46] Leff, *Medieval Thought*, p. 86.

MET ON THE *VIA MODERNA*

by JOHN BOSSY

SOMEWHERE about 1970 Gordon Leff changed his mind about William of Ockham. Earlier, in the article 'The fourteenth century and the decline of scholasticism' and the survey *Medieval Thought*, Ockham had appeared in the conventional role of demolisher of the scholastic synthesis of reason and revelation; apologist of pure will in God and man; lock-picker of the Pandora's box of moral and theological bugs in which the teaching of his successors consisted. Sceptic and/or fideist, he might be credited with clearing the way for natural science, and indeed for Renaissance and Reformation; but in himself he was an apostle of negation, carrying a whiff of the diabolic. Leff made public his change of heart in the massive exposition of Ockham of 1975 and the essay, *The Dissolution of the Medieval Outlook*, which came out the following year. Ockham was still the author of a 'metamorphosis of scholastic discourse' because he had excluded all but empirical knowledge of individual things and had refused to accept that rational proof could be found for more than marginal items of revealed truth. But he had, it seems, believed that 'nature' and 'right reason' were terms which might be properly used of the physical and moral worlds; random incursions of God's *potentia absoluta* (what God might do) into the system of salvation constructed by his *potentia ordinata* (what God had actually done) were no longer to be anticipated; and Ockham was not responsible for the aberrations of some followers.

Here I shall not exactly be asking why he changed his mind, but wondering about some of the circumstances surrounding the change; then I shall be speculating about whether, in the long term, the change was a good idea. It was certainly going with the scholarly consensus, as we can check from William Courtenay's important piece on 'Nominalism and late mediaeval religion', given in 1972 and published in 1974. Courtenay was generally happy with the conventional picture of Ockham's terminism and epistemological scepticism, and of the hostility to metaphysics which abolished natural theology as practised by Aquinas. He was not happy with the conviction that Ockham's distinction of God's two powers, absolute and ordained, meant that there could be no natural ethics or natural law since ethics and laws had been ungroundedly produced, and might be ungroundedly overturned, by the free will of God. The distinction of the two powers was a dialectical instrument, used by Aquinas to explain that God did not act of necessity, and by Ockham and his successors to distinguish the essential from the accidental in the object of investigation: the *potentia absoluta* did not describe a mode in which God might *now* act. These points are also found in Leff's *Ockham*. But Courtenay's account cannot have been the source of Leff's change of mind. I should think that the 666 pages of *Ockham* had been written before it came to Leff's notice. In his first published effort on the subject he had noted the defence of Ockham put up by the Franciscan Philotheus Boehner and the unattached Paul Vignaux, which lies at the bottom of Courtenay's critique, but had thought it a feeble effort to keep under control the ungovernable force of the *potentia absoluta*. He was also unsympathetic to the revised version of nominalism proposed by Courtenay and his ally Heiko Oberman.[1]

If we wish to go farther, we can consult Steven Ozment's admirable *The Age of Reform* (1980), an account of the intellectual background to the Reformation in late medieval thought and religion. Ozment is one of the few scholars to have taken a careful look at the corpus of Leff's contributions, and he had two things to say. He noted Leff's change of mind about Ockham, and suggested that what it amounted to was getting out from under the shadow of Etienne Gilson, whose Aquinas-centred view of medieval thought, expounded in *La Philosophie au Moyen Age* and in a shelf of monographs, was virtually compulsory for anyone starting to study medieval thought in the 1950s. He also took on board an area of Leff's writings which historians of medieval thought generally did not consider: the subject of his other monumental work, *Heresy in the Later Middle Ages* (1967).[2] As a historian of the Reformation, Ozment naturally warmed to the sympathetic view of late-medieval unorthodoxy elaborated in the book, as to the change of mind about Ockham. It was not his business to make a connection between the two, but perhaps he might have done.

[1] William J. Courtenay, 'Nominalism and late mediaeval religion', in Charles Trinkaus and Heiko A. Oberman, eds, *The Pursuit of Holiness in Late Mediaeval and Renaissance Religion* (Leiden, 1974), pp. 26–59; Leff, 'Decline', p. 33, and below, pp. 314 f.

[2] Steven Ozment, *The Age of Reform, 1250–1550: An Intellectual and Religious History of Late Mediaeval and Reformation Europe* (New Haven, CT, and London, 1980), pp. 9, 18 n. 29, 94, 110, 168; Etienne Gilson, *La Philosophie au Moyen Age* (Paris, 1944; 2nd edn 1952), translated as *History of Christian Philosophy in the Middle Ages* (London, 1955).

Gilson was a distinguished product of the revival of scholasticism launched by Pope Leo XIII's canonization of Thomism in 1879. Preceded by the aggressive Heinrich Denifle and by Maurice de Wulf, he was flanked by a string of more or less polemical Catholic historians whose business was to denigrate late medieval thought and practice as a comedown from the heights of the thirteenth century and a pathfinder for the Reformation and other misfortunes: Pierre Imbart de la Tour's *Les Origines de la Réforme*, Georges de Lagarde's *Naissance de l'esprit laïque au déclin du Moyen Age* and Joseph Lortz's *Die Reformation in Deutschland* were three of them. They generally featured attacks upon those who had 'let the genie of individualism out of the scholastic bottle'. Imbart deplored the 'organic anarchy' of the fifteenth-century Church. Lagarde expounded Ockham as the prophet of a philosophical and social atomism mining away at a synthesis which had embraced the personality of collective entities as well as the unity of reason and revelation. Lortz wrote him off as a 'fundamentally unCatholic' mind, a wrecker of true Catholic thinking and a direct precursor of Luther.[3] Of these, I do not know whether Leff had read Imbart; his notion of the relation between late scholasticism and the Reformers was different from Lortz's both before his change of mind about Ockham and after it; he thought Lagarde attractive in detail but unreliable in general drift.[4]

Leff might well have fought shy of Gilson had he detected in him such evidently propagandist and, in the 1940s, fairly alarming motifs. But Gilson seems to have been a loyal citizen of the French Republic, and no such nervousness was called for. Nevertheless, there was an equally distinguished influence closer at hand: his Cambridge supervisor David Knowles. Knowles put him on to the topic of his first book, Thomas Bradwardine, and he is mentioned warmly in the prefaces to it (1956) and to *Gregory of Rimini* (1961); *Bradwardine* appeared in a series edited by Knowles. Both Courtenay and Ozment,

[3] Pierre Imbart de la Tour, *Les Origines de la Réforme: 2, L'Eglise catholique* (2nd edn, Melun, 1946), pp. 181–212; Georges de Lagarde, *La Naissance de l'esprit laïque au déclin du Moyen Age*, 6 vols (Saint-Paul-Trois-Châteaux, 1934–46); 2nd edn, 5 vols (Paris, 1956–63); Joseph Lortz, *Die Reformation in Deutschland*, 2 vols (Freiburg-im-B., 1939–40; 2nd edn, 1949); English translation, *The Reformation in Germany*, 2 vols (London and New York, 1968), I, pp. 195–8, 200. One might add, from a High-Anglican point of view, Gregory Dix, *The Shape of the Liturgy* (London, 1945), pp. 546–612. Quotation from Charles T. Davis in Trinkaus and Oberman, *Pursuit of Holiness*, p. 59.

[4] Leff, 'Decline', p. 39; *Ockham*, p. 470; *Dissolution*, p. 52; for Lagarde, see below n.12.

commenting on the conservatism of Knowles's opinion about Ockham, connect it with Leff's original view; the ideas about the fourteenth century expressed in his article of 1956 sound very much like Knowles's, and he observed in the course of it that the century was not Gilson's strong point.[5]

Knowles's dislike of Ockham is evident enough in his *Evolution of Medieval Thought* (1962), but not half so evident as it was in the lecture series from which the book emerged. I can testify to this, because I went to those lectures in 1954, as I suppose Leff had done a little earlier, and I have kept a respectable set of notes on the last of them, about Ockham. It was a powerful performance, and even in an undergraduate's notes one can sense Knowles putting all his talent and charisma into demolishing his subject. Ockham's flight from Avignon to Munich was an event in history of the same order as Lenin's train from Zürich to St Petersburg. He was a spoiled theologian. He was something like a logical positivist, sweeping sure-footed thought and spiritual concern out of the schools, reducing judgements of value to mindless exclamations. His doctrines of God's omnipotence and unknowability left a schizophrenic generation bisected between the theoretical possibility that God is always putting his boot into the things of the world and the practical assumption that he has nothing to do with it.[6]

This was adding a good deal of acid to Gilson's measured sorrow; it can hardly have failed to impress the young scholar. And Knowles did not, any more than Gilson, encumber himself with a lot of 'Catholic' baggage: in his lecture he warned us not to go drawing straight lines from Ockham to Luther; he suggested a general effect of secularization. Here he may have been drawing on Lagarde; if so, it was with his own gloss. There is no sign at all in Knowles of the corporatism which inspired so many of his Catholic contemporaries. His view of the history of the Church and of spiritual experience could happily accept the modulation of these, during the fifteenth century, into the individualistic mode which his friend Outram Evennett had recently expounded in his Birkbeck Lectures on the Counter-Reformation.[7]

[5] Prefaces to Leff, *Bradwardine* and *Gregory*; Courtenay, in *Pursuit of Holiness*, p. 27, n.4; Ozment, *Age of Reform*, pp. 8–9 and n.5; Adrian Morey, *David Knowles: a Memoir* (London, 1979), p. 104; Leff, 'Decline', p. 30.

[6] Cf. Knowles, *The Evolution of Mediaeval Thought* (London, 1962), pp. 318–26, where the spoiled theologian has gone, but Lenin remains.

Relieved of some incubi, and represented by Gilson and Knowles, the 'Catholic' consensus about Ockham was available to be recycled in Leff's *Medieval Thought* of 1958.[8]

I guess that his parting from it had something to do with Knowles as well. In *Heresy in the Later Middle Ages* (1967) his thesis was that heresy was an interior growth in Catholic Christianity, arising from the tension between Christian precept and ecclesiastical practice; an upshot of piety, not of Lagarde's 'lay spirit' or of unbelief; a 'catholic phenomenon' driven into anti-sacerdotal and sectarian opposition by Church repression after 1215. His heretics were sympathetic: the Spiritual Franciscans St Francis's true heirs; the condemners of Wyclif wreckers of real thought at Oxford; the burners of Huss guilty of tyranny and hypocrisy. Knowles and Beryl Smalley, his earlier readers, had read the manuscript; but so had Margaret Aston and Marjorie Reeves, who may be thought to represent the other side. Knowles reviewed the book tepidly in the *Times Literary Supplement*, and it had a very different dedicatee, Leff's former headmaster A. S. Neill of Summerhill, 'who has shown the perennial need for dissent'.[9] I doubt if Knowles was convinced of this need and, *propter hoc* or otherwise, it does not seem that he and Leff had much contact in the remaining years of Knowles's life.

There is something else to remember here. In 1969 Leff published a second edition of his attack on Marxism, *The Tyranny of Concepts*. It takes no great perception to read the book as subintending the sort of view of Catholicism expounded in *Heresy*: Marxism is 'one more closed system', a secular faith or religion, an orthodoxy creating heretics. 'The lesson of the failure of Marxism is that of any orthodoxy. The personal insights of the founder become lost and only its formal expression remains.' This was good news for Ockham, and not only because of his anti-papalism. The title of the book was something of a general philosophical programme: the trouble with Lenin, as with William of Champeaux, was that he '[took] mental categories for reality', a 'bondage' from which 'Ockham . . . and Bertrand Russell . . . have

[7] H. O. Evennett, *The Spirit of the Counter-Reformation* (Cambridge, 1968), ed. J. Bossy with a foreword by David Knowles, pp. 36, 41.

[8] Leff, *Medieval Thought*, pp. 279–91.

[9] Leff, *Heresy*, preface, pp. 1–22, 63, 573, 650–5; Ozment, *Age of Reform*, pp. 110 n.95, 168 n.83; *Times Literary Supplement*, 27 January 1968 – where Ockham the 'spoilt theologian' reappears. In *Paris and Oxford*, p. 308, Leff says, a year later, that he has changed his mind about Wyclif.

attempted to deliver men'. This was turning Knowles's parallel of Ockham and Lenin upside-down.[10]

While he was now being more chummy with Ockham, Leff does not yet seem to have changed his mind about what Ockham had said. The change was evidently the result of his re-immersing himself in Ockham's texts, and completed by October 1974, when he signed the preface to *William of Ockham*: his 'retraction' as he said. The revised Ockham, who was not a destroyer of scholasticism but a pruner of some of its more unwelcome growths, needed a new perspective on late medieval thought, of which Leff gave a rough sketch in *The Dissolution of the Medieval Outlook*. We were to think of this dissolution as: not achieved with a bang by Ockham but as taking more than three centuries to accomplish; limited, before the sixteenth century, by a clinging to the axioms of earlier scholasticism, Christian and Aristotelian; inhibited by an incoherent pluralism of initiatives, a loss of intellectual nerve and a lack of first-class minds; effected, eventually, by the Reformation and the scientific revolution; and, last, obstructed by a force of wilful inertia illustrated by the defence of geocentrism and the Counter-Reformation.[11] The last two points extended the impatience with Catholic orthodoxy expressed in *Heresy*, but look like shots in the dark; the first three amount to saying, I think, that there was no such thing as a coherent Ockhamism or nominalism which might colour much or most of late medieval thinking and have something to contribute to the theological future.

This negative conviction appears to have governed the three instances where the new vista entailed criticism of individuals. Two of them were from the Catholic side. Lagarde, in so far as he expounded a late-medieval individualism launched by Ockham, got short shrift in a brisk passage of *The Dissolution*. Lortzianism, as represented by Erwin Iserloh, was the object of almost the only polemic in *Ockham* for equating Ockham with Luther and claiming that he revolutionized ethics for the worse by substituting a subjective for an objective standard of value.[12] The third victim was a newcomer to the scene, Heiko Oberman, who had used the term 'nominalism' to

[10] *Tyranny*, pp. 1–3, 16, 44, 47. The first two quotations are from the 'Introduction' of 1969; the others I take it from the edition of 1961, which I have not seen.

[11] *Ockham*, p. xxiii; *Dissolution*, pp. 145–7.

[12] On Lagarde, *Dissolution*, pp. 22–3; *Heresy*, p. 10; *Ockham*, pp. 615–16, 620, 632, 643; on Iserloh, *Ockham*, pp. 470, 496–7, 500.

describe a theological tradition running from Ockham to the teachers of Luther via Pierre d'Ailly, Jean Gerson, and Gabriel Biel. 'The label of Nominalism', wrote Leff, 'lies like a pall – recently renewed – across the philosophy and theology of the fourteenth century.' True, he conceded that there might be some justification for it in the fifteenth and sixteenth centuries, which was what Oberman was writing about; but that was only because the 'philosophical context' of the fifteenth century was so feeble that it did not matter much what one said about it. Leff gave a strong impression that the term, and the idea that it described an identifiable tradition of thought, ought to be abandoned altogether.

That impression may be incorrect, but in any case the reaction seems excessive, and puzzling. Oberman was defending the 'catholicity of nominalism' against Lortz; so, crudely speaking, was Leff now defending the catholicity of Ockham. Oberman's ally Courtenay, in the article I have cited, was saying the same thing as Leff about the relation of the *potentia absoluta* and the *potentia ordinata* in Ockham's thought. It is true that Courtenay said something that Leff did not: that Ockham's legacy was theological rather than philosophical, and that its crux as a theology was the *pactum* or covenant embodied in 'verbal, contractual agreements' between God and man. But this was a fairly simple conclusion from the previous point about the *potentia ordinata*, on which Leff and Courtenay were agreed. So far as I know, Leff has not discussed the point; but it appears to contradict his general line about the fifteenth century which, as Ozment suspects, may still have owed a good deal to Gilson.[13]

I ought to explain why I should be venturing, as one not wise, into this debatable land. Some while ago, when trying to describe to myself some of the ways in which the transformation of western Christianity in the sixteenth century could be said to have elements which were common to all mainstream participants, I came upon what seemed to be a general shift in the moral system. In practice, the moral system of pre-Reformation Christianity seemed to me to turn on the Seven Deadly Sins, the moral system of all post-Reformation churches on the Ten Commandments. Looking for an explanation for this

[13] Heiko Augustinus Oberman, *The Harvest of Medieval Theology: Gabriel Biel and Late Medieval Nominalism* (Cambridge, MA, 1963; repr. Durham, NC, 1983); Leff, *Dissolution*, pp. 12–13. Oberman, pp. 423–8, on the 'catholicity of nominalism'; Courtenay, 'Nominalism and late medieval religion', pp. 50–1; Ozment, *Age of Reform*, p. 18 n.29.

alteration, I was pushed back behind the Reformation because to some degree the transition seemed to have happened already. The place I found to start was Ockham, interpreted fairly conventionally:

> If something was good, or conducive to human salvation, it was because God had sovereignly willed it so. . . . Hence there was no method by which Christians could determine what was good or bad, except to discover what God had actually commanded to be done or avoided. Ethics was a matter of faith, not of reason. This pointed to the Decalogue as the . . . moral code . . . for Christians, and not as a summary of what was naturally so [Aquinas's view], but as a free . . . expression of God's legislative will.

I then traced the conversion of this doctrine into practice via an apostolic succession in the *via moderna*, which resembled that of Oberman and Courtenay but proceeded via d'Ailly to Gerson, whom I thought central, and from Gerson to his German followers, among them the pre-Reformation preacher, Johannes Geiler.[14] I did not include Gabriel Biel, though it seems that I might have done. I illustrated its consequences by the well-known history of the sin of witchcraft during the fifteenth century, promoted from a shadowy and insecure place among the deadly sins to the prominent status of one of the principal forms of disobedience to the first commandment, against worshipping false gods. I took the process to be completed by the catechisms of the sixteenth century, and in the first place by Luther's *Shorter Catechism* of 1529, which began with the Commandments and owed a good deal to Gerson, whom Luther greatly respected. One of the things it owed to Gerson and his pre-Reformation successors was the version of the Commandments which it used, a non-scriptural form which went back to Augustine and was silent on the prohibition of graven images.[15]

This line of thought has been found fruitful by two sixteenth-century historians, one of whom has wondered about the particular genealogy I constructed.[16] It seems fairly clear that my story is

[14] 'Moral arithmetic: Seven Sins into Ten Commandments', in Edmund Leites, ed., *Conscience and Casuistry in Early Modern Europe* (Cambridge and Paris, 1988), pp. 214–34, quoted at pp. 221–2.

[15] Ibid., pp. 222–32.

[16] Stuart Clark, *Thinking with Demons: the Idea of Witchcraft in Early Modern Europe* (Oxford, 1997), and Fernando Cervantes, *The Devil in the New World: the Impact of Diabolism in New Spain* (New Haven, CT, and London, 1994); for whom see below, nn.27 and 28.

incompatible with Leff's later view of Ockham and his aftermath: for one thing, it claims that Ockham's ethics are purely supernatural, which Leff denies. It is ignorant of his warning against reviving the spectre of nominalism. Perhaps it reveals an unacknowledged debt to Knowles or Lortz or Lagarde; but in the present state of the field its most obvious affinity is to Oberman and Courtenay. They do not expressly affirm anything of the kind, indeed my suspicion is that they would find it unscholarly; but it sits rather comfortably with several items in their description of nominalist theology. I cite four such items: that in the *via moderna* morally commendable behaviour consists in obedience to God's commands; that the relation between it and human salvation depends, *stante lege* or under the present dispensation, on the pact(s) or covenant(s), the explicitly verbal agreements between God and man by which obedience to the Commandments is enjoined; that the concept of the *pactum* applies as much to the New Testament as to the Old; and that therefore the ethics of the New Testament is a New Law, the 'Law of Christ', and, to quote Gerson, 'sufficiently contained in the precepts of the Decalogue'.[17]

I can now add something particular to this general sense of affinity: it concerns my illustrative example of the consequences of Decalogue ethics, the history of the sin of witchcraft. In 1972 the Reformation historian Erik Midelfort, in the course of an account of the witch-hunt in south-western Germany, floated the idea that in the fifteenth-century formation of the updated witch-syndrome there might be a difference of *via moderna* and *via antiqua* traditions. His evidence was a set of sermons by the Tübingen theologian Martin Plantsch, published in 1507. His point was taken up by Oberman in an essay on Plantsch, and from the two of them the following things are clear. Plantsch was a theologian loyal to the *via moderna*, a pupil of Gabriel Biel and a fan of Gerson. He claimed that witches could not cause the *maleficia* they were supposed to effect: these were caused directly by God's will as a punishment for people's sins, and any other belief was 'vain credulity'. Oberman takes this to be an Ockhamist position about the non-independence of secondary causes. What was the matter with witches, according to Plantsch, was that they had violated the Commandments by entering into an alternative Church headed by the devil and a mirror-image of the true one, and had sought to use the real Church's

[17] Oberman, *Harvest of Medieval Theology*, pp. 108–19, 337 n.46.

sacraments and other rites to produce noxious effects. They could not actually do this because, short of a direct intervention of God's absolute power, sacraments and rituals did not work mechanically but in virtue of God's covenant.

As Midelfort and Oberman indicated, the object of Plantsch's polemic was the celebrated *Malleus maleficarum*, which could now be seen as a distinctive product of the *via antiqua*. This was evident from its Dominican authorship, its notion that witchcraft was principally sexual malefice, an offence against nature and charity, perhaps from its attitude to causality. It might also be detected from the papalism which sheltered its arguments under the umbrella of a papal bull: extreme papalism was a mark of the Dominican order around 1500. Free of such embarrassments, Plantsch's arguments could be picked up in Tübingen later on by Lutheran theologians following the authority of Johannes Brenz, who claimed that witches could not do the things they were alleged to do, but thought that they deserved death because of their apostasy and evil will.[18] Here we have a nominalist theory of witchcraft which amounted to the view that it was an offence against the first Commandment, and was acceptable to Lutherans. It seems a satisfactory confirmation of my proposal, as well as of the continuity and coherence of the nominalist tradition.

In other respects the proposal does not sit down so happily with Oberman–Courtenay: indeed a close investigation reveals divergences which, if there is something to be said for both sides, may suggest that Leff was correct to dismiss the theology of the fifteenth century as an incoherent pluralism. One of the difficulties arises from the importance in the history of Decalogue ethics which I attribute to another Dominican, Johannes Nider. Nider was, about equally it seems, a follower of Gerson and of Aquinas: he used their joint authority to compose a system of popular ethics which seems principally Gersonian; but in his compilation of evidence about witchcraft, in which he was a pioneer, he had rather more to say about its maleficent effects than about its entailment of apostasy in religion, and so provided a good deal of material for the authors of the *Malleus*. There were nominalist Dominicans, but it does not seem that Nider was one of them; despite

[18] H. C. Erik Midelfort, *Witch-Hunting in South-West Germany* (Stanford, CA, 1972), pp. 34–5 and n.7; Oberman, *Werden und Wertung der Reformation: vom Wegestreit zum Glaubenskampf* (Tübingen, 1977), pp. 201–33, English translation, *Masters of the Reformation* (Cambridge, 1981), pp. 158–83.

his veneration for Gerson he does not appear in the nominalist tradition as described by Oberman and Courtenay but, if anywhere, in the opposition to it from the *via antiqua*.[19] This seems unwarranted; but since I cannot claim to have found him a coherent position I had better admit that he may show that my story is too simple, and also exemplify Leff's strictures on fifteenth-century theology.

He also brings up a major difficulty of principle, which is that both Ockham and Biel seem determined to run together a voluntaristic account of God's commands with a substantial resort to the idea of natural law. In Ockham's case the term only appears in his political writings, where it is polemically used as a weapon against the papacy, and is said to be equivalent to divine law and deducible from the scriptures; what stands in for it in his moral doctrine is the notion of right reason as, to cite Leff revised, the immutable 'criterion of what should and should not be done'. Coplestone has scratched his head to try and reconcile this with the voluntarism of the divine commands, and we may feel much the same.[20] But in Biel's case the term 'natural law' is explicitly incorporated into the moral teaching, and is virtually identified with the Ten Commandments in what seems a quasi-Thomistic move.[21] Oberman says that this is not inconsistent with the voluntarist notion of good and evil to which Biel announces his firm allegiance, but it seems to require an act of faith to believe this. We have, at least I have, two problems. Either we have a persistent, and coherent, notion of natural law embedded in the moral teaching of the *via moderna*, in which case my idea of the primacy of the Commandments in its moral teaching proves inaccurate. Or we have a moral doctrine incoherent because attempting to please everyone, which would not have the strength to launch the transformation of popular morality for which I was arguing. The Leff of 1976 would be amply vindicated: at the climax of the *via moderna*, its moral doctrine either clings to outdated axioms, or timidly syncretizes. Perhaps it does both at once.

19 K. Schieler, *Magister Johannes Nider* (Mainz, 1885); A. Vacant, E. Mangenot et al., *DTC*, 11 (Paris, 1931), cols 851–4 ('Nyder, Jean'); Joseph Hansen, *Quellen und Untersuchungen zur Geschichte des Hexenwahns* (Bonn, 1901; repr. Hildesheim, 1963), pp. 88–99; 'Moral arithmetic', pp. 225, 231; Oberman, *Masters of the Reformation*, p. 174.

20 *Ockham*, pp. xxiii–xxiv, 620ff., esp. pp. 622, 476–526; F. C. Coplestone, *A History of Philosophy*, 3, *Ockham to Suarez* (London, 1960), pp. 104–9.

21 Oberman, *Harvest of Medieval Theology*, pp. 96, 101–2, 105, 107, 110; Alister McGrath, *The Intellectual Origins of the European Reformation* (Oxford, 1987), p. 85.

In this tight corner I look for a rescuer, and find him in a historian whose grasp on late medieval thought and religion is as strong as anyone else's, and whose thoughts about the *via moderna* embody a more worked-out story than theirs. I mean Francis Oakley, who has offered a solution to the problem about natural law. In an article published as long ago as 1961, whose conclusions he repeated in a short book twenty years later, Oakley claimed that when Ockham and his followers spoke of natural law they meant something different from what it had meant to Aquinas. He had meant, in a quasi-Platonic sense, 'external manifestations [laws] of an indwelling and immanent reason', something embedded in the constitution of the created universe; what they meant was a law externally imposed on man and the universe by divine *fiat*: 'The dictates of natural law, the rectitude of right reason, the very fact that it is virtuous to act according to right reason – all these amount from the human point of view to nothing more than inscrutable manifestations of the divine omnipotence.'[22] That being so, the problem about the survival of the concept of natural law in the *via moderna* seemed to disappear.

Oberman seems to have thought Oakley's original piece a shot from the 'Catholic' or Lortzian side, but I do not think that can be right. There are indeed differences between them. Oakley has a more active notion of the *potentia absoluta* than Oberman–Courtenay: it is not simply a theoretical possibility *dépassé* by God's actual decisions or a 'dialectical standby', but may entail actual interventions in the present universe of a miraculous kind. But altogether Oakley goes along quite happily with Oberman–Courtenay's revised nominalism, agrees that the notion of a *pactum* or covenant is central to the theology of the *via moderna*, and is particularly complimentary to Courtenay.[23] I shall assume that his distinction of different meanings of the term 'natural law' is correct. By the same token I seem bound to say that Leff's rejection of the idea of a coherent and even creative 'nominalist' tradition looks premature. Hence I may stick, more or less and until further notice, to my claim about the *via moderna* and the practical transformation of Christian ethics.

22 Francis Oakley, 'Christian theology and the Newtonian science: the rise of the concept of the laws of nature', *Church History*, 30 (1961), pp. 433–57; Idem, *Omnipotence, Covenant and Order* (Ithaca, NY, and London, 1984), pp. 52–6, 79–84, quotations at pp. 80, 82.

23 Oberman, *Harvest of Medieval Theology*, p. 91 n.5 (over page); Oakley, *Omnipotence*, pp. 50, 52, 61ff., 141 n.68.

This may be a conclusion more gratifying to my *amour-propre* than to a larger understanding of the legacy of Ockham. I am certainly not competent to write its history in the sixteenth and seventeenth centuries; but I think I can show that there are other, and probably better, reasons for believing that Leff's dismissal of an Ockhamist/nominalist tradition, if that was what he meant to do, was hasty. Taking my cue from his schema of the long-term 'dissolution of the medieval outlook', I divide them into reasons to do with the Reformation; with the Counter-Reformation; and with seventeenth-century philosophy, natural and other.

The relation between nominalism and the Reformation remains a problem. On the traditional 'Catholic' view there were two effects, positive and negative, and the positive effect was the more important. This was held to lie in a general similarity to Luther's of Ockham's view of God's relation to mankind. The negative effect lay in the particular idea of this relation under the Christian dispensation which was professed by Luther's nominalist teachers, and in Luther's explicit reaction against it when arriving at the doctrine of justification by faith. The positive and negative effects argued for are connected to the ideas of God's absolute and his ordained power respectively, and this line implies that the absolute power is the only one that really matters.

At the moment, the dominant voice on the topic in the English-speaking world is that of Alister McGrath, who appears to hold, in respect of Luther, that there is no good evidence for a positive input from nominalist theology by way of the *potentia absoluta*; he puts all the weight on the negative input, which turns on Luther's total rejection of the idea of a *pactum* or covenant governing human salvation, which is a matter of the *potentia ordinata*. He does, it is true, catch us on the wrong foot by wondering at some length whether what he has said is not true of Luther, is actually true of Calvin, to whom nominalist ideas may have been mediated in Paris by John Mair and others; or, to be more exact, whether the positive influence does not come from what he calls the *schola Augustiniana moderna* and its leading light Gregory of Rimini. Leff has deprecated such connections as being 'neither ascertainable nor particularly fruitful', and I should be bold indeed to offer a view here about Gregory, about Gregory's relation with Ockham, or about the well-foundedness of the term used to describe his 'school'. But I shall add that after a lot of head-scratching Steven Ozment does come out with a positive judgement: 'From Luther to the American Puritans the central religious problem of mainstream Protestantism became the certitude of salvation . . ., the trustworthiness of God's word and promises. It is not far-fetched to see here the legacy of Ockham.' We have seen good reason to respect Ozment's judgement in such matters, as indeed has Leff.[24]

Second, the Counter-Reformation. It will surprise not a few to find that there may be a subject here. One thing we all know about Luther is that he could not abide Dominican theology: the *via moderna* was gravely weakened among Catholics by his connection with it, and fell victim to the landslide which opened the way for the *reconquista* launched by the *via antiqua* from its redoubts in Italy and Spain. It reconquered the remaining Catholic world when the Jesuits took it up. Ockham's anti-papalism was enough in itself to damn him in this age of papalist *revanche*: at the Council of Trent there were Thomists and Scotists, but no Ockhamists. The only person connected with the Council who has been convincingly claimed to be an Ockhamist is its enemy Paolo Sarpi, in whose order of Servites the *via moderna* appears to have survived.[25]

But there is a group of credible authors who detect a nominalist underground persisting beneath the official doctrine of the Counter-Reformation. The line has been pursued independently by Coplestone, Francis Oakley, and most recently by Fernando Cervantes. It relates to Francisco Suarez. All of them agree that Suarez's apparent Thomism conceals an eclectic mixture of contributions from Thomas, Scotus, and Ockham. Suarez goes on about natural law, and explicitly rejects Ockham's will-founded notion of divine law; but none of the three believes that he really means what he says. Coplestone says that when he speaks of 'natural law' he really means what nominalists called the 'lex Christi'; Oakley takes him to be expounding the view of natural law as imposed on the Creation, not as immanent in it. If either of them is right, Suarez's Thomism is paper-thin.[26] Cervantes treats the question at some length in the context of a close discussion of theological attitudes to the Indians of New Spain: he is pleasing to

[24] McGrath, *Intellectual Origins*, pp. 94–121; Leff, *Gregory*, pp. 1–28, 235–42, quoted at p. 237; Ozment, *Age of Reform*, p. 244, and see the extract from Leff's review on the back cover.

[25] David Wotton, *Paolo Sarpi* (Cambridge, 1983), pp. 8, 17, 152 n.19. Perhaps the Servite theologian Mazocchi, who appears at Trent as a Scotist, was actually an Ockhamist: H. Jedin, *Papal Legate at the Council of Trent: Cardinal Seripando* (Saint Louis, MO, and London, 1947), pp. 366–9.

[26] Coplestone, *History of Philosophy*, 3, pp. 353–405, at p. 386; Oakley, *Omnipotence*, p. 82.

me because he takes up what I have had to say about the *via moderna* and the Ten Commandments. This concerns him because he finds Jesuit eclecticism exemplified generally by Suarez and particularly in the treatment of Indian religion by his fellow-Jesuit José de Acosta. Acosta is best known for his sympathetic, and no doubt Thomist, account of Indian civil culture and institutions; he should also be known for his contrasting conviction that Indian religion was a diabolically inspired parody of Christianity, which he borrowed, Cervantes thinks, from the witchcraft theory of the *via moderna*. This seems a good example of Jesuit theology that, as Cervantes says of Suarez, is particularly un-Thomist in its separations between the natural and the supernatural, matter and spirit, body and soul: in a climate of 'zeal for souls', which the Jesuits had largely created, it could hardly have been otherwise. We can expect Dominicans to have reasoned differently: I doubt if I shall be the only person to be tempted by Cervantes's notion of the Jesuit theology of the Counter-Reformation as being in good part a nominalism that dared not speak its name.[27]

Some of the same voices are also to be found in the small chorus which is now telling us that a condition *sine qua non* of the scientific revolution was the replacement of the Aristotelian by the Ockhamist notion of God: a being of will, decisions, and direct action imposing by his ordinary power the laws of nature and of mathematics, and reserving his absolute prerogative to suspend or change them, or to put things right when they went wrong. The notion was put forward by Oakley in 1961 in respect of Boyle and Newton; it has been taken up by Cervantes, proceeding forward from his account of Suarez to Cartesian philosophy, whose 'impetus came from an anti-teleological morality which found its source in the nominalist revolt against Aristotelian naturalism and the threat it seemed to pose to the sovereignty of God'. On the resurgence of Ockhamist ethics Oakley has a persuasive authority in the Cambridge Platonist Ralph Cudworth, and Cervantes another in Pierre Bayle. Most recently Stuart Clark in a weighty book on the idea of witchcraft has concluded that until perhaps 1720 the background of the new natural philosophy was a 'theology of nominalism and voluntarism' which was perfectly compatible with the modern idea of witchcraft. Clark, like Cervantes,

[27] Cervantes, *The Devil in the New World*, pp. 20–1, 23, 27–34.

has also found congenial the argument about Decalogue ethics outlined above.[28]

Many students, though perhaps not so many students of medieval thought, will be familiar with Michael Oakeshott's classic portrayal of the Thomas Hobbes of *Leviathan* as a nominalist. He is a nominalist: strictly, in his notions of the relations between names and things, and of insignificant speech; because he reasserts, in 'civil' philosophy, the grand tradition of Will and Artifice against the other grand tradition of Reason and Nature; and because, theologically, he holds that faith and 'reasoning' are opposites, since we can know nothing of God but his omnipotence and his revealed will, by which he has set up the 'law' called Christianity. For Christians, all law, including 'natural' law, is a divine command. He shifts, or perhaps simply extends, the burden of pre-Reformation nominalism by attributing to the mortal God, Leviathan, the power of saying what this law is, effectively of making it. This is the ungrounded sovereign will to whose commands, simply because they are commands, obedience is obligatory. We should be sorry to say goodbye to our nominalist Hobbes; and so would Leff, if we are to judge by the epigraph to *The Tyranny of Concepts*: 'For words are wise men's counters, they do but reckon by them; but they are the money of fools, that value them by the authority of an Aristotle, a Cicero, or a Thomas, or any other doctor whatsoever, if but a man.'[29]

[28] Oakley, 'Christian Theology and the Newtonian Science', and *Omnipotence*, pp. 69–92; Cervantes, *The Devil in the New World*, pp. 134, 144; Clark, *Thinking with Demons*, pp. 299, 502–5, and in general pp. 489–508.

[29] Thomas Hobbes, *Leviathan*, ed. M. Oakeshott (Oxford, 1946), pp. vii–lxvii, 22; Leff, *Tyranny*, title-page, which leaves out Cicero.

BIBLIOGRAPHY OF THE WRITINGS OF GORDON LEFF, 1956–98

by SIMON DITCHFIELD[1]

1956

'The fourteenth century and the decline of scholasticism', *P&P*, 9, pp. 30–41.

'Thomas Bradwardine's *De Causa Dei*', *JEH*, 7, pp. 21–9.

REVIEWS

E. Gilson, *History of Christian Philosophy in the Middle Ages* (London, 1955), *The Cambridge Review*, 77, 10 March 1956, pp. 446–7.

J. H. Mundy, R. W. Emery and B. N. Nelson, eds, *Essays in Medieval Life and Thought Presented in Honor of Austin Patterson Evans* (New York, 1955), *JEH*, 7, p. 27.

1957

Bradwardine and the Pelagians: a study of his De Causa Dei and its opponents, Cambridge Studies in Medieval Life and Thought, 2nd ser., vol. 5 (Cambridge University Press, Cambridge).

'A History of the Millennium', *Cambridge Review*, 79, 26 October, pp. 77–9.

REVIEWS

E. R. Fairweather, ed. and tr., *A Scholastic Miscellany: Anselm to Ockham*, Library of Christian Classics, 10 (London, 1956), *JEH*, 8, p. 270.

D. Roth, *Die Mittelalterliche Predigttheorie und das Manuale Curatorum des Johann Ulrich Sargant*, Basler Beiträge zur Geschichtswissenschaft, 58 (Basle and Stuttgart, 1956), *JEH*, 8, pp. 242–3.

1958

Medieval Thought: St Augustine to Ockham (Penguin Books, Harmondsworth).

'In search of the Millennium', *P&P*, 13, pp. 89–95.

'Manchester University', Cambridge Review, 79, 26 April, pp. 476–9.

REVIEWS

R. H. C. Davis, *A History of Medieval Europe from Constantine to St Louis* (London, 1957), *Cambridge Review*, 79, 25 Jan, p. 272.

P. Molinari, *Julian of Norwich: the teaching of a fourteenth-century English mystic* (London, 1958) and

[1] This bibliography could not have been compiled without the extensive collaboration of the dedicatee. My sincere thanks to him.

A. M. Reynolds, ed., Julian of Norwich, *A Shewing of God's Love: the shorter version* (London, 1958), *JEH*, 9, p. 243.

S. Runciman, *The Sicilian Vespers: A History of the Mediterranean World in the Later Thirteenth Century* (Cambridge, 1958), *Cambridge Review*, 79, 3 May, p. 513.

R. Vaughan, *Matthew Paris* (Cambridge, 1958), *Cambridge Review*, 10 May, p. 532.

R. Weiss, *Humanism in England during the fifteenth century*, 2nd edn (Oxford, 1957), *JEH*, 9, pp. 97–9.

1959

Medieval Thought: from Augustine to Ockham, hardback edition (Merlin Press, London).

'Faith and Reason in the Thought of Gregory of Rimini', *Bulletin of the John Rylands Library*, 42, pp. 88–112.

REVIEWS

S. M. Afnan, *Avicenna: his life and works* (London, 1958), *Cambridge Review*, 80, 17 January, p. 235.

K. Foster, ed. and tr., *The Life of St Thomas Aquinas: Biographical Documents* (London, 1959), *Cambridge Review*, 80, 13 June, p. 622.

H. A. Oberman, *Archbishop Thomas Bradwardine: A Fourteenth-Century Augustinian: A Study of His Theology in Its Historical Context* (Utrecht, 1958), *JThS*, ns, 10, pp. 188–90.

H. O. Taylor, *The Emergence of Christian Culture in the West: the classical heritage of the middle ages* (New York, 1958), *JEH*, 10, pp. 123–4.

1960

REVIEW

R. B. Brooke, *Early Franciscan Government: Elias to Bonaventure*, Cambridge Studies in Medieval Life and Thought, 2nd ser., 7 (Cambridge, 1959), *Cambridge Review*, 81, 20 February, p. 381.

1961

Gregory of Rimini: Tradition and Innovation in Fourteenth-Century Thought (Manchester University Press, Manchester).

The Tyranny of Concepts: a Critique of Marxism (Merlin, London).

'Heresy and the decline of the medieval Church', *P&P*, 20, pp. 36–51.

'The changing pattern of thought in the earlier fourteenth century', *Bulletin of the John Rylands Library*, 43, pp. 354–72.

'Gregory of Rimini: a fourteenth-century Augustinian', *Revue des Études Augustiniennes*, 7, pp. 153–70.

REVIEWS

M. Bloch, *Feudal Society* (London, 1961), *The Guardian*, 2 June, p. 9.

C. N. L. Brooke, *From Alfred to Henry III, 871–1272* (Oxford, 1961), *The Guardian*, 3 November, p. 8.

L. Hödl, *Die Geschichte der scholastischen Literatur und der Theologie der Schlüsselgewalt*, Beiträge zur Geschichte der Philosophie und Theologie des Mittelalters, Texte und Untersuchungen, 38 (Münster, 1960), *JThS*, ns, 12, pp. 124–5.

J. C. Holt, *The Northerners: a Study in the Reign of King John* (Oxford, 1961), *The Guardian*, 3 November, p. 8.

J. Huizinga, *Men and Ideas: History, the Middle Ages, the Renaissance; Essays* (London, 1960), *New Statesman*, 61, 20 January, pp. 104–6.

E. F. Jacob, *The Fifteenth Century* (Oxford, 1961), *The Guardian*, 24 November, p. 12.

M. H. Keen, *The Outlaws of Medieval Legend* (London, 1961), *The Guardian*, 30 June, p. 7.

B. Smalley, *English Friars and Antiquity in the Early Fourteenth Century* (Oxford, 1960), *JEH*, 12, pp. 241–2.

W. L. Warren, *King John* (London, 1961), *The Guardian*, 10 March, p. 7.

1962

REVIEWS

F. Heer, *The Medieval World, Europe 1100–1350* (London, 1961), *The Guardian*, 1 June, p. 6.

M. W. Labarge, *Simon de Montfort* (London, 1962), *Spectator*, 2 February, p. 146.

K. Popper, *The Poverty of Historicism*, 2nd edn (London, 1960), *Manchester Independent*, 2, p. 9.

J. A. Robson, *Wyclif and the Oxford Schools: the Relation of the 'Summa de Ente' to Scholastic Debate in the Later Fourteenth Century*, Cambridge Studies in Medieval Life and Thought, 2nd ser., 8 (Cambridge, 1961), *EHR*, 77, pp. 721–3.

M. Seidlmayer, *Currents of Medieval Thought with Special Reference to Germany* (Oxford, 1960), *EHR*, 77, pp. 138–9.

1963

Richard Fitzralph, Commentator of the Sentences: a Study in Theological Orthodoxy (Manchester University Press, Manchester).

The Tyranny of Concepts: a critique of Marxism (Philadelphia, Dufour editions), reprint of 1961 edn.

'Richard Fitzralph's "Commentary on the Sentences"', *Bulletin of the John Rylands Library*, 45, pp. 390–422.

REVIEWS

J. G. Bougerol, *Introduction à l'étude de saint Bonaventure* (Paris, 1961), *JThS*, ns, 14, pp. 213–14.

H. Cam, *Law-finders and Law-makers in Medieval England: Collected Studies in Legal and Constitutional History* (London, 1962) and.

D. Knowles, *The Evolution of Medieval Thought* (London, 1962), *New Statesman*, 11 January, p. 50.

A. duPont Breck, ed., *Johannis Wyclyf: Tractatus de Trinitate*, Studies and Texts in Medieval Thought, 3 (Boulder, CO, 1962), *JEH*, 14, pp. 96–7.

J. Pieper, *Scholasticism: personalities and problems of medieval philosophy*, trans. R. and C. Winston (London, 1961), *Philosophical Quarterly*, 13, p. 176.

R. Ridolfi, *The Life of Niccolò Machiavelli* (London, 1963), *The Guardian*, 15 February, p. 7.

1964

REVIEWS

W. Breuning, *Die hypostatische Union in der Theologie Wilhelms von Auxerre, Hugos von St Cher und Rolands von Cremona*, Trierer Theologische Studien (Trier, 1962), *JThS*, ns, 15, pp. 199–201.

D. Knowles, *The Evolution of Medieval Thought* (London, 1962), *EHR*, 79, pp. 577–8.

H. A. Oberman, *The Harvest of Medieval Theology: Gabriel Biel and Late Medieval Nominalism*, (Cambridge, MA, Oxford, and London, 1963), *JEH*, 15, pp. 108–9.

L. R. Wynar, *S. Harrison Thomson: Bio-bibliography*, Bio-bibliographical Series, 1 (Boulder, CO, 1963), *Medium Aevum*, 33, pp. 242–3.

1965

REVIEWS

R. Guardini, *Systembildende Elemente in der Theologie Bonaventuras: die Lehren vom lumen mentis, von der gradatio entium, und der influentia sensus et motus*, Studia et Documenta Franciscana, 3 (London, 1964), *JThS*, ns, 16, pp. 531–2.

J. Hofmeier, *Die Trinitätslehre des Hugo von St Viktor dargestellt im Zusammenhang mit den trinitarischen Strömungen seiner Zeit*, Münchener theologische Studien, II, Systematische Abteilung, 25 (Munich, 1963), *JThS*, ns, 16, pp. 238–9.

Oxford studies presented to Daniel Callus, Oxford Historical Society, ns, 16 (Oxford, 1964), *JEH*, 16, pp. 239–40.

William of Ockham, *Opera Politica*, vol. 2, ed. R. F. Bennett and H. S. Offler (Manchester, 1963), *EHR*, 80, p. 150.

J. R. Weinberg, *A Short History of Medieval Philosophy* (London, 1963), *JThS*, ns, 16, pp. 532–3.

1966

'John Wyclif: the Path to Dissent' (Raleigh Lecture), *PBA*, 52, pp. 143–80.

BROADCASTS

'The Medieval Crisis I: William of Ockham and his School' (The Third Programme, BBC), printed in *The Listener*, 75, 13 January, pp. 61, 68.

'The Medieval Crisis II: Nicholas of Cusa' (The Third Programme, BBC), printed in *The Listener*, 75, 10 February, pp. 203–5.

REVIEWS

W. H. Principe, *The Theology of the Hypostatic Union in the Early Thirteenth Century*, vol. 1, *William of Auxerre's Theology of the Hypostatic Union*, Pontifical Institute of Medieval Studies, Studies and Texts, 7 (Toronto, 1963), *JThS*, ns, 17, p. 273.

J. B. Russell, *Dissent and Reform in the Early Middle Ages* (Berkeley and Los Angeles, CA, 1965), *Theology*, 49 (November), p. 521.

J. D. Tooke, *The Just War in Aquinas and Grotius* (London, 1965), *History*, 51, pp. 211–12.

C. Wackenheim, *La faillité de la religion d'après Karl Marx* (Paris, 1963), *Philosophical Quarterly*, 16, p. 92.

1967

Heresy in the Later Middle Ages: the Relation of Heterodoxy to Dissent c. 1250–c. 1450, 2 vols (Manchester University Press, Manchester; Barnes & Noble, New York).

Middeleeuwse wijsbegeerte, Aula boeken, 312 (Het Spectrum, Antwerp and Utrecht), Dutch translation of *Medieval Thought: St Augustine to Ockham*.

'The Apostolic ideal in later medieval ecclesiology', *JThS*, ns 18, pp. 58–82.

In P. Edwards, ed., *Encyclopedia of Philosophy* (Macmillan, London and New York):

- 'D'Ailly, Pierre' (1, pp. 61–2).
- 'Albert of Saxony' (1, pp. 63–4).
- 'Thomas Bradwardine' (1, p. 363).
- 'Burley, Walter' (1, pp. 431–2).
- 'Giles of Rome' (3, pp. 331–2).
- 'Gregory of Rimini' (3, p. 390).
- 'John of Mirecourt' (4, pp. 282–3).
- 'Marsilius of Inghen' (5, p. 166).
- 'Swineshead', Richard (8, p. 53).

REVIEWS

E. Anagnine, *Dolcino e il movimento ereticale all'inizio del trecento* (Florence, 1964), *JEH*, 18, p. 278.

F. Heer, *The Intellectual History of Europe* (London, 1966), *History*, 52, pp. 405–6.

J. B. Russell, *Dissent and Reform in the Early Middle Ages* (Berkeley and Los Angeles, CA, 1965), *Medium Aevum*, 36, pp. 100–1.

W. Ullmann, *A History of Political Thought* (Harmondsworth, 1965), *EHR*, 82, pp. 378–9.

1968

Paris and Oxford Universities in the Thirteenth and Fourteenth Centuries: an Institutional and Intellectual History (John Wiley, New York, London, and Sydney).

'Wyclif and Hus: a doctrinal comparison', *Bulletin of the John Rylands Library*, 50, pp. 387–410.

'Hérésie savante et hérésie populaire dans le bas moyen âge', J. Le Goff, ed., *Hérésie et sociétés dans l'Europe préindustrielle, 11e–18e siècles. Communications et débats du Colloque du Royaumont* (Mouton, Paris, and the Hague), pp. 219–25, comments and reply, pp. 226–17, comments on other papers, pp. 103, 136–7, 216–17, 301.

REVIEWS

F. Rörig, *The Medieval Town* (London, 1967), *Times Literary Supplement*, 6 June, p. 573.

G. Schrimpf, *Die Axiomenschrift des Boethius (De Hebdomadibus) als Philosophisches Lehrbuch des Mittelalters*, Studien zur Problemgeschichte der antiken und mittelalterlichen Philosophie, 2 (Leiden, 1966), *Philosophical Quarterly*, 18, pp. 364–5.

W. Ullmann, *The Individual and Society in the Middle Ages* (London, 1967), *History*, 53, p. 414.

1969

History and Social Theory (Merlin, London; University of Alabama Press, University, Alabama).

The Tyranny of Concepts: a Critique of Marxism, 2nd edn (Merlin, London; University of Alabama Press, Alabama).

'Knowledge and its relation to the status of theology according to Ockham', *JEH*, 20, pp. 7–17.

'The Birth of Oxford and Cambridge', *History of the English Speaking Peoples* (Purnell, London), 2, pp. 619–22.

'Wyclif and his heresy', ibid., pp. 749–52.

In A. Richardson, ed., *A Dictionary of Christian Theology* (London, 1969),
'Nominalism-Realism', pp. 232–3.
'Thomism', pp. 236–9.

BROADCAST

'The Past and the New' (The Third Programme, BBC), printed in *The Listener*, 81, 10 April.

REVIEWS

William of Ockham, *Opera theologica*, vol. 1, *Scriptum in librum primum sententiarum, Ordinatio, Prologus et Distinctio prima*, ed. S. Gál and S. Brown (New York, 1967), *JEH*, 20, p. 172.

W. H. Principe, *The Theology of the Hypostatic Union in the Early Thirteenth Century*, vol. 2, *Alexander of Hales' Theology of the Hypostatic Union*, Pontifical Institute of Medieval Studies, Studies and Texts, 12 (Toronto, 1967), *JThS*, ns 20, pp. 673–4.

G. L. Seidler, *The Emergence of the Eastern World: Seven Essays on Political Ideas* (Oxford, 1968), *History*, 54, pp. 267–8.

1970

'Wyclif and the Augustinian tradition, with special reference to his *De Trinitate*', *Medievalia et Humanistica*, ns, 1, pp. 29–39.

BROADCAST

Participant in 'Evil in History', BBC 1, 10 March.

REVIEW ESSAYS

'The Medieval University', *History of Education Quarterly*, 10, pp. 492–5.

'When History (and God) is on your side', *Encounter*, 35, November, pp. 83–6.

REVIEWS

R. R. Betts, *Essays in Czech History* (London, 1969) and

M. Spinka, *John Hus: a biography* (Princeton, NJ, 1968), *History*, 55, pp. 103–4.

Pierre Falco, *Questions disputées ordinaires*, ed. A.-J. Gondras, 3 vols. Analecta Mediaevalia Namurcensia, 22, 23, 24 (Louvain and Paris, 1968), *JEH*, 21, pp. 183–4.

M. E. Reeves, *The Influence of Prophecy in the Later Middle Ages: a Study in Joachism* (Oxford, 1969), *Medium Aevum*, 38, pp. 351–5.

E. A. Synan, ed., *The Works of Richard Campsall*, vol. 1, *Questiones super Librum Priorum Analeticorum*, Pontifical Institute of Medieval Studies (Toronto, 1968), *JEH*, 21, pp. 283–4.

C. Thouzellier, *Catharisme et valdéisme en Languedoc à la fin du XIIe siècle et au début du XIIIe siècle*, Publications de la Faculté des lettres et sciences humaines de Paris, Recherches, 27, 2nd edn (Louvain and Paris, 1969), *Medium Aevum*, 39, pp. 364–6.

1971

History and Social Theory (Doubleday, Garden City, NY), Anchor paperback reprint of 1969 edition.

'The making of the myth of a true Church', *Journal of Medieval and Renaissance Studies*, I, pp. 1–15.

REVIEWS

M. L. Colish, *The Mirror of Language: A Study in the Medieval Theory of Knowledge* (New Haven, CT, and London, 1968), *EHR*, 86, pp. 161–2.

William of Ockham, *Opera Theologica, 2, Scriptum in librum Primum Sententiarum, Ordinatio, Distinctiones II–III*, ed. S. Gál and S. Brown (New York, 1970), *JEH*, 22, p. 282.

H. Heimpel, ed., *Drei Inquisitions-Verfahren aus dem Jahr 1425: Akten der Prozesse gegen die deutschen Hussiten Johannes Drändorf und Peter Turnau sowie gegen Drändorfs Diener Martin Borchard*, Veröffentlichungen des Max-Planck-Instituts für Geschichte, 24 (Göttingen, 1969), *EHR*, 86, p. 613.

D. Luscombe, *The School of Peter Abelard: The Influence of Abelard's Thought in the Early Scholastic Period*, Cambridge Studies in Medieval Life and Thought, 2nd ser., 14 (Cambridge, 1969), *EHR*, 86, pp. 160–1.

A. Marwick, *The Nature of History* (London, 1970) and

J. H. Plumb, *The Death of the Past* (London, 1969), *History*, 56, pp. 326–7.

I. Mészáros, ed., *Aspects of History and Class Consciousness* (London, 1971), *Times Literary Supplement*, 9 July, p. 801.

W. L. Wakefield and A. P. Evans, eds, *Heresies of the High Middle Ages: selected sources translated and annotated*, Records of Civilization, Sources and Studies, 81 (New York and London, 1969), *JEH*, 22, pp. 139–140.

1972

'Models inherent in history', *The Rules of the Game: Cross-Disciplinary Essays on Models in Scholarly Thought*, ed. T. Shanin (Tavistock Publications, London), pp. 149–60.

REVIEWS

G. R. Elton, *Political History: principles and practice* (London, 1970), *History*, 57, pp. 92–3.

R. A. Humphreys, *The Royal Historical Society 1868–1968* (London, 1969), *History*, 57, p. 94.

R. E. Lerner, *The Heresy of the Free Spirit in the Later Middle Ages* (Los Angeles, Berkeley, and London, 1972), *Times Literary Supplement*, 27 October, p. 1295.

T. Manteuffel, *Naissance d'une hérésie: les Adeptes de la pauvreté volontaire au moyen âge* (Paris and The Hague, 1970), *EHR*, 87, p. 606.

C. Thouzellier, *Hérésies et hérétiques: vaudois, cathares, patarins, albigeois*, Storia e Letteratura, 116 (Rome, 1969), *EHR*, 87, pp. 165–6.

1973

'Christian thought', in *Literature and Western Civilization*, ed. D. Daiches and A. K. Thorlby (Aldus, London, 1972–), 2, *The Medieval World* (1973), pp. 191–243.

REVIEWS

F. C. Copleston, *A History of Medieval Philosophy* (London, 1973), *JEH*, 24, p. 436.

W. Eckermann, *Der Physikkommentar Hugolins von Orvieto OESA: ein Beitrag zur Erkenntnislehre des spätmittelalterlichen Augustinismus*, Spätmittelalter und Reformation, Texte und Untersuchungen, 5 (Berlin and New York, 1972), *JEH*, 24, pp. 436–7.

The Letters of John Hus, trans. M. Spinka (Manchester, 1972), and

R. Friedenthal, *Ketzer und Rebell: Jan Hus und das Jahrhundert der Revolutionskriege* (Munich, 1972), *Times Literary Supplement*, 2 February, p. 127.

S. Ozment, *Mysticism and Dissent: Religious Ideology and Social Protest in the Sixteenth Century* (New Haven, CT, and London, 1973), *Times Literary Supplement*, 1 June, p. 619.

E. Peters, *The Shadow King: 'Rex Inutilis' in Medieval Law and Literature, 751–1327* (New Haven and London, 1970), *EHR*, 88, pp. 162–3.

1974

In P. P. Wiener ed., *Dictionary of the History of Ideas. Studies of Selected Pivotal Ideas* (Charles Scribner's Sons, New York, 1973–):

'Heresy in the Middle Ages', 2, pp. 416–24.

'Prophecy in the Middle Ages', 3, pp. 664–9.

REVIEWS

F. de Boor, *Wyclif's Simoniebegriff: die theologischen und kirchenpolitischen Grundlagen der Kirchenkritik John Wyclifs*, Arbeiten zur Kirchengeschichte und Religionswissenschaft, 3 (Halle, 1970), *EHR*, 89, p. 164.

A. S. McGrade, *The Political Thought of William of Ockham: Personal and Institutional Principles*, Cambridge Studies in Medieval Life and Thought, 3rd ser., 7 (Cambridge, 1974), *Times Literary Supplement*, 2 August, p. 827.

Hayden V. White, *Metahistory: the Historical Imagination in Nineteenth-Century Europe* (Baltimore and London, 1973), *Pacific Historical Review*, 43, pp. 598–600.

M. E. Reeves and B. Hirsch-Reich, *The Figurae of Joachim of Fiore* (Oxford, 1972), *Medium Aevum*, 43, pp. 885–8.

J. B. Russell, *Witchcraft in the Middle Ages* (Ithaca, NY, and London, 1972), *EHR*, 89, pp. 884–5.

1975

William of Ockham: the Metamorphosis of Scholastic Discourse (Manchester University Press, Manchester; Rowman and Littlefield, Totowa, NJ).

Paris and Oxford Universities in the Thirteenth and Fourteenth Centuries: an Institutional and Intellectual History (R. E. Krieger Pub. Co., Huntingdon, NY), reprint of 1968 edition.

REVIEWS

R. B. Brooke, *The Coming of the Friars*, Historical Problems: Studies and Documents, 24 (London and New York, 1975), *The Times Higher Education Supplement*, 28 November, p. 22.

B. Smalley, *The Becket Conflict and the Schools. A Study of Intellectuals in Politics in the Twelfth Century* (Oxford, 1973), *EHR*, 90, pp. 360–1.

W. Ullmann, *Law and Politics* (London, 1975), *The Times Literary Supplement*, 8 August, p. 901.

W. L. Wakefield, *Heresy, Crusade and Inquisition in Southern France, 1100–1250* (Berkeley, Los Angeles and London, 1974), *EHR*, 90, p. 883.

1976

The Dissolution of the Medieval Outlook: an Essay on Intellectual and Spiritual Change in the Fourteenth Century (Harper & Row, New York and London), Harper Torchbook paperback.

'Augustinianismus im Mittelalter', *Theologische Realenzyklopädie* (Walter de Gruyter, Berlin and New York), 4, pp. 699–717.

'Ockham and Wyclif on the Eucharist', *Reading Medieval Studies*, 2, pp. 1–13.

REVIEWS

A. B. Cobban, *The Medieval Universities: their Development and Organisation* (London, 1975), *History*, 61, p. 248.

N. Cohn, *Europe's Inner Demons: an Enquiry Inspired by the Great Witch-Hunt* (London, 1975), *EHR*, 91, p. 412.

C. Erickson, *The Medieval Vision: Essays in History and Perception* (Oxford, 1976) and

E. Power, *Medieval Women* (Cambridge, 1975), *Times Higher Education Supplement*, 18 June, p. 17.

A. S. McGrade, *The Political Thought of William of Ockham. Personal and Institutional Principles*, Cambridge Studies in Medieval Life and Thought, 3rd ser., 7 (Cambridge, 1974), *Ampleforth Journal*, 81, pp. 47–8.

R. I. Moore, ed. and trans., *The Birth of Popular Heresy*, Documents of Medieval History, 1 (London, 1975) and

H. R. Loyn and J. Percival, ed. & trans., *The Reign of Charlemagne: Documents on Carolingian Government and Administration*, Documents of Medieval History, 2 (London, 1975), *Times Higher Education Supplement*, 9 January, p. 15.

J. A. Weisheipl, *Friar Thomas D'Aquino: his Life, Thought and Works* (Oxford, 1975), *EHR*, 91, p. 895.

1977

REVIEWS

M. D. Lambert, *Medieval Heresy. Popular Movements from Bogomil to Hus* (London, 1977), *Times Literary Supplement*, 1 July, p. 811.

A. Patschovsky, *Die Anfänge einer ständigen Inquisition in Böhmen. Ein Prager Inquisitoren – Handbuch aus der ersten Hälfte des 14. Jahrhunderts*, Beiträge zur Geschichte und Quellenkunde des Mittelalters, 3 (Berlin and New York, 1975), *EHR*, 92, p. 888.

1978

REVIEWS

R. I. Moore, *The Origins of European Dissent* (London, 1977), *Times Literary Supplement*, 26 May, p. 588.

N. H. Steneck, *Science and Creation in the Middle Ages: Henry Langenstein (d. 1397) on Genesis* (Notre Dame and London, 1976), *British Journal for the History of Science*, 11, pp. 285–7.

1979

REVIEW ARTICLES

'The diversity of history', *Encounter*, 52, April 1979, pp. 50–8, 'Catching up: Europe in the Middle Ages': a composite review of the following works:

J. Richards, *The Popes and the Papacy in the Early Middle Ages* (London, 1979).

F. Barlow, *The English Church, 1066–1154* (London, 1979).

T. N. Bisson, *Conservation of Coinage: Monetary Exploitation and its Restraint in France, Catalonia and Aragon (c. A. D. 1000–c. 1225)* (Oxford, 1979).

H. Soly and C. Lis, *Poverty and Capitalism in Pre-Industrial Europe, 1350–1850* (Brighton, 1979).

L. White, Jr, *Medieval Religion and Technology* (California, 1978).

L. K. Little, *Religious Poverty and the Profit Economy in Medieval Europe* (London, 1978).

J. Le Goff, *The Dawn of Modern Banking* (New Haven, CT, and London, 1979).

D. Baker, ed., *Medieval Women: dedicated and presented to Rosalind M. T. Hill on the occasion of her seventieth birthday*, SCH. S, 1 (Oxford, 1978).

REVIEWS

M. T. Clanchy, *From Memory to Written Record 1066–1307* (London, 1979), *Times Literary Supplement*, 2 December, p. 169.

R. Kalivoda, *Revolution und Ideologie: der Hussitismus* (Cologne and Vienna, 1976), *EHR*, 94, pp. 75–6.

1980

'The Franciscan Concept of Man', in A. Williams, ed., *Prophecy and Millenarianism: Essays in Honour of Marjorie Reeves* (Longman, London), pp. 219–37.

REVIEWS

G. R. Evans, *Anselm and a New Generation* (Oxford, 1980), *Times Literary Supplement*, 4 July, p. 767.

S. Ozment, *The Age of Reform, 1250–1550* (New Haven, CT, and London, 1980), *Times Literary Supplement*, 31 October, p. 1232.

M. E. Reeves, *Joachim of Fiore and the Prophetic Future* (London, 1976), *Medium Aevum*, 49, p. 168 and *Ampleforth Journal*, 86 (1980), p. 129.

N. P. Tanner, *Heresy Trials in the Diocese of Norwich 1428–31*, RHS, Camden 4th ser., 20 (London, 1977), *Medium Aevum*, 49, p. 168.

E. P. Thompson, *The Poverty of Theory and Other Essays* (London, 1980), *Cambridge Quarterly*, 9, pp. 173–6.

Gregory of Rimini, *Lectura super primum et secundum sententiarum*, 4, *Super secundum (dist. 1–5)*, ed. A. D. Trapp, Spätmittelalter und Reformation, Texte und Untersuchungen, 9 (Berlin and New York, 1979), *JEH*, 31, pp. 385–6.

1981

REVIEWS

A. Black, *Council and Commune: the Conciliar Movement and the Fifteenth-Century Heritage* (London, 1979), *Times Higher Education Supplement*, 8 February, p. 21.

J. Marenbon, *From the Circle of Alcuin to the School of Auxerre: Logic, Theology and Philosophy in the Early Middle Ages*, Cambridge Studies in Medieval Life and Thought, 3rd ser., 15 (Cambridge, 1981), *British Book News*, September 1981, p. 526.

T. C. Potts, *Conscience in Medieval Philosophy* (Cambridge, 1980), *Times Higher Education Supplement*, 3 April, p. 16, and *British Book News*, March 1981, p. 143.

D. C. Steinmetz, *Luther and Staupitz: an Essay in the Intellectual Origins of the Protestant Reformation*, Duke Monographs in Medieval and Renaissance Studies, 4 (Durham, NC, 1980), *American Historical Review*, 86, pp. 1107–8.

B. Tierney and P. Linehan, eds, *Authority and Power: Studies on Medieval Law and Government Presented to Walter Ullmann on his Seventieth Birthday* (Cambridge, 1980), *Times Literary Supplement* 13 March, p. 276.

K. Walsh, *A Fourteenth-Century Scholar and Primate: Richard FitzRalph in Oxford, Avignon and Armagh* (Oxford, 1981), *Times Literary Supplement*, 20 November, p. 1371.

William of Ockham, *Opera philosophica et theologica*, 9, *Quodlibeta septem*, ed. J. C. Wey (New York, 1980), *JEH*, 32, pp. 554–5.

1982

REVIEWS

C. H. Clough, ed., *Profession, Vocation and Culture in Later Medieval England: Essays Dedicated to the Memory of A. L. Myers* (Liverpool, 1982), *Times Higher Education Supplement*, 8 October, p. 22.

J. Cohen, *The Friars and the Jews: the Evolution of Medieval Antijudaism* (London, 1982), *Times Literary Supplement*, 5 November, p. 1208.

M. Gibson, ed., *Boethius. His Life, Thought and Influence* (Oxford, 1981) and

H. Chadwick, *Boethius. The Consolations of Music, Logic, Theology and Philosophy* (Oxford, 1981), *Times Higher Education Supplement*, 15 January, p. 12; also reviewed together in *British Book News*, March, p. 144.

Hugolino of Orvieto, *Commentarius in Quattuor Libros Sententiarum*, 1, ed. W. Eckermann, Cassiciacum, Supplement volume, 8 (Würzburg, 1980), *JEH*, 33, pp. 327–8.

Richard Kieckhefer, *Repression of Heresy in Medieval Germany* (Liverpool, 1979), *EHR*, 97, pp. 176–7.

N. Kretzmann, A. Kenny, and J. Pinborg, eds, *The Cambridge History of Later Medieval Philosophy. From the Rediscovery of Aristotle to the Disintegration of Scholasticism, 1100–1600* (Cambridge, 1982), *Times Higher Education Supplement*, 7 May, p. 22; also in *British Book News*, June, pp. 344–5.

J. McEvoy, *The Philosophy of Robert Grosseteste* (Oxford, 1982), *Times Higher Education Supplement*, 5 November, p. 17.

B. McGinn, *Visions of the End: Apocalyptic Traditions in the Middle Ages*, Records of Civilisation, 96 (New York, 1979), *Literature and History*, 8, pp. 257–8.

1983

REVIEWS

J. Croall, *Neill of Summerhill: the Permanent Rebel* (London, 1983), *Times Higher Education Supplement*, 15 July, p. 16.

G. E. Hughes, ed. and trans., *John Buridan on Self-Reference: chapter eight of Buridan's Sophismata* (Cambridge, 1982), *British Book News*, March, p. 155.

H. A. Oberman, ed., *Gregor von Rimini: Werk und Wirkung bis zur Reformation*, Spätmittelalter und Reformation, Texte und Untersuchungen, 20 (Berlin and New York, 1981), *JEH*, 34, p. 304.

V. J. Scattergood and J. Sherborne, eds, *English Court Culture in the Later Middle Ages* (London, 1983), *Times Higher Education Supplement*, 25 March, p. 21.

1984

'John Wyclif's religious doctrines', *Churchman*, 98, pp. 319–28.

'John Wyclif as a religious reformer', *Lambeth Palace Library: Annual Report* (1984), pp. 21–9.

REVIEWS

J. I. Catto, ed., *The Early Oxford Schools* (Oxford, 1984), in T. H. Aston, ed., *The History of the University of Oxford*, 1, *Times Higher Education Supplement*, 2 November, p. 31.

H. E. J. Cowdrey, *The Age of Abbot Desiderius: Montecassino, the Papacy and the Normans in the Eleventh and Early Twelfth Centuries* (Oxford, 1983) and

J. H. Van Engen, *Rupert of Deutz*, Publications of the Center for Medieval and Renaissance Studies, 18 (California, 1983), *Times Literary Supplement*, 3 February, p. 122.

D. L. Wagner, ed., *The Seven Liberal Arts in the Middle Ages* (Indiana, 1983), *Times Higher Education Supplement*, 27 April, p. 16.

1985

'The Bible and rights in the Franciscan disputes on poverty', in K. Walsh and D. Wood, eds, *The Bible in the Medieval World: Essays in Memory of Beryl Smalley*, SCH. S, 4 (Blackwells; Oxford), pp. 225–35.

REVIEWS

A. Kenny, *Wyclif* (Oxford, 1985), and

I. J. Mueller, together with A. Kenny and P. V. Spade, ed. and trans., John Wyclif, *Tractatus de Universalibus*, 2 vols (Oxford, 1985), *Times Literary Supplement*, 9 August, p. 885.

M. Oakeshott, *On History and Other Essays* (Oxford, 1983), *EHR*, 100, pp. 953–4.

J. Pelikan, *The Christian Tradition: a History of the Development of Doctrine*, 4, *Reformation of Church and Dogma (1300–1700)* (Chicago, 1984), *Theology*, 88, pp. 468–71.

1986

'Wyclif and Hus: a doctrinal comparison', in A. Kenny, ed., *Wyclif in His Times* (Clarendon Press, Oxford), pp. 105–25 (an updated version of the article which originally appeared in the *Bulletin of the John Rylands Library*, 50, 1968).

REVIEWS

R. Brecher, *Anselm's argument: the Logic of Divine Existence*, Avebury Series in Philosophy (Aldershot, 1985) and

R. Gruner, *Philosophies of History: a Critical Essay*, Avebury Series in Philosophy (Aldershot, 1985), *British Book News*, January, p. 19.

R. E. Lerner, *The Powers of Prophecy: the Cedar of Lebanon Vision from the Mongol Onslaught to the Dawn of the Enlightenment* (California, 1985), *History*, 71, pp. 84–5.

J. Pelikan, *The Christian Tradition: a History of the Development of Doctrine*, 4,

Reformation of Church and Dogma (1300–1700) (Chicago, 1984), *International History Review*, 8, pp. 158–60.

1987

'The place of metaphysics in Wyclif's Theology', in A. Hudson and M. Wilks, eds, *From Ockham to Wyclif*, SCH. S, 5 (Blackwells, Oxford), pp. 217–32.

'Herejía culta y herejía popular en la Baja Edad Media', in J. Le Goff, ed., *Herejías y sociedades en la Europa preindustrial, siglos XI–XVIII. Comunicaciones y debates del Coloquio de Royaumont (1962)*, Historia de los Movimentos Sociales (Siglo Veintiuno de España Editores, Madrid), pp. 167–71, translation of 'Hérésie savante et hérésie populaire dans le bas moyen âge', in J. Le Goff, ed., *Hérésie et sociétés dans l'Europe préindustrielle, 11e–18e siècles: Communications et débats du Colloque du Royaumont* (Mouton, Paris, and The Hague, 1968), pp. 219–25.

In M. Eliade, ed., *Encyclopedia of Religion* (Macmillan, London and New York):
'Cathari' (3, pp. 115–17).
'Waldensians' (15, pp. 327–8).
'William of Ockham' (15, pp. 383–4).

1988

In J. Cannon, *et al.*, eds, *The Blackwell Dictionary of Historians* (Blackwell, Oxford):
'Wilhelm Dilthey' (pp. 106–7).
'Charles Howard McIlwain' (pp. 262–3).
'Philosophy of History' (pp. 323–5).

REVIEWS

J. A. Burrow, *The Ages of Man: a Study in Medieval Writing and Thought* (Oxford, 1986),
M. Dove, *The Perfect Age of Man's Life* (Cambridge, 1986) and
E. Sears, *The Ages of Man: Medieval Interpretations of the Life Cycle* (Princeton, 1986), *EHR*, 103, pp. 101–4.

A. E. McGrath, *The Intellectual Origins of the European Reformation* (Oxford, 1987), *Theology*, 91, pp. 431–3.

H. A. Oberman, *The Dawn of the Reformation: Essays in Late Medieval and Early Reformation Thought* (Edinburgh, 1986), *Theology*, 91, pp. 229–32.

1989

'Inventions of Medieval Minds', *Times Higher Education Supplement*, 'Europe's Universities' supplement, p. viii.

REVIEWS

J. H. Burns, ed., *The Cambridge History of Medieval Political Thought c. 350–c.1450* (Cambridge, 1988),

P. Dronke, ed., *A History of Twelfth-Century Philosophy* (Cambridge, 1988), and

J. J. O'Meara, *Eriugena* (Oxford, 1988), *Times Literary Supplement*, 7 July, p. 756.

Hugolino of Orvieto, *Commentarius in Quattuor Libros Sententiarum*, 2, ed. W. Eckermann, Cassiciacum, Supplement volume, 9 (Würzburg, 1984), and

3, ed. W. Eckermann and V. Marcolino, Cassiciacum, Supplement volume, 10 (Würzburg, 1986), *JEH*, 40, pp. 307–8.

P. Gradon ed., *English Wycliffite Sermons*, 2 (Oxford, 1988), *JThS*, ns 40, pp. 667–8.

P. Raedts, *Richard Rufus of Cornwall and the Tradition of Oxford Theology* (Oxford, 1987), *History*, 74, pp. 294–5.

1990

REVIEWS

M. H. Shanks, *'Unless You Believe, You Shall Not Understand': Logic, University and Society in Late Medieval Vienna* (Princeton, NJ, 1988), *AHR*, 95, pp. 484–5.

D. D. Smeeton, *Lollard Themes in the Reformation Theology of William Tyndale*, Sixteenth Century Essays and Studies, 6 (Kirksville, MO, 1986), *EHR*, 105, pp. 171–2.

1991

'St Augustine's Concept of Man', in R. G. Benson and E. W. Naylor eds, *Essays in Honor of Edward B. King* (The University of the South, Sewanee, TN), pp. 173–86.

REVIEWS

A. Hudson, ed., *English Wycliffite Sermons*, 3 (Oxford, 1990), *JThS*, ns, 42, p. 841.

D. Wilcox, *The Measure of Times Past* (Chicago, 1987), *EHR*, 106, pp. 425–6.

1992

'The *Trivium* and the Three Philosophies', in H. De Ridder-Symoens, ed., *A History of the University in Europe*, 1 (Cambridge University Press, Cambridge), pp. 307–36.

REVIEWS

A. J. Freddoso and F. E. Kelley, trans., William of Ockham, *Quodlibetical Questions*, Yale Library of Medieval Philosophy, 2 vols (New Haven, CT, and London, 1991), *JEH*, 43, p. 681.

R. D. Sorrell, *St Francis of Assisi and Nature* (New York and Oxford, 1988), *EHR*, 107, p. 697.

1993

'Gerald Aylmer in Manchester and York', in J. Morrill, P. Slack, and D. Woolf, eds, *Public Duty and Private Conscience in Seventeenth-century England: Essays Presented to G. E. Aylmer* (Clarendon Press, Oxford), pp. 9–17.

1994

REVIEWS

A. Black, *Political Thought in Europe, 1250–1450* (Cambridge, 1992) and
M. Viroli, *From Politics to Reason of State: the Acquisition and Transformation of the Language of Politics 1250–1600*, Ideas in Context, 22 (Cambridge, 1992), *Times Literary Supplement*, 2 September, p. 23.

O. Capitani and J. Miethke, eds, *L'Attesa della fine dei tempi nel medioevo* (Bologna, 1990), *EHR*, 109, p. 411.

K. Kerby Fulton, *Reformist Apocalypticism and Piers Plowman*, Cambridge Studies in Medieval Literature, 7 (Cambridge, 1990), *EHR*, 109, pp. 703–5.

J.-F. Genest, *Prédétermination et liberté créée à Oxford au XIVe siècle: Buckingham contre Bradwardine*, Études de Philosophie Médiévale, 70 (Paris, 1993), *Vivarium*, 32, pp. 122–5.

K. Pennington, *The Prince and the Law, 1200–1600: Sovereignty and Rights in the Western Legal Tradition* (Berkeley, CA, and Chichester, 1993), *Times Literary Supplement*, 14 January, p. 24.

1995

'Wilhelm Dilthey', *History Review*, 21, March, pp. 17–20.

'Ockham/Ockhamismus', *Theologisches Realenzyklopädie*, 25 (Walter de Gruyter, Berlin and New York), pp. 6–14.

REVIEWS

F. Seibt, *Hussitica* 2nd edn (Cologne and Vienna, 1990) and
E. Werner, *Jan Hus* (Weimar, 1991), *EHR*, 110, pp. 166–7.

1996

REVIEW

D. Burr, *Olivi's Peaceable Kingdom: a Reading of the Apocalypse Commentary* (Philadelphia, 1993), *EHR*, 111, pp. 682–3.

1997

'John Wyclif', *Medieval Life*, 6, pp. 19–25.

REVIEW

P. Gradon and A. Hudson, eds, *English Wycliffite Sermons*, 3–4 (Oxford, 1996), *JThS*, ns, 48, pp. 732–3.

1998

'Alcuin of York', in P. Bulzer, *et al.*, eds, *Charlemagne and His Heritage*, 2, *The Mathematical Arts* (Brepols, Turnhout), pp. 3–9.

'Learning and intellectual life, 1050–1200', in *Medieval England: an Encyclopedia* (Garland, New York), vol. III, pp. 415–17.

FORTHCOMING

'Heresy' and 'Ockham', in A. McGrath, ed., *Blackwell's Encyclopedia of Medieval, Reformation and Renaissance Thought* (Blackwell, Oxford).

'Duns Scotus' and 'Thomas Bradwardine', in C. Matthew, ed., *New Dictionary of National Biography* (Oxford University Press, Oxford).

INDEX

Note: Page references in *italics* indicate tables.

Abelard, Peter, *Letter 10* 17 n. 16
Abels, R. 20 n. 71
Accolti, Benedetto 295
Adam of Belsham 44
Adam (Cathar) 43–4
Adam de Easton 249 n. 37
Alain de Lille 52–3
De fide catholica contra haereticos 28–30, 45–6
Quoniam homines 28–30, 46
Regulae caelestis iuris 38
Albanenses 7–8, 11 n. 35
Albert of Aachen 300, 302
Albertus Magnus 77, 88
Albigenses 50
Alcock, John, bishop of Ely 268
Alexander V, Pope
and mendicant orders 229–33, 234
Regnans in excelsis 229–37
Alexander of Hales
Glossa in IV Libros Sententiarum 64
and the Jews 64–6, 69, 74
Summa theologiae (attributed) 65–6, 74–5
Alexander Nequam
and Cathars 35, 37, 40, 44, 46, 48–9
Sacerdos ad altare accessurus 37
Speculum speculationum 35
Alington, Robert 145, 151
Determinacio de adoracione ymaginum 148
Allegationes de potestate imperiali 102–6, 108–9
Alnwick, William, bishop of Norwich 251
Alverny, M.-T. d' 45
Ambrose of Milan, St 151
Ambrosiaster, *Quaestiones veteri et novi testamenti* 62 n. 19, 64 n. 26
Andreas, Antoine 89
Anselm of Alessandria 40–1, 51
Tractatus de hereticis 19 n. 67, 20 n. 69, 41 n. 67
Anselm of Canterbury, St
Cur Deus Homo 64 n. 26
and the Jews 64
Anselm of Laon (*et al.*), *Glossa ordinaria* on the Bible 55, 57–8, 59–60, 62 n. 19, 64 n. 25, 66 n. 29, 175
anti-Lollard verses 175
Apologia for the Church of God (Cathar work) 6, 15, 16, 22 n. 77
Aquinas, St Thomas 77, 147, 318
canonization 93
Catena Aurea 151
and dualism 25–6
and ecclesiastical hierarchy 102, 105
and ethics 318
Expositio et Lectura super Epistolas Paulii 66
and heresy 111, 117, 128, 130–3, 168
and the Jews 64, 66–8
Lectura super Matthaeum 68
and natural law 320
and nominalism 322
and Peter Lombard 55
Quaestiones disputatae de veritate 131
Scriptum super libros Sententiarum 25, 128, 130–1
Summa theologiae 67–8, 102, 105–6, 111, 130–3, 168
and virtue 130–3
and William of Ockham 309–10
see also Thomism
Arians, Arius 112, 119 n. 24, 120, 167
Aristotle
and Cathar use of maxims 25, 29, 36–40, 43, 49, 51
commentaries on 87, 200

Aristotle (*cont.*):
  De anima, possible lost commentary 200
  Latin translations 36–8
  Metaphysics 25, 37
  Meteora, Wyclif's commentary on 200 n. 22
  and monarchy 181
  Nichomachean Ethics 36, 99 n. 21
  On generation 36–8
  Physics 39
    Wyclif's commentary on 200 n. 22
  and scientific revolution 323
  and virtue 132
  see also *Auctoritates Aristotelis*
Arius *see* Arians
Arnaud de Clermont 84
Arundel, Thomas, archbishop of Canterbury 146, 154, 159, 171–2
  Constitutions 169
asceticism, Cathar 13–14
Asshefeld, John 243
Aston, John 144, 145–6, 155, 187, 190
Aston, Margaret 163–91, 313
Aston, T. H. 258
atonement, in Catharism 11–12
Auctoritates Aristotelis 39
Audelay, John, poem 186
Augustine of Hippo, St 3, 62 n. 19, 64 n. 26, 147, 151, 234
  City of God 123–4
  Confessions 124
  Contra Cresconium 123 n. 32
  De haeresibus 122
  De trinitate 104, 108, 124–5
  De vera religione 122
  Enarratio in Psalmos 57–9, 69–71
  Epistle 185 121 n. 27
  Epistle 93 121 n. 27
  and heresy 117, 119, 121–5, 131, 137, 168
  and the Jews 57–60, 61, 68–71, 73, 75
  and Manichees 26
  On the advantage of believing (De utilitate credendi) 121–2, 131
  On Free Will 124, 129
  and Ten Commandments 316
  Tractatus in Johannem 57–8
Augustinian canons
  in late medieval Cambridge 240, 242–3, 247, 249, 254, 256, 258–60, 262, 266, 267
  and the 'mendicant problem' 222–3, 232, 233, 237
  in Yorkshire [illegible]–3
    geographical origins 282–3
    social origins 286–7
    and university education 289–90
Augustinian hermits, and education 77, 79–81, 89
Augustinus de Ancona, *Summa de ecclesiastica potestate* 115 n. 13, 129–30
Augustinus Triumphus 100
Auriol, Pierre 84, 87, 88–9
authority
  episcopal 217, 220, 226–7, 229, 238
  of monarch 305
  papal 101–6, 128–30, 133, 218, 229–30, 233–4, 236, 294–5
Avignon, papal court 87, 93
Aylmer, Gerald x, 1–4

baccalaureat, and mendicant orders 79–81, 82–8, 90–2
Bacon, Francis, *Advertisement Touching on Holy Warre* 297, 306
Baldric of Dol 302
Baldwin, John 47
Bale, John 199, 289
Bardney, Richard
  Historia Sancti Hugonis Martyris 262
  verse life of Grosseteste 262
Barnwell Priory, and university of Cambridge 242–3
Barnwell Process (1430) 243
Basle, Council (1431-49) 237
Bayle, Pierre 323
Beauchamp, Sir William 154 n. 35, 155, 157, 158
Beaufort, Lady Margaret 240
Bedale (Stapleton), William 282
Bede, Venerable 65, 151, 179
Belgrave, John 183
Benedict XII, Pope
  and education 80, 246, 259, 266
  Redemptor noster 81 n. 7

Benedict XIII, Pope, and mendicant orders 233
Benedictine order
and education 90, 266
in late medieval Cambridge 240–1, 246–54, 256, 259–62, 268
statutes (English) 252
in Yorkshire 250, 256, 272, 280–2, 287
Berengar of Landorra 85
Berger, Peter 111 n. 2
Berkley, Gilbert, bishop of Bath and Wells 288
Berlière, Ursmer 264
Berlin, Isaiah 2
Bernard of Arezzo 89
Bernard of Clairvaux, St
and Catharism 45
and crusades 296
De consideratione 129
and Lollards 151
Bernard Lombardi 84, 88
Bertolf (canon of Bonn) 44
Bible
in Catharism 7–8, 12, 44, 48
and heresy 14–15, 116, 117–18, 167, 174–5
vernacular 151–3, 154, 160, 188–9
Biel, Gabriel 315, 316, 317, 319
Biller, Peter 25–53
bishops
Cathar 12, 13, 19–20, 41–2
and heresy 120, 127
and Lollards 149
and mendicant orders 217, 220, 223, 226–7, 229, 235, 238
Blackfriars Council 148, 173, 175
Blacman, John 147
blasphemy, and the Jews 74–5
Blund, John, *De anima* 37
Blyton, Roland, abbot of Rievaulx 275
Boehner, Philotheus 310
Boethius, Anicius Manlius Severinus, *De hebdomadibus* 38
Bologna
Dominican convent 31
university 60
Bolton, John, prior of Watton 245
Bonaventure, St 77, 88
Commentaria in quatuor libros sententiarum 26, 128, 131 nn. 53-4
Bongars, Jacques, *Gesta Dei Per Francos* 293–4, 301–6
Boniface IX, Pope, and heresy 170
Boniface VIII, Pope 88
Super cathedram 217, 220, 222–3, 230, 235
Unam sanctam 104, 108 n. 44
gloss on 106
Book of the Two Principles (Cathar work) 6, 9, 10, 39, 51
Boniface of Savoy, archbishop of Canterbury 95, 97
Borst, Arno 27, 51
Bossy, John 309–24
Bourdeille, Pierre de 306
Bowland, Robert 146–7
Bozoun, Thomas 261
Bradwardine, Thomas 311
Brenon, Anne 6, 20 n. 71
Brenz, Johannes 318
Brethren of the Common Life 144
Bridgettine order, and medieval intellectual life 266
Brook, Sir Thomas 158
Brown, Robert McAfee 111 n. 2
Browne, William, prior of Monk Bretton 291
Brundage, J. A. 242
Brut, Walter 147
Buckingham College, Cambridge 248, 250–4, 261
Burci, Salvo 11 n. 35
Suprastella 6, 21 n. 76, 22–3 n. 82
burial, in mendicant houses 217, 220, 221, 223–4, 228, 230–1, 236, 238
Burton, Henry, prior of St Mary Overy 247
Bury St Edmunds Abbey 221–2, 249, 256
Byland Abbey 276–7, 285, 291

Calvin, John
and nominalism 321
and Ottoman empire 295, 303
Calvinism, and crusading history 293, 301–4

Cambridge, university
compared with Oxford 239–40, 246, 257–8
and mendicant orders 91, 240, 288, 289
and monastic orders 239–69, 287, 290
canon law
and heresy 94–5, 114–15, 171, 174–5, 187, 190
and human rights 129 n. 48
and mendicant orders 217–18
and papacy 104, 115
and theology 93–5, 98–9
and university of Cambridge 249, 250, 258, 263
Capgrave, John, *Life of St Norbert* 265
Caprone, Thomas 275
Carmelites
and apostolic poverty 218, 225
and education 77, 288–9
and the 'mendicant problem' 224–5 n. 34, 225, 232
Carthusian order 13, 146, 147–8
in late medieval Cambridge 247, 255, 266
in Yorkshire *272*, 273–4, 282
Cathars
believers 13–14
in England 43, 46
in *Francia* 30, 34–6, 38, 40–3, 47–8, 50
bishops 37, 41
La Charité 35, 50
notary 43
as heretics 120, 131
and higher learning 25–7, 40–53
in Italy 7–9, 27, 30, 33, 36, 37–9, 41, 43, 50–1
in Languedoc 7, 14, 25–7, 41, 43, 47, 50
maxims 27–30, 32–3, 36–40, 43, 45–6, 49, 51
name used of 4th-century heretics 120
name used of medieval heretics 120
and *perfecti* 12–17, 19–21, 35, 43
service-book 40–1, 43–4
and sources 5–7, 15, 18, 25–33, 41–2
spirituality 5–23
texts 6–7, 15
anonymous treatise 6, 9, 10, 23 n. 83
see also *Apologia for the Church of God*; *Book of Two Principles*; Desiderius; *Ritual*; *Stella*; Tetricus
wealth 43
Catto, Jeremy 141–61
celibacy
Cathar 13
clergy 304
Cervantes, Fernando 322–3
Chatteris, John 243
Chaucer, Geoffrey, *Clerk's tale* 166
Chénon, É. 42
Chenu, M.-D. 38
Cheyne, Sir John 154 n. 35, 155, 156–7, 159
Chichele, Henry, archbishop of Canterbury 154
Chichele, William 257
choice, and heresy 116, 135–6, 167–8
Chronicle of St André de Castres 127 n. 42
Chronicon Hierosolymitanum 299–301
Church
and apostolic ideal 126–8, 129, 138, 182–3, 217, 218–19, 225, 227
in Catharism 12, 16, 18–19
in early Protestantism 141, 142, 143
and heresy 313
and reform 154, 160–1, 217, 234, 268–9, 288–9, 304–5
Church and state, and Lollards 170–3
Cicero, Marcus Tullius, *De oratore* 32
Cistercian order
and education 89, 246–7
in late medieval Cambridge 240, 247–8, 254–5
in Yorkshire 271–3, *272*
geographical origins 271, 274–80, 282
university education 287, 289
Clanvowe, Perryne 159
Clanvowe, Sir John 154 n. 35
The Two Ways 155–6
Clark, James 250
Clark, Stuart 323–4
Clarkson, Simon, prior of York Carmelites 288

Clédat, L. 8 n. 13
Clementines *see* John XXII, Pope
clergy
  and apostolic ideal 126–8
  and concubinage 233
  and Lollards 148–9, 154
  secular, and mendicant orders 217–18, 220–6, 227–31, 233, 235–6, 238
  see also sacraments
Clermont, Arnaud de 84
Clifford, Sir Lewis 154 n. 35, 155, 156–8, 159
  'book of tribulation' 159
Cluniac order
  in late medieval Cambridge 250
  in Yorkshire *272*
    geographical origins 281–2
    social origins 282
Cockerell, James, prior of Guisborough 288, 289
Codenham (Buntying), William 257 n. 62
Coluthus 122
conciliarism, and the 'mendicant problem' 229, 233–7
confession
  and Cathars 18
  and Lollards 144
  and mendicants 217, 220, 221–2, 227–8, 229–34, 237–8
consolamentum 10 n. 30, 12–14, 15 n. 49, 16, 18, 21, 42, 44
Constance, Council (1414-18) 160, 228, 233–6
Constantine the Great, Emperor 119
Constantinople, First Council (381) 120
convenanza, Cathar 14
conventicles, and sects 165, 171, 174, 187
Coplestone, F. C. 319, 322
councils, ecumenical
  and heresy 119–21, 138
  and the 'mendicant problem' 229, 233–7
Counter, William, collection of moral works 155, 156, 157, 159
Counter-Reformation, and nominalism 314, 322–3
court, English, and Lollard knights 145, 154–9
Courtenay, William, archbishop of Canterbury 146, 172 n. 33, 173, 190–1
Courtenay, William J. 77–92, 309–10, 311–12, 315–17, 318–20
Cowper, Christabel, prioress of Marrick 283
Cresconius 123 n. 32
Crespet, Pierre 304
Cromwell, Thomas 255, 275, 289–90
Cross, Claire 271–91
cross-referencing, in works of Wyclif 193–215
Crowland Abbey 247, 249, 251–2, 256
crusades
  early modern views 293–307
  Fifth 302
  First 41, 299
    chronicles 300, 302–3, 306
    see also Guibert de Nogent; Jacques de Vitry; William of Tyre
  and the Jews 68–9, 71, 74–5
  Second 40
  Third 299
Cudworth, Ralph 323
Cunich, 251 n. 42, 252–4

Daniel of Morley 37
Dassel, Rainald 45
De heresi Catharorum in Lombardia 22 n. 81
death, in Catharism 10, 14, 22–3
Decalogue ethics 315–19, 323–4
Declaration on Religious Freedom 111
Decretals *see* Gregory IX, Pope
Denifle, Heinrich 311
Denis the Areopagite
  Celestial Hierarchy see Grosseteste, Robert
  and Grosseteste 97, 98–9
  and Ockham 93, 101–6, 108–9
Desenzano, Church of (Albanenses) 7–8
Desiderius (Cathar author) 33
Diceto, Ralph, *Ymagines historiarum* 72 n. 43
Digoun, John 147–8
Dionysius, Pope 228, 234
Disputatio inter clericum et militem 305
Ditchfield, Simon 325–42

Dobson, Barrie 239–69, 280
doctorate, and mendicant orders 78–81, 83–92
Dominican order
  and anti-Cathar polemic 27, 31, 33, 44
  and education 77, 79–86, 88–91, 241, 288
  and the 'mendicant problem' 221, 232
  and nominalism 318–19, 322, 323
  and provincial centres of learning 31, 83–5, 91
Donatists 121, 167
Douais, C. 14
Doyle, Eric 197
Drayton, Thomas 144
Dresser, Matthew, commentary on *Chronicon Hierosolymitanum* 299–301, 303, 305
dualism
  absolute, in Catharism 7–15, 18–20, 23, 25–8, 40–6
  moderate 7, 43
  and universities 25–6, 28, 38–9, 45–6
Dubois, Pierre, *De recuperatione terrae sanctae* 302, 304–5
Duns Scotus, John 87–8, 134
  In IV libros Sententiarum (Reportatio Parisiensia) 132–3
  lecturing on the *Sentences* 87
  see also Scotists
Durand of Huesca, and anonymous Cathar treatise 6, 9, 10, 23 n. 83
Durand of St Pourçain 84, 88
Durham Priory 251, 280, 285
Duvernoy, Jean 5–6, 16 n. 54
Dworkin, Ronald 139 n. 64
Dziewicki, 198

Eccleston, Henry 255
Eckbert of Schönau 44–5, 48
  Sermones XII contra Catharos 44
Eckhart, Meister 85
ecumenism, European 297–8, 304
education
  and Cathars 25–7, 40–53
  and mendicant orders 77–92, 240–1, 287–8
  and monastic orders 239–69, 287
  see also Cambridge, university; Oxford, university; Paris, university
Edward the Black Prince, and Lollards 145, 154
Ely cathedral priory, and university of Cambridge 247, 249, 256, 259, 261–2, 264–5
Emden, A. B. 248
Empire, Holy Roman
  and Ottoman threat 295
  and papacy 101–6, 108–9, 134–5, 219, 295
endura, Cathar 14
England
  and Cathars 43, 46
  and the 'mendicant problem' 220–6, 238
English
  and Bible translation 151–3, 154, 160, 188–9
  in wills 156–8
Épernon, Robert d' 42
Epiphanius of Salamis
  and heresy 117, 118–19, 122 n. 31
  Panarion 117–18
Erasmus, Desiderius, and holy war 295, 298
Ereth, William 256
Ermengaud of Béziers, *Manifestatio haeresis Albigensium et Lugdunensium* 10 n. 25, 12 n. 37
ethics
  and heresy 111–12, 113–14, 127, 135–6
  and reason 319
  and William of Ockham 309–10, 314, 316–18, 323
  see also theology, moral
Eucharist
  in Catharism 16–18
  and Lollards 143–4
  and Wyclif 214
Eudes de Châteauroux 47
Eugenius IV, Pope, and mendicant orders 237
Eulogium historiarum 185 n. 75
Europe, and crusades 293–7, 306–7
Eustache, *Gesta* of bishops of Auxerre 34

Evennett, Outram 312–13
Eversin of Steinfeld 40
Évrard of Béthune 48
  Liber antihaeresis 43 n. 76, 46–7
Évrard of Chateauneuf 34–5, 47, 50
Exmewe, William 255

factiousness, and heresy 115, 119–20, 122–3, 125, 128–9
faith
  and heresy 111, 117–19, 122–5, 130–2, 134–5, 168
  and reason 27, 132–3, 134, 309, 311, 316, 324
Farewell, John 258
Fasciculi Zizaniorum 163, 172, 176
fasting, in Catharism 13, 14, 19
Fawkes, Nicholas 214
Ferrar, Robert, prior of Nostell 283, 290
Fidem catholicam (imperial manifesto) 103
Filastrius of Brescia, and heresy 122 n. 31
FitzRalph, Richard, archbishop of Armagh 219
  writing against friars 220–1
Flacius Illyricus, Matthias, *Magdeburg Centuries* 141
Fleming, Richard 153
Floretum 150, 179–80
Florimond de Raimond 304
Folkingham, Robert 157, 159
Forde, Simon 148
Fort, Thomas 256–7
Fountains Abbey
  geographical origins of religious 279–80
  numbers of religious 271–3
  social origins of religious 285
  university education of religious 287
Fox, Richard, bishop of Winchester 268
Foxe, John
  Acts and Monuments (Foxe's *Book of Martyrs*) 142, 143
  History of the Turks 298–9
  and the true Church 141, 142, 143
France
  and crusade history 301, 303–5
  northern, and Cathars *see* Cathars, in *Francia*
  see also Languedoc; Paris, university
Francis of Assisi, St, Rule and Testament 218
Francis of Marcia 89
Francis of Meyronnes 88, 89, 100
Franciscan order
  and apostolic poverty 218
  and education 77, 79–86, 88–91, 240–1, 288
  and Joachism 218
  and the 'mendicant problem' 221–2, 224–5, 228–30, 232
  and Michael of Cesena 88, 102–6, 108–9
  Observant 220, 226, 232–3
  and Ockham 99–100, 103, 115
  and papacy 218–19
  and provincial centres of learning 84–7, 91, 103
  Spirituals 88, 218–19, 225, 313
fraticelli 219
freedom
  academic 232, 237
  religious 111–13, 129 n. 48, 137
Fuer, William 143–4
Fulcher of Chartres 302

Gairdner, James 141
Gamylgay, John 150
Garret, Thomas 290
Geiler, Johannes 316
Gerard of Borgo San Donnino, *Liber introductorius ad Evangelium Aeternum* 183–4, 189, 218
Gerard (Cathar) 43
Gerard of Zutphen, *De spiritualibus ascensionibus* 148
Germany
  and Catharism *see* Rhineland
  and crusade history 294, 299–301, 302, 305
  and the 'mendicant problem' 226–7
Gerson, Jean
  De statu papae et minorum praelatorum 229
  De visitatione praelatorum 228
  Discours sur le fait des mendiants 231

Gerson, Jean (*cont.*):
and mendicant orders 228, 229, 231, 234
and Ockham 315–19
Gewirth, Alan 139 n. 64
Gieben, Fr Servus 96, 97 n. 12
Gil de Torres, Cardinal 96
Gilbertine order
in late medieval Cambridge 240, 244–6, 262
in Yorkshire *273*
geographical origins 273–4, 282
social origins 283, 286–7
university education 290
Giles of Rome 77, 100
De ecclesiastica potestate 108 nn. 44–5, 129
Gilson, Etienne 310–13, 315
Gloss on the Lord's Prayer (Cathar) 6, 14, 18, 20 n. 73
Glossa ordinaria see Anselm of Laon
Glossa ordinaria on Gratian's *Decretum* 127 n. 43
Glossa ordinaria on *Libri quinque decretalium* (Decretals) 127–8 n. 43
gnosticism
in Catharism 11
and Irenaeus 118, 119
Godard, Jean 304
Godfrey of Fontaines 90
Godson, Brian, prior of York Dominican house 285, 288
Goldast, Melchior 93
Goldwell, James, bishop of Norwich 266
Gonteri, Anfredus 84, 89
Gorel, Jean 228–31
Gower, John 163
Confessio amantis 169
Grandimontine order 13
in Yorkshire *272*, 281–2
Gratian
Decretum 60, 121 n. 28
and natural law 95
and responsibility for death of Christ 60
Gray, William, bishop of Lincoln 260
Greatrex, Joan 261
Gregory I, Pope (St Gregory the Great) 151, 179
Moralia on Job 44
Gregory VII, Pope
and clergy 127, 128
and papal power 128, 129
Registrum 127 n. 42
Gregory IX, Pope
and heresy 43, 174
Libri quinque decretalium (Decretals) 127–8 n. 43, 263
Gregory XI, Pope, and Wyclif 170, 207, 213
Gregory of Rimini 88, 321
Groote, Gerard 144
Grosmont Abbey 281
Grosseteste, Robert, bishop of Lincoln
De cessacione legalium 199
and heresy 93–4, 168
Letter 128 96, 99
and Lollards 151
and Ockham 94–100, 107
Super Angelicam Hierarchiam 95, 97 n. 11, 98
verse life of 262
see also Marsh, Robert
Gui, Bernard, *Practica inquisitionis* 171, 172
Gui de Orchelles, *Tractatus de sacramentis* 31
Guibert de Nogent
and crusades 302
and dualism 26, 48
Guido de Baysio (Baisieux), *Lectura super Sexto* 172
Guillaume d'Auvergne
De legibus 47
De universo 29 n. 18, 46–7, 51
Guillaume d'Auxerre, *Summa aurea* 26–32, 33–6, 38–40, 46, 52–3
Guillaume de Laon 84
guilt, and responsibility for death of Christ 59, 61–5, 68, 72
Guisborough Priory 283, 288, 289

Hallum, Robert, bishop of Salisbury 154, 160
Hamilton, Bernard 5–23, 40–1, 43

Harris, M. R. 8 n. 13, 22 n. 80
Harrison, E. 20 n. 71
Haskins, C. H. 37, 42
Hayton, prince of Armenia, *Flowers of the History of the East* 300
Heloise, and Lord's Prayer 17
Henri de Villeneuve, bishop of Auxerre 35
Henry of Ghent 90
Henry IV of England, and Lollardy 169
Henry IV of France 301, 303–4
Henry IV of Germany 299
Henry of Susa *see* Hostiensis
Henry V of England, and reform of the Church 154
Henry VII of England, and university education 240, 258
Henryson, Robert, poem 185
Hereford, Nicholas 144, 145–8, 150, 152, 155
  possibly author of *Opus arduum* 146
heresy
  and apostolic ideal 126–8, 129, 138, 182–3
  and communal ideal 128–30, 138
  as created by orthodoxy 112, 313
  definitional problems 113–16
  in early Church 11–25
  and enlightenment 126–35
  medieval idea 111–39
  and mendicant orders 177–82, 188, 225, 233
  papal 93–4, 115–16, 129–30, 133–4, 230
  and sect 119, 167–8, 172–6, 179
  twentieth-century views 111–13
  and virtue 111, 130–5, 138
  and William of Ockham 93–4, 115–16, 133–4
  see also Cathars; ethics; faith; Lollards
Hervé, count of Nevers 34–5
hierarchy, ecclesiastical 97, 102–6, 108–9, 230–1, 234–5, 237
Higden, Ranulf
  Polychronicon 100
  see also Trevisa, John
Hilary of Poitiers, St 45
Hildegard of Bingen, St, and Cathars 40, 41
Hill, Edmund 125 n. 38
Hinnebusch, W. A. 80 n. 4
Hippolytus of Rome
  Adversus omnium haeresium 117–18
  and heresy 117, 118–19
Historia Eliensis 26
historiography
  and crusades 293–4, 296–307
  Marxist 1–3, 313
  and Protestant continuity 293–4
Hobbes, Thomas 3, 324
Hockey, S. F. 248 n. 32
Holgate, Robert, prior of Watton 246, 283, 290
Holinshead, Raphael 297
holy war
  crusades as 293–4, 296–7, 299, 303–4, 306
  and Ottoman threat 294–5, 297–8, 305
Hook, Robert 155, 160
Hostiensis 128–9 n. 46, 172
Hothom, Walter 262
Houghton, John 255
Howlett, D. 49 n. 116
Hudson, Anne 142, 187, 193–215
Hugh de Marciaco 84
Hugh of Noyers, bishop of Auxerre, and Cathars 34–5, 50 n. 117
humanism
  and the crusades 295
  and monasticism 258, 289–90
Humiliati 171
Hus, Jan
  condemnation 313
  and mendicant orders 236
  and universities 25
Hussites, catalogues of works of Wyclif 206, 215 n. 61
Hutten, Ulrich von 297

identity
  national 294, 300–1, 303–45
  religious 142–61
Ignatius of Antioch, and heresy 117
ignorance, and responsibility for death of Christ 61–8

Imbart de la Tour, Pierre 311
Incarnation, in Catharism 10–12
individualism, and William of Ockham 311, 312, 314
indulgences, and crusades 294, 295, 296
initiation, Cathar 5 n. 1, 14, 16, 20
Innocent III, Pope 128 n. 46, 187 n. 86
  and crusades 296
  and heresy 174, 187
Innocent IV, Pope, and Robert Grosseteste 95–6, 98–9
Inquisition
  and Catharism 6, 15, 41
  and mendicant orders 129
intercession, in Catharism 20–1
Irenaeus of Lyons, *Adversus haereses* 117, 118–19
Iserloh, Erwin 314
Isidore of Seville, St 179
  Etymologies 167–8, 183
Italy, and Catharism 7–9, 27, 30, 33, 36, 37–9, 40–1, 43, 50–1
Ivo of Narbonne, letter 50–1

James VI of Scotland, *Lepanto* 297
Jacques de Vitry, bishop of Acre, *Historia Orientalis* 298, 302, 305
James, Eric (later Lord James of Rusholme) 4
James of Esculo 89
James of Lausanne 84, 88
James of Metz 88
James of Spinello 89
James of Viterbo 100
James, William 150, 151, 153, 160
Jean de Pouilly 227, 237
Jean-Aimes de Chavigny 304
Jerome, St
  Commentary on St Paul's Epistle to the Galatians 120 n. 25
  and Lord's Prayer 17
Jervaulx Abbey 277, 278
Jesuits, and nominalism 323
Jewell, John, bishop of Salisbury 297
Jews
  and Christian society 68–76, 166
  and Paris theologians 55–76
  and responsibility for death of Christ 56, 57–68, 72
Joachim of Fiore
  and barefoot preaching 183–4, 189
  and Franciscans 218
Joan, countess of Hereford 155
Joan, Princess of Wales, and Lollards 145, 154
Johan de Thorley 242
John XXII, Pope
  Constitutiones Clementinae (Clementines) 217
  and mendicant orders 218–19, 230
  and Ockham 93, 101, 104, 106, 115–16, 133
  Vas electionis 217, 227, 230
John XXIII, Pope
  and Council of Constance 234
  and mendicant orders 232–3
John Chrysostom, St 44
John de Bardney 251, 262
John de Craudon, prior of Ely 247
John de Usk 206 n. 38
John of Gaunt, and Lollards 145
John of Jandun 170
John of Luchembergh 85
John of Lugio 8
John of Paris, *De potestate regia et papali* 106
John of Parma 88
José de Acosta 323
Josephus 166
Juan de Segovia 295
Justinian I, Emperor, and heresy 117

Kaluza, Zenon 89
Kempe, Margery 156
Kempis, Thomas, *Imitation of Christ* 148
Kenningham, John 189 n. 89
Kightly, Charles 154 n. 35
Kilcullen, John 107, 134 n. 58
killing, Cathar prohibition 13, 21–2
Kirkby (Cowper), Edward, abbot of Rievaulx 275, 287–8
Kirkham (Kirkby), Thomas 289
Kirkstall Abbey 278, 285, 291
Knighton, Henry 154, 182, 184–90
  Chronicon 186–90

Knowles, David 2, 264, 271, 311–14, 317
Krämer, Henry and Sprenger, Jacob, *Malleus Maleficarum* 318
Kretz, Matthias, sermon 296
Kyrketon, Alan 263

Lagarde, Georges de 100, 311, 313, 314, 317
laity
  and ecclesiastical hierarchy 103–6
  and Lollards 144, 161
  and mendicant preaching 224, 225
Landulf of Caracciolo 89
Langland, William, *Piers Plowman* 224
Langley, Thomas, bishop of Durham 251
Langton, Stephen, archbishop of Canterbury 69
  Expositio super Genesim 73
Languedoc, and Catharism 7, 14, 25–7, 41, 43, 47, 50
Lateran Councils
  Third (1179) 120–1, 183
  Fourth (1215) 75, 120 n. 26, 217
    Omnius utriusque sexus 217, 230, 234
  Fifth (1512-17) 295–6
    Dum intra mentis arcana 238
Latimer, Sir Thomas 154 n. 35, 155, 156–8
law, natural 324
  in William of Ockham 95, 97, 309–10, 319–20, 322
Layton, Richard 258
lectorate, and mendicant orders 77, 79–82, 83–7, 91–2
Leff, Gordon ix–xi, 25, 164, 239, 306–7, 324
  appreciation 1–4
  bibliography 325–42
  and fifteenth-century theology 30, 311–12, 315, 318–21
  and William of Ockham 309–15, 317, 319, 321
Legger, Thomas 258
Leo X, Pope, and crusades 295–6
Leo XIII, Pope, and scholasticism 311
Liber de causis 38–9
Liber de duobus principiis see *Book of the Two Principles*
Liber XXIV philosophorum 38
liberalism, and heresy 113, 123–4, 130, 136–9
libraries
  cathedral 147
  college 154, 293
  conventual 89–90, 99–100
  monastic 243, 263–5, 290–1
  private 155, 157, 290, 301
Lincoln, diocese 96, 98
Litlington, John, abbot of Crowland 247, 251, 260
Loades, David 164
logic, in mendicant education 78, 83
Lollards
  beliefs and practices 143–4
  and court support 145, 154–9
  defectors 145–50, 155
  early martyrs 141–2
  and English Bible 151–3, 154, 160, 188–9
  literature 144–5, 150–2, 160, 177
  and mendicant orders 177–82, 185, 188–91, 225
  preachers 144–5, 148–9, 150–1, 153–5, 159–60, 180, 182–3, 187–9
  and religious identity 142–61
  and rising of 1414 146, 158
  as sect 143–4, 163–5, 168–91
  vocabulary 186–7
  writings *see* Wycliffite writings
Longère, Jean 47
Longland, John, bishop of Lincoln 143
Lord, Elizabeth, prioress of Wilberfoss 286
Lord's Prayer, in Catharism 17
Lortz, Joseph 311, 314–15, 317, 320
Loserth, 199 n. 19, 201 nn. 25,26
Louis IV (the Bavarian), Emperor 102, 104, 219
Louis IX of France 74, 302
Louis XIII of France 303–4
love, in Catharism 18, 21
Lowth, John, abbot of Thornton 261
Loyola, St Ignatius 298
Lucas, Thomas 150
Lucius III, Pope
  Ad abolendam (bull) 187

Lucius III, Pope (*cont.*):
  and heresy 171, 174, 187
Luscombe, David 93–109
Luther, Martin
  and Gerson 316
  and nominalism 321
  and Ockham 311–12, 314–15, 321
  and Ottoman empire 295, 298
  Shorter Catechism 316
Lutheranism
  and crusading history 293, 299, 302
  in Oxford 290
Lydgate, John, *Life and Passion of St Alban* 263–5
Lyndwood, W. 172
Lyons, papal court 94–100

Macedonians 120
McFarlane, K. B. 141, 154, 156–7, 159
McGrade, Arthur Stephen 111–39
McGrath, Alister 321
Mackarall, Mathew 258
Mair, John 321
Maleverer, Ralph, prior of Hull 282
Malleus maleficarum 318
Malton Priory 274, 286
Manicheanism
  and Augustine 121–2
  and dualism 25–6, 28–30, 45–7
Mannying de Brunne, Robert, *Handlyng Synne* 262
Map, Walter, *De nugis curialum* 183
Mare magnum (papal bull) 237
Marsh, Robert, collection of Grosseteste's writings 96–100
Marsilius of Inghen 90
Marsilius of Padua 133, 170
Marxism, and historiography 1–2, 313
Mayronis, Francis *see* Francis of Meyronnes
Meaux Abbey 278, 279, 287, 289
Mede, John, commonplace book 146
mendicant orders
  and apostolic ideal 129, 217, 218–19, 225, 227, 235–6
  and Cambridge university 240, 288, 289
  and Denis the Areopagite 101
  and Inquisition 129
  and leadership roles 81, 84–5, 87, 90–2
  and Lollards 177–82, 185, 188–91, 225
  and the 'mendicant problem' 217–38
  and Observer movements 226, 232–3
  and Oxford university 288
  and papacy 217, 218–20, 222–3, 227, 229–37
  and Paris University 77–92, 218
  and patronage 87–8, 90, 91–2
  and preaching 175, 180, 184, 188, 217, 220, 224–5, 228, 231, 238
  and provincial centres of learning 31, 78–9, 81–7, 91, 103
  and secular clergy 217–18, 220–6, 227–31, 233, 235–6, 238
  and tertiaries 235–6
  in Yorkshire 288–9
Mersche, Thomas 258 n. 63
Merton College, Oxford, and Lollards 150, 151, 153
Meyronnes, François de *see* Francis of Meyronnes
Michael of Cesena 88
  and Ockham 93, 102, 106
Michel, John 255
Midelfort, Erik 317–18
Millyng, Thomas 257
ministry, Cathar 14, 20–1
monarchy, papal 100–5
monasticism
  and dissolution of monasteries 269, 289–90
  and financial resources 267–8
  and intellectual life 262–6, 267, 287, 289–91
  and late medieval Cambridge 239–69
  in Yorkshire 271–91
    geographical origins 271, 275–82, 291
    social origins 271, 282–7
    university connections 250, 256, 262, 287–8, 289, 291
  see also mendicant orders
Moneta of Cremona 36, 40, 51, 52–3
  Adversus Catharos et Valdenses 6, 10 n. 29, 13 n. 41, 15 n. 52, 22 n. 79, 23 n. 83, 27, 28–33

Monk Bretton Abbey 280–1, 290–1
Mont-St-Michel 36–7
Montagu, Sir John (later earl of Shrewsbury) 154 n. 35, 155
Moore, R. I. 114, 136–7
Moschus, François 306
  edition of Jacques de Vitry, *Historia Orientalis* 298
Moston, Thomas 153
Mueller, I. J. 200, 214
Multon, Roger 267–8
Mynde, Thomas 256

Nandyke, Katherine, prioress of Wykeham 284
Neill, A. S. 1, 313
Nestorians 167
Netter, Thomas 153, 191, 215 n. 61
  Doctrinale 179 n. 55, 201
  letters 225 n. 34
Neville, Anne, dowager duchess of Buckingham 253
Neville, Sir William 154 n. 35, 155
New Testament
  and Cathars 6–8, 17
  and heresy 116–18, 167, 174–5
Nicaea, First Council (325) 119–20
Nicetas (dualist) 42
Nicholas IV, Pope, and monastic orders 244
Nicholas of Autrecourt 89
Nicholas of Cusa, and mendicant orders 237
Nicholas of Lyra, *Postilla* on the Bible 175
Nider, Johannes 318–19
Noël, Hervé 88
nominalism
  and Counter-Reformation 314, 322–3
  and Reformation 321
  and scientific revolution 323–4
  and William of Ockham 309–10, 314–15, 317–21
Normavale, Eleanor, prioress of Nun Appleton 284
Norreys, Philip 237
Norwich cathedral priory, and university of Cambridge 248, 249, 256, 259, 265, 287
Nostell Priory 283, 290
Noue, François de la 297, 304
nuns, social origins 283–5, 286–7
Nykke, Richard, bishop of Norwich 266

Oakeshott, Michael 324
Oakley, Francis 320, 322, 323
Oberman, Heiko 310, 314–20
Observant movements 220, 226, 232–3
Ockham *see* William of Ockham
Octavian, Cardinal (papal legate) 34
Odonis, Gerard 89
Offler, H. S. 102–3, 108
Oldcastle, Sir John 142, 146, 150, 158, 159–60
Oliver of Paderborn 302
Olivi, Peter John (Peter of John Olivi) 218
omnipotence of God 103, 309–10, 312, 315, 317–18, 320, 324
Omnis utriusque sexus 217, 227, 230, 231, 234
Oresme, Nicole 90
orthodoxy, and heresy 6, 112, 120, 123, 131, 313, 314
Osney Priory 242, 243–4 n. 15
Otto, bishop of Freising 300
Ottoman empire
  and crusades 294–7, 305
  and Protestantism 298, 300, 303–5
Oxford, Franciscan convent library 99–100
Oxford, university
  Arts student's notebook 153
  and Grosseteste 99–100
  and knowledge of Aristotle 37
  and Lutheranism 290
  and mendicant orders 77, 79, 84, 91, 234, 288
  and monastic orders 239–41, 246–50, 252, 254–8, 260, 266, 287–8, 290
  and Wyclif 208, 214, 313
  and Wycliffites 150–4, 160, 170, 173, 182, 184
Ozment, Steven 310, 311–12, 315, 321–2

Palud, Pierre de la 88
Pantin, W. A. 96, 241, 264

Paolini, Lorenzo 33
papacy
  and crusades 293, 294–6, 298–300, 303, 305–6
  and Empire 101–6, 108–9, 134–5, 219, 295
  and Grosseteste 93–100, 107
  and heresy 94, 114–15, 128–30, 170–1, 174
  and Lollardy 169
  and mendicant orders 217, 218–20, 222–3, 227, 229–37
  and Ockham 100–6, 115–16, 133–4, 313, 319, 322
  and papal heresy 93–4, 114–15, 129–30, 133–4, 219, 230
  and plenitude of power 103–6, 108–9, 128, 134
  and Wyclif 99, 170, 206, 207, 213
Paris, Matthew 294
  Chronica Majora 44, 51 n. 121, 96
  Liber Additamentorum 185
  and Robert Grosseteste 96, 97, 99–100
Paris, university 31, 32, 44
  and Cathar learning 27, 45–7, 49, 50–1
  chancellors *see* Eudes de Châteauroux; Prévostin of Cremona
  and dualism 25–7, 30, 33–4, 36–7, 40
  and the Jews 55–76
  and Joachim of Fiore 183–4
  and mendicant orders 77–92, 218, 227–34, 237
  and monastic orders 241, 244 n. 17, 268 n. 95
  and papal authority 229–30, 233–4
  Quodlibets 87
  regent masters 77, 82, 83, 85, 87
Parker, Matthew, archbishop of Canterbury 294, 301
Pastor de Serrescuderio 84, 89, 90 n. 22
Patridge, Peter 153
Patrington, Stephen 190
Paul, St, and heresy 116, 137–8, 176
Paul III, Pope, and indulgences 296
Payne, Peter 150, 209 n. 44
Pelagius, Alvarus, *De planctu ecclesiae* 266
Pelagius, Pelagians 121, 167
Pelikan, Jaroslav 112
penance, in Catharism 19–20
perfection, and the Cathars 5–23
Péronne 46, 48
persecution
  of Cathars 14, 21, 23, 34–5
  of heretics 111, 114, 116, 121, 126, 130, 135–9
  of Jews 68, 71
Perte (Thirsk), William, abbot of Fountains 287
Peter of Aquila 89
Peter the Chanter (Petrus Cantor)
  and heretics 47
  and the Jews 55–6, 63–4, 68–9, 72–3, 75
  Summa Abel 56, 72–3
  Summa de sacramentis et animae consiliis 56, 63
Peter of Corbara 219
Peter Lombard
  commentaries 55, 56, 57
  Glossa in Epistolas Beati Pauli (Magna glossatura) 55, 61–3, 71
  Glossa in Psalmos 55, 58–9, 71–2
  and the Jews 55, 58–9, 61–2, 63, 66, 71–2, 74–5
  Sententiae in IV Libris Distinctae (Sentences)
    lectures and commentaries on 83–5
    see also Alexander of Hales; Aquinas, St Thomas; Bonaventure, St; Peter of Tarentaise; Duns Scotus, John
Peter of Tarentaise 30 n. 20
  In IV. Libros sententiarum commentaria 26, 29 n. 16
Peter of Vaux-de-Cernay, *Historia Albigensis* 50
Peterborough Abbey, and late medieval Cambridge 249–50, 256
Philip the Chancellor 47
Philip the Fair of France 88
philosophy, natural
  in mendicant education 78, 81, 83, 86
  and nominalism 323–4
Pickering, John, prior of York Dominican house 288
Pierre d'Ailly 90, 315, 316

Pierre de Courtenay, count of Auxerre 34
Pilate, Pontius, and responsibility for death of Christ 57, 68
Pilgrimage of Grace 258, 288
Pisa, Council (1409) 154, 160, 229
placenames, as surnames 271, 274–82
Plantsch, Martin, sermons 317–18
Plumpton, Lawrence 282–3
Pollard, Alfred 207, 215 n. 60
Pontefract Abbey 281, 282
Poor Men of Lyon 170–1, 174
Popper, Karl 2
Porcari, Giovanni 84
potentia absoluta/ordinata 309–10, 315, 317–18, 320–1, 323
poverty, evangelical 101, 103, 115, 126–7, 133
  and Lollards 170, 182–6, 188
  and mendicants 217, 218–19, 225, 235–6
prayer, in Catharism 20–1, 22–3
preaching
  barefoot 182–5
  Lollard 144–5, 148–9, 150–1, 153–5, 159–60, 177, 180, 182–3, 187–9
  mendicant 175, 180, 184, 188, 190, 217, 220, 224–5, 228, 231, 238
  and sects 171–4
  by university monks 261–2
Premonstratensian order
  in France 34
  in late medieval Cambridge 240, 247–8, 258, 265, 267
  in Yorkshire *273*, 282
Prévostin of Cremona 35–6, 47
  'Mainz' sermons 36
  Summa contra haereticos (attributed to) 36
Priscillian, Priscillianists 117, 167
property, ecclesiastical 93, 219
Protestantism
  and continuity with past 141–3, 179, 293–4, 301, 305
  and crusades 293–4, 296, 297, 298–307
  and Ottoman threat 297–300, 303–5
  and William of Ockham 314–15, 321–2
  and Yorkshire religious 290
Pseudo-Chrysostom 151
pseudo-Dionysius, *Celestial Hierarchy* 18
Purgatory, and Catharism 22
Pursglove (Sylvester), Robert, prior of Guisborough 283, 289
Purvey, John 146–7, 187, 190

Queen's College, Oxford, and Lollards 148–9, 152–4, 160

Raemond, Florimond de 304
Rahner, Karl 111
Ramihrdus 127–8
Raymond of Aguilers 302
reason
  and ethics 63, 319
  and faith 27, 132–3, 134, 311, 324
  in William of Ockham 309, 316, 319–20
Redman, Richard, bishop of Ely 249 n. 33
Reeves, Marjorie 313
Reformation
  and Decalogue ethics 315–16
  and nominalism 321–2
  and William of Ockham as precursor 309, 310, 311–12, 314–15, 321–2
  see also Protestantism
regent masters 77, 82, 83, 85, 87
Regnans in excelsis (papal bull) 229–30, 232–7
reincarnation, in Catharism 9–10, 13, 23, 35
Reineck, Reiner (editor of medieval chronicles) 299–302, 305, 306
religion, freedom of 111–13, 129 n. 48, 137
Réné de Lucinge 296, 304
Repingdon, Philip 144, 145–6, 148–50, 152–3, 160, 183, 190
  Sermones dominicales 149, 153
resurrection, in Catharism 13, 27–8
Rex pacificus 106
Rhineland, and Catharism 35–6, 40, 44–5
Richard II of England, and Lollards 154, 169
Richard of Bury, bishop of Durham, *Philobiblon* 262
Richmond, Thomas 224–5

Rievaulx Abbey
- geographical origins of religious 274–6, 282
- social origins of religious 285–6
- university education of religious 287–8

Rigord, *Gesta Philippi Augusti* 74
Rimington, William 175
Ritual, Cathar 5 n. 1, 6, 9–10, 12, 13 n. 43, 14, 17, 18 n. 63, 22
Robert of Anjou 88
Robert of Auxerre, *Chronicon* 34, 43
Robert of Courson 47
Robert le Bougre 43–4, 50
Robert of Rheims 300, 302
Robert of Torigny 36–7
Robinson, Robert 289
Roche Abbey 278–9
Roger, Pierre 90
Roland of Cremona 31–2
Rolle, Richard 157, 264
- *Form of Living* 156
- works 159

Roman Catholicism
- and crusading history 298–300, 303
- and orthodoxy and heresy 6, 114–15, 128–30, 313, 314
- and scholasticism 311

Romans, and responsibility for death of Christ 57–9
Rorty, Richard 124
Russell, Jeffrey B. 114
Russell, William 225
- sermon 224

Sacconi, Rainier 44
- *Summa de Catharis et de Pauperibus de Lugduno* 7 n. 9, 9, 12 n. 37, 16 n. 57, 19, 22 n. 78, 41

sacraments
- in Catharism 12, 16–18
  - see also *consolamentum*
- and Lollards 143–4
- and unworthy clergy 127–8, 225

St Albans Abbey 36, 256, 263, 264, 265
St Andrew's Priory, York 274, 286
St Edmund's Priory, Cambridge 244–5, 246
St Félix-de-Caraman, Cathar council 42, 50
St Mary's Abbey
- geographical origin of religious 281
- numbers of religious 271, 273, 281
- social origins of religious 283, 287
- university education of religious 250, 256, 262, 288

Salcot (Capon), John, bishop of Salisbury 259
Salerno, university 37
Salimbene 33–4
Sanudo Torsello, Marino 305
- *Secreta Fidelium Crucis* 302

Sarpi, Paolo 322
Savile, Sir Henry 302
Sawley Abbey 277–8, 285
Sawtry, William 142
Sayle, Charles 207
scholasticism
- and intellectual community 130
- and Suarez 322–3
- and William of Ockham 102, 309–14

Scotists 322
Scott, John 107
sect
- and heresy 119, 167–8, 172–6, 179
- Lollards as 143–4, 163–91
- meanings 165–7, 171–2, 176–8
- and mendicant orders 177–82, 188
- and preaching 171–4
- and sect of Christ 177–81

secularization
- of holy war 295–7
- and Reformation 312

Selby Abbey 247, 256, 280
Selling, John 258
sententiae, and Cathar maxims 25, 39
Sermon against Cathars (anonymous) 42
Sermon against Cathars of Arras (anon.) 42
Serrurier, Nicholas 233, 236
Seyton, Edward 267
Sharpe, John 152–3
- *De oracionibus sanctorum* 153

Simon de Asceles 242
Simon Magus 118
simony, and heresy 118, 127, 130–1

sin
  in Catharism 9, 14–16, 18–20, 35
  and guilt 61, 63, 68
  and ignorance 61–8
  in William of Ockham 315–16
  and witchcraft 316, 317–18, 323
Sixtus IV, Pope, *Mare magnum* 237
Skryvener, Thomas 143
Smalley, Beryl 313
Smith, Ralph, prior of Hull 282
Smith, William 142, 143, 182, 186–7
society, and heresy 123–5, 138
Socrates Scholasticus, *Ecclesiastical History* 119 n. 24
soul, in Catharism 9–10, 13–16, 18, 20–3, 28, 35
Southern, R. W. 96 n. 9, 99
Speculum peccatoris 157
Spiritual Franciscans 88, 218–19, 225, 313
spirituality, Cathar 5–23
Stella (Cathar work) 6, 21 n. 76
Stokes, Peter 173
Stonham, Robert 160
Stopes, Richard, abbot of Meaux 287
Strayer, J. R. 20 n. 70
studia generalia et provincialia
  and mendicant orders 78, 79–81, 86–7, 91
  and monastic orders 243–52
Suarez, Francisco 322–3
succession, apostolic 103, 227–9, 231, 234, 237
Sudbury, John 251
Suleiman the Magnificent 295
Super cathedram (papal bull) 217, 220, 222–3, 230, 235
surnames, placenames as 271, 274–82
Swaffham, Richard 261–2
Swanson, R. N. 217–38
Swinderby, William 168, 186
Swynborn (Gwynborne), William 289
Szitta, Penn 174 n. 40, 175, 185 n. 77

Talmud 74
Tanner, N. P. 120
Tasso, Torquato, *Gerusalemme Liberata* 294, 306
Taylor, William 142, 144, 150
Ten Commandments *see* Decalogue ethics
tertiaries 235–6
Tertullian, Quintus Septimus Florens 175
Tetricus (Cathar) 6, 15 n. 52, 22 n. 79, 33
Theodosian Code 167, 174 n. 40
Theodosius II, Emperor, and heresy 117
theology
  and canon law 93–5, 98–9
  and heresy 93–5
  and Judaism 55–76
  and the laity 224
  and mendicant orders 77–91
  and monastic orders 258
  moral 61–8
  and use of maxims 38–40, 45, 51
Thetford, John 259
Thierry (Cathar) 6, 50
Thomas of Chobham 47, 69
  Summa confessorum 73–4
Thomas de la Mare, abbot of St Albans 250
Thomas de Stewkley, abbot of Colchester 260–1
Thomas, Peter 89
Thomas, W. E. S. 3
Thomism 322–3
Thomson, J. A. F. 141, 168
Thomson, S. Harrison 96
Thomson, W. R. 193 n. 1, 198, 215
Thorpe, William 144, 145–6, 150, 159–60
  Testimony 146
Thoresby, John, archbishop of York, *Lay Folk's Catechism* 224
The Three Arrows 157, 159
Tierney, Brian 112, 116 n. 15, 129 n. 48, 137
tithes, and mendicant orders 224, 228, 231
toleration
  and heresy 111–13, 127, 139
  of Jews 56, 68–76
toponymics, and Yorkshire religious 271, 274–82
Trefnant, John, bishop of Hereford, *Register* 147, 168–9
Trent, Council (1545-63) 296, 322

Trevisa, John
dialogue on translation 152
translation of Hugden's *Polychronicon* 166–7
Trinity
in Augustine 124–5
in Catharism 10–11
and Lollardy 158
Turkenbuchlein 296
Tyerman, Christopher 293–307

Ullerston, Richard 152–4
De translacione sacre scripture in vulgare 152
Defensorium dotacionis ecclesie 153
Petitiones quoad reformationem ecclesie militantis 160
Unam sanctam 104, 108 n. 44
gloss on 106
Underwood, M. G. 240
Unger, Dominic J. 119 n. 22
universities
and heretical dualism 25–7, 30, 33–4, 36–7, 40
and knowledge of Aristotle 36–8
and mendicant orders 240–1, 288–9
and Yorkshire religious 271, 287–91
see also Cambridge, university; Oxford, university; Paris, university
Urban II, Pope, and First Crusade 299
Urban VI, Pope, and Wyclif 206

Valdes *see* Waldensians
Vas electionis 217, 227, 230
Vavasour, Richard 282
Vavasour, William 282, 288, 290
via moderna and *via antiqua* 316–23
Vienne, Council (1311-12) 217 n. 2
Religiosi 235
Vignaux, Paul 310
virtue, and heresy 111, 130–5, 138
voluntarism, and ethics 309, 319, 323–4
Vorgrimler, Herbert 111
Vowell, Richard, prior of Walsingham 262

Wakeham, William 143
Waldensians, as heretics 170–1, 172, 183
Walsingham, Thomas
Chronicon Anglie 182 n. 63, 185–6
Historia anglicana 146, 182, 185–6
and Lollards 146, 154, 155, 158, 182, 184–5
Walter, William 293, 303
Walther, 128–9 n. 46
Ward, Isabel, prioress of Clementhorpe 283
Watt, Jack 55–76
Watton Priory 245–6, 274, 283, 290
Waytestathe, Richard 186, 187
wealth
Cathar 43
clergy 231
monastic 268
Wells, Robert 264–5
Wessington, John, prior of Durham 251
Westhaugh, Thomas 148
Whelpington, Richard 150
Whethamstede, John, abbot of St Albans 239, 265
Whitby Abbey
geographical origins of religious 281
social origins of religious 285
White, William 142, 161
Whitehead, John 230
Wiles, Maurice F. 112
Wilks, Michael 214
William of Alnwick 84, 89
William of Kilkenny, bishop of Ely 242
William of Malmesbury 299
William of Newburgh 44
William of Ockham
De imperatorum et pontificum postestate 135 n. 61
and Denis the Areopagite 93
Dialogus 93–9, 101–2, 107, 115–16, 134
and ethics 309–10, 314, 316–19, 323
and Franciscans 99–100, 103, 115
and Grosseteste 93–100, 107
and heresy 93–4, 115–16, 133–4
and Michael of Cesena 93, 102, 106
and natural law 95, 97, 309–10, 319–20, 322
and nominalism 309–10, 314–15, 317–21
ordination 79

and papacy 100–6, 115–16, 133–4, 313, 319, 322
political writings 115 n. 14
and reason and revelation 309, 311
and scholasticism 310–14
William of St Amour 175, 184, 189
De Pharisao 184
William of Tyre, *Historia Ierosolymitana* 293, 300, 302, 304, 305
Williams, Gwyn x
Williams, Rowan 112
wills
and geographical origins of Yorkshire religious 282
'Lollard' 155, 156–9
and social origins of Yorkshire religious 271, 284–6
witchcraft, and sin 316, 317–18, 323
Wodard, John 155
Wodeham, Adam 84
women, in Catharism 20
Woodford, William 197, 213, 215 n. 61
Woodhull, John 143
Worcester cathedral priory, and university education 287
Workman, Herbert 146–7
Wulf, Maurice de 311
Wych, Richard 144, 145, 160
Wyclif, John
and English Bible 152, 189
and eucharist 214
followers 141–2, 144–61
and Grosseteste 99–100
and heresy 25, 154, 168, 170, 313
and mendicants 177–9, 236
and papacy 99, 170, 206, 207, 213
and sects 164–5, 173, 175–8, 182
writings
chronology 194–5
commentary on Aristotle's *Meteora* 200 n. 22
commentary on Aristotle's *Physics* 200 n. 22
and cross-referencing 193–215
De accione 200
De actibus anime 200
De adnichilacione 198, 212
De anima 200
De apostasia 196, 197
De benedicta incarnacione 196, 198, 200, 212, 213–14
De blasphemia 196, 197, 213
De cessacione legalium 199
De Christo 200
De civili dominio 99, 193, 196, 197, 206–8, 209 n. 45, 210–14
De continuacione 200
De dominio divino 200, 210–11, 212–13
De ecclesia 193, 194 n. 5, 196, 198–202, 205–8, 213–14
De ente in communi 212
De ente predicamentali 200, 212
De eucharistia 193, 198, 212, 213
De fide catholica 195
De fundacione sectarum 177–8
De heresi 198
De intelleccione dei 196, 210, 212
De logica (De arte sophistica) 200, 214
De mandatis 206–7, 209 n. 45, 210, 213
De maximo et minimo 200
De mendacio 199
De officio pastorali 193 n. 1, 207
De officio regis 199, 206–8, 210
De perplexitate 200
De potencia productiva dei 196, 198, 212
De potestate pape 195, 205, 208, 213
De privilegiis 199–200
De quattuor sectis novellis 195
De religione 197–8, 200
De sacramentis 195, 213
De scientia dei 198 n. 14, 210, 212
De statu innocencie 195, 198, 206, 210–11
De symonia 196, 199, 210, 213
De tempore 196, 212
De trinitate 193 n. 1, 198 n. 15, 212
De universalibus 192 n. 1, 195, 212
De veritate sacre scripture 176, 193, 196, 198–9, 200, 202–8, 210–14
De volucione dei 212
De ydeis 195, 212
Dialogus 215
Opus evangelicum 194

Wyclif, John (*cont.*):
Purgans errores circa veritates in communi 196, 212
Responsio ad decem questiones 160
Sermones 199
Sermones quadraginta 193, 197, 213 n. 55, 214–15
Sermones viginti 193 n. 2, 197
Summa de ente 193 n. 1, 196–8, 200, 210, 212, 213
Summa theologie 193, 196, 197–215
Trialogus 193 n. 1, 194, 195
see also Hussites, catalogues; Lollards
Wycliffite writings
Floretum 150, 179–80
glossed gospels 149
Jack Upland 180–2
'Of the leaven of the Pharisees' 176
Rosarium 179
sermons 144–5, 150–1, 160, 163, 177
Tractatus de Pseudo-freris 178–9
Wygenhale, John, *Historia* of West Dereham 265
Wyllis, James 142, 143–4

Yorkshire, university connections of religious 250, 256, 262, 271–91
Ypma, Eelcko 79–80

Compiled by Meg Davies
(Registered Indexer, Society of Indexers)